UNDERSTANDING PHENOMENOLOGY

Michael Hammond, Jane Howarth, Russell Keat

Basil Blackwell

Copyright © M.A. Hammond, Jane M. Howarth and R.N. Keat 1991

First published 1991

Basil Blackwell Ltd
108 Cowley Road, Oxford, OX4 1JF, UK

Basil Blackwell, Inc.
3 Cambridge Center
Cambridge, Massachusetts 02142, USA

British Library Cataloguing in Publication Data
A CIP catalogue record for this book is available from the British Library.
Library of Congress Cataloging in Publication Data
Hammond, Michael
    Understanding phenomenology/Michael Hammond, Jane Howarth, Russell Keat.
        p.   cm.
    Includes bibliographical references and index.
    ISBN 0-631-13282-1: $70.00. — ISBN 0-631-13283-X: $25.90
    1. Phenomenology. I. Howarth, Jane. II. Keat, Russell.
III. Title.
B829.5.H345 1991
142' .7—dc20   90-43857
                                                                                        CIP

Typeset in 10 on 12 pt Ehrhardt
by Graphicraft Typesetters Ltd., Hong Kong
Printed in Great Britain by T. J. Press Ltd., Padstow, Cornwall.

Contents

Preface

The main aim of this book is to provide an introduction to phenomenology that will help its readers to understand and evaluate the work of phenomenological philosophers. We try to do this by presenting an account of the central concepts and arguments of two major texts of the phenomenological movement, Edmund Husserl's *Cartesian Meditations* and Maurice Merleau-Ponty's *Phenomenology of Perception*, together with less detailed analyses of two others – Husserl's *The Crisis of European Sciences* and Jean-Paul Sartre's *Being and Nothingness*. Our reasons for selecting these particular texts will be presented in the Introduction.

A major problem facing the English-speaking student of phenomenology is that, despite the existence both of translations of most of the classical phenonemonological texts and of a considerable volume of secondary literature, making sense of those texts remains a daunting task. Their difficulty, especially to the reader with little background in post-Kantian European philosophy, is due largely to a combination of esoteric terminology, opaque style, and apparently unfamiliar philosophical concerns. Hence most of this book is directed at these problems of intelligibility, and involves explaining technical concepts, articulating lines of argument, and identifying the issues being addressed, often by locating these in relation to more familiar philosophical positions and debates.

In this way we hope to contribute something to the study of phenomenology which is arguably somewhat lacking in the existing literature, despite its usefulness in other respects. There are, for example, general introductions to the field which, whilst intellectually accessible, still leave one floundering when trying to read the primary texts. There are mainly historical accounts which, though informative about who wrote and read what, and when, provide rather little in the way of philosophical illumination. There are accounts of particular texts which sometimes stay so close to the structure and terminology of the original that their main virtue seems to consist in their relative brevity. And there are the critical debates of the continuing phenomenological movement, which inevitably presuppose an understanding of its classical texts and their theoretical concepts.

In writing this book, then, our primary concern has been to provide an intelligible and reasonably accessible account of the texts we examine. Partly because of this, our analyses often fall short of what would be required by a full-scale scholarly commentary. But we hope that these shortcomings are redressed by our often going beyond what would be involved in this: for example, by trying to provide reconstructions of implicit lines of argument, and by drawing attention to their parallels with, and differences from, analogous arguments to be found in other philosophical traditions, especially those of a broadly analytical character.

As the discerning reader will already have noticed, this is a co-authored book; and at least one advantage of this is that we can employ the authorial 'we' without undue impropriety. Nonetheless, for obvious reasons, each chapter has been written primarily by one of us: Chapters Three, Seven, Nine, and section 1 of the Conclusion by Michael Hammond; Chapters Two, Four, Eight, and section 3 of the Conclusion by Jane Howarth; and Chapters One, Five, Six, section 2 of the Conclusion, and the Introduction by Russell Keat.

Finally, our thanks: to our students in courses over the past ten years, whose difficulties in understanding phenomenology made us think that a book of this kind was worth writing, even if it is not this book; to our publishers and colleagues who, over a similar period, have displayed great patience and support; to Margaret Gudgin, Maggie Lackey, and Ivy Thexton, who typed earlier drafts of various chapters; and to Roslyn Platt, who typed a final draft of them all.

Department of Philosophy, University of Lancaster. May 1990

Abbreviations and Acknowledgements

The following abbreviations are used throughout the text.

CM: Husserl, Edmund, *Cartesian Meditations*, trans. Dorion Cairns, Martinus Nijhoff, The Hague, 1977.

CES: Husserl, Edmund, *The Crisis of European Sciences and Transcendental Phenomenology*, trans. David Carr, Northwestern University Press, Evanston, IL, 1970.

BN: Sartre, Jean-Paul, *Being and Nothingness*, trans. Hazel Barnes, Methuen, London, 1958.

PP: Merleau-Ponty, Maurice, *Phenomenology of Perception*, trans. Colin Smith, Routledge & Kegan Paul, London 1981 (includes revisions to translation in 1962 edition).

The authors are grateful to the following publishers for the use of copyright material: passages from Husserl's *Cartesian Meditations* appear by permission of Routledge; those from Sartre's *Being and Nothingness* by permission of Methuen & Co.; and those from Merleau-Ponty's *Phenomenology of Perception* by permission of Kluwer Academic Publishers.

Introduction

1 Understanding Phenomenology

What is phenomenology? To answer that question directly, even if it were possible, would require the introduction of too many technical concepts to be helpful at this point. So we shall begin instead by making some remarks about its overall philosophical character which are designed to remove some possible sources of initial misunderstanding.[1] A convenient starting-point is the following story recounted by Simone de Beauvoir in her autobiography, which tells of how Sartre's interest in phenomenology was first aroused by their mutual acquaintance, Raymond Aron, in 1932:

> Raymond Aron was spending a year at the French Institute in Berlin and study-ing Husserl simultaneously with preparing a historical thesis. When he came to Paris he spoke of Husserl to Sartre. We spent an evening together at the Bec de Gaz in the Rue Montparnasse. We ordered the speciality of the house, apricot cocktails; Aron said, pointing to his glass: 'You see, my dear fellow, if you are a phenomenologist, you can talk about this cocktail and make philosophy out of it!' Sartre turned pale with emotion at this. Here was just the thing he had been longing to achieve for years – to describe objects just as he saw and touched them, and extract philosophy from the process.[2]

No doubt there is something a little contrived about this story. But it provides a quite helpful initial characterization of phenomenology – 'to describe objects just as one experiences them, and to extract philosophy from the process' – even if one feels rather less excited by the prospect than was Sartre. Taken fairly literally, 'phenomenology' means 'the study or description of phenomena'; and a 'phenomenon' is simply anything that appears or presents itself to someone (and so does not involve any sense of the strange or spectacular). Thus phenomenology involves the description of things as one experiences them, or of one's experiences of things: the slight differences in these two formulations can be ignored here. One important class of such experiences of things is perception – seeing, hearing, touching, and so on. But it is by no means the only one. There are also phenomena such as believing, remembering, wishing, deciding and imagining things; feeling apprehensive, excited, or angry at things; judging and evaluating things; the experiences involved in one's bodily actions, such as lifting or pulling things; and many others.

How exactly one is to 'extract a philosophy' from this process of description is something we will not try to explain here – though certainly phenomenology does not consist merely of an indefinitely long list of descriptions of particular phenomena. But there are several important points to be made at the outset about how this phenomenological programme of description is to be understood.

The first concerns the term 'phenomenon' itself, and especially its near-equivalent, in some cases at least, namely 'appearance'. In both ordinary and many philosophical uses, the concept of appearance is often defined through an implicit or explicit contrast with that of reality, such that what is apparent, or appears to be the case, is taken to be other than what is real, or really the case. Especially in philosophy, this kind of contrast is often associated with a view of reality as something that lies 'behind' or 'beyond' the realm of mere appearances (phenomena); and even of the former being 'hidden' or 'misrepresented' by the superficial or misleading character of the latter. But this is not the sense of 'phenomena' involved in phenomenology. Its descriptions of phenomena are not of what is distinct from the real, but simply of how one experiences things; and included here is how in some cases one in fact distinguishes between the experience of what is real and of what is *only* apparent. That is, any distinction between the real and the apparent is one that operates *within* the more general category of 'the phenomena', all of which phenomenology is concerned to describe.

The second point concerns the use we have been making of the term 'experience', in talking for example of 'perceptual experience'. Just as there are philosophical traditions endorsing a dichotomy between appearance and reality, which phenomenology rejects, so also is there a well-known (though often challenged) dichotomy between an inner world of 'private experience' and an outer world of 'public objects'. This latter dichotomy, probably best represented in Descartes' dualism of mind and body, consciousness and matter, is also rejected by phenomenologists. Hence the description of phenomena, of what is experienced, is not regarded by them as the description of a separate, subjective realm by contrast with the objective realm of the external world. Rather, it is maintained, any such separation is philosophically untenable; and this is revealed by the fact that the description of experience shows it always to be experience *of* something. Experience, as it were, always refers to something beyond itself, and therefore cannot be characterized independently of this. (Conversely, it is claimed, no straightforward sense can be given to an outer, external world of objects which are not the objects *of* such experiences.) One cannot, for example, characterize perceptual experience without describing what it is that is seen, touched, heard, and so on. This feature of conscious experience is called by phenomenologists its 'intentionality'; and what it is that is experienced – such as the cocktail that Sartre perceived – is often termed the 'intentional object'.

The third point is connected with the first two, and concerns the relationship between phenomenology and the empirical sciences, especially the physical sciences. At least since the time of the seventeeth-century scientific revolution, the distinction between appearance and reality has often been interpreted by philosophers so as to ascribe a privileged status to the accounts of 'reality' provided by the physical sciences, and hence to regard the way in which the world is experienced in everyday perception as 'mere appearance'. This view – which can roughly be called 'scientific realism' – was adopted by, for example, both Galileo and Descartes; and in both it was associated with a distinction between two 'worlds', of private experience and public objects. As might already be expected, this is a view which phenomenologists reject: for them, the account of the external world provided by the sciences has no such privileged philosophical status, and is to be seen instead as a kind of abstraction from the only 'real' world, namely that which is pre-scientifically experienced.

The final point is this. The phenomenologists' insistence on the careful description of ordinary conscious experience is partly motivated by their sense that previous philosophers have either ignored this altogether, or described it in an inaccurate or misleading fashion. In particular, it is claimed that they have allowed their prior philosophical commitments to distort this descriptive enterprise so that, for example, their accounts of perceptual experience have been influenced more by what this 'should' be like, given those commitments, than by what it is actually like. The avoidance of this kind of distortion is at least part of what is meant by the phenomenologists' insistence that these descriptions must be 'presuppositionless', or 'free from prejudices' – the term 'prejudice' here having its fairly literal sense of 'prior judgement'. One important example of such a prejudice is the empiricists' tendency to characterize perception as consisting in 'ideas' or 'sense-data', in individual 'atoms' of experience such as patches of colour or particular shapes. Indeed, the term 'phenomenon' has often been used to refer to these items. But this is not how it is used by phenomenologists, who deny that one's normal perceptual experiences are of this kind, and are likely to suspect that some philosophical prejudice is at work here in the empiricists' 'descriptions': for example, a commitment to some scientific theory of perception, which explains it in terms of the impingement upon the sense-organs of discrete external stimuli.

2 The Choice of Texts

So far we have talked about phenomenology as if it were a single, relatively unified philosophical standpoint. But this is by no means so; and in choosing the particular texts for examination here, we have tried to select works that will illustrate some of the diversity, and indeed conflict, to be found within the phenomenological movement. Probably the most important contrast is between the 'transcendental' phenomenology of the first of our two main main texts, Husserl's *Cartesian Meditations*, and the 'existential' phenomenology of which our second main text, Merleau-Ponty's *Phenomenology of Perception*, represents one influential form and Sartre's *Being and Nothingness* another.[3] There is considerable debate about the relationship between transcendental and existential phenomenology, including whether they are so much at odds with each other that they cannot properly be regarded as two sub-classes of a single category, 'phenomenology'. We shall consider this question more directly in section 1 of the Conclusion. But some initial sense of the differences between them should emerge from the following comments about the texts we have chosen for discussion.

To the extent that it is ever legitimate to talk of the 'founder' of a philosophical movement, Husserl is the recognized founder of phenomenology. So there is no difficulty in justifying the use of his writings for an introduction to phenomenology. But the same cannot be said about the choice of any particular text by him for these purposes. As with most philosophers, his work developed and changed in complex ways through his lifetime; and, equally unsurprisingly, there is much argument about the identification of various 'stages' in his thought, the relationship between them, and so on. One central question here has been whether the best-known text of his 'final' stage, *The Crisis of European Sciences and Transcendental Phenomenology*, involved a radical break with the preceding stage represented by the *Cartesian Meditations*; and this is one reason for our including it along with the latter, though we shall be discussing it far more briefly.

In the *Cartesian Meditations* Husserl presents phenomenology as a form of transcendental idealism, and hence as closely related to Kant's philosophy – though he is also keen to emphasize the differences between them. This transcendental phenomenology is crucially opposed to philosophical realism, according to which there can straightforwardly be said to exist an external world that is quite separate from one's knowledge of it. Realism, for Husserl, involves a philosophically naive misinterpretation of what he calls 'the natural attitude', the everyday assumption of the independent existence of what is perceived, thought about, and so on. To avoid this misinterpretation one must, as a philosopher, 'suspend' or 'put into abeyance' this assumption, and investigate these experiences without it. This suspension is termed the phenomenological *epoché* or 'bracketing', which is closely related to the concept of 'reduction'.

As its title suggests, Husserl draws attention in the *Cartesian Meditations* to some important parallels between transcendental phenomenology and Descartes' *Meditations*. In particular he sees himself as following Descartes in adopting the standpoint of the meditating philosophical 'I' or Ego, who is concerned to establish secure foundations for knowledge; and he introduces the *epoché* by partial analogy with the Cartesian method of doubt. But he goes on to argue that Descartes drew the wrong conclusions from this self-reflective procedure: for instance, the dualism of mind and body and, most importantly, the attempted 'proof' of the existence of the external world. For Husserl, this proof failed to escape from the standpoint of philosophical realism. Transcendental phenomenology, by contrast, ascribes to the reflecting Ego a *constitutive* role with respect to the 'real world': the sense or meaning of the latter is provided by the former, the transcendental ego, which is not itself a part of that world, but rather is presupposed by it. Furthermore, Husserl maintained that this transcendental ego has various essential 'structures', whose nature can be investigated by a second level of phenomenological reduction which he termed 'eidetic', involving the discovery of 'essences'.

This concept of the transcendental ego, and its associated transcendental form of phenomenology, was rejected by the existential phenomenologists. Indeed Sartre's first work on phenomenology, *The Transcendence of the Ego*, contained a detailed argument designed to show that no such concept could be arrived at by properly phenomenological methods; and in the *Phenomenology of Perception* Merleau-Ponty assigned transcendental idealism (and, by implication, transcendental phenomenology) to the category of 'intellectualism', one of the main targets of his philosophical criticism. Yet – rightly or wrongly – Merleau-Ponty did not regard this transcendental element as essential to Husserl's conception of phenomenology; and in the *Phenomenology of Perception* he spared little effort in proclaiming his allegiance to the 'true spirit' of Husserl's philosophy.

One reason for this was his interest in developing a central theme in the final period of Husserl's work, represented by *The Crisis*. This concerns the relationship between the picture of the world provided by the empirical sciences, especially physics, and the way in which the world is actually experienced in everyday life: between the 'scientific' and 'lived' worlds. Husserl considers this question by examining Galileo's attempt to establish a 'mathematized' conception of nature, according to which the only real properties of things are those that can be measured and quantified – the so-called primary properties such as size, shape, position, and so on. By contrast, the 'secondary' properties such as colour, taste or smell are deemed by Galileo to be unreal: they are to be understood as merely the subjective effects of the real world upon the perceiver, 'existing' only in the realm of private experience.

Against this Husserl argues that the only real properties of things are those that are experienced in everyday life, and hence include both primary and secondary qualities. Galileo's mathematized nature must be regarded as only a (predictively useful) *abstraction* from the lived world which, philosophically speaking, has ontological priority (priority in its claims to existence) over the scientific world. It is this general endorsement of the philosophical primacy of the lived world that provides the most obvious, though not the only, common theme between *The Crisis* and Merleau-Ponty's *Phenomenology of Perception*. Much of this latter text consists in the detailed description of that world as it is revealed in everyday perception; and also in showing how previous philosophers and psychologists have misdescribed it, largely because of their 'scientific prejudice', their attempt to fit the perceived world into the frame-work assumed by the sciences – for instance, in taking it for granted that the perceived shapes and sizes of objects conform to the laws of geometrical optics. Such assumptions are part of what Merleau-Ponty calls 'objective thought', an erroneous view which he sees as being shared by philosophers who in other respects are largely at odds with one another: in particular, both by 'empiricists', such as Locke, and by 'intellectualists', such as Kant.

But the description of this lived world is not Merleau-Ponty's only concern in the *Phenomenology of Perception*. He is equally interested in the nature of the human 'subject' for whom this world exists. It is here that the more obvi-ously existentialist character of Merleau-Ponty's philosophy emerges, with its emphasis upon active engagement in the world by individuals exercising their capacity to make choices and 'impose meanings'. In effect, it is this existential subject that replaces Husserl's transcendental ego, and arguably leads to a fun-damental departure from, or at least reconstruction of, his phenomenology. Unlike Sartre, however, Merleau-Ponty devotes relatively little attention to providing a systematic justification of this existentialist standpoint; and it is partly for this reason that we have included an account of some central themes from *Being and Nothingness*.

Drawing upon what he took to be the defensible elements, not only of Husserlian phenomenology, but also of Heidegger's *Being and Time*, Sartre developed a radical conception of human freedom based on a distinction between two kinds of being, the for-itself (*pour-soi*) and the in-itself (*en-soi*). These map on, very roughly, to the everyday concepts of 'humans' and 'the world'; but their precise philosophical character can be understood only by reference to the way Sartre relates them to the more fundamental categories which provide the title of his book. In particular the for-itself, as Nothingness, is said to have the power of 'nihilating Being'; and it is through such acts of nihilation that its freedom is expressed, and the in-itself is constituted.

We shall make no attempt to explain these claims at this point. Instead we will merely note two important ways in which the existentialism of *Being and Nothingness* relies upon Sartre's understanding of Husserl's phenomenology. First, the relationship between the for-itself and the in-itself is characterized as an 'intentional' one, with the former's acts of consciousness having the latter as their 'objects'. Second, Sartre is concerned to provide detailed phenomenological descriptions of many concrete human experiences, aiming to 'extract' from them philosophical accounts of the character of human existence and especially of its freedom. The accuracy, or at least the typicality, of these descriptions has often been questioned by Sartre's critics. But a more radical challenge has concerned whether his account of the distinction between the for-itself and the in-itself can be justified by reference to phenomenological procedures of description and explication – and hence, in effect, whether his existentialist categories can be phenomenologically supported.

Merleau-Ponty is one such critic – though mainly, in the *Phenomenology of Perception*, only implicitly. A central aim of this text is to reject, on phenomenological grounds, any philosophical dichotomy between a conscious subject, reflectively transparent to itself, and a world of objects whose nature can be identified in scientific terms. (Whether Sartre's dichotomy is in fact of this kind is, however, debatable.) In place of this dichotomy Merleau-Ponty develops a view of the human subject as essentially 'embodied', and hence neither entirely free nor self-transparent; and of its 'world', consisting of the intended objects of bodily action and perception, as neither fully determined, causally, nor determinate ('clear-cut'), and hence not straightforwardly accessible to the empirical sciences. Thus, although both *Being and Nothingness* and the *Phenomenology of Perception* can reasonably be seen as works of existential phenomenology, there are significant differences between them; and so a further reason for including a brief account of the former is to enable these differences to be explored.

3   The Background to the Texts

(With a few exceptions, we include here only information that is directly relevant to the particular texts we are discussing. Unless specified otherwise, the translations referred to are into English; full publication details are provided in the Bibliography.)[4]

Both the *Cartesian Meditations* and *The Crisis* were written after Husserl's retirement in 1928 from the professorship he had held at Freiburg since 1916. He had moved there from Gottingen, where he had been an associate professor since 1900, the year in which the first volume of his *Logical Investigations* was published (translated 1970). In this he rejected the 'psychologism' of his earlier work in the philosophy of mathematics.[5] The second volume, published in 1901, is normally taken to mark the beginnings of his phenomenological work, with its introduction of the concept of intentionality, derived partly from his earlier teacher Franz Brentano's *Psychology from an Empirical Standpoint* (1874, translated 1973). In 1907 Husserl delivered a series of five lectures at Gottingen, in which several further basic phenomenological concepts were introduced, including the epoché, reduction and essences. (These lectures were published only posthumously, in 1950, and translated in 1964 as *The Idea of Phenomenology*.) By 1913, with the publication of the first volume of *Ideas* (translated 1931), Husserl's phenomenology had taken a recognizably transcendental form.

The *Cartesian Meditations* had their origin in two lectures, given at the Sorbonne in 1929, entitled 'Introduction to Transcendental Phenomenology'. (These came to be called the 'Paris Lectures', translated with this title in 1970: it is thought that Merleau-Ponty attended them.) After giving the lectures, Husserl began to rework and expand them considerably for publication; and in a letter to Roman Ingarden in March 1930 he wrote of this project that

> it will be the major work of my life, a basic outline of the philosophy that has accrued to me, a fundamental work of method and of philosophical problematics. At least for *me* [it will represent] a conclusion and ultimate clarity, which I can defend and with which I can lie contented.[6]

But as with similar hopes in the past, these were not to be fully realized. For although at one stage in his work on the manuscript Husserl released it for translation into French (*Meditations Cartesiennes*, published in 1931), he was never sufficiently happy with it to allow publication in German; and eventually he stopped working on it. The text from which the English translation was made, in 1960, was published only posthumously, in 1950; and it contains many passages marked for deletion, proposed emendations and other marginal comments.

There is disagreement as to why Husserl gave up his attempt to produce a final text for the *Cartesian Meditations*: all that is certain is that he turned instead to the work that led to *The Crisis*. One possibility is that he became dissatisfied with the long Fifth Meditation, where he had tried to show that his position did not entail solipsism, and to describe in some detail how the individual transcendental ego can know of the existence of other such egos. But another possibility is that the new project represented by *The Crisis* seemed to him a more urgent and politically significant one.

Like the *Cartesian Meditations*, *The Crisis* was based on a series of lectures – this time given in Prague, in November 1935, and entitled 'The Crisis of European Sciences and Psychology'. Their opening remarks addressed the general intellectual and cultural crisis of contemporary Europe, as had another lecture given earlier that year in Vienna, 'Philosophy and the Crisis of European Humanity'. It seems likely that Husserl began the work leading to these lectures in response to an invitation in 1934, from the organizing committee for the International Congress of Philosophy in Prague, to comment upon 'the mission of philosophy in our time' (*CES*, p. xvi). In a letter read out at the Congress that September, Husserl wrote of philosophy as the force which has transformed mere internationality through power into a completely new sort of internationality, and sustains it, namely a solidarity through the spirit of autonomy;

but he went on to note 'the influence of great fateful events that completely upset the international community', and to warn that, at present,

we are faced with the imminent danger of the extinction of philosophy in this sense, and with it necessarily the extinction of a Europe founded on the spirit of truth. (*CES*, p. xxvii)

Amongst those 'great fateful events' was presumably the coming to power of the Nazi Party in the March elections of 1933. Husserl himself was barred from lecturing and publishing in Germany and removed from the list of emeritus professors at the University of Freiburg: his parents were Jews, though he had converted to Lutheranism in his twenties. On his retirement in 1928, he had been succeeded as professor of philosophy by Heidegger, who from April 1933 till February 1934 also held the position of Rector, joining the local Nazi Party in May 1933. In earlier years, especially during the period between 1916 and 1923 when Heidegger had worked with Husserl at Freiburg, Husserl had regarded the former as a loyal disciple and potential successor. But these hopes proved unfounded when, with the publication of *Being and Time* in 1927, the radical differences between their positions became apparent to him.[7]

Indeed some commentators have viewed *The Crisis* as in part a critical response to the growing popularity of existential philosophy which, to Husserl, represented one form of the intellectual and political irrationalism that he was concerned to diagnose and combat. This irrationalism he saw as due to a loss of faith in the ability of the empirical sciences to provide answers to

precisely the questions which man, given over in our unhappy times to the most portentous upheavals, finds the most burning: questions of the meaning or meaninglessness of the whole of this human existence. (*CES*, p. 6)[8]

But, Husserl argued, this lost faith had always been misplaced, to the extent that it had depended on viewing the empirical sciences as embodying the sole form of rationally grounded human knowledge or 'science' (*Wissenschaft* – the German term having a much broader meaning than the English 'science', and not limited to the empirical sciences such as physics or astronomy). This positivist limitation of knowledge to the 'facts' discovered by these sciences excluded value questions from the realm of rational enquiry, and more generally excluded philosophy itself: positivism, he says, 'in a manner of speaking decapitates philosophy'. To challenge this positivism, and the irrationalism

and cultural crisis consequent upon it, Husserl thought it necessary to undermine the scientific realism which positivism mistakenly assumed, and replace
it with transcendental phenomenology. But exactly how this would enable
'European humanity' to answer its 'most burning questions' remains unclear.
For Husserl never completed a full draft of *The Crisis*. He died in 1938,
having become seriously ill the previous year whilst at work on it.

The English translation of *The Crisis* is based on the posthumous German
edition of 1954, and consists of three parts. The first two, deriving from the
Prague lectures, had been published in 1936 in *Philosophia*, an international
year book edited in Belgrade. The text of the much longer third part required
considerable work on the manuscripts by its editor, Walter Biemel, and
remains incomplete. There were probably two more parts projected, but no
drafts for either these or the conclusion to Part III were found amongst the
vast amount of manuscript material existing at the time of Husserl's death.
This material was smuggled out of Germany later in 1938, and removed to
Louvain. It was there that Merleau-Ponty first came across some of the
unpublished manuscripts of the last period of Husserl's work, including Part
III of *The Crisis*, when he made a brief visit to Louvain in April 1939.

This visit had apparently been prompted by the publication in 1938 of
a special memorial issue of the *Revue internationale de philosophie*, which
contained information about the new developments of Husserl's phenomenology in *The Crisis*. This was also the year in which Merleau-Ponty's
first book, *The Structure of Behaviour*, was completed, though it was not
published until 1942 (translation 1963). Unlike the *Phenomenology of Perception*, which was published in 1945, *The Structure of Behaviour* was not presented or conceived as a specifically phenomenological work. Nonetheless it
was clearly influenced by his study of several of Husserl's earlier writings up
to and including the 1931 *Meditations Cartesiennes*; and many of its arguments
were taken over in the *Phenomenology of Perception*.

The main concern of *The Structure of Behaviour* was to show the inadequacy of various behaviourist and neurophysiological accounts of both
human and animal activity, and to demonstrate instead the need to articulate
the meaning of that activity for the organism performing it. Here Merleau-
Ponty drew substantially, though not uncritically, on the anti-reductionist,
holistic biology of Kurt Goldstein, and on the Gestalt psychologists such as
Wolfgang Kohler. But in the final chapter he addressed more systematically
the question of 'naturalism' (roughly equivalent to scientific realism), arguing
against the philosophical primacy of scientific conceptions of reality, and
instead for that of the world as actually experienced in action and perception.

From this brief sketch of *The Structure of Behaviour*, one can at least see
how attractive to Merleau-Ponty the work of Husserl's last period would be.
As he puts it in the Preface to the *Phenomenology of Perception*:

Husserl's first directive to phenomenology, in its early stages, to be a 'descriptive psychology', or to return 'to the things themselves', is from the start a foreswearing of science. (*PP*, p. viii)

However, many commentators have been sceptical about the accuracy of Merleau-Ponty's interpretations of Husserl's work, and even about the existence of some of the passages cited or quoted from the (then) unpublished manuscripts.[9]

Sartre's enthusiasm for phenomenology, unlike that of Merleau-Ponty, was based on Husserl's work before the period of *The Crisis*. We quoted earlier from de Beauvoir's account of her and Sartre's meeting with Aron, on his return to Paris in 1932 from the French Institute in Berlin. In the following year Sartre too went to Berlin, for nine months. Whilst in Berlin he read work by Husserl, Scheler, Jaspers and Heidegger, all apparently for the first time. But his main interest was probably in Husserl (de Beauvoir records that he made no serious study of Heidegger until 1939); and when he came back to Paris in 1934 he particularly recommended Husserl's *Ideas* to Merleau-Ponty – the two having become friends whilst students at the Ecole Normale in the late 1920s.

The most celebratory of Sartre's published discussions of Husserl's philosophy was probably the brief article in the *Nouvelle revue française* in 1939, 'A Fundamental Idea of Husserl's Phenomenology: Intentionality' – though his interpretation of that concept is far from orthodox. Two years earlier the more important, and more critical, essay 'The Transcendence of the Ego' had been published in *Recherches philosophiques*. This had been written whilst he was in Berlin, in 1934. After his return to Paris he produced two phenomenological studies of the imagination – *The Imagination* (1936) and *The Psychology of Imagination* (1940) – and one of the emotions, the *Sketch for a Theory of the Emotions* (1940). *Being and Nothingness* was published in 1943; and, in addition to its phenomenological inspiration, the influence of Heidegger's *Being and Time* should be noted, along with the interpretation of Hegel developed by Alexandre Kojève in his lectures between 1933 and 1939.[10]

As we noted earlier, Merleau-Ponty's *Phenomenology of Perception* (published in 1945) is at least implicitly highly critical of Sartre's distinction between the for-itself and the in-itself, and of its associated conception of freedom. Later, in the *Adventures of the Dialectic* (published in 1955), Merleau-Ponty addressed Sartre's position more systematically and explicitly, criticizing his political views and their supposed basis in this philosophical distinction.[11] Three years earlier Merleau-Ponty had resigned as co-editor, with Sartre, of *Les Temps modernes*, the journal which they had founded at the end of the war. It was here that de Beauvoir responded to Merleau-Ponty's attack on Sartre, in 'Merleau-Ponty et le pseudo-Sartrisme', arguing that he had thoroughly misrepresented Sartre's position, including his conception of freedom. When Merleau-Ponty died, in 1961, Sartre contributed a long article to the special memorial issue of *Les Temps modernes*, 'Merleau-Ponty vivant'. It said a good deal about their personal relationship, but little about Merleau-Ponty's philosophy – though there is rather more about this in an earlier version of the article, published only after Sartre's own death in 1980.[12]

4   Outline of the Book

Each chapter of this book consists largely in the explication and analysis of specific parts of the texts we have chosen for discussion; and these are identified, for each chapter, in the Table of Contents above, using the title-abbreviations listed on page x. Since all the chapters themselves contain brief outlines of the main themes and issues they address, we shall confine ourselves here to outlining the overall structure of the book, and to noting a number of conventions we employ throughout.

Chapters One to Three deal exclusively with the *Cartesian Meditations*, working straight through this text up until the final Fifth Meditation, which deals with the question of the individual subject's relation to other subjects. We defer discussion of this Meditation until Chapter Eight, so that we can consider Husserl's treatment of this issue alongside those of Sartre and Merleau-Ponty. Having examined the nature of Husserl's transcendental phenomenology in these first three chapters – dealing respectively with his 'Cartesian' characterization of the phenomenological project, his account of intentionality and existence, and his particular form of transcendental idealism – we move on in the following chapters to the existential phenomenologies of Merleau-Ponty and Sartre.

We begin, in Chapter Four, by examining Sartre's criticisms of Husserl, his alternative view of phenomenology, and his account of human freedom – which is later contrasted with that of Merleau-Ponty, in Chapter Nine. Chapters Five to Seven deal mainly with the *Phenomenology of Perception*, though there is a brief discussion of *The Crisis* in Chapter Six. Chapter Five provides an overall characterization of Merleau-Ponty's philosophical position and method of argument. Chapter Six discusses his conception of the human body and its intentionality; and Chapter Seven examines his account of the perception of material objects and their properties. But, unlike our treatment of the *Cartesian Meditations*, which is a relatively brief but very densely written text, we do not try to provide a 'complete' account of the *Phenomenology of Perception*. Instead we focus mainly on a few particular chapters, chosen to illustrate central features of Merleau-Ponty's overall argument.[13]

In the Conclusion, we begin by returning to the question, noted earlier in this Introduction, of the relationship between transcendental and existential phenomenology – at least, in so far as they are represented by the texts we have examined. We then consider some of the broader issues raised by the phenomenologists' rejection of scientific realism. Finally, we explore the potential relevance of Merleau-Ponty's position for recent debates within analytical philosophy about the nature of the mind.

Throughout the book, quotations from the texts are from their standard available English translations. For purposes of clarification we occasionally insert our own remarks in the passages being quoted. These are always indicated by the use of square brackets. Where there are already square brackets in the translated text, these are preserved, but explicitly noted as such. We also provide a considerable number of cross-references between our own chapters. The numbering of these chapters is presented as 'One', 'Two', etc., to avoid confusion with the numbers of the chapters in the texts we are discussing, which are presented in arabic numerals. Finally, we have tried to confine the use of 'we' to what we, as authors, are saying; and to use 'one' or 'it' when describing the supposed experiences of the phenomenological 'I' or subject. Given the phenomenologists' focus upon the *first*-person standpoint, this convention is not ideal, but it seemed the most convenient to adopt.

1

The Project of Phenomenology

1 Husserl and Descartes

At the outset of the *Cartesian Meditations*, Husserl pays tribute to 'France's greatest thinker, René Descartes', and declares that

> one might almost call transcendental phenomenology a neo-Cartesianism, even though it is obliged – and precisely by its radical development of Cartesian motifs – to reject nearly all the well-known doctrinal content of the Cartesian philosophy. (*CM*, p. 1)

As soon emerges in the Introduction (sections 1–2), the Cartesian motifs which Husserl wishes to develop radically are twofold: they concern both the aims and the methods of Descartes' *Meditations*. The central aim of the *Meditations*, says Husserl, was 'a complete reforming of philosophy into a science grounded on an absolute foundation' (*CM*, p. 1); and in addition to this there was the further aim of establishing this philosophical science as the foundation of all other sciences. The method to be employed was a certain kind of self-reflective procedure: more specifically, the 'method of doubt', in practising which the individual meditating philosopher 'refuses to let himself accept anything as existent unless it is secured against any conceivable possibility of becoming doubtful' (*CM*, p. 3).

What Husserl will argue, mainly in the First Meditation, is that, had Descartes applied this method consistently, and followed through its implications, he would, in achieving these aims, have arrived at substantive conclusions quite different from those to which he in fact came. The first such conclusion was: 'I exist'. Husserl accepts this, provided that it is understood in a certain way. But he rejects most of the further doctrines which Descartes, having misunderstood this initial claim, thought he could derive from it. In particular, Husserl refuses to accept the doctrines of what he terms 'Objective Nature' and 'the duality of finite substances' (*CM*, p. 3): the existence of a subject-independent world, populated by two kinds of entities, minds and bodies.

We will now elaborate this sketch of how Husserl presents his relationship to Descartes, partly by reference to the text of his Introduction, and partly by providing some necessary philosophical background.[1] We can begin with Husserl's Cartesian aim of constructing philosophy as 'a science with absolute foundations'. The first point to note is that the term translated here as 'science', namely '*Wissenschaft*', has a much broader sense than is normal for the English term 'science'. The latter typically implies the use of empirical methods – observation and experimental testing. It is hence applied primarily to those forms of enquiry which employ such methods: to physics, chemistry, physiology, etc,; and also to the human or social sciences such as psychology, sociology and history, to the extent that they share these methods with the natural sciences.

By contrast, the term '*Wissenschaft*' refers to any systematic, rational form of enquiry with rigorous and objective (in the sense of inter – subjectively agreed and applicable) procedures of validation. Hence the term is not reserved exclusively for the empirical sciences, but may also be applied to the formal, a priori 'sciences' such as mathematics and logic, and to the various 'hermeneutic' disciplines concerned with the interpretation of meanings – such as the study of literary texts and, according to at least some philosophical views, the human and social 'sciences'. Thus in order to merit the status of *Wissenschaft*, a form of enquiry is not, as such, required to employ empirical methods.[2]

So in adopting the aim of establishing a 'scientific' philosophy, Husserl is not saying that philosophy should share its methods, let alone its content, with any of these specific kinds of science – empirical, formal, hermeneutic, and so on. This has important implications for how one should understand his further Cartesian aim, that this philosophical science is to provide the foundation for all other sciences. For example, some philosophers have argued that, amongst the empirical sciences, physics has a 'foundational' role, meaning by this that the laws of all the other empirical sciences are somehow reducible to the laws of physics. But this is not the sense in which, for Husserl, philosophy is to be the foundation of the sciences: it is not a basic empirical science from which the theories of other such sciences can be derived.

What kind of foundation this might instead be we shall leave aside for the moment, as does Husserl at this point in the *Cartesian Meditations*. (We shall also, for the sake of convenience, focus mainly upon the empirical sciences when we discuss the relationship between Husserl's phenomenology and 'other sciences'.) But what of his view that philosophy itself should have an 'absolute' foundation? What Husserl means by this emerges mainly in his discussion of 'the idea of science' at the beginning of the First Meditation, and we shall examine this in the next section. For now it can simply be said that an absolute foundation has two main characteristics: it depends upon nothing else; and it is itself indubitable.

We can now consider the second Cartesian 'motif', namely Descartes' philosophical *method*. According to Husserl, Descartes believed that, if philosophy is to have foundations that depend upon nothing else, and which are indubitable, then anyone engaging in philosophy had only themselves to rely upon. Philosophy, as Husserl puts it, must be 'the philosopher's quite personal affair' (*CM*, p. 2); and only that which he finds himself unable to doubt can be accepted. Further, says Husserl, had Descartes been faced with the objection that all intellectual work is necessarily collaborative, and hence cannot be performed by 'an individual', he might well have replied:

> I, the solitary individual philosophizer, owe much to others; but what they accept as true, what they offer me as allegedly established by their insight, is for me at first only something they claim. If I am to accept is, I must justify it by a perfect insight on my part. Therein consists my autonomy – mine and that of every genuine scientist. (*CM*, p. 2, note 2)

Two points can be noted about this passage. The first is that Husserl clearly attaches some considerable normative, moral significance to the Cartesian method. In refusing to accept what one cannot establish for oneself, one is displaying most fully one's individual autonomy, and making oneself accountable for one's beliefs: Husserl refers to this as 'self-responsibility' (*CM*, p. 6). Second, the refusal to accept without questioning what others claim to have established is an important application of Husserl's principle that the meditating philosopher must, in engaging in the Cartesian project, free himself from all 'prejudices'; and later on he will argue that Descartes failed to do this.

The term 'prejudice' means literally, 'pre-judgement'.[3] In requiring that all prejudices be discarded, Husserl is here concerned to eliminate any prior judgements or assumptions that have not been adequately justified. Hence, at the very outset of this 'complete reforming of philosophy' (*CM*, p. 1), it is particularly important not to assume, not to take for granted, any of the concepts or doctrines supposedly established by other philosophical schools or traditions. Indeed, Husserl expresses a certain disdain for the (then) current state of philosophy, with its fragmentation into competing schools, many of which gave a 'mere semblance of philosophizing seriously' (*CM*, p. 5). This makes avoiding prejudices and 'starting anew' all the more vital. It is, says Husserl, a fitting time

> to subject to a Cartesian overthrow the immense philosophical literature with its medley of great traditions, of comparatively serious new beginnings, of stylish literary activity (which counts on 'making an effect' but not on being studied),

and to begin with new *meditationes de prima philosophia* [the full Latin title of Descartes' *Meditations*]. (*CM*, p. 5)

In the First Meditation, Husserl introduces the key phenomenological procedure of 'bracketing', the *epoché*, by analogy with Descartes' method of doubt; and he claims that in both cases what is first established, indubitably, is 'the pure Ego', the 'I' of the meditating philosopher.[4] But he criticizes Descartes for the further doctrinal conlusions he went on to draw from this: above all, for their *realist* character. (Husserl normally uses the term 'objectivist', and sometimes 'naive objectivist': see, e.g. *CM*, p. 4. But we will use 'realist' because of its greater familiarity.) What is this realism, which Husserl so strongly rejects?

The realist believes that there is an external world, whose nature and existence are independent of one's knowledge of, or beliefs about, it. Thus, for the realist, what is known about the world would be true of it even if there were no one to know this: knowledge involves the discovery of what is there quite independently of its being discovered. Further, those who in fact happen to acquire such knowledge (in particular, human beings) are just as much part of this world as are the other entities about which this knowledge is gained. Hence they, too, are legitimate 'objects' of knowledge. It may well be that, in order to acquire knowledge of reality, various specific characteristics are required: certain mental capacities, a brain and sense-organs of a particular kind, and so on. But these characteristics can themselves be investigated and understood in essentially the same way as anything else, for example by empirical sciences such as psychology and physiology.

It should be noted that, in this fairly minimal characterization of realism, nothing has been said about what *sorts* of entities belong to the real world. In the *Cartesian Meditations* Husserl considers realism mainly in the specific form of (Cartesian) dualism, according to which there are two basic kinds of entity, namely 'minds' and 'bodies', which can interact causally with each other. Nonetheless his rejection of realism applies also to other forms of it, with different ontologies: for example to materialism, with its exclusion of the mental, or to realist philosophies which accept the independent existence of abstract objects such as numbers, and so on.[5]

Husserl believes that, had Descartes kept consistently to his method and its implications, he would have avoided realism. At least potentially, says Husserl:

the *Meditations* were epoch-making in a quite unique sense, and precisely because of their going back to the pure *ego cogito*. Descartes, in fact, inaugurates an entirely new kind of philosophy. Changing its total style, philosophy takes a radical turn: from naive objectivism [i.e. realism] to transcendental subjectivism. (*CM*, p. 4)

Husserl's philosophy, then, is a form of 'transcendental subjectivism', or of transcendental idealism – as is Kant's, with which it has much in common. (A comparison between the two will be made in Chapter Three, section 5.) There are two key features of transcendental subjectivism which make it so radically at odds with realism. First, the existence of a 'real world' that is wholly independent of the 'subject' that knows or experiences this world is denied. Second, it is claimed that this knowing subject does not itself belong to the world which it knows or experiences. This subject of knowledge or experience is termed by Husserl the 'pure' or 'transcendental' Ego – the relatively slight differences in meaning of these terms need not concern us yet. Far from being a part of the (known or experienced) world of objects, this Ego is presupposed by the world, which therefore cannot be said straightforwardly to exist by or in itself.

We can now proceed to the First Meditation, where many of the ideas briefly sketched or alluded to in the Introduction begin to be developed. In the next section, we consider Husserl's account of what exactly would be required for philosophy to be a genuine science. In section 3, we turn to his presentation of the phenomenological epoché. We then examine, in section 4, his criticism and diagnosis of Descartes' dualistic realism. We conclude, in section 5, by noting certain problems with Husserl's 'Cartesian' presentation of the epoché, and sketch an alternative to this.

2   The Idea of Science

In the opening sections of the First Meditation (*CM*, sections 3–6) Husserl sets out to articulate 'the idea of science', and hence what philosophy would have to be in order for it to be a science – though he notes that one cannot assume it will in fact be possible to develop a philosophy that meets these requirements, whatever they turn out to be. But the first question is how one is to go about discovering what this idea of science consists in.

Husserl says that one must take care to avoid adopting without critical reflection any particular conception of science already developed by philosophers; to do so would involve 'prejudices'. Instead he proposes that one should examine the sciences that actually exist, and try to identify the idea of science which is implicit in them. That is, one should explore those forms of enquiry which are generally recognized *as* sciences (which, as we have noted, include both empirical and non-empirical sciences), and try to discover those features by virtue of which they are deemed to have this status. In doing so, Husserl emphasizes, one is not automatically accepting that they deserve this status, since they may in fact fail to achieve their own aims. But one can at least discover what it is that is aimed at, and which would, if achieved, make them (at least in their own terms) 'genuine sciences'.

With these qualifications in mind, Husserl proposes that one should proceed by 'immersing' oneself in the various sciences, trying to explicate the general conception of science implicit in the actual practice of scientific enquiry. It is, he says, a matter of

> 'immersing ourselves' in the scientific striving and doing that pertain to them [the sciences], in order to see clearly and distinctly what is really being aimed at. If we do so, if we immerse ourselves progressively in the characteristic intention of scientific endeavour, the constituent parts of the general final [i.e. 'aimed at'] idea, genuine science, become explicated for us. (*CM*, p. 9)

The overall picture that Husserl claims to emerge from this procedure is this: any science aims at achieving a hierarchically ordered structure of *judgements*, which rests ultimately upon *evidential* foundations that are both *apodictic* (indubitable) and *first in themselves* (dependent on nothing else).[6]

Let us now examine the main elements in this picture of science. Husserl begins by introducing the ideas of '"judicative" doing and the "judgement" *itself*' (*CM*, p. 10). In making a judgement one claims that something is the case: one makes a truth-claim. An example might be the judgement that all metals expand when heated. (This is our example, not Husserl's – there is a marked lack of examples in the *Cartesian Meditations*.) The making of the claim, a conscious mental act, is the 'judicative doing'; whilst what is claimed is the 'judgment itself'.

But in science one not only makes judgements but also tries to support or justify them. Husserl calls this the 'grounding' of judgements, 'in which the *"correctness"*, the *"truth"*, of the judgment should be shown' (*CM*, p. 10). He distinguishes, in effect, between two kinds of grounding, and correspondingly between two sorts of judgements, 'mediate' and 'immediate'. The grounding of mediate judgements consists in their support by other judgements, whose relevance is indicated by the meaning or 'sense' of what is being claimed in the judgement that is to be grounded. Thus:

> mediate judgments have such a sense-relatedness to other judgments that believing them 'presupposes' believing those others – in the manner characteristic of a believing on account of something believed already. (*CM*, p. 10)

So, continuing with our example, the mediate judgement that all metals expand on heating 'presupposes', and is hence to be grounded by reference to, the further judgements that copper, iron, and so on behave in this way. These latter judgements might themselves be mediate, and hence grounded in other judgements. But there is also a distinct set of judgements, the 'immediate' ones, upon which all mediate judgements ultimately depend, and which involve some kind of direct encounter with the states of affairs to which these judgements refer. It is at this point that Husserl introduces the idea of *evidence*:

> there is sometimes a pre-eminent judicative meaning [*Meinen*], a judicative having of such and such itself. This having is called *evidence*. In it the affair, the complex (or state) of affairs, instead of being merely meant 'from afar', is present as the affair 'itself', *the affair-complex or state-of-affairs 'itself'*; the judger accordingly possesses it itself. (*CM*, p. 10; square brackets in translated text)

For instance, one might actually be heating a piece of iron, and see its expansion; and, in making the judgement that it had expanded, this state of affairs would be 'evident' to one. It is this idea of something's being *evident to* someone that is the central feature of Husserl's concept of evidence.[7] In this respect it differs from the more familiar understanding of evidence as whatever is cited to support or dispute some claim. On this latter view, the main emphasis is upon something's being *evidence for* or *against* such a claim: for example, experimental evidence that might confirm or refute a scientific hypothesis.

But there is another, and more important, feature of Husserl's conception of evidence that distinguishes it from more familiar ones: in particular, from the sense of 'evidence' associated with empiricist theories of knowledge, where all evidence is regarded as essentially perceptual or sensory in character. For Husserl, by contrast, there is no such limitation upon what can be found to be evident, and hence be counted as evidence. Rather, what is evident may include anything that might naturally be said to be 'seen', where this term refers, not just to visual perception, but to any kind of direct and immediate mental grasp or intuition of something. For example (again ours), one might in this sense 'see' that one proposition does or does not follow from another; or that there is an ambiguity in some passage in a text. As Husserl puts it:

> Evidence is, in an *extremely broad sense*, an '*experiencing*' of something that is, and is thus; it is precisely a mental seeing of something itself. (*CM*, p. 12)

This broad sense of evidence corresponds, it should be noted, to the broad range of sciences whose 'idea of science' Husserl is attempting to explicate. This idea of science, which Husserl will take as defining what philosophy should 'strive to be', is not derived exclusively from the empirical sciences. It should, for example, be equally applicable to an axiomatic formal science, such as Euclidean geometry. Hence, in particular, to talk about immediate judgements being grounded in evidence does not, as such, mean their being grounded in empirical sensory evidence.

Judgements, then, are to be grounded ultimately in evidence. But Husserl claims that one can distinguish, within the category of evidence, between what is 'merely' evident and what is *apodictically* so. The term 'apodictic' comes from the Greek *'apodeiktikos'*, meaning 'clearly demonstrating'. It has been given a number of more technical philosophical senses including, in logic, 'necessarily true'. But Husserl says that what he means by the idea of apodicticity is 'absolute indubitability' (*CM*, p. 15), the impossibility of doubting something; and he contrasts apodictic with non-apodictic evidence in the following way:

> Any evidence is a grasping of something that is, or is thus, a grasping in the mode of 'it-itself', with full certainty of its being, a certainty that accordingly excludes every doubt. But it does not follow that full certainty excludes the conceivability that what is evident could subsequently become doubtful, or the conceivability that being could prove to be an illusion – indeed sensuous experience furnishes us with cases where that happens.... An *apodictic* evidence, however, is not merely certainty of the affairs ... evident in it; rather it discloses itself, to a critical reflection, as having the signal peculiarity of being *at the same time* [i.e. as well as being certain] *the absolute unimaginableness* (inconceivability) of their *non-being*, and thus excluding in advance every doubt as 'objectless', empty. (*CM*, pp. 15–16)

To understand the distinction Husserl is making here between apodictic and non-apodictic evidence, one has to avoid thinking of the concept of certainty as implying that what is said to be 'certain' cannot be possibly false. Certainty, in this sense, is a concept of epistemic 'success', of unassailable truth. For Husserl, by contrast, certainty is a feature that may characterize some of one's experiences of things – it is, one might say, a phenomenological rather than an epistemological matter. Thus, when something is evident, it is 'certain'; and it 'excludes doubt' in the sense that in experiencing something as certain one does not at the same time experience it as doubtful. But later, of course, such doubts or uncertainties may arise, and even turn out to be justified: that something is certain, or evident, does not exclude this possibility.

However, says Husserl, there are some cases of evidence where, upon critical reflection, one sees that doubt is not just absent but impossible. This 'critical reflection' involves one trying to *imagine* that what is evident might be other than it presents itself as being. If this cannot be imagined, the evidence is apodictic; if it can be, the evidence is non-apodictic. Hence apodicticity, like evidence and certainty, is also understood by reference to a specific kind of experience, in this case 'imagining'; and indubitability is a matter of one's actually being unable to doubt something, i.e. to imagine it as other than it is.

Husserl introduces the idea of apodictic evidence as one of two kinds of 'perfection' that evidence may have. The other kind he calls 'adequacy' or 'completeness'. Evidence is incomplete or inadequate, he says, when there is a one-sidedness and ... a relative obscurity and indistinctness that qualify the givenness of the affairs themselves ... i.e. an infectedness of the 'experience' with *unfulfilled components*, with *expectant* and *attendant meanings*. Perfecting then takes place as a synthetic course of further harmonious experiences in which these attendant meanings become fulfilled in actual experience. (*CM*, p. 15)

It is difficult to understand this fully without reference to Husserl's accounts of 'horizonality' and 'truth' in the Second and Third Meditations, which we shall examine in the next chapter. But what he has in mind here can be illustrated by the following example. Suppose that one is looking at a tree. Not every feature of the tree will be directly evident: for instance, one will not be able to see the back of it, or the detailed texture of the bark. Hence the evidence of 'the whole tree' is incomplete or inadequate. Nonetheless, many of these additional features of the tree will be 'implicit' in this visual experience of it, and may themselves become evident in further such experiences (for instance, looking from another angle, or from a shorter distance). This is what Husserl means by the 'expectant and attendant meanings' becoming 'fulfilled in actual experience'.

The main elements of the idea of science that have so far emerged, then, are as follows. A science must consist of a set of judgements making truth-claims; these judgements are to be grounded – Husserl calls a grounded judgement a 'cognition' (*CM*, p. 10) – either mediately, in other judgements, or immediately, in evidence; and ideally this evidence should be both apodictic and complete. Taken together, these imply a further requirement: that there should be what Husserl terms 'a systematic order of cognitions' (*CM*, p. 14), a hierarchically ordered structure of grounded judgements; and hence, in particular, a basic level of cognitions upon which all others depend. These Husserl refers to as cognitions that are 'first in themselves' (*CM*, p. 14); and, given the role of evidence in grounding judgements, there will likewise have to be evidence or, as Husserl often puts it, evidenc*es*, that are 'first in themselves'.

Husserl presents this further requirement in the following passage, considering it from the standpoint of the philosophical meditator's aim of constructing philosophy as a science:

Since the form belonging to a systematic order of cognitions – genuine cognitions – is part of this idea [of a science], there emerges, as the *question of the beginning*, the inquiry for those cognitions that are first in themselves and support the whole storied edifice of universal knowledge [i.e. philosophy]. Consequently, if our presumptive aim is to be capable of becoming a practically possible one, we meditators ... must have access to evidences that already bear the stamp of fitness for this function, in that they are recognizable as preceding all other imaginable evidences. (*CM*, p. 14)

In saying that the evidence which is 'first in itself' must 'bear the stamp of fitness' for its function, Husserl means that it must be *evident* that it does; and he later goes on to add that ideally this should be apodictically so.

Husserl concludes his account of the idea of science by formulating its implications for the possibility of constructing philosophy as a science in the following way:

> In accordance with what has already been said, we now formulate, as an initial definite question of beginning philosophy, the question whether it is possible for us to bring out evidences that, on the one hand, carry with them – as we must now say: apodictically – the insight that, as 'first in themselves', they precede all other imaginable evidences and, on the other hand, can be seen to be themselves apodictic. (*CM*, p. 16)

It is this question that Husserl addresses in the next three sections (7–9) of the First Meditation, and which leads him to introduce the fundamental phenomenological procedure of the epoché. But before examining this, we shall note one other distinction that Husserl makes in explicating the idea of science: between *predicative* and *pre-predicative* evidence and judgement.

'Predicative' means 'expressed in the form of a statement'. In a statement, something is predicated of something else: for example, in the statement 'the tree has green leaves', 'has green leaves' is predicated of 'the tree'. Correspondingly, 'pre-predicative' means 'not (yet) expressed in the form of a statement'. So pre-predicative evidence is the actual experiencing of something that is evident to one, whilst predicative evidence is the expression or representation of this experience in a statement. The same distinction can be applied to judgements; for Husserl distinguishes the mental act of judging that something is the case (pre-predicative) from the statement in which this judgement is expressed (predicative).

Further, Husserl maintains that whether or not a particular experience is adequately represented by its predicative expression will itself be evident. Thus:

> That which is meant [in a pre-predicative judgement] or, perchance, evidently viewed [in a pre-predicative evidence] receives predicative expression; and science always intends to judge expressly [to make predicative judgements] and keep the judgment or the truth fixed, as an express judgment or an express truth. But the expression as such has its own comparatively good or bad way of fitting what is meant or itself given; and therefore it has its own evidence or non-evidence, which also goes into the predicating. (*CM*, p. 11)

This passage, it should be noted, seems to present a view of the relationship between language and experience which is both characteristic of Husserl's phenomenology and philosophically quite problematic. For Husserl appears to ignore the possibility of 'language preceding experience' – of the conceptual resources of a particular language in some way determining the character of what is experienced. Rather, his concern is with how well or badly such experience is predicatively expressed in language.[8]

3 The Epoché and Transcendental Subjectivity

In sections 7–9 of the First Meditation, Husserl considers how the conditions that must be satisfied for philosophy to be a genuine science might actually be met. He has claimed that, at least as a starting-point, a realm of evidence must be identified which meets three requirements. Replacing the rather cumbersome phrase 'first in itself' by the term 'primary', we can state these requirements as follows. This realm of evidence must be primary; it must be apodictic; and its primacy must itself be apodictic. But Husserl in effect ignores the third of these, noting in a later marginal comment that he has done so (*CM*, p. 21, note 4); and we shall follow him in this.

His overall argument in these sections is this. It might initially seem that the existence of the world qualifies as primary evidence. But it is far from clear that, even if this were so, it would also satisfy the requirement of apodicticity. So, since the existence of the world is not obviously apodictic, one should, as a meditating (Cartesian) philosopher, 'suspend judgement' about its existence. This is the phenomenological epoché, the procedure of 'bracketing'. What emerges from this procedure is twofold. First, there is the vast realm of one's conscious acts or experiences, such as perceiving or remembering something, now describable in a way that does not assume the world's existence. Husserl refers to these as '*cogitationes*', using the plural form of the Latin term '*cogitatio*', which means literally a 'thought' or 'act of thinking'. Second, there is what Husserl calls the 'pure' or 'transcendental' Ego, the 'I' which is reflecting upon these (its) experiences. Both the Ego and its cogitationes can be shown to satisfy the requirement of primacy, and in particular to have priority with respect to 'the world'. Further, says Husserl, this Ego is apodictically given. The question of the apodicticity of the Ego's cogitationes, however, he defers until later in the '*Cartesian Mediations* (see Chapter Three, section 2, below).

Let us now examine these claims in more detail. 'The question of evidences that are first in themselves', says Husserl,

> can apparently be answered without any trouble. Does not the *existence of the world* present itself forthwith as such an evidence? The life of everyday action relates to the world. All the sciences relate to it. ... It is so very obvious that no one would think of asserting it expressly as a proposition. After all, we have our continuous experience in which this world incessantly stands before our eyes, as existing without question. (*CM*, p. 17)

The existence of the external world, Husserl is suggesting, would seem to be evident, and an evidence that is primary. It is evident in that our perceptual experience constantly presents us with a world of objects that exist independently of us. That it is also primary is supported by the fact that both scientific and everyday activity seem to depend on assuming its existence. For instance, the empirical sciences apparently describe and explain the world; and in everyday life one apparently relies upon there being a world to be perceived and acted upon, with respect to which one makes one's plans, and so on.

However, Husserl continues, this evidence does not straightforwardly meet the second requirement, namely apodicticity. Echoing Descartes, he notes that perceptual experience is prone to error, sometimes of a very extensive nature:

> Not only can a particular experienced thing suffer devaluation as an illusion of the senses; the whole unitarily surveyable nexus [a connected group or series of things], experienced throughout a period of time, can prove to be an illusion, a coherent dream. (*CM*, p. 17)

But Husserl insists that one cannot immediately conclude from this that the evidence of the world's existence is *not* apodictic. Apodicticity means indubitability; and the test for indubitability is whether one can imagine something being other than it is. Hence this evidence would only be non-apodictic if one really could imagine the non-existence of the world. To show this would require a careful process of what Husserl terms 'critical reflection' (in effect, carefully conducted thought-experiments in the imagination), and not merely the noting of actual errors and illusions. Thus, for the moment, he says:

> We shall only retain this much: that the evidence of world- experience would, at all events, need to be criticized [i.e. subjected to critical reflection] with regard to its validity and range, before it could be used for the purpose of a radical grounding of science, and that therefore we must not take that evidence to be, without question, immediately apodictic. (*CM*, pp. 17–18)

But this task of critical reflection turns out to be unnecessary. For Husserl now argues that there is another realm of evidence which undermines the initially plausible claim to primacy of the world's existence, since this new realm can be shown to have priority with respect to 'the world'. This is the realm of 'transcendental subjectivity' (*CM*, p. 18), the pure Ego and its cogitationes. It is made accessible by the phenomenological epoché, a procedure that is introduced by Husserl as a response to the apparent lack of apodicticity in the evidence of the world's existence. What he proposes is that one should 'suspend judgement' about its existence, and 'parenthesize' (put into brackets, put to one side) the existential assumptions made in everyday life and the sciences.

To get some initial sense of what Husserl is proposing here, the following remarks may be helpful. Consider an everyday experience such as seeing a tree. In having this experience one 'naturally' assumes that the tree one sees exists, that it belongs to a world that is independent of one's perceptual experience of it. This is a central assumption of what Husserl terms 'the natural attitude' (e.g. *CM*. p. 20). But now, as a 'meditating philosopher', one suspends judgement about this assumption: one no longer *makes* it. What one needs to do, therefore, is to find a way of describing this perceptual experience that does not commit one to the tree's existence. It might at first be thought that the only way of doing this would be to avoid any mention of the tree in this 'philosophical', reflective description. But that, in effect, would be to distort or misrepresent the very experience one is trying to describe: a proper description of this experience must retain the fact that it was a 'seeing-of-a-tree'. One must, therefore, give the experience that description, whilst at the same time remaining neutral about, i.e. neither affirming nor denying, the existence-assumption concerning the tree.

That this is not an impossible task might be suggested by an analogy with familiar features of reported speech (though it must be emphasized that this analogy is not used by Husserl). Suppose that on some occasion one says: 'There is a dog in the garden'; and that later on one wishes to report the making of this claim. One might then say: 'I said that there was a dog in the garden'. In making this report one is not committing oneself to the truth or falsity of the claim itself, but only to one's having made it. Thus the truth of the report is independent of the truth of the claim reported; and hence also of the existence or otherwise of the dog and the garden. The report is 'neutral' with respect to these. To be neutral here is not to cast doubt on the initial claim, but to put this matter aside – to 'bracket' or 'parenthesize' it, for the purposes of a correct report.

We can now consider what Husserl actually says about the epoché, in section 8. 'As radically meditating philosophers', having suspended judgement about the world's existence,

> we now have neither a science that we accept [since it assumes the world's existence] nor a world that exists for us. Instead of simply existing for us – that is, being accepted naturally by us in our experiential believing in its existence – the world is for us only something that claims being. (*CM*, p. 18)

Husserl is saying something like this. The philosopher no longer accepts that the world exists, or 'has being', but wishes to register the fact that in everyday experience it is nonetheless taken to exist or 'have being'. So instead of talking about 'the world' as if it *does* exist, one must talk about it as that which is taken to exist – as that which 'claims being'.

The same idea is put in several other passages here. For instance, Husserl says: 'The being of the world ... must be for us, henceforth, only an acceptance-phenomenon' (*CM*, p. 18) – that is, something which is in fact accepted in everyday experience, with this acceptance now being noted, but not endorsed, by the philosopher operating the phenomenological epoché. Likewise, he says that this world 'is for me, from now on, only a phenomenon of being, instead of something that is [i.e. exists, 'has being']' (*CM*, p. 19). It appears to one, in everyday experience, as existing; but now, as a meditating philosopher, one restricts oneself to registering the fact of its appearing as such, without thereby actually accepting (or rejecting) its existence.

But Husserl is concerned to emphasize that, whilst 'the world' is now only something which 'claims being', the fact that it does 'claim being' must nonetheless be preserved in the phenomenological description – otherwise this would not be a correct description of experience. So, although in performing the epoché, the existence-assumptions of the natural attitude are no longer made, the fact that they *are* made in the natural attitude must still be registered. In a sense, therefore, 'nothing has changed':

> the world experienced in this reflectively grasped life goes on being for me (in a certain manner) 'experienced' as before, and with just the content it has at any particular time. It goes on appearing as it appeared before; the only difference is that I, as reflecting philosophically, no longer keep in effect (no longer accept) the natural believing in existence involved in experiencing the world – though that believing too is still there and grasped by my noticing regard. (*CM*, pp. 19–20)

Husserl notes that this 'reflectively grasped life' consists not only of perceptual experience, but also of all the other kinds of conscious acts (cogitationes), such as remembering, deciding, willing, valuing, judging, expecting, hoping, and so on. He refers to these as 'concrete subjective processes' (*CM*, p. 20), and says that the phenomenological epoché is to be applied to all of them. For, as he argues in the Second Meditation, all such conscious experiences are 'of' or 'about' something: they have 'objects' (for instance, what it is that is experienced or remembered) whose existence is to be bracketed in phenomenological reflection. We shall examine this in the next chapter.

Having now introduced the epoché, the procedure of phenomenological reduction, Husserl goes on to claim that it not only opens up this realm of cogitationes, but also reveals what he calls 'the pure ego', the 'I' that is performing the epoché and reflecting upon its own subjective processes. Thus:

> If I put myself above all this life [of ordinary experience of the world] and refrain from doing any believing that takes 'the' world straightforwardly as existing – if I direct my regard exclusively to this life itself, as consciousnes *of* 'the' world – I thereby acquire myself as the pure ego, with the pure stream of my *cogitationes*. (*CM*, p. 21)

Husserl's point here is that, in the very process of one's suspending judgement about the existence of the world, one must inevitably recognize the 'I' that is engaged in this process, and which can now reflect upon its own cogitationes. Both the Ego and its cogitationes are 'pure' in that they have, as it were, survived the parenthesizing of the world's existence: they are thus free from the (philosophical) 'impurities' of the existential assumptions made in the natural attitude.

More light is shed on this idea of 'purity' in the next stage of Husserl's argument to which we now turn. The question he addresses is whether the Ego and its cogitationes meet the requirements of primacy and apodicticity that have been identified as the key elements of the idea of science. He begins by considering primacy, and argues that, whilst it had initially seemed that the existence of the world satisfied this requirement, it can now be seen that what emerges from the epoché – the Ego and its cogitationes – has priority with respect to this. There are, in effect, two distinguishable aspects of this priority, and we shall examine each in turn.

The first is that the Ego and its cogitationes are not dependent upon the existence of the world. This, he thinks, follows directly from what has already been said about the nature of the epoché. The Ego and its cogitationes are what emerge from the procedure of suspending judgement about the 'world's existence; and hence they 'exist' whether or not it exists. As Husserl puts it:

> If I keep purely what comes into view – for me, the one who is meditating – by virtue of my free epoché with respect to the being of the experienced world, the momentous fact is that I, with my life [my cogitationes], remain untouched in my existential status, regardless of whether or not the world exists. (*CM*, p. 25)

And likewise:

> If I abstained – as I was free to do and as I did – and still abstain from every believing involved in or founded upon sensuous [perceptual] experiencing, so that the being of the experienced world remains unaccepted by me, still this abstaining is what it is; and it exists, together with the whole stream of experiencing life [cogitationes]. (*CM*, p. 19)

The second aspect of this priority is rather more difficult to specify. Husserl initially introduces it in the following way:

> Anything belonging to the world, any spatio-temporal being, exists for me – that is to say, is accepted by me – in that I experience it, perceive it, remember it, think of it somehow, judge about it, desire it, or the like. (*CM*, p. 21)

Taken by itself, this passage might be read as asserting an *epistemic* relationship between the Ego's conscious experiences and the world: that it is only by reference to the former that its claims to knowledge of the latter can legitimately be made. But this is not what Husserl has in mind, as can be seen from the way he then continues. 'The world', he declares,

> gets its whole sense, universal and specific, and its acceptance as existing, exclusively from such *cogitationes* ... by my living, by my experiencing, thinking, valuing, and acting. I can enter no world other than the one that gets its sense and acceptance or status [*Sinn und Geltung*] in and from me, myself. (*CM*, p. 21; square brackets in translated text)

The claim being made here is not that one can only know about the world via one's conscious experiences, but rather that it is they which provide the very sense or meaning of 'the world' and its 'existence'. That is, whatever can be meant by ascribing existence to the world must be rooted in the various kinds of experience of 'it' that one has or can have. In this respect, therefore, the Ego and its cogitationes are 'prior' to the world. As Husserl puts it:

> Thus the being of the pure ego and his *cogitationes*, as a being that is prior in itself, is antecedent to the natural being of the world – the world of which I always speak, the one of which I *can* speak. Natural being is a realm whose existential status [*Seinsgeltung*] is secondary; it continually presupposes the realm of transcendental being. (*CM*, p. 21; square brackets in translated text)

This 'realm of transcendental being' is that of the pure Ego and its cogitationes, now described as 'transcendental' precisely because of its presuppositional relationship to the world, its providing the basis for the world's 'existential status'. Thus Husserl's claims about this second aspect of the pure Ego's priority commit him, in effect, to a form of transcendental idealism.[9] We shall not comment on this here, since it will be discussed in Chapter Three below.

Husserl now goes on to consider whether this realm of transcendental subjectivity, having been shown to meet the requirement of primacy, can also be shown to meet the second requirement for a genuine science, namely apodicticity. That the pure Ego, at least, is apodictically evident can be established quite easily, he believes – the apodicticity of its cogitationes is to be examined separately. Endorsing Descartes' famous demonstration that 'I exist' is indubitable, Husserl says:

> That *ego sum* or *sum cogitans* must be pronounced apodictic, and that accordingly we get a first apodictically existing basis to stand on, was already seen by Descartes. As we all know, he emphasizes the indubitability of that proposition and stresses the fact that 'I doubt' would itself presuppose 'I am'. For Descartes too, it is a matter of that Ego who grasps himself after he has deprived the experienced world of acceptance, because it might be doubtful. (*CM*, p. 22)

It may be helpful at this point to note the following passage from *The Crisis*, where Husserl spells out this argument in his own terms, making explicit reference to the phenomenological epoché rather than to Descartes' method of doubt. Thus:

> If I refrain from taking any position on the being or non-being of the world, if I deny myself any ontic validity [assumption of existence] related to the world, not *every* ontic validity is prohibited for me within this epoché. I, the ego carrying out the epoché, am not included in its realm of objects but rather ... am excluded in principle. I am necessary as the one carrying it out. It is precisely herein that I find just the apodictic ground that I was seeking, the one which absolutely excludes every possible doubt. (*CES*, p. 77)

Hence unlike the existence of the world – whose apodicticity, it will be remembered, had earlier been deemed to be at least problematic – the pure Ego is apodictic; and its apodicticity is, indeed, established by reflecting upon the implications of just that procedure, the epoché, which had been introduced in response to the apparent 'failure' of the world in this respect.

However, says Husserl, despite this Cartesian demonstration of the pure Ego's apodicticity,

> the problem of apodicticity – and consequently the problem of the primary basis on which to ground a philosophy – is not thereby removed. (*CM*, p. 22)

This is because it is far from clear how extensive is 'the range covered by our apodictic evidence' (*CM*, p. 22). The problem here is twofold. First, even the 'extent' of the pure Ego's apodicticity has not yet been considered. For instance, this Ego might plausibly be thought to have temporal continuity, and memories of its own past (see Chapter Two, section 2); yet such memories are not obviously apodictic. Second, it is by no means clear that apodicticity can be ascribed to this Ego's particular cogitationes. This is an issue which Husserl considers more fully in later Meditations, and which we shall therefore leave aside at present (see Chapter Three, section 2).

4 Descartes' Errors and his Axiomatic 'Prejudice'

In the final stage of this First Meditation (sections 10–11), Husserl, having so far emphasized the parallels between himself and Descartes, now focuses upon their differences, and diagnoses the sources of what he regards as the latter's errors. For, as we noted earlier, it is Husserl's view that Descartes somehow misapplied his philosophical method, and thereby arrived at substantive conclusions with which Husserl radically disagrees, despite accepting Descartes' aims of establishing philosophy as a science with absolute foundations, and also as the foundation of the other sciences:

> It seems so easy, following Descartes, to lay hold of the pure Ego and his *cogitationes*. And yet it is as though we were on the brink of a precipice, where advancing calmly and surely is a matter of philosophical life and death. (*CM*, p. 23)

Continuing this metaphor briefly: to go over the precipice is to fall into the abyss of (dualistic) realism; and the fateful step which Descartes unfortunately took was to characterize the 'I' whose existence had been established by the method of doubt as a mind – *res* (or *substantia*) *cogitans*, a thinking 'thing' or 'substance'. In doing so, says Husserl, Descartes mistakenly ascribed to the pure Ego the status of an object in the world; and the fact that he characterized it as mental rather than physical in no way mitigates the error. The source of this error, Husserl argues, was Descartes' 'prejudice' in adopting an axiomatic conception of science, and hence also of philosophy. This same axiomatic prejudice also led him to misrepresent the foundational role of philosophy in relation to the sciences, and to ignore the philosophical possibilities presented by the vast new realm of evidence, the realm of transcendental subjectivity, that emerges from the phenomenological epoché.

Let us now look at these claims in more detail, starting with what was supposedly Descartes' central error, concerning the ontological status of the Ego. Having arrived at the indubitable 'I exist', says Husserl,

> Descartes introduced the apparently insignificant but actually fateful change whereby the ego becomes a *substantia cogitans*, a separate human *'mens sive animus'* ['mind or soul']. (*CM*, p. 24)

A brief sketch of the view here being attributed to Descartes, and its relation to his dualistic realism, may be helpful at this point. Having argued from the indubitable 'I think' to its supposed consequent, 'I exist', Descartes posed the question of the nature of this 'I', or ego. His answer was that this ego is a mind or mental substance, a particular concrete entity enduring through time, whose defining characteristic is that it 'thinks', or is conscious. Further, each individual human was regarded as consisting in some form of union between one such mind, and a body, or *res extensa* – a different kind of entity, whose defining characteristic is that it has extension in space. As such, each human belongs to a world comprising both other humans and various non-human beings which, unlike humans, are bodies without minds. Causal interactions can take place both between bodies and between the mind and body of each individual human; and all these interactions can be scientifically investigated and explained.

In criticizing Descartes, Husserl is not concerned with the well-known problems of dualistic interactionism, such as the intelligibility of mind-body causation. Rather his concern is exclusively with the mistake he detects in Descartes' identification of the Ego that is established by the method of doubt, either specifically with a mind, or more broadly with an individual human (a union of mind and body), belonging to a 'real world' open to scientific investigation. Restating his earlier claims about the epoché and the primacy of the pure Ego *vis-à-vis* the world, Husserl says:

> This Ego, with his Ego-life, who necessarily remains for me, by virtue of such epoché, is not a piece of the world; and if he says, 'I exist, *ego cogito*', that no longer signifies, 'I, this man, exists'.... Nor am I the separately considered psyche itself. (*CM*, p. 25)

For 'this man', or this 'psyche' (mind), belong to that very world of objects whose assumed existence has been subjected to the epoché, and cannot therefore be identified with the 'I' that performs the epoché, and which, far from being bracketed, necessarily emerges through that procedure.

Much the same criticism is made in the following passage from *The Crisis*, though this time relying on the transcendental, 'sense-giving' role of the Ego, and not merely on its 'purity':

> Descartes does not make clear to himself that the ego, his ego deprived of its worldly character [*entweltlicht*] through the epoché, in whose functioning *cogitationes* the world has all the ontic meaning [sense of 'existence'] it can ever have for him, *cannot possibly* turn up as subject-matter *in* the world, since everything that is of the *world* derives its meaning precisely *from these functions* – including, then, one's own psychic being, the ego in the usual sense. (*CES*, pp. 81–2)

In other words, what Descartes has done is to transform the 'I' which performs the epoché and gives the world (including 'one's own psychic being') its existence-sense into a part of that very world which in fact presupposes it.

It may be useful at this point to comment on the rather complex set of terms employed by Husserl in his talk of various 'egos'. The central distinction is between the ego that belongs to the world, and whose existence is therefore parenthesized in the epoché, and the Ego which is not a part of the world, and which emerges in the performance of the epoché. (We normally mark this distinction, as in the preceding sentence, by the use of 'ego' and 'Ego' respectively.) But within the framework provided by this basic distinction, a number of further differentiations are made.[10]

In the *Cartesian Meditations*, Husserl sometimes calls the former 'worldly' ego 'my natural human Ego' (*CM*, p. 26). Another appropriate name for this, which we shall sometimes use, is 'the empirical ego', thereby indicating its suitability for investigation by the various empirical sciences including, as Husserl notes, biology and psychology (*CM*, p. 25). Assuming, for these purposes, a dualistic 'division' of the empirical ego into its mental and bodily components, one can then abstract from this ego a specifically 'psychological ego', which corresponds roughly to Descartes' 'mind'. In the above passage from *The Crisis*, 'one's own psychic being, the ego in its usual sense', is this psychological ego; and in both *The Crisis* and the *Cartesian Meditations*, Husserl criticizes Descartes, as has been seen, for identifying the pure or transcendental Ego with either the psychological or the empirical ego.

Turning now to the 'non-worldly' Ego, one finds that three main designations have been given to it by the end of the First Meditation (others are introduced later, and will be noted as they occur). These are: 'philosophizing' (or 'meditating'); 'pure' (or 'reduced'); and 'transcendental'. At the risk of over-simplification, one can say that all these terms are different names for, or ways of referring to, one and the same Ego; and the significance of the different 'names' is that they each imply, or rather draw attention to, specific claims that Husserl wishes to make about this Ego. In other words, one is not being confronted with a host of different Egos, but rather with the same Ego varyingly characterized so as to emphasize the particular philosophical status or function being ascribed to it in a given context.

We can now consider each designation in turn. The 'philosophizing Ego' and 'meditating Ego' refer to the 'I' who is engaging in the kind of philosophical reflection endorsed and practised in the *Cartesian Meditations*, and initially introduced, as we have seen, by analogy with Descartes' conception of 'meditation': a process that anyone, as a philosopher, is to conduct in a first-person, self-reflective form, as a 'quite personal affair' (*CM*, p. 2). By the time one gets to the middle of the First Meditation, this idea of a philosophical meditation has been given a more specific sense through the introduction of the phenomenological epoché, or reduction. The philosophizing Ego is now seen to be the pure Ego – the Ego which, as it were, emerges unscathed from the bracketing of the world's (including the empirical ego's) existence, and can now reflect upon its (pure) cogitationes. It can also be termed 'the reduced Ego' (e.g. *CM*, p. 26), drawing attention to its emergence from the process of reduction.

Finally, there is the transcendental Ego. In talking of the Ego as transcendental, Husserl is emphasizing its sense-giving, presuppositional role: as that through which the objects in the world gain their status *as* existent objects, and which their being experienced as such therefore presupposes. (Correspondingly, when he talks of the 'transcendental phenomenological reduction' (e.g. *CM*, p. 21), he is alluding to the claim that this enables one to investigate how this 'sense-giving' is achieved.) Thus the distinction between the pure and the transcendental Ego maps onto the two aspects of the primacy that this Ego is said to have with respect to the world, which we discussed in the preceding section. The purity of the Ego indicates its 'independence' of the world's existence, and its transcendental character, the 'dependence' of the world's existential status on this Ego (and its cogitationes).

Two further points can be noted about this ego-terminology. First, it is difficult to avoid talking explicitly or implicitly of the Ego's *existence*: for instance, in saying, as we did, that 'the pure Ego' and 'the transcendental Ego' are different names that refer to the same Ego. But one must be careful not to be misled by doing so. For this is *not* the 'existence' of the world and its constituent objects, which has been parenthesized in the epoché, and whose 'sense' is, according to Husserl, to be understood by transcendental phenomenological reflection. If the transcendental Ego 'gives the world its existence-sense', then its own 'existence' cannot be said to have the same character as the world's.

Second, it should be noted that in Husserl's work the term 'transcend*ental*' has a quite different meaning from another that he also uses, namely 'transcend*ent*'. These are terms that have been given various meanings by different philosophers, for some of whom the two are distinct and for others not. The literal meaning of both is the same, viz. 'going beyond'; and for many (though not all) philosophers, including Husserl, what it is 'beyond' which something is said to 'go' is experience, or what is experienced. But this 'going beyond' can be given a number of more specific philosophical interpretations; and Husserl employs two, marked by 'transcendental' and 'transcendent'. The former, as we have seen, means 'being presupposed by one's experience of the world'. Hence the transcendental Ego 'goes beyond' the experienced world in that it is necessary for, and thus not itself a part of, that world. By contrast, transcend*ence* is a feature of the 'objects' of experience, of what is experienced; and these objects are transcend*ent* in that they 'go beyond', are 'more' or 'other' than, any particular experience or set of experiences one has or can have of them.

This distinction between 'transcendental' and 'transcendent' may become clearer by considering the following passage at the end of the First Meditation, where Husserl first uses the latter term:

> Just as the reduced Ego is not a piece of the world, so, conversely, neither the world nor any worldly object is a piece of my Ego, to be found in my conscious life as a really inherent part of it.... This *'transcendence'* is part of the intrinsic sense of anything worldly, *despite* the fact that anything worldly necessarily acquires all the sense determining it, along with its existential status, exclusively from my experiencing. (*CM*, p. 26)

To understand this passage, it is helpful to remind oneself of a central feature of the natural attitude. In, for example, everyday visual perception, one assumes that what is perceived exists independently of the act of perceiving it, that it belongs to a 'real' world of objects. Husserl – as will be seen in the next chapter – insists that this assumption is a perfectly 'natural' one: it is, as it were, built into the very character of these perceptual experiences. What is seen is seen as something that is 'more' or 'other' than one's seeing of it – as something that 'transcends' any perception of it. Thus, as he puts it in the passage just quoted, this transcendence is 'part of the intrinsic sense of anything worldly', i.e. of anything accepted by one as belonging to the world.[11]

Moreover, as we emphasized in our account of the epoché in the previous section, whilst the existence-assumptions of the natural attitude are no longer *made* once this operation is performed, the fact that they *are* made in the natural attitude is preserved. 'The world is for us only something that claims being' (*CM*, p. 18). But that it *does* claim being is something which must be recognized; and it is in the transcendence of the objects of experience that this claim to being at least partly resides. That the world's 'existential status', including this 'sense' of transcendence, is itself provided by the transcendental Ego and its cogitationes does not in Husserl's view undermine any of this. In particular, as he puts it here, it should not be taken to imply that the world is 'a really inherent part' of 'my conscious life', or 'a piece of my Ego'.

We can now return to Husserl's criticism of Descartes' errors, and to the diagnosis he suggests for these. By identifying the Ego with the mind, or psychological ego, says Husserl, Descartes became 'the father of transcendental realism, an absurd position.' (*CM*, p. 24). What Husserl means is this. Employing his method of doubt, Descartes arrived at the indubitable 'I exist', and thereby in fact established the transcendental Ego. But he then attempted to deduce from this the existence of a subject-independent world, dualistically populated by minds and bodies, and including within it his own Ego, now mistakenly given the status of a psychological, worldly ego. Thus a realist position emerged from what was, properly understood, a transcendental starting- point. This 'transcendental realism' is 'absurd' because realism can give no place to a transcendental subject; and any form of transcendental idealism, such as Husserl's, must give a non-realist interpretation of 'the real world'. (We shall examine these issues in more detail in Chapter Three below.)

Husserl maintains that Descartes went wrong because, despite his declared intention of making a 'radical new beginning' in philosophy, he failed to free himself altogether from various philosophical prejudices (*CM*, p. 10). In particular, he accepted without question a specific idea of science, and hence of what philosophy as a science would have to be like: namely an axiomatic system, modelled upon geometry and the newly emerging mathematical natural science of the time. In an axiomatic system there is a set of basic assumptions (the axioms) which operate as premises, from which, in accordance with certain principles of inference, other propositions (the theorems) can be derived, as the conclusions of deductively valid arguments. The axioms themselves cannot be proved within the system; but they may in some cases be regarded, as Descartes regarded his own, as self-evident, undeniably true, or suchlike. (In presenting his claim that this was Descartes' model for philosophy, Husserl on some occasions talks of the initial axiom as 'I think', and on others as 'I exist'. The former is, strictly speaking, preferable; but we shall for convenience follow the latter.)

As we saw in section 2, Husserl takes the two key requirements for a science to be evidence that is primary and apodictic. His ascription to Descartes of an 'axiomatic prejudice' thus consists, in effect, of charging him with unjustifiably interpreting these requirements in such a way that they could be met only by the formulation of a set of axioms which were themselves indubitable. (An 'empiricist prejudice' would involve, presumably, interpreting the requirements as having to be met by epistemically unchallengeable sense-experience, e.g. by so-called sense-data.)

Adopting this model for philosophy, says Husserl, Descartes took the indubitable 'I exist' as the axiomatic starting-point for a series of deductively valid arguments:

> The course of the argument is well known: first God's existence and veracity are deduced and then, by means of them, Objective Nature [the existence of the external world], the duality of finite substances – in short, the Objective field of metaphysics and the positive sciences, and these disciplines themselves. All the various inferences proceed, as they must according to guiding principles that are immanent, or 'innate', in the pure ego. (*CM*, p. 3)

The 'guiding principles' to which Husserl refers are what Descartes terms 'the principles of natural light', such as 'nothing can be the cause of nothing', 'if there are qualities there must be a substance', the principle of non-contradiction, and so on. They operate, in effect, as the principles of inference in an axiomatic system.[12]

Husserl does not explain exactly how this axiomatic prejudice was responsible for Descartes' realist misidentification of the pure Ego with the mind. He confines himself to warning that one should not assume, as Descartes did, that:

> with our pure apodictic ego, we have reserved a little *tag-end of the* world, ... and that now the problem is to infer the rest the world by rightly conducted arguments, according to principles innate in the ego. (*CM*, p. 24)

But a possible line of argument to support Husserl's criticism of Descartes might be this. If 'I exist' is taken as an axiomatic premiss, from which 'the world exists' is to be deduced as a conclusion, then the meaning of the term 'exists' must remain the same throughout – otherwise the argument would not be valid. Thus the ontological status of the 'I', and of the world, would have to be the same; and, given Descartes' realist understanding of the world's existence, that of the Ego would be assimilated to this, thereby denying its 'purity'. Further, if the existence of the Ego is regarded in this way as an axiom from which the existence of the world can be inferred, its transcendental status with respect to this world will inevitably not be recognized.

In the opening section of the Second Meditation (section 12) Husserl returns to this issue, in discussing the concept of *grounding*. He declares that he does not intend to abandon

> the great Cartesian thought of attempting to find in transcendental subjectivity the deepest grounding of all sciences and even of the being of an Objective world.

But perhaps, he says,

> with the Cartesian discovery of the transcendental ego, *a new idea of the grounding of knowledge* also becomes disclosed: the idea of it as a transcendental grounding.

And he goes on to contrast this with:

> attempting to use *ego cogito* as an apodictically evident premise for arguments supposedly implying a transcendent subjectivity. (*CM*, p. 27)

This 'transcendent subjectivity' is the psychic life of the empirical ego, the Cartesian *res cogitans*; and what Husserl is suggesting here is that, instead of trying to deduce its existence from an apodictic premiss, thereby 'grounding' it by (axiomatic) deduction, he will instead explore the possibility of a transcendental grounding.

Further (and this has been implicit in several of the passages quoted above), Husserl's rejection of Descartes' axiomatic ideal for philosophy involves a corresponding rejection of his view of how philosophy is to ground, to provide foundations for, the various empirical sciences. For Descartes this grounding would take the form of providing the axioms for these sciences, from which their specific laws and theories can be deduced – though, as Husserl notes, these axioms may need to be augmented by various 'inductively established hypotheses' (*CM*, p. 24). In other words, the theorems that have been deductively established on the basis of philosophy's own axioms are then to be used, along with these additional hypotheses, as the axioms from which the laws of these particular sciences (physics, optics, physiology, etc.) can be derived as theorems.[13]

But Husserl is no more willing to accept this axiomatic account of philosophy's grounding of the sciences than he is to accept Descartes' axiomatic account of the pure Ego's grounding of the world. In both cases, he wishes to propose instead a transcendental grounding. What this would be like in practice can be seen only in the light of the following Meditations. But clearly Husserl is concerned neither to prove the truth of the basic theories of the empirical sciences, nor to prove the existence of the world, at least as this would be understood by realists. Transcendental phenomenology does not aim to provide, by means of a priori philosophical arguments, the kind of knowledge of the world gained by the empirical sciences. Nor does it aim, for example, to defeat scepticism by showing that the world's existence can be established by valid arguments from indubitable premises.

There is one final aspect of Husserl's criticisms of Descartes that needs to be considered here. In the second section of the Second Meditation (section 13), Husserl suggests that, as a result of his axiomatic idea of a philosophical science, Descartes failed to explore the vast (indeed infinite) realm of the pure Ego and its cogitationes. 'Unlike Descartes,' he declares,

> we shall plunge into *the task of laying open the infinite field of transcendental experience*. The Cartesian evidence – the evidence of the proposition, *ego cogito, ego sum* – remained barren because Descartes neglected, not only to clarify the pure sense of the transcendental epoché, but also to direct his attention to the fact that the ego can explicate himself *ad infinitum* and systematically by means of transcendental experience, and therefore lies ready as a possible *field of work*. (*CM*, p. 31)

What Husserl is saying is this. Since Descartes made use of his method of doubt only to establish an axiomatic premiss from which the existence of the world, the basic laws of the sciences, etc., could be inferred, he did not bother to investigate the character of all those particular cogitationes which this method potentially revealed. For him they were of interest only in establishing that 'I exist'. For Husserl, by contrast, they constitute an 'indefinite field' to be investigated in their own right; and it is this investigation that is pursued in most of the Second and Third Meditations, and which we shall examine in the next chapter. It involves not only careful attention to the character of particular experiences, such as 'seeing a house', 'remembering a conversation', etc., but also the discovery of their 'universal properties' (*CM*, p. 29), including their intentionality.

But this, he says, is only the first of two distinct stages of phenomenological enquiry. There is also a second stage of work, which he calls the '*criticism of transcendental experience*'; and only this second stage is '*philosophical in the full sense*' (*CM*, p. 29). The term 'criticism' here means something like 'critique' in the Kantian sense – the identification of 'conditions for the possibility of experience'; though Husserl will emphasize a number of important differences between his own position and Kant's. But at this point, near the beginning of the Second Meditation, he gives only the barest indication of what is involved, namely the construction of

> an a priori science, which confines itself to the realm of pure possibility (pure imaginableness) and, instead of judging about actualities of transcendental being i.e. the particular cogitationes which actually occur, judges about its a priori possibilities and thus at the same time prescribes rules a priori for actualities. (*CM*, p. 28)

This second stage is developed mainly in the Fourth Meditation, and we shall discuss it in Chapter Three. Its central procedure is what Husserl terms 'the eidetic reduction', whereby the so-called essences of things are identified. The procedure for identifying essences is said to consist in the imagination of possibilities, and thereby the discovery of necessities, of what cannot be imagined otherwise.[14] Thus it is only at this second, eidetic stage, that the problem noted earlier (at the end of section 3 above) about the apodicticity of the Ego's cogitationes can adequately be met. Further, this eidetic stage leads to a much more complex account of the transcendental Ego than has so far been suggested.

5   An Alternative to the Cartesian Way

In the *Cartesian Meditations*, as we have seen, Husserl introduces the key phenomenological procedure of the epoché by analogy with Descartes' method of doubt. But it is sometimes claimed by Husserl's commentators that this 'Cartesian way' to transcendental phenomenology is at best highly misleading, and at worst inevitably distorts or misrepresents the basic philosophical character of Husserl's phenomenology. Further, such critics note that, although the *Cartesian Meditations* is not the only text in which this Cartesian way is followed, significantly different routes are at least sometimes taken by Husserl. For instance, in Part IIIA of *The Crisis* – entitled 'The Way into Phenomenological Transcendental Philosophy by Inquiring back from the Pregiven Life-World' – he introduces the epoché via a fairly detailed account of the natural attitude; and at one point he declares that the Cartesian way, by comparison, 'has a great shortcoming' (*CES*, p. 155).[15]

Whether or not the Cartesian way is fundamentally misconceived, it is certainly easy for the reader of the *Cartesian Meditations* to be misled by it. The problem is this. In introducing the epoché by analogy with Descartes' method of doubt, Husserl suggests that one should suspend judgement about the existence of the world because it is not obviously apodictic. This makes it hard to avoid expecting that he will eventually return to the question of the world's existence, and tell one either that it does exist or that it does not. Initially, that is, one almost inevitably thinks of the bracketing of existence as a temporary matter, which will eventually enable a correct decision to be made. Indeed Husserl makes several remarks that reinforce this impression. For instance, he says that, having performed the epoché,

> the momentous fact is that I, with my life, remain untouched in my existential status, regardless of whether or not the world exists and regardless of what my eventual decision concerning its being or non-being might be. (*CM*, p. 25)

And likewise:

> no matter whether, at some future time, I decide critically that the world exists or that it is an illusion, still this phenomenon itself [the 'reduced' world], as mine, is not nothing but is precisely what makes such critical decisions at all possible. (*CM*, p. 19)

Thus the epoché, and the consequent exploration of the field of transcendental subjectivity, might seem to be presented as enabling one eventually to make this 'decision'. Understood in this way, the reader is then bound to be disappointed by the absence of any such decision in the later Meditations. But even to expect this involves a basic misunderstanding of Husserl's transcendental phenomenology. For it soon emerges that what Husserl is concerned to do is not to determine 'whether or not the world exists', but rather both to identify exactly what is involved in the sense that one does in fact have, in the natural attitude, of the world's existence, and also to provide a transcendental account of how this 'sense' of existence arises.

That these, and not some proof (or disproof) of the world's existence, are Husserl's concerns is made particularly clear in the following passage from *The Crisis*, where he emphasizes that, unlike Descartes, he is not aiming to provide some kind of justification for a belief in the existence of the world – as it were, to remove the brackets and decide in favour of the world. Thus:

> It is naturally a ludicrous, though unfortunately common misunderstanding, to seek to attack transcendental phenomenology as 'Cartesianism', as if its *ego cogito* were a premise or set of premises from which the rest of knowledge ... was to be deduced, absolutely 'secured'. The point is not to secure objectivity [the 'objective existence' of the world] but to understand it.... To deduce is not to explain.... The only true way to explain is to make transcendentally understandable. (*CES*, p. 189)

It may be helpful, therefore, to sketch out briefly a rather different way of introducing the epoché, which does not generate the misleading expectations of the Cartesian way. This involves presenting the epoché as a means of avoiding well-known problems for realism that may be claimed to arise from its failure to achieve the necessary philosophical 'distance' from the natural attitude. The account that follows draws upon some of the lines of thought in the opening lecture of the set of lectures later published as *The Idea of Phenomenology*. But it is not intended as a faithful exegesis of this; and it should anyway be noted that in the following lecture Husserl moves on to a version of the Cartesian way.

In the natural attitude, the attitude of everyday life, one takes it for granted that there is an external world of (various kinds of) objects, which exists independently of one's experience of it, and that knowledge of this world is possible. One is aware that, in any particular perceptual experience of something, by no means 'all' of it is directly revealed. But one assumes that, for example, by changing one's position or employing a different perceptual sense, more can be discovered about the same object – indeed this is part of what is meant by talking of these *as* objects that belong to an independent world. Mistakes, of course, both can be and sometimes are in fact made; but there are standardly accepted means by which these can be detected and rectified. Much remains unknown; but one knows roughly how to go about increasing one's knowledge and testing one's claims to have done so. And, in most if not all these respects, the same is true of scientific, as distinct from everyday, knowledge: this attitude is common to both science and everyday life.

Thus although in the natural attitude many particular problems may arise about what one knows and what exists, there are no general problems about knowledge and existence. Problems of the latter kind arise only when one poses, as a *philosophical* question, how such knowledge of the world is possible. More specifically, they arise when first of all one makes explicit the taken for granted existence of an external world, now asserting this as a philosophical basis (the thesis of realism), and then poses the question: how is knowledge of this world possible? The apparently major difficulty here is that there seems to be an unbridgeable 'gap' between the beliefs or experiences of the knower and the objects supposedly known. How can one 'pass' from one to the other, or know that the former in some way correspond to, or adequately represent, the latter? For, surely, to claim justifiably that any such relations of correspondence or representation obtain, one would need access both to the beliefs or experiences and to the world of objects. Yet to assume such access is possible would be to beg the question.

Husserl describes these problems for realism in the following passage from *The Idea of Phenomenology*:

But how can we be certain of the correspondence between cognition and the object cognized? How can knowledge transcend itself [i.e. 'get beyond' itself] and reach its object reliably? The unproblematic manner in which the object of cognition is given to natural thought to be cognized now becomes an enigma. In perception the perceived thing is believed to be directly given. Before my perceiving eyes stands the thing. I see it, and I grasp it. Yet the perceiving is simply a mental act of mine, of the perceiving subject.... How do I, the cognizing subject, know if I can ever really know, that there exist not only my own mental processes, these acts of cognizing, but also that which they apprehend? How can I ever know that there is anything at all which could be set over against cognition as its object? (*IP*, pp. 15–16)

Husserl maintains that no satisfactory answer to this question can be given, so long as the thesis of realism is retained. What would have to be accepted is some form of radical scepticism about the possibility of knowledge; and he regards any such position as clearly absurd (see *IP*, p. 17). Hence realism requires one to think of the existence of the world in a way that makes it impossible to give any account of how knowledge of this world can be achieved. To avoid scepticism it is therefore necessary to reject realism. But realism itself is apparently no more than the articulation, as a philosophical thesis, of what is taken for granted in the natural attitude. So perhaps what is basically wrong with realism is that it has not achieved sufficient philosophical 'distance' from this natural attitude: that it has not adopted what Husserl terms the 'specifically philosophical attitude of mind' (*IP*, p. 19) which would enable it seriously to reflect upon the natural attitude, rather than merely to endorse it.

If this is so, then what is needed is some way of disengaging oneself from the natural attitude so as to explore it in a suitably neutral, disinterested manner. In particular, it will be essential to find a way of reflecting upon its existential assumptions, and upon its assumption that knowledge of an independent world is possible, a way that does not commit one to any explicit or implicit judgement about these. At the same time, of course, the fact that such assumptions are made is itself a central feature of the natural attitude which must not be omitted from these reflective descriptions. What is required, then, is a 'suspension of judgement': not because these assumptions are inherently dubious, and need to be critically assessed as to their truth or falsity, but solely in order to achieve a reflective standpoint which is appropriately 'uncommitted'. And this is precisely what is achieved by the phenomenological epoché.

What kind of philosophical work could be done by adopting this procedure? An important possibility would seem to be this: that one could investigate the character of the various kinds of experience that occur in the natural attitude and consider, for example, what exactly is involved in perceiving an object, or in discovering that something exists. In doing this one would, in effect, be 'exploring the possibility of knowledge', but in a specific manner – namely, exploring the character of those experiences in which, as a matter of fact, such epistemic 'achievements' are regarded as taking place. So, for example, one would need to examine the ways in which such experiences are related to their 'objects', the general nature of such objects, and so on. As Husserl puts it in *The Idea of Phenomenology*, one could explore

> the problems of the relations among [i.e. between] cognition, its meaning and its object by inquiring into the essence of cognition. Among these, there is the problem of explicating the essential meaning of being a cognizable object or, what comes to the same thing, of being an object at all. (*IP*, p. 17)

This concludes our account of an alternative way of introducing the phenomenological epoché. It is designed both to correct the misleading expectations that are easily generated by the Cartesian way, and also to indicate, in a preliminary fashion, the relationship between Husserl's phenomenology and some traditional philosophical problems and responses to them. (We shall say more about this relationship in Chapter Two, section 4.) But this alternative account stops well short of the point Husserl has reached near the beginning of the Second Meditation, with his introduction of the pure Ego, the idea of a transcendental grounding of knowledge, and the identification of two stages of phenomenological enquiry. It is this first stage that we shall be examining in Chapter Two, to be followed by the second in Chapter Three.

2

Intentionality and Meaning

The central aim of this chapter is to explicate Husserl's Second and Third Meditations. We shall explore how Husserl develops what he regards as a radically new, phenomenological, method of philosophy. In so doing, we shall look at Husserl's interpretation of the claim that consciousness is intentional, and at his rejection of realism. The chapter will conclude with two brief comparisons: the first, between Husserl's treatment of intentionality and modern attempts to analyse intentional language; the second, between Husserl's phenomenological method and its results and those of ordinary language philosophy.

The programme for Husserl's Second and Third Meditations is to sketch how a phenomenological description of experience would proceed. The Second Meditation divides into three main parts. Sections 12–16 are introductory, reminding the reader of what has gone before in the First Meditation and describing the aims and methods of the Second and Third Meditations. In sections 17 and 18, Husserl sketches a method for describing phenomena or experiences. In sections 19–22, he shows how this method can be used to achieve a more general level of description. The Third Meditation aims chiefly to explore the meaning of two higher level concepts involved in the assumptions made in the natural attitude: these are the concepts of existence and truth. Husserl finds their meaning to be explicable in terms of their 'phenomenological origins' – namely, evidence and verification. This Meditation contains an important part of Husserl's opposition to realism.

1 Intentional Analysis

The opening section, section 12, of the Second Meditation restates the Cartesian aim expressed in the First Meditation. We explored in Chapter One (section 1) how Husserl presented his aim as like that of Descartes: to ground objective knowledge on subjective certainty. We explored there also (section 4) how Husserl departs from Descartes in rejecting the kind of grounding Descartes offers: that of deriving objective knowledge from the premise 'ego sum'. Husserl now suggests that an alternative *kind* of grounding can be given: this he terms 'transcendental' grounding. He then sketches a programme for the next stage of his meditations. The epoché opens up a realm of 'transcendental' experience. One should now explore this whole realm looking for something, other than 'ego sum', which is both indubitable and could serve to ground objective knowledge.

Husserl expresses two hopes. The first is that he can find some a priori rules which govern experience. He bases this hope on the fact that there are limits to the range of possible or imaginable experiences. These are limits, not on the *contents* of particular experiences, but on their *'structure'*:

> .he bare identity of the 'I am' is not the only thing given as indubitable in transcendental self-experience. Rather there extends through all the particular data of actual and possible self-experience – even though they are not absolutely indubitable in respect of single details – a *universal apodictically experienceable structure* of the Ego.... (*CM*, p. 28)

Husserl's second hope is that he will be able to show that our *experiences* have this structure because *the Ego* has this structure:

> Perhaps it can also be shown, as something dependent on that structure, and indeed as part of it, that the Ego is *apodictically predelineated*, for himself, as a concrete Ego existing with an individual content made up of subjective processes, abilities, and dispositions. (*CM*, pp. 28–9)

These a priori rules or apodictic truths about the structure of experience can then serve as a grounding for objective knowledge.

In section 13, Husserl says that he will proceed in two stages. The first stage involves describing experiences, aiming to discover universal features of them. The Second and Third Meditations are concerned with this first, descriptive stage. This, he says, is not 'philosophical in the full sense', but is a necessary preliminary to the fully philosophical second stage where the two hopes, outlined above, will be realized. The second stage involves what he calls the 'criticism' or 'critique' of experience. The aim of criticism is to show that the universal features of experience revealed in the first stage are necessary or a priori features and correspond to necessary structures of the Ego. Husserl, while frequently alluding to this second stage during the Second and Third Meditations, does not embark upon it in a systematic way until the Fourth Meditation. This will be the subject matter of the next chapter.

In this first stage of phenomenological research, that of pure phenomenological description, Husserl says, the philosopher is to proceed like the natural scientist, simply describing experiences, and doing so in increasingly general terms. In section 14, Husserl notes the similarity between his phenomenological description and the natural science of empirical psychology: both aim to produce accurate descriptions of subjective experiences:

> pure psychology of consciousness is a *precise parallel* to transcendental phenomenology of consciousness ... the contents to be described on the one hand and on the other can correspond. (*CM*, p. 32)

However, though there is this similarity of content, what Husserl emphasizes, in sections 13–15, is the crucial difference between the ways the descriptions are regarded by psychologists and phenomenologists respectively. The difference, in short, is that the empirical pyschologist will have the 'natural attitude', that is, will assume that the field of enquiry – minds and mental states (one's own and those of others) – exists; the phenomenologist, in contrast, has bracketed this assumption. The psychologist aims to describe a part, the psychic part, of the existent world; the phenomenologist aims to describe how the whole world, no longer assumed to exist, appears to consciousness:

> In the one case we have data belonging to the world, which is presupposed as existing – that is to say, data taken as psychic components of a man. In the other case the parallel data, with their like contents, are not taken in this manner, because the whole world, when one is in the phenomenological attitude, is not accepted as actuality, but only as an actuality-phenomenon. (*CM*, p. 32)

Husserl terms psychology a science of 'objective subjectivity', and contrasts it with his own study, which is to be 'absolutely subjective'. Husserl then voices a natural worry that his science of subjectivity, which he calls 'egology', will be solipsistic, will be able to give no account of other egos. But he raises this worry only to put it aside. He returns to it in the Fifth Meditation which we discuss in Chapter Eight, section 2, below.

In section 15, Husserl aims to show how the reflecting phenomenologist, precisely because he has bracketed these assumptions about existence implicit in 'straightforward' experiences, can explore these very assumptions and come to describe them in an unprejudiced way, thereby producing the 'pure' descriptions necessary for the second 'critical' stage of phenomenological research. Husserl describes phenomenological reflection as involving a 'splitting of the Ego'. In 'naive' experience, the ego is 'immersed', 'interested' in the world. Reflection involves a split between this 'immersed' ego and a 'disinterested' ego which looks at the immersed ego. The phenomenologist must then further reflect upon the fact that this split has taken place and, retaining disinterestedness in the world, set about the task of describing:

> to see and to describe adequately what he sees, purely as seen, as what is seen and seen in such and such a manner. (*CM*, p. 35)

Husserl then puts forward a positive methodological principle to guide this enterprise of describing experiences in an unprejudiced way. Each experience – each *cogitatio* – has two sides: the *cogito*, or experiencing, and the *cogitatum*, or what is experienced. The descriptions must, correspondingly, fall into two groups. Husserl calls these '*noetic*' and '*noematic*' descriptions. The *noetic* descriptions will describe 'modes' of the *cogito*, 'modes'[1] of consciousness, the ways in which one is experiencing (e.g. perceiving or remembering). The *noematic* descriptions will be descriptions of *cogitata*, of intentional or meant objects, of what it is that one is experiencing (e.g. the perceived or remembered object):

> If we follow this methodological principle in the case of the dual topic *cogito – cogitatum (qua cogitatum)*, there become opened to us, first of all, the general descriptions to be made, always on the basis of particular *cogitationes*, with regard to each of the two correlative sides. Accordingly, on the one hand, descriptions of the intentional object as such, with regard to the determinations attributed to it in the modes of consciousness concerned, ... which stand out when attention is directed to them.... This line of description is called *noematic*. Its counterpart is *noetic* description, which concerns the modes of the *cogito* itself, the modes of consciousness.... (*CM*, p. 36)

It may aid mastery of this unfamiliar terminology to note that 'noetic' is the adjectival form of 'noesis', which is the Greek noun corresponding to the Latin verb 'cogito'. 'Noematic' is the adjectival form of 'noema', which again is Greek, and means the same as 'cogitatum' in Latin. We can illustrate this terminology with reference to one of Husserl's own examples (p. 33). One's perceiving a house is a *cogitatio* (pl. cogitationes). *Noematic* description describes the object of consciousness, the *cogitatum* (pl. cogitata): the house (as one perceives it). *Noetic* description describes the mode of consciousness, the *cogito*:[2] one's perceiving (of the house).

At several points during these opening sections of the Second Meditation, Husserl issues the reminder that consciousness is intentional:

> Conscious processes are also called *intentional*; but then the word intentionality signifies nothing else than this universal fundamental property of consciousness: to be consciousness *of* something. (*CM*, p. 33)

He elaborates this earlier in the same section, section 14. After one has dropped all assumptions that the world exists, one turns one's attention to one's conscious experience and discovers, in effect, that nothing has changed. One's experience is still 'of' things which appear to be 'outside'. One is not conscious only of mental items; one is conscious of physical and abstract objects also:

> It must not be overlooked that epoché with respect to all worldly being does not
> at all change the fact that ... e.g. the perception of this table still is, as it was
> before, precisely a perception of this table. In this manner, without exception,
> every conscious process is, in itself, consciousness *of* such and such, regardless
> of what the rightful actuality-status of this objective such-and-such may be....
> (*CM*, pp. 32–3)

Being conscious of objects, of an external world, does not require that one
believes that objects exist. Consciousness is 'directed outward' whether one is
assuming that there exists anything outside of one or not.

In section 16, Husserl cites a particular tradition[3] in philosophy and
psychology which has, he claims failed to observe that consciousness is intentional. He diagnoses this failure as being due to a prejudice shared by
exponents of this tradition: the prejudice of sensualism. The model of the
mind underlying sensualism is that mental life is made up of 'sensations',
purely mental items such as pains, feelings of hot or cold, sensations of
colour, mental images. Husserl's claim is that this theory has no foundation
in experience:

> In advance, as though this were obviously correct, one misinterprets conscious
> life as a complex of data of 'external' and (at best) 'internal sensuousness'; ...
> But, when descriptive theory of consciousness begins radically, it has before it
> no such data ... except perhaps as prejudices. (*CM*, p. 38)

That is to say, if one looks without prejudice at one's experience, it is not
confined to purely mental items: it appears as intentional, as relating to things
other than sensations: tables, dice, houses.

A second feature of intentionality which Husserl notes is the inseparability
of consciousness and its objects:

> Each *cogito*, each conscious process, we may also say, '*means*' *something or other*
> and bears in itself, in this manner peculiar to the *meant*, its particular *cogitatum*.
> Each does this, moreover, in its own fashion. The house-perception means a
> house – more precisely, as this individual house – and means it in the fashion
> peculiar to perception. (*CM*, p. 33)

Acts of consciousness and objects of consciousness are essentially interdependent: the relation between them is an 'internal' not an 'external' one. That
is to say, one cannot first identify the items related and then explore the
relation between them; rather one can identify each item in the relation only
by reference to the other item to which it is related. Acts of consciousness are
directed upon objects such that one cannot investigate the acts independently
of their objects; and objects are always objects *for* consciousness such that one

cannot investigate objects independently of investigating the conscious acts of which they are the objects.

This inter-relatedness of consciousness and its objects must be reflected in any phenomenological description:

> Inquiry into consciousness concerns *two sides*...; they can be characterized descriptively as *belonging together inseparably*. (*CM*, p. 39)

In Husserl's terminology, noetic description describes acts of consciousness, but in so doing will make reference to *objects* of consciousness; noematic description describes the objects of consciousness, but in so doing will make reference to acts of consciousness. In section 20, Husserl calls the sort of description he gives of consciousness and objects 'intentional analysis'. Acts of consciousness 'point beyond' themselves, intend or mean objects; and objects 'point beyond' themselves to the acts of consciousness which intend or mean them. Also, acts of consciousness may point beyond themselves to other acts of consciousness; and objects to other objects. This 'pointing beyond' is, for Husserl, central to the notion of intentionality. The aim of intentional analysis is to reveal the full range of what the analysandum, that which is to be analysed or described, points to beyond itself: what, in Husserl's terms, it means.

Husserl issues a reminder that, having performed the epoché, the next stage in his meditations is to reflect upon experience and describe it in a way which does not presuppose that the natural world exists. The assumptions that objects exist and that conscious subjects, with their mental states, exist as parts of a natural world must be dropped. These are 'prejudices' of the natural attitude.

What Husserl hopes to discover is that this 'pure' unprejudiced reflection upon experience will reveal it to be, not a 'chaos', but an organized structure, exemplifying certain patterns or 'forms'.

2 Phenomenological Description

In sections 17–19 of the Second Meditation, Husserl gives, in outline, a particular phenomenological description. His aim is twofold: to display the structure of the particular experience selected for description; and to introduce, via this particular example, his method for producing all phenomenological descriptions.

The specific example Husserl selects for phenomenological description is that of 'perceiving a die'.[4] Perceiving a die is what he calls the 'theme' of the description. To remind his reader that the actual die as an object in the natural world has been bracketed, Husserl calls the perceived die the 'intentional object' of perception.

Husserl begins with the noematic description – the description of the die, the cogitatum. He lists a variety of appearances of the die involved in perceiving it. We shall elaborate a little on Husserl's list. Watch someone throwing a die. The die appears far away, then close to; different sides of the die appear successively as it rolls over; the die makes a sound as it hits the table; it is hard to the touch as it brushes the hand; its shape appears differently in different orientations, and its colour appears differently in different lights.

This description reveals the 'noematic structure' of perceiving a die. It indicates what the structure or 'constitution' of the die is: the die appears as having orientations in space, as having six sides, etc. But this constitution of the die is not independent of consciousness: the noematic description is always a description of the die as it appears to the consciousness which perceives it.

Having listed diverse appearances of the die, the next thing Husserl notes is that they are experienced as a 'collective *unity*'. That is to say, they are all experienced as appearances of the same die. This unity is reflected in the description which must, if it is to be accurate, characterize the various appearances as appearances of the same (intended) die. This unified collection Husserl calls a 'synthesis', and its structure, a 'synthetic structure'. Since what unifies the collection in this case is its being a collection of appearances of the same identical die, Husserl calls this kind of synthesis a 'synthesis of identification': the die when, for example, it appears close by is 'identified' with the die when it appears further away.

Husserl concludes section 17 with the claim that all examples of consciousness of objects are like the example he has described of perceiving a die in that they all involve the synthesis of identification. At the beginning of section 18, Husserl refers to identification as the 'fundamental form of synthesis': it is the kind of synthesis involved in all consciousness of objects, and hence, since all consciousness is consciousness of objects (i.e. intentional), it is the kind of synthesis involved in all consciousness.

Husserl's avowed aim at this stage is simply to describe experience, and, like the natural scientist, to look for universal patterns in what he describes. So, one must regard this general claim – that all consciousness of objects involves the synthesis of identification – as a hypothesis which Husserl is putting forward as true, but which could in principle be falsified by counter-example. The appropriate sort of counter-example would have to be an example of being conscious of an object without experiencing a collection of appearances of the *same* object, a collection unified by the synthesis of identification. Husserl believes that no such counter-example exists.

In section 18, Husserl turns his attention to noetic description. The aim now is to describe the other side of perceiving a die: the perceiving of the die rather than the die perceived. His aim is to describe the noetic structure of the perceiving. What he first discovers is that the perceiving also involves a 'collection', this time of 'phases'. We can list some of these on Husserl's behalf. They would include seeing the die close to, seeing it far off, seeing one side of the die, seeing another side, hearing the die as it hits the table, seeing it come to rest on the table, feeling the die as it hits one's hand, etc.

These phases, Husserl claims, like the appearance of the die, form a unity, a synthesis, and not merely a disconnected series. Reflection reveals that what unifies this collection is that they are ordered in time. Seeing the near die precedes (or succeeds) seeing the far die; whilst hearing the die and seeing the die drop on the table are simultaneous. (Indeed, if this were not so, there would be no synthesis of identification: for example, simultaneously seeing a near die and a far die would not be experienced as perceiving one and the same die.) Noetic description will reveal facts of synthetic structure concerning the temporal order of the phases of the perceiving.

Husserl next, just as he did following the noematic description, moves from concrete description to make a universal claim. This claim is that one's experiences are never a mere 'collection', but always form a unity. This unity is another synthesis:

> Synthesis, however, does not occur just in every particular conscious process, nor does it connect one particular conscious process with another only occasionally. On the contrary, as we said beforehand, the *whole of conscious life is unified synthetically*. (*CM*, p. 42)

This synthesis, which unifies one's entire conscious life, is a temporal one. Conscious life is experienced as a unity because it is ordered in time. The appropriate sort of counter-example to this universal claim would be an experience which was one's own but was neither earlier, nor later, nor simultaneous with one's other experiences. Husserl again believes that no such counter-example exists.

Husserl calls this temporal ordering of conscious processes 'internal time', and the consciousness of internal time 'the fundamental form of universal synthesis.'[5] It is 'fundamental' because it is involved in all syntheses of conscious processes or their phases, as identification is involved in all syntheses of appearances of objects.

Husserl ends section 18 by pointing out a seeming paradox involved in this claim that the whole of conscious life constitutes a unity. The air of paradox derives from the fact that the experience of reflecting upon this unity is itself one of the elements in the unity. Husserl regards this air of paradox, not as indicating any fault in his description of the unity of conscious life, but as resulting from the character of what is being described: the capacity of conscious subjects to be self-aware. Husserl calls this 'the ego's marvellous being-for-himself' (*CM*, p. 43). He returns to this at the beginning of the Fourth Meditation, where he describes the *subject* of experience (see Chapter Three, section 1). Here, in the Second Meditation, he is aiming to describe the experiences, and not the experiencing subject.

In section 19 Husserl returns from these universal claims to his description of concrete experience. The description of perceiving a die which he sketched in sections 17 and 18 confined itself to actual appearances of the die and actual temporal phases of the perceiving. These are elements explicitly involved in perceiving a die; but, Husserl now claims, they are not the only appearances and perceivings involved in perceiving a die. Other possible appearances and possible perceivings are implicitly involved, and these too must be characterized in a complete description. These implicit appearances and perceivings Husserl calls 'horizons'. The horizons of perceiving a die would be, on the noematic side, appearances one might experience as appearances of the same die; and on the noetic side, perceivings one might have of the die. While any single experience of a die explicitly involves, as an actual appearance, one aspect of the die, it also involves implicitly, as possible appearances, the other aspects of the die. Similarly, while a single experience of a die explicitly involves actually seeing it from a certain angle, it also involves implicitly a possible perceiving of the same die from a different angle. If one were to walk around the die or turn it over, one could make these possibilities actual:

> Every subjective process has a process 'horizon'.... For example, there belongs to every external perception its reference from the 'genuinely perceived' sides of the object of perception to the sides 'also meant' – not yet perceived, but only anticipated.... Furthermore, the perception has horizons made up of other possibilities of perception, as perceptions that we *could* have, if we *actively directed* the course of perception otherwise: if, for example, we turned our eyes that way instead of this, or if we were to step forward or to one side, and so forth. (*CM*, p. 44)

In his later work, *The Crisis*, Husserl writes, in the following way, about horizons and their role in the syntheses which constitute the sense of object in the world:

> the pure thing seen, what is visible 'of' the thing, is first of all a surface, and in the changing course of seeing I see it now from this 'side', now from that, continuously perceiving it from ever differing sides. But in them *the* surface exhibits itself to me in a continuous synthesis; each side is for consciousness a manner of exhibition *of* it. This implies that, while the surface is immediately given, I mean more than it offers. (*CES*, Part IIIA, section 45, pp. 157–8)

Perceiving this die involves, as part of its sense, definite expectations concerning likely future experiences. It is part of one's perceiving a die that one expects it to go on looking like a die from other angles, in other places, at other times:

> We can *ask any horizon what 'lies in it'*, we can *explicate* or unfold it, and *'uncover'* the potentialities of conscious life at a particular time. Precisely thereby we uncover the *objective sense meant implicitly* in the actual cogito. . . . (*CM*, p. 45)

The fact that perceiving this die has horizons referring beyond one's set of actual experiences indicates that what one means by 'die' is something which goes beyond one's actual experience of it. One perceives it as something with aspects which one does not and may never actually perceive. For example, if one perceives a die, one will expect the other side of it to look like a die and not a mouse, and one will expect it to be solid to the touch and not soft or explosive. Of course, one can be fooled: there are even 'trick' objects designed specifically for that purpose. But it is one's expectations, and not these trick objects, which reveal what one means by a die. If one did not have these expectations, one would not be perceiving a die. One's expectations may not be very precise: one may have no expectations about all manner of detail of the die, but one's expectations have what Husserl calls a 'determinate' structure:

> the die leaves open a great variety of things pertaining to the unseen faces; yet it is already 'construed' in advance as a die. . . . (*CM*, p. 45)

In the final paragraph of this section, section 19, Husserl writes of the object as a 'pole of identity'. The object, that is to say, is what is experienced in any one of a collection of experiences of the same object. These experiences, as it were, 'cluster round' the object. One might have any of these experiences; but one can never actually have all of them. The 'reality' of an object consists precisely in its having unexperienced aspects:

> The object is, so to speak, *a pole of identity*, always meant expectantly as having a sense yet to be actualized. (*CM*, pp. 45–6)

In the Fourth Meditation, which we shall discuss in Chapter Three, Husserl introduces the notion of a 'subject-pole' also. These 'poles', object and subject, are best seen as the guiding principles of the noematic description and the later descriptions of the subject (see Chapter Three, section 1). The descriptions are to be descriptions of the object and subject respectively.

Section 20 begins with a review of the method Husserl has just introduced and an indication of the scope he believes this method to have. The central features of the method which Husserl now calls 'intentional analysis' are these. First, one selects as a theme a concrete example of being conscious of an object; next, one reflects upon this experience, aiming to describe it free from the prejudices of the natural attitude; and then one describes actual and possible appearances which one takes to be appearances of the same object. This is the noematic description. Next, one gives a noetic description, describing the actual and possible modes of consciousness of the object, and the temporal order of the appearing to consciousness of the appearances of the object. In this way one can explicate *what* the constitution of the intentional object is – what one means or intends by, or constitutes as, the same object; and also *how* one constitutes the object – what conscious processes are involved in meaning, intending or constituting it.

The example Husserl gives of perceiving a die is intended to introduce this method. Clearly that particular example is otherwise of no great philosophical interest. But Husserl goes on to indicate how this same method can be employed to explore issues of more obvious philosophical concern. If one were to take as a theme 'perceiving a spatial thing', one could reveal what meaning or sense attaches to classifying an object as spatial. Ignoring what particular kind of spatial thing it is, one could describe both the actual and expected appearances which one would identify as appearances of the same spatial object. In this way, Husserl claims, one can explicate what one means by 'spatial thing'. Husserl does not elaborate, but one can speculate. One would expect to find, by bringing out the horizons of such experiences, that spatial things are three-dimensional, exclude other spatial things from the space they occupy, are spatio-temporally continuous, etc.

The same method, Husserl further claims, can be used to explicate philosophically problematic notions such as 'real and ideal actuality, possibility, necessity, illusion, truth' (*CM*, pp. 48–9). In each case, what the method will reveal will be the 'subjective origins' of these notions, i.e. what one means when one employs these categories in attempting to understand the world. Finding these 'subjective origins' is a crucial stage in Husserl's avowed Cartesian project of grounding all knowledge on subjective certainty. Husserl does not here indicate precisely how the intentional analysis of these very general categories is to proceed. The Third Meditation deals with two important such categories: existence and truth. We shall discuss Husserl's treatment of these in section 3 below.

At the end of section 20, Husserl asks if the same method of exploring horizons can be used in noetic description, i.e. for describing experiences. In outline, what he claims is that one cannot use precisely the same method because consciousness is a 'flux'. Consciousness can, nonetheless, be explored, as it were, indirectly. To do this one can proceed either via the analysis of objects of experience, or by reflecting on one's experience.

We shall explore this in a little more detail. As we noted earlier, Husserl

(*CM*, section 18) detected a 'unity' in all experience. This consisted in their temporal order. The problem Husserl now raises is that consciousness is a 'Heraclitean flux'.[6] Heraclitus' claim, crudely, was that, since all physical objects are in a state of continuous change, it cannot be accurate to speak of the *same* object persisting through time. We have just, in effect, outlined what Husserl's answer to that problem would be. It is that sets of changing appearances do nonetheless have a unity. They are experienced or expected as different appearances of the same object, and this is because they are structured by the synthesis of identification.

Experiences, in contrast, are not structured in this way. Conscious life is ever changing, and the events in it do not persist as objects to be expected or reidentified as the same at different times. One might, for example, have exactly similar experiences at different times; but they are not the same experience, not identical – there are two experiences, not one.

Husserl concludes section 20 with the claim that, despite this disanalogy, intentional analysis can still explore the structure of consciousness.

> the idea of an intentional analysis [for processes of consciousness] is legitimate, since, in the flux of intentional synthesis (which creates unity in all consciousness and which, noetically and noematically, constitutes unity of objective sense), *an essentially necessary conformity to type* prevails and *can be apprehended in strict concepts*. (*CM*, p. 49)

He goes on to explain how one can discover this 'conformity to type'. In section 21, Husserl observes that what corresponds, for experiences, to horizons of objects is that there is implicit in the experience of an object expectations of different possible kinds of experience one might have of the same object. He gives as examples: 'possible perception, retention, recollection, expectation'. So, to elaborate, implicit in one's actual experience of hearing, for example, a car, are possible experiences of seeing it, smelling its exhaust fumes, remembering it later, having expected it earlier, and so on.

Husserl then shows how this method can be applied to reveal general truths just as the method of noematic description was generalized from the particular description of the die to an analysis of spatial object. One might take, as one's theme, experiencing a spatial object. One could then describe the kinds of experience which one would expect to have of such an object. These would include seeing it, hearing it, touching, tasting, smelling it. These are all ways of perceiving. They are seen to be grouped together as all experiences of what Husserl calls the same 'type'. One reveals them as of the same type – perception – by revealing them to be possible experiences of the same type of object – spatial.

Noetic description, then, reveals that consciousness, though a 'flux', is not a chaos. It is not made up of persisting objects; but its constituents are 'tokens' (though Husserl does not use the word) of types. Experiences of the same type form a synthesis. This Husserl calls a 'synthesis of types of modes of consciousness'.

Husserl's focus has so far been on just one type of object – spatial – and one type of experience – perceiving. But there are different types of objects and correspondingly different types of experience of them. One different type of object of experience is, Husserl notes, state of affairs; and the corresponding type of experience is judgement.

This way of analysing experience into types is indirect. One must begin from the type of object and use it as what Husserl calls a 'clue' to the type of experience. Husserl ends this discussion of how one can use objects as clues to exploring types of experience by stating, without illustration, that not only objects intended as 'Objective' but also 'merely subjective objects' can be taken as clues. These 'merely subjective objects' are the objects of self-reflection and, as objects of consciousness, they have horizons which further explicate the type of experience involved. An example (ours) would be remembering. One could take as the theme for one's description a memory. One could then reflect on a memory, revealing horizons such as believing one did something in the past, recognizing something as familiar, feeling satisfaction or regret, nostalgia or relief. One would thereby reveal that remembering was of a different type from, for example, perceiving, expecting or imagining.

Husserl ends his Second Meditation with the claim that intentional analysis will not only reveal different types of object and different types of experience, it will also show that the whole of the objective world and the whole of conscious life constitute a unity. He then looks ahead to the Fourth Meditation, where he will try to show that this unified structure and its constituent structures are not only *universal* but *essential* features of consciousness of the world: that they function as a priori rules governing what experiences are possible, and that the source of these rules lies in the structure of the transcendental Ego. We shall discuss this second stage of Husserl's programme in Chapter Three, sections 2 and 3.

3   Existence, Evidence and Truth

In the Third Meditation, Husserl outlines phenomenological accounts of 'actuality', which he also calls 'existence' or 'being', and of truth – two of the concepts which in section 20 of the Second Meditation he claimed that his phenomenological method could be used to investigate. Husserl concentrates his attention mainly on actuality rather than truth, and we shall follow him in this. He also talks mainly in terms of 'being' rather than 'actuality' or 'existence'.[7] In this, we shall not follow him, but will instead employ the more familiar locution 'existence'.

Husserl begins with the reminder that, following the epoché, the phenomenologist's concern has been only with the meaning of objects, and not with their existence or being; and with how those objects are meant or intended, and not with whether the intending, for example believing or judging, is true. Husserl now claims that phenomenology can still explore what these existential claims mean, and what is involved in truly believing that an object exists. In the natural attitude, true existential beliefs are, at least when rationally held, held as a result of having certain kinds of experiences. That is to say, they have what Husserl calls a 'phenomenological origin': an origin, that is, which survives the epoché. Husserl argues in sections 23–5 that the phenomenological origin of all existential claims is what he calls 'evident verification'. In sections 26–8 he argues that the sense of existential claims can be explicated in terms of their phenomenological origins, namely in terms of 'evident verification'. In short, the programme is to explicate what is meant by 'existence' by explicating the phenomenon of evident verification.

We explained in Chapter One (section 2) that, by 'evidence', Husserl means, not a relation between experience and the conclusion it supports, but rather a feature of the experience: the intentional object's being clearly present – as we might say, being 'in evidence' or 'evident'. In section 24 he describes evidence as 'the *self-appearance*, the *self-exhibiting*, the *self-giving*, of an affair' (*CM*, p. 57), when that affair is presented as ' "itself there", "immediately intuited", "given originaliter" ' (*CM*, p. 57), to a consciousness which intends its object as 'being with it itself, viewing, seeing, having insight into, it itself' (*CM*, p. 57).

By 'evident verification', Husserl means a process of investigation, or 'verification', which leads to the intentional object's being 'evident' to consciousness. Evident verification is what Husserl in the Second Meditation calls a 'type' of synthesis of modes of consciousness. It is, that is to say, a particular kind of collection of experiences of the same object. What is common to all such evidently verifying syntheses is that they culminate in making their object evident to consciousness. For example (ours), one might catch a glimpse of something but be uncertain as to what it is or even whether there is anything there at all. This 'glimpse' may have implicit horizons. These will be possible experiences which, if one actually had them, would establish both that there is something there and also what it is. If one actually had all these further experiences, one would have 'evidently verified' the existence of the object.

The specific modes of consciousness involved in an evidently verifying synthesis will be different for different types of object. For example (ours), the conscious processes involved in making and having evident a physical object will be different from those involved in making and having evident an abstract object, such as the 100th digit in the decimalization of π. The former will typically involve perception; the latter, calculation.

In the case of perception, one often does not get evident verification. One's senses may be deficient, conditions may be poor, or one's attention may wander. Husserl claims, however, that, though evidently verifying syntheses may rarely take place in experience, they nonetheless feature as horizons of all consciousness:

> Any consciousness, without exception, either is itself already characterized as evidence (that is, as giving its object originaliter) [without any need for analysis] or else has an essential tendency toward conversion into givings of its object originaliter – accordingly, toward syntheses of verification, which belong essentially in the domain of the 'I can'. (*CM*, p. 58)

Whenever one is conscious of an object, there is, at least implicit in that consciousness, an awareness of what one would need to do to make the object evident, and what would count as success: what it would be like for the object to be evident to one. For example (ours), if one is hunting a thimble, the thimble is not yet evident, but one must be implicitly aware of the sort of thing one must do to make it evident – look for it; and what would count as success – seeing and touching an object with a certain shape, size, use, etc. If one does not know what would count as finding the thimble, one can scarcely be said to be hunting it. Awareness of what it would be like to make an object evident is a necessary condition of being conscious of the object. Husserl calls this a 'fundamental trait of all intentional life'; and evidence a 'universal primal phenomenon of intentional life' (section 24).

Evident verification, Husserl now claims, is the phenomenological origin of the existential claims made in the natural attitude. When, in the natural attitude, one posits the existence of some object, one does so when one has evidently verified the object, or when one expects that one would get evident verification of that object if one performed the appropriate actions.

So far, this is an accout of the phenomenological origins of positive existential claims. In section 24, Husserl extends this account to other existential claims, such as claims that an object does not exist, or that its existence is probable or doubtful. These claims also have phenomenological origins, and these too can be characterized in terms of evident verification. These different kinds of existential claims have their origins in different outcomes of the process of verification. For example, the claim that an object does not exist has its phenomenological origin in completing all the stages of the process of verification, the process which aims at making the object evident to consciousness, and discovering that this last state does not occur. Husserl calls this an 'evidently nullifying synthesis'. It is a synthesis which nullifies the original positing of the existence of the object. Husserl does not spell out how judgements of probable, doubtful or other modes of existence have their phenomenological origins in evident verification. But it is not difficult to speculate in general terms. One judges that an object, for example a virus, probably exists when the process of verification is, in a sense which would be clear in the particular enquiry, going well, seems likely to lead to making the object evident. Similarly, one judges that it is doubtful that an object exists when the process is not going well.

Husserl completes this stage of his discussion by outlining, in section 25, how one can use a version of evident verification to decide whether a proposed object or kind of object could *possibly* or *conceivably* exist. One does this by a process of 'clarification', which follows the same course as the process of verification, but takes place in the imagination or 'phantasy.' For example (ours), if one were trying to decide whether there existed any non-human persons, or any disembodied persons, one might imagine processes of investigation, of trying to find such objects, along with their outcomes. One might find that one could imagine what it would be like to find a non-human person, to have such a person evident to consciousness. In contrast, one might discover that one could not imagine what it would be for a disembodied person to be evident to consciousness. These processes of imagination would then result in one's claiming that a non-human person could possibly exist, but a disembodied person could not.

Husserl has so far written of a 'correlation' between existential claims and their phenomenological origins in evident verification. His overall aim is to explicate the sense or meaning of existential claims. He now turns directly to this project. In section 26, he expresses a possible objection to regarding these phenomenological origins as constituting the meaning of the existential claims with which they are correlated. The objection is, in effect, that one can believe that an object exists without having evidence or even believing that one has evidence that it does. So, evidence for that belief cannot be part of its meaning.

Husserl's response to this is to point out that, though having a belief that an object exists may not obviously mean the same thing as having evident verification of it, nonetheless there is a relation of meaning between the two in virtue of the fact that belief is answerable to evident verification:

> To be sure, that objects ... exist for me is a statement that says nothing immediately about evidence; it says only that objects are accepted by me – are, in other words, there for me as cogitata intended in the positional mode: certain believing. But we do know also that we should have to abandon such acceptance forthwith, if a course of evident identifying synthesis were to lead to conflict with an evident datum, and that we can be sure something is *actual* only by virtue of a synthesis of evident verification, which presents rightful or true actuality itself. (*CM*, pp. 59–60)

That is, one must give up one's belief that an object exists when the process of verification fails to make it evident. To continue our earlier example: if the search for the virus goes badly enough, one has to give up the belief that it exists. Further, Husserl claims, the rational basis for believing that objects exist is that they be made evident. These connections between belief and making evident, Husserl claims, show that a belief that an object exists has, as a horizon, as part of its sense, evident verification of that object.

In sections 27 and 28 of the Third Meditation, Husserl makes two vital additions to his account of evident verification. With these additions, he concludes, he has supplied an account of the sense of existential claims: an account of what he calls 'existence-sense'. Explication of evident verification reveals it to have, as part of its implicit meaning, two kinds of horizon or potential experience, neither of which can be actualized, since to do so would involve having infinitely many experiences.

The first kind of horizon is that the experience is repeatable. To experience an object as evident involves, as a horizon, the expectation that the object could be made evident again by repeating the process of verification:

> Every evidence 'sets up' or 'institutes' for me an *abiding possession*. I can 'always return' to the itself-beheld actuality, in a series of new evidences as restitutions of the first evidence. (*CM*, p. 60)

This is so, however many times one repeats the actual process of making evident. Hence the potential repetitions involved in an object's being evidently verified are infinite. This infinite potential is an implicit part of one's experience of persisting objects, and more generally of a 'fixed and abiding' world.

The second kind of infinite horizon involved in evident verification comes to light when one recognizes the 'one-sidedness' of one's experience. Whenever an object is evident, there are, implicit in that experience, other potential experiences of the same object from different perspectives or at different times. There are, Husserl claims, for any object *actually* evident to one, infinitely many such *potential* evidences as horizons:

> evidences refer us to infinities of evidences relating to the same object, wherever they make their object itself-given with an essentially necessary *one-sidedness*. (*CM*, p. 61)

This infinite unfulfillable potential is an implicit part of one's experience of independently existing objects and, more generally, of the objective, transcendent world.

Persistence and independence are parts of 'existence-sense'. Both point to experiences beyond any number of actual ones. So, to experience the world as existing is to experience it as affording, in prospect, more experiences than one can ever actually have.

The permanent and independent existence of the objective world is something whose sense is 'constituted' in consciousness. What one means by such a world is that it can go beyond any actual investigation one can make of it. The horizonality of one's experience guarantees that one knows how the investigation should proceed and also that the investigation is not completable:

> That the being of the world 'transcends' consciousness in this fashion (even with respect to the evidence in which the world presents itself), and that it necessarily remains transcendent, in no wise alters the fact that it is conscious life alone, wherein everything transcendent becomes constituted, as something inseparable from consciousness, and which specifically, as world-consciousness, bears within itself inseparably the sense: world – and indeed: 'this actually existing' world. (*CM*, p. 62)

The situation is exactly parallel in the case of objective truth. We shall not go into the details of Husserl's account. In broad outline, it is that truth is the goal of a search, the search for complete verification, revealing as evidence all horizons of a state of affairs. But it is part of the sense of objective truth that the search can never be completed. Objective truth is constituted as essentially transcending one's powers of discovery.

In the final section, section 29, of the Third Meditation, Husserl indicates how this account of existence-sense gives rise to a method for detailed study of objectivity. What one needs to explore are the structures of the different systems of evidences which constitute objective existence for different kinds of objects. Husserl calls the theories which we should thereby develop 'constitutional theories'.

> Naturally it [constitutional theorizing] is everywhere a matter of uncovering the intentionality implicit in the experience itself as a transcendental process, a matter of explicating systematically the predelineative horizons by a conversion into possible fulfilling evidence, and then incessantly explicating in like manner the new horizons that indeed incessantly arise within the old, according to a definite style. (*CM*, p. 64)

Each kind of object will have its own constitutional theory. Husserl here adds to the list of kinds of objects he gave in section 21 of the Second Meditation 'man', 'human community' and 'culture'. The implication of this is that not only objective reality but social reality is to be explained in terms of how experiences of it are constituted into systems. Husserl discusses these kinds of objects in the Fifth Meditation (see Chapter Eight, section 2 (d)).

We are now in a position to sum up in very broad terms the fundamental difference between Husserl's phenomenology and realism. Both can agree that one experiences the world as 'other than oneself'. The difference lies in the explanations as to the source of this experience of otherness. For the realist, one experiences the world that way because it *is* that way, it *is* other than oneself. Phenomenology explores the *sense* of this realist belief. What does 'the world is other than us' mean? Husserl believes his phenomenological descriptions have revealed that this sense or meaning is, as all meaning, the result of acts of consciousness. Hence, *to that extent*, the otherness of the world is for Husserl something which conscious subjects constitute. But, it is not only the realist as characterized in Chapter One who differs from Husserl. As we shall see in Chapter Four, Sartre takes issue with Husserl on this point.

4 Phenomenological Description and Conceptual Analysis

We can now make some comparisons between Husserl's work and some results of analytic philosophy.[8] We shall first contrast the different interpretations of the concept of intentionality by Husserl and certain analytic philosophers. Second, we shall look at some similarities between Husserl and some analytic philosophers in their claims about perception, truth and existence.

In the Second Meditation, Husserl credits his teacher, Franz Brentano, with the insight, crucial for Husserl's phenomenology, that consciousness is intentional or possesses intentionality, referring to

> Franz Brentano's significant discovery that 'intentionality' is the fundamental characteristic of 'psychic phenomena' – and actually lays open the method for a descriptive transcendental-philosophical theory of consciousness.... (*CM*, p. 41)

Brentano himself had stated the thesis of intentionality as follows:

> Every mental phenomenon is characterized by what the Scholastics of the Middle Ages called the intentional (or mental) inexistence of an object, and what we might call, though not wholly unambiguously, reference to a content, direction toward an object (which is not to be understood here as meaning a thing), or immanent objectivity. Every mental phenomenon includes something as object within itself, although they do not all do so in the same way. In presentation something is presented, in judgement something is affirmed or denied, in love loved, in hate hated, in desire desired and so on. This intentional inexistence is characteristic exclusively of mental phenomena. No physical phenomenon exhibits anything like it. We can, therefore, define mental phenomena by saying that they are those phenomena which contain an object intentionally within themselves.[9]

Brentano's examples give us some initial understanding of his claim: belief is always *about* something, and fear *of* something; when one perceives or imagines, one perceives or imagines something; and so on. We are not concerned with whether Brentano's claim is true for all mental processes, but with how it has been interpreted by different philosophers.

The most familiar statements of Brentano's thesis are that consciousness is 'intentional', or that it is 'object-directed'. Both terms are open to misunderstanding. For Brentano, as for Husserl, to say that conscious acts are intentional is not to say that they are intended or deliberate acts, but that they point to, reach out towards, objects. The claim that conscious acts are 'object-directed', or directed towards objects', is not to be understood straightforwardly as meaning that conscious acts relate thinkers to existent things. This is why Brentano speaks of intentional or mental inexistence. The distinction in German between 'Objekt' and 'Real' may facilitate expression of this point. 'Real' means existent thing: conscious acts do not have objects in this sense. 'Objekt' has no such existential commitment. Hence the use of the term 'Objekt' leaves open the question of the actual existence of the object. It is in this sense that conscious acts have objects.

The influence of Brentano upon Husserl can be formulated as follows. Husserl performs the epoché precisely in order to leave open questions about existence. What the phenomenological method aims to explore is the remaining sense in which conscious acts have objects.

Since these objects of consciousness are not objects in the world, it is convenient to introduce a name for them. Philosophers have introduced the term 'intentional object'. This expression should be seen as a way of posing certain questions, and not as a substitute for answering them. The chief questions will be: how do intentional objects relate to existent objects; how do they relate to conscious acts; and how do they relate to each other? Parallel questions will arise with respect to acts of consciousness. As we noted above, these are just the questions which Husserl's phenomenological descriptions aim to answer.

We are now in a position to compare Husserl's phenomenological study of the intentionality of consciousness with one influential way in which certain recent analytic philosophers have studied intentionality. Following Chisholm's[10] interpretation of Brentano's thesis, they have interpreted it as a thesis about language. The thesis can be stated thus: the intentionality of consciousness displays itself in the language used to ascribe mental states. Chisholm calls such language 'intentional' language. The quest is then to discover the logical form of intentional language. The logical peculiarity of intentional language consists in two facts: the object-expressions of verbs used to ascribe mental states are indifferent to existence; and they are referentially opaque. What do these mean?

We might begin with grammar. Verbs which are used to ascribe states of consciousness are frequently followed by a noun or preposition and noun. For example: 'He was thinking about his future', 'She was angry at the insult'. When they are not so followed, it is nonetheless often in point to ask 'about what?', 'by what?' etc.: e.g. 'About what is he thinking, or surprised, or pleased?', 'By what is she amused, deafened, convinced?'. So stated, however, this does not distinguish these verbs from others which do not ascribe conscious states. For it is also in point to ask 'On what did the ball bounce?', 'By what was the butter melted?', 'What was the story about?', etc.

So, one must look beyond grammar for a satisfactory characterization of 'intentional' language. One must look to its logical form. Chisholm noted that intentional language features differently in inference from non-intentional language. Two forms of inference which one would expect to be valid, judging by the apparent form of the sentences, turn out not to be so when the sentences ascribe conscious states. One concerns existential commitment; the other, substitution. We shall look at each of these in turn.

With most sentences which comprise subject, verb, and object, one can validly infer from the truth of the sentence, the truth of another sentence which says that the object exists.

> e.g. The cat sat on the mat
> implies
>> A mat exists.
>
> The formal representation of this inference pattern is
>> a R b   – an object 'a' bears a relation 'R' to an object 'b'
>> $\therefore (Ex)(x = b)$ – the object 'b' exists

But this inference pattern is not valid for instances where one replaces 'R' by a verb ascribing a state of consciousness.

> e.g. Jones thought about a mat
> does not imply
>> A mat exists.

Jones *may* be thinking about a mat which exists; but he may equally well be thinking about a fictional mat, an imagined mat, a hallucinated mat, a mat he intends to weave. The mat might exist or it might not, Jones may believe that the mat he is thinking about exists, or he may not; but whichever of all these possibilities is the case, his thinking does not logically require a mat in the way the cat's sitting does.

One natural conclusion to draw is that sentences ascribing states of consciousness of objects are not of the logical form 'a R b'. Questions then arise about what their logical form is: what contribution do the parts of the sentence make to the truth value of the whole, and in what valid inferences do the sentences feature? In particular, does the object expression refer to some other object, or does it play some role other than referring in the sentence? In addressing themselves to such questions, analytic philosophers engage with issues in the philosophy of mind and metaphysics, which we shall not pursue here.[11]

The second logical oddity (referential opacity) about sentences ascribing conscious states points to the same conclusion: that objects of mental states are not objects in an ordinary sense. Once again, for sentences comprising subject, verb, and object, one can normally substitute for the object expression in the sentence a different expression and, provided that the new expression refers to the same thing, the truth value of the whole sentence will not be affected.

> e.g. The cat sat on the mat in the garden.
> The mat in the garden is the mat I wove last year.
> These two together imply
> The cat sat on the mat I wove last year.
> The formal representation of this inference pattern is
> a R b – object 'a' stands in the relation 'R' to the object 'b'
> b = c – object 'b' is identical with object 'c'
> ∴ a R c – object 'a' stands in the relation 'R' to the object 'c'

But this inference pattern is not valid for instances where 'R' stands for a verb ascribing a conscious state.

> e.g. Jones was thinking about the mat in the garden.
> The mat in the garden is the mat I wove last year.
> These do not imply
> Jones was thinking about the mat I wove last year.

The conclusion need not give a version of the thought which Jones would recognize or acknowledge – it does not say *how* Jones is thinking of the mat; whereas the original version, one is to suppose, does.[12] It is a peculiarity of sentences ascribing conscious states that the object expression can indicate *how* the object is regarded by the subject. This is not the case for other sentences. How the cat either regarded or sat on the mat is not indicated by the sentence 'The cat sat on the mat in the garden'. There, the expression 'the mat in the garden' simply refers to an object – its occurrence is 'referentially transparent'. Hence any expression with the same referent would fulfil exactly the same role in the sentence; and so the truth value of the sentence would remain unchanged by substitution of any such expression.

In the sentence ascribing a conscious state, the expression 'the mat in the garden' does not simply refer – its occurrence is 'referentially opaque'. The expression also, or instead, in some sense 'characterizes' the thought. Other expressions with the same referent may fail to fulfil that role. Hence it is not obvious that truth value is preserved when a different expression with the same referent is substituted for the original one. One natural conclusion to draw is, again, that sentences ascribing conscious states and their objects do not have the logical form 'a R b'. Here again, analytic philosophers go on to ask what _is_ their logical form: how does the referentially opaque expression serve to characterize the thought? Again, this takes the enquiry into the area of philosophy of mind and metaphysics which again we shall not investigate.

Our concern is to explore the contrast with Husserl. The way in which these problems about intentional language are set up could easily be seen as ignoring the real significance of the thesis that consciousness is intentional, for the analytic approach might seem to presuppose that one can study the object meant without reference to _how_ it is meant. Intentional language is presented as a problem, as deviating from the well-established rules that referring expressions carry existential import, and that expressions with the same reference can be inter-substituted without affecting the truth value of the sentence in which the substitution is made. Since these rules do not apply to intentional language, the acceptance of the rules presupposes an at least implicit acceptance that non-intentional language is primary, in that it constitutes the norm and its logical form can be settled without looking at its logical relations with intentional language.

Thus, in our example of indifference to existence, it is presupposed that one can assess the truth value of 'the mat exists' independently of the truth-value of 'Jones is thinking about the mat'. Husserl would, of course, agree with the particular example: one can think about things which do not exist, and no single act of consciousness directed towards an object guarantees the existence of that object. What he would contest, however, given his arguments in the Third Meditation, is that the general philosophical questions about existence can be settled without looking at what is meant by 'existence', without looking at the phenomenological origins of existence: that is, looking at acts of consciousness directed towards existent objects.

Similarly, the above presentation of the problem of referential opacity in intentional language suggests that the logical form of identity statements, what other statements they imply or are implied by, is regarded as settled in essentials, though how they relate to intentional statements is not settled. Husserl's claim in section 18 of his Second Meditation, that the identity of objects is something that conscious subjects constitute, indicates that he would disagree with that suggestion.

In terms of understanding intentional language, Husserl's work suggests that, rather than regarding non-intentional or 'extensional' language as primary and intentional language as logically deviant, one should look at this distinction as one which is made _within_ the natural attitude, and that one should seek to understand it from the philosophical standpoint as a distinction which one constitutes oneself. To do this would be, in a way, to regard all language as intentional in a very wide sense of 'intentional', that is, as depending upon consciousness. The rules of extensional language depend upon consciousness as much as do the 'deviations' of intentional language (now in its narrow sense). One should, as Husserl does in his Second and Third Meditations, examine the phenomenological origins of the concepts of 'object', 'existence', 'identity' and 'truth'. These origins will be revealed by describing how one experiences objects as existent, and how one experiences different aspects as aspects of the *same* object. In doing this, one must not ignore the possibility that one may uncover grounds for revising the accepted norms concerning extensional language, and so also the customary way of presenting intentional language as problematic.

Both phenomenologists and analytic philosophers aim to explore meanings, but they differ in their interpretation of 'meaning'. For Husserl, the source of meaning is the conscious subject. One reveals meanings by examining the structure of one's conscious experience, how and what one means. Analytic philosophy holds the bearer of meaning to be language; meaning is revealed by examining the structure of language and how it is used.

One kind of analytic philosophy is ordinary language philosophy. We shall conclude this chapter by comparing the approach of some ordinary language philosophers with the first, descriptive stage of Husserl's phenomenological approach to philosophical problems.[13] Despite their radically different methods, they both aim to reveal philosophical truths by focusing upon and exploring presuppositions which are so commonly held and so familiar that one does not ordinarily notice them. For Husserl, these are the assumptions of the natural attitude; for ordinary language philosophy, they are assumptions embedded in our language as one unreflectingly uses it. Some ordinary language philosophers would also agree broadly with Husserl's results. We shall look briefly at three areas of philosophical enquiry where similarities are evident: theories of perception, of existence and of truth.

Ordinary language philosophers have often explored the meaning of perceptual claims. One critical direction of their work is very similar to that of Husserl. They have aimed to defeat philosophical theories of perception which construe perception as the passive reception of data from the external world, what Husserl terms 'sensualism'. Such, they concede, may be a correct causal account of perceiving, but it is not a proper philosophical account. Philosophers should ask about the meaning of perceptual claims; the causes of perception are no part of this meaning.

The positive results of some ordinary language philosophy also closely resemble those of Husserl, though they are expressed in different terms. Where Husserl seeks the meaning of experience, the ordinary language philosopher asks: what does the claim 'X sees a die' commit one to? Three kinds of such commitment are often noted.

(1) X has identified, conceptualized something as a die, as an object in the world. X sees the whole die, not just the facing surface. Only this surface

is revealed to X's eyes; but 'see' does not mean 'have revealed to one's eyes'. 'X sees a die-front' means something different from 'X sees a die'.

(2)	What X perceives has a past and a future; it is reidentifiable and persists through time.

(3)	The die is solid and would be resistant if one touched it; it has a back with other faces on it; it will not disappear into thin air; it is not an illusion, hallucination or dream object.

All these are claims to which one commits oneself in making the original claim: they are part of the sense of the claim 'X sees a die'. One test for showing this is that if any of the commitments turned out to be misplaced – if the die had no back, or disappeared as a dream – one would be logically required to retract the original claim.

Notice, now, how similar these three commitments are to the features which Husserl's phenomenological description revealed. One's experiences of the die have *unity*; the die is experienced as having *identity*; and the experience has horizons which could be actualized, but may not be. The different methods produce remarkably similar accounts of perception.

Ordinary language philosophers have also explored the meaning of existential claims. We shall outline the sort of account some of them have given of claims that physical objects in the world exist. We noted earlier (section 3 above) that, for Husserl, to experience an existing object is to have an experience which has implicit in it infinite 'horizons' of the same object. Since these horizons, the possible experiences of the object, are infinite, they can never all become actual. Hence an objective existent is always intended as impossible to experience fully: it always 'goes beyond' any number of experiences one can have of it. There is a close parallel between this and Wittgenstein's criterial account of meaning. The account states that the meaning of a statement is given in terms of the criteria for its proper use. A criterial account of the meaning of an existential claim about an object in the world, such as 'this die exists', will thus include:

(1)	Predictions concerning future experiences which, if false, will cast doubt on the claim that this die exists.

(2)	The recognition that the statement is not conclusively verifiable: we can never check all its criteria, it remains always defeasible in the light of future experience, any of the criteria may turn out not to hold – one might wake up, etc.

Condition (1) articulates the meaning of the claim that the die exists. Condition (2) states that it is an empirical claim not susceptible to conclusive verification: it is a claim about objective existence. That it cannot be conclusively verified is not due to an inadequacy in human powers of discovery, but is part of what is meant by the claim that the die exists. These two claims correspond to Husserl's account of the existence of 'transcendent' objects in terms of infinite horizons. Thus the positive accounts of meaning run parallel, despite the difference in the methods of producing them. They also have similar critical force. Both are intended as weapons against realism and Berkeleyan idealism, or its progeny, verificationism.

Finally, ordinary language philosophers have often explored the concept of truth; and some have reached conclusions broadly similar to those of Husserl. The study of ordinary language may reveal grounds for endorsing a coherence theory of truth and rejecting a correspondence theory. For Husserl, that truth corresponds to reality is one of the assumptions characteristic of the natural attitude. From a transcendental standpoint, one can examine this assumption. One finds that what one means by it is not that certain experiences, the 'true' ones, correspond to facts in a realm independent of experience, but rather that a judgement is true when it is an element in a set of judgements which together characterize a coherent system of experiences.

Ordinary language philosophy might set out to challenge the correspondence theory of truth by asking what it means. This theory says that 'p' is true just in case 'p' corresponds to reality. But if this is to be developed into a theory, it must be further articulated. One must ask how reality must be in order for it to correspond to 'p'. The obvious answer is that reality must be such that p is a fact, or it is a fact that p. But now it is noted that the two claims 'p is true' and 'p is a fact' are used in common parlance entirely interchangeably: they are used to mean the same thing. Ordinary language, therefore, in this trivial and innocuous way, assumes something like a correspondence theory of truth. As long as this stays embedded in ordinary language it does no harm. It misleads only when it is taken as the basis of a philosophical claim about the nature of truth. The agreement with Husserl at this point should be clear: there is nothing wrong with the natural attitude or with ordinary linguistic usage in their proper place, and *proper* interpretation of these practices can reveal error in philosophical theories, error which can often be seen to have its source in a misinterpretation of ordinary practice.

Ordinary language philosophers might then go on to explore some less vacuous articulation of the correspondence theory of truth: e.g. 'p' is true just in case 'q', 'r', and 's' are facts where 'q' 'r' and 's' result from analysing what 'p' means. But now, since 'is a fact' means what 'is true' does, one has as an account of the truth of 'p', ' "p" is true just in case "q", "r" and "s" are true'. But the theory of truth to which this commits one is not a correspondence but a coherence theory. For 'p' to be true, it must cohere with certain other sentences. The correspondence theory collapses into a coherence theory of truth just as it did for Husserl. What is supposed to cohere differs: for Husserl it is experiences, for the ordinary language philosophers it is sentences or propositions; but the form of the reasoning is clearly similar. This rejection of the correspondence theory of truth is thus another aspect of the attack on realism launched both by Husserl and by some practitioners of ordinary language philosophy.

We have now explored how intentionality lies behind phenomenological method for Husserl. Further, we have examined how this method is used by Husserl to explore the meanings of 'object', 'existence' and 'truth', and thereby to produce a philosophical position which is neither realist nor Berkeleyan idealist. It avoids realism because it rejects the correspondence theory of truth and the intelligibility of a realm wholly independent of consciousness. We shall discuss how Husserl's position differs from Berkeleyan idealism in the next chapter.

3

Phenomenology and Transcendental Idealism

The main aim of this chapter is to provide an account of the 'transcendental' character of Husserl's phenomenology which involves his adopting a form of transcendental idealism.[1] To do this we have to elucidate two themes which emerge most explicitly in the Fourth Meditation. The first is implicit in Husserl's 'Cartesian' approach to phenomenology: it concerns the role of the subject in experience (see Chapter One, section 3). The second theme concerns the move to the second, 'philosophical', stage of phenomenological analysis (see Chapter Two, section 1): this involves what Husserl calls the 'critique' of the descriptions of experience performed in the first, 'descriptive' stage (see Chapter Two, section 2).

Both these themes figure in the opening section (30) of the Fourth Meditation, where Husserl points out what is required in order to give concrete meaning to the following claim:

> Objects exist for me, and are for me what they are, only as objects of actual and possible consciousness. (*CM*, p. 65)

What needs to be shown in more detail is what this existence is, what sort of actual and possible consciousness is concerned, and what 'possibility' signifies here. This involves two things. First – and this is the first theme referred to above – it involves looking at how the world is constituted in order to discover how the subject, the transcendental Ego, is constituted. The subject can be fully described only via the objects it experiences. The transcendental Ego cannot be *independently* identified and individuated; it can only be seen as a 'pole' of experiences.

The second thing involved – and here emerges the second theme – is the discovery of not just universal but *essential* (necessary, a priori) properties of experience. These are discovered by discovering essential properties of the Ego. One of these essential properties is that the structure of the objective world is a correlate of the structure of the Ego:

It is thus an essential property of the ego, constantly to have systems of intentionality – among them, harmonious ones – partly as going on within him ⟨actually⟩, partly as fixed potentialities, which, thanks to predelineating horizons, are available for uncovering. Each object that the ego ever means, thinks of, values, deals with, likewise each that he ever phantasises or can phantasy, indicates its correlative system and exists only as itself the correlative of its system. (*CM*, p. 65)

This chapter follows the course of the Fourth Meditation. In the first section we present some features of the subject of experience noted by Husserl in sections 31–3. In section 2, we introduce the method of 'eidetic' description, which marks the move to the level of critique, and which aims to discover the necessary or essential elements of experience. In section 3, this eidetic method is applied to the Ego, the subject of experience, thus providing the basis for the fully fledged account of transcendental idealism, given in section 4, according to which the world of objects, and the world of possible objects, is necessarily the correlate of the system of the constituting ego, and that system can itself be seen to have essential structures. The final section examines the similarities and differences between Husserl's transcendental idealism and that of Kant.

1   The Description of the Subject

In sections 31–3 Husserl turns his attention to the subject of experience. Hitherto he has been examining the subject's experiences; but now he wants to focus on the subject whose experiences they are. The description of the subject is still at the level of analysis employed in the Second and Third Meditations, viz, that of the first stage of phenomenological description, in which one looks at one's own experience 'with simple devotion to the evidence inherent in the harmonious flow of such experience' (*CM*, p. 29). We noted in Chapter Two (section 2) that noetic description reveals this 'harmonious flow' as always having a temporal order, being sythesized in 'internal time' and as having a 'conformity to type'. Husserl now highlights three features of the subject: the identity of the subject, the individuality of the subject, and the connection between the subject and the objective world constituted by the subject. We shall look at each of these in turn.

Husserl introduces the first feature thus:

The ego grasps himself not only as a flowing life but also as *I*, who live this and that subjective process, ... *as the same I.* (*CM*, p. 66)

Husserl is saying that there is, in the multitude of one's experiences, an awareness that those experiences belong to a single identical subject. All experiences, all the different kinds of experience, all possible experiences, are seen to be those of an identical subject of consciousness. We have already noted (Chapter Two, section 2) that, for Husserl, synthesis, as applied to objects, means that reflection discovers that an object is identical for a variety of different experiences of it. He now introduces (section 31) a second kind of identifying synthesis: the identity of the subject.

Corresponding to these two sytheses, there are two 'poles' of experience: the object-pole and the subject-pole. Neither of these can be discovered without reference to the other, nor without reference to the experience which link them. All experience, Husserl now claims, has a tri-partite structure: the 'ego-cogito-cogitatum' (*CM*, p. 50). The subject-pole is the experiencing subject, the transcendental Ego; the object-pole is the cogitatum, the object experienced; and the cogito is the stream of experiences which link ego and cogitatum.

The second feature of the subject which emerges from phenomenological reflection concerns its 'individuation' or individuality: what distinguishes that subject from others. The subject is not just an 'empty pole of identity' (*CM*, p. 66). It is seen to have a history, a personal style or character. The way this 'personal character' comes about is by the subject's past, present and future *acts*. In each act, the subject either develops new characteristics or reinforces old ones; but, in either case, there is a continuity of character, what Husserl calls an 'abiding style'. For example:

> If, in an act of judgment, I decide for the first time in favor of a being and a being-thus, the fleeting act passes; but from now on *I am abidingly the Ego who is thus and so decided*, (*CM*, p. 66)

If the act of judgement is not revoked, it forms part of the history of that subject. One finds oneself convinced by a certain judgement and this affects one's other judgements or opinions. Decisions, likewise, influence one's life. Consider, for example (ours), the decision to become a socialist. From then on, one's life and activities are to be seen in that light. It is possible for one to cease to be a socialist, either by another decision, or by simply failing to live up to the prior decision. In either case, one has changed, but not into a different person: one is still oneself. Husserl believes that, despite one's decisions and convictions often being only temporary, only 'relatively abiding', 'the Ego shows, in such alterations, an abiding style with a unity of identity throughout all of them: a "personal character"' (*CM*, p. 67). Husserl also believes that this character is something one actively produces. One's 'abiding style' is the result of the active constitution of the self.

The third feature (section 33) of the subject concerns the role of objects in this individual 'style'. A full individuation (the second feature) of the subject depends upon a full account of the experiences of that subject:

> The Ego can be concrete only in the flowing multiformity of his intentional life, along with the objects meant – and in some cases constituted as existent for him – in that life. Manifestly, in the case of an object so constituted, its abiding existence and being-thus are a correlate of the habituality constituted in the Ego-pole himself by virtue of his position-taking. (*CM*, p. 68)

The reference to 'habituality' is important. It is an extension of the idea of personal character contained in the second feature of the subject. The subject identifies objects, builds up experience of similar objects, and so develops a repertoire of experiences of objects. One is then faced with a 'distinction between those objects with which I am acquainted and those only anticipated as objects with which I may become acquainted' (*CM*, p. 68). Those objects of which a subject has had experience, for example (ours) the tables and chairs of everyday experience, form part of the description of the self who has had those experiences. A subject who has had such experiences will have expectations and beliefs about future perceptions of chairs that someone who has never seen a chair would not have. Their 'habitualities' will be different. But the important point is that these 'habitualities' are identified by reference both to what one has experienced and to what one has not yet experienced. The world of objects with which the subject is not yet actually acquainted is a world which is nonetheless a possibility for that subject. It is the nature and significance of such possibilities which are explored in the second 'critical' stage of phenomenological description.

The individual subject, which Husserl calls the 'monadically concrete Ego' (*CM*, p. 68), consists of the whole of actual and potential conscious life. This potential life is made up of objects one has not actually experienced, but one anticipates experiencing. One's anticipation is based on one's actual experience as a particular subject with its distinctive way of experiencing the world. These anticipations are horizons (see Chapter Two, section 2) 'implicit' in one's actual experience of objects. The naming of the concrete ego by the Leibnizian[2] term 'monad' is suggestive, because Leibnizian monads 'mirror' the whole universe, and are individuated by what they mirror. At any moment, a Leibnizian monad contains its whole past and is pregnant with its entire future; and every monad contains within itself its relation to every other monad. Analogously, Husserl wants to emphasize that the concrete Ego 'contains within itself', and is individuated by, all the experiences it could possibly have – all the ways it can constitute the actual or possible world.

It is at this point that Husserl provides the first hint of his transcendental idealism:

> the problem of *explicating this monadic ego phenomenologically* ... must include *all constitutional problems without exception.* Consequently the phenomenology of this *self-constitution* coincides with *phenomenology as a whole.* (*CM*, p. 68)

The three features of the self, its identity, its individuality and its monadic qualities, indicate that one might be able to uncover the essential structure of the world by uncovering the structures of the constituting self. To develop this, Husserl has to turn to the second stage of phenomenology, involving the method of eidetic description, which discovers that there are essential structures to the experiences of the self.

2 The Method of Eidetic Description

Thus far in the *Cartesian Meditations*, Husserl has simply been describing experience. And one might expect that the content of such descriptions would be contingent upon the life experiences of the person whose experience is being described, the philosophical meditator. If this were so, then the aim, articulated in the First Meditation, of building an apodictically secure philosophy could not be achieved. However, Husserl is convinced that these descriptions of experience do contain elements that are essential. He says:

> By the method of transcendental reduction each of us, as Cartesian meditator, was led back to his transcendental ego – naturally with its concrete-monadic contents as this de facto ego, the one and only absolute ego. When I keep on meditating, I, as this ego, find descriptively formulable, intentionally explicatable types; and I was able to progress step by step in the intentional uncovering of my "monad" along the fundamental lines that offer themselves. For good reasons, in the course of our descriptions such expressions as "essential necessity" and "essentially determined" forced themselves upon us – phrases in which a definite concept of the Apriori, first clarified and delimited by phenomenology, receives expression. (*CM*, p. 69)

But so long as one confines oneself to description, it remains a mystery what these 'good reasons' are for such phrases as 'essentially determined' being unavoidable. One requires a method for discovering what is and what is not essential in the descriptions. If one had such a method and applied it, one could uncover these 'essential necessities' and therefore become aware why these phrases signifying such necessities 'force themselves' upon one. Such a method would also clarify the concept of the a priori.

Husserl's method, in outline, is this: as meditator, one 'imaginatively varies' the case from which one starts, viz. one's own, so that the descriptions of the variations will no longer be descriptions of one's own experiences. His justification of this method as one which will reveal necessary truth is, roughly, this: the descriptions of these 'imaginatively varied' experiences will pick out not only features which all actual experience in fact has; they will also pick out features which all imaginable experience has. But features of all imaginable experience (that is to say, all conceivable, or all possible, experience) are precisely essential features of experience, features 'contingent upon' neither the existence of the world (for that has been bracketed), nor the existence of experiences. They will be necessary, or a priori. And if one can discover these necessities, one has discovered the apodictically secure foundations for philosophy. It is the aim of the second stage of phenomenological research, the 'criticism of transcendental experience' (*CM*, p. 29), to discover these essential elements of experience. The method of discovery Husserl calls the method of 'eidetic description'. Its key is the imagination. We shall now look in more detail at this method.

Husserl has already made implicit use of imagination in his phenomenological descriptions. Noematic and noetic descriptions (see Chapter Two, section 2) included 'horizons', experiences which one expects – that is to say, 'imagines' – one would have if, for example, one moved in relation to the experienced object. Similarly, the description of the subject's 'habitualities' (see section 1, above) implicitly involves anticipating – that is to say, imagining – objects one has not yet experienced. So, one can imagine both hitherto unexperienced experiences and hitherto unperceived objects. Husserl's second stage of phenomenology involves making explicit and additional use of this imaginative process. If one can see how far imagination can take one, then one would not be confined to the actual, which would be a slim basis for discovering necessities.

Husserl introduces this explicit appeal to the imagination via an example:

> Starting from this table-perception as an example, we vary the perceptual object, table, with a completely free optionalness, yet in such a manner that we keep perception fixed as perception of something, no matter what. Perhaps we begin by fictively changing the shape or the color of the object quite arbitrarily, keeping identical only its perceptual appearing.... We, so to speak, shift the actual perception into the realm of non-actualities, the realm of the as-if, which supplies us with "pure" possibilities, pure of everything that restricts to this fact or to any fact whatever. (*CM*, p. 70)

A more readily graspable example (ours) would be that of seeing. One can imagine a wide range of physical objects as being possible objects of seeing but one cannot imagine seeing sounds. These unimaginable experiences are excluded from the possible or 'ideal' extension of seeing. So, by discovering what one can and what one cannot imagine, one builds up a list of what one can imagine, a list of possible experiences. Since one can do this, one intuits that there is a principle at work governing what is imaginable. This principle is the eidos. One knows that it is possible to see trees but not sounds because one has a universal principle which enables one to make this distinction. To have such a universal principle is to be aware of the 'essence' of seeing. It is this awareness that enables one to generate the list of possible experiences of the type under consideration.

This more specific example of seeing has just the same form as Husserl's example of perception. By imaginatively varying *what* is perceived while retaining the process of *perceiving*, one can construct a list of possible perceptions. The construction of this list is governed by a principle. To be able to use such a principle is to know what the essence of perceiving is. This is what Husserl calls the 'eidetic' analysis of perception.

> Perception, the universal type, … has become the pure "*eidos*" perception, whose "*ideal*" extension is made up of all ideally possible perceptions, as purely phantasiable processes. (*CM*, p. 70)

By 'purely phantasiable process', Husserl is not referring to any specific phantasy of the kind one might have in dreams, or in fairy stories, or in sexual life; he is referring to the process of imagining a whole set of experiences, including some which are different both from any actual experience and from any experience implicit as a horizon in an actual experience. This is the set of 'ideally possible perceptions'. The basis on which one constructs the set is 'intuitive and apodictic consciousness' (*CM*, p. 70). Husserl's understanding of 'apodicticity' is introduced in the First Meditation (*CM*, pp. 15–16), which we discussed in Chapter One, section 3. Something is apodictic if it is not possible to doubt it, or if it is absolutely impossible to imagine it otherwise. So, if one is concerned with the pure 'eidos' perception, one is looking for properties of perception, e.g. horizonality, which would be impossible to imagine as not being properties of perception. If one found any, then the claim that perception had those properties would be based on apodictic consciousness. It would not just be universal in the sense of being a property which every actual perception in fact has. No counter-example could possibly be discovered. These properties, so based, Husserl sees as 'essentially necessary' and 'essential universal' properties. One acquires consciousness of these essentially necessary properties via the process of imaginative variation outlined in the discussion of the table-perception. These essential properties of something are its 'eidos'. One can discover the eidos of a mode of experience, such as perception, the object of perception, such as table, or the subject of experience.

It may be helpful at this point to compare eidetic description with conceptual analysis. In the latter, the philosopher analyses concepts such as 'perceive', 'see', 'physical object', 'appearance', 'reality', etc., in order to determine their structure, their relations to one another, and their presuppositions; and in order to determine whether or not there are any necessary rules governing their use. One can arrive at conclusions similar to the ones we have just shown to result from eidetic descriptions: e.g. a rule governing the word 'see'; part of the meaning of the word is that it is not possible to apply it to a process which has certain kinds of objects (sounds). So if one says 'I can see a sound' one is misusing (or misunderstanding) the word 'see'. Similarly, it might be argued that part of the meaning of 'perceive' involves the presupposition that there is something perceived. Further, conceptual analysis, like eidetic description, involves a kind of imaginative variation. So, for example, if one were trying to discern whether or not the concept of 'physical object' necessarily included reference to the spatial features of objects, one would have to appeal to 'linguistic intuitions' by imagining applying the term 'physical object' without, at least implicitly, employing the concept 'space'.

Whether there *are* any strictly necessary rules governing the use of such terms, and what the status of such rules is (e.g. are they linguistic conventions?), is a matter for debate within analytic philosophy. However, Husserl would be convinced that there are such necessities to be discovered, and that one realizes why when one recognizes that eidetic description is logically prior to conceptual analysis.

> It [the eidos] is *prior to all* "*concepts*", in the sense of verbal significations; indeed, as pure concepts, these must be made to fit the eidos. (*CM*, p. 71)

Husserl is saying that the ability to conceptualize, and therefore the ability to engage in conceptual analysis, comes from experience. For example, if one had not first seen things, one would not have the concept of 'seeing'. The eidetic description of seeing is based upon one's experience of seeing; for one realizes that it is implicit in one's ability to distinguish seeing from other kinds of experience, and in one's ability to limit the possible range of objects which are visible, that one operates with an intuitive awareness of the essential nature of the process of seeing. It is this which is the basis for one's use of the term 'see'. Conceptual analysis, at best, could only be a clue to the eidetic description. But one must avoid putting the cart before the horse. For Husserl, philosophy, as a rigorous study, has to be rooted in the essential necessities of experience and it is these which ground one's concepts.

3   Eidetic Description of the Ego

Eidetic description can now be taken a step further. Not only can particular types of experience be given eidetic descriptions, but one can attempt to describe the eidos of the subject. Here it is important to remember that because of its 'monadic' qualities (the third feature of the subject noted by Husserl in the first stage of his analysis: see section 1, above) focus on the subject will lead to the unfolding of the whole of experience of the world. One will thus discover how the world is constituted by the subject. So, if there are any necessary determinants in the Ego, these will be the basis for any necessary structures of the world – for the two cannot be separated. The way to discover these necessities is to find out whether or not what one says about one's experiences is dependent upon their being one's own. If it is not so dependent, then what one says about these experiences would hold for any subject of experience. To discover these necessities Husserl applies the method of imaginative variation to the subject.

When referring to the realm of non-actualities, which supplies one with the 'pure' possibilities (pure of everything that restricts them to any particular fact), Husserl writes:

> we keep the aforesaid possibilities, not as restricted even to the co-posited de facto ego, but just as a completely free "imaginableness" of phantasy. Accordingly from the very start we might have taken as our initial example a phantasying ourselves into a perceiving, with no relation to the rest of our de facto life. (*CM*, p. 70)

It is clear how this method of eidetic description connects with the phenomenology of self-constitution; for we can see how the procedure of imaginative variation can have, as its starting point, an imaginary experience that bears no relation to any actual experiences of the concrete subject which is performing the imaginative procedure. But Husserl emphatically points out that this does not involve other selves:

> I phantasy only myself as if I were otherwise; I do not phantasy others. (*CM*, p. 72)

Each type of experience which would be revealed by an eidetic description would be a possible type of experience of a possible subject. Indeed if one had a list of all possible types of experiences (perceptions, memories, touchings, etc.), with their appropriate objects, and a list of all possible types of objects (physical objects, imaginary objects, numbers, etc.), with their appropriate experiences, then one would have a complete list of all the possible states of an Ego. However, not any collection of such states, in any order, is a possible or imaginable Ego. What eidetic description of the Ego aims to provide is a list of all possible Egos. It can then discover the rules or principles which guide one's recognition that some collections are possible Egos whilst others are not. This principle is an essential a priori one. This list is what Husserl calls the 'ideal extension of the Ego'. The governing principle of this extension he calls the 'eidos or 'eidetic' principle.

One's own *de facto* Ego is included on the list generated by the eidos principle, because the eidos principle is what determines which transcendental Egos are possible, and this includes all actual transcendental Egos. The list also includes any number of possible variants of a *de facto* Ego. This means that the eidos Ego is an analysis of the eidos (essential universalities) of a transcendental Ego. Any particular transcendental Ego must be an instance of this universal type (and hence displays '*essential universality*'), because the eidetic description includes a principle (or set of principles) which generates all possible transcendental Egos.

Although there is a vast number of possible transcendental Egos as possible variants for any particular transcendental Ego – and it is important to remember that a transcendental Ego is a concrete-monadic Ego, with habitualities – Husserl thinks that there are limits to the range of possible features that any particular transcendental Ego could have. He says:

> in a *unitarily possible* ego not all singly possible types are *compossible*, and not all compossible ones are compossible in just any order, at no matter what loci in that ego's own temporality. If I form some scientific theory or other, my complex rational activity, with its rationally constituted existent, belongs to an essential type that is possible, not in every possible ego, but only in one that is "rational" in a particular sense, (*CM*, p. 74)

For example (ours), if one starts from the *de facto* transcendental Ego that is a philosopher in a particular English language-speaking culture, with a whole set of habitualities, expectations and experiences, etc., then it is possible, by imaginative variation, to conceive of a variety of other states one might have been in – in which case one would have been a different transcendental Ego, e.g. a French philosopher or a Chinese philosopher. Similarly, one could imagine oneself as a physicist. But these possibilities could only be realized for a particular transcendental Ego if that Ego had undergone successfully certain training and experience.[3] One could only be a French philosopher, say, had one been born in France, spoke French and had a French education. One could only be a physicist if one had a certain background in mathematics and physics. What one can phantasize (thereby generating the 'ideal' extension of the universal Ego), and what one can realize, differ, in that the latter is structured by the requirements of the universal type under consideration, e.g. 'physicist'. Whether or not a particular transcendental Ego satisfies these requirements is a matter of its history: of what apparatus it has acquired or developed during the course of its life. A blind man can imagine seeing, but he could not see unless certain facts in his history (e.g. his congenital eye defect, his detached retinas or his undetected glaucoma) had been different.

What Husserl nonetheless hopes can emerge from the reflective, 'imaginative' awareness of a particular transcendental Ego is a consciousness of the universal principles which operate for any transcendental Ego. His search is for eidetic laws 'that govern simultaneous or successive existence and possible existence together' (*CM*, p. 75). His concern is with the relationship between the eidos Ego and the transcendental Ego. To understand the universal principles which govern the eidos Ego *is* to discover the nature of the a priori rules governing how any *de facto* Ego can be an instance of the eidos Ego.

Husserl has already indicated that these rules concern the history of any particular Ego, and concern how this Ego acquires its features. These features, and the universal principles underlying them, are discovered by examining their genesis. It is to these concerns which Husserl turns in sections 37–9.

Here, Husserl wants to discover universal principles which govern any evolving transcendental Ego such that its past, present and future experiences are experienced as being those of a single subject. Husserl has already noted that one does implicitly experience the world from a single point of view; and he is now concerned to discover the necessary elements of this fact. He has already claimed, in particular cases, that it is only when certain kinds of experiences have occurred in the past that certain kinds of experience are possible in the future: e.g. that only if X had done high level mathematics could X do physics. Only if X has had certain experiences is a range of possibilities open to X, which would not be open to someone who had not had those experiences. The laws relating to these possibilities, the laws which govern the possibility of unifying experiences which occur at different times within a single life, are the eidetic laws for which Husserl is searching. They are 'laws for an If and Then' (*CM*, p. 75), which Husserl does not want to call 'causal laws' because of the naturalistic overtones. He prefers to call them laws of *motivation* (in the transcendental sphere). The intentional (motivational) stance of a subject and the world that subject constitutes are determined (though not causally) by laws which relate the kind of experience the subject has had in the past to present and future experiences.

Earlier, in the first stage of the analysis, Husserl claimed that the subject faces the world with certain habitualities. Now the claim is that the subject necessarily faces the world with habitualities. If it did not, it would not be a subject. But, Husserl notes, habitualities must be acquired. It is part of the essential feature (eidos) of a single unified self (transcendental Ego) that the principle of unification relates in part, but in a very important part, to the history (or genesis) of that self. The kind of experience a subject has is limited by the kind of experience it has had in the past:

> That a Nature, a cultural world, a world of men with their social forms, and so forth, exist for me signifies that possibilities of corresponding experiences exist for me, as experiences I can at any time bring into play and continue in a certain *synthetic style*, whether or not I am at present actually experiencing objects belonging to the realm in question. (*CM*, p. 76)

Husserl wants to push this analysis further. He wants to discover necessary features of how habitualities are acquired, about their 'genesis'. He wants to discover eidetic laws governing this genesis. The task of discovering such laws is, Husserl concedes, difficult for any particular meditating transcendental

Ego, because of the difficulty of transcending one's particular habitualities, one's particular style. One can overcome this properly only by a rigorous attempt to provide an eidetic description of the Ego.[4]

However, Husserl believes that it is possible to discover universal principles governing the genesis (i.e. how one is the subject one is, and how this subject remains the same even though it has new experiences). These are the principles of active and passive genesis (see *CM*, section 38). These two sets of principles concern what is presented in experience (passive) and what is made of what is presented (active). In active genesis the Ego produces new objects for consciousness through being presented with some more basic experiences. Husserl gives some examples of this:

> in collecting, the collection is constituted; in counting, the number; in dividing, the part; in predicating, the predicate; ... in inferring, the inference; and so forth. (*CM*, p. 77)

Each of these examples involves the Ego being presented with some object(s) and then performing some act of consciousness on what is presented. For instance (ours), one could have consciousness of the series of natural numbers, and then further notice that some of them have the property of not being divisible by any other natural number greater than one. In this way one would have actively produced the series of prime numbers. Similarly one could have been presented with a complete jumble of stamps; it is then possible to conceive of this set of stamps as a collection. This would involve a certain attitude towards acquiring stamps one has not already got in one's possession: it would involve sorting the stamps into country of origin, date, etc. In this way one divides the set of stamps into parts. One creates subsets of stamps. These subsets did not exist, for one as a subject, prior to one's treating the set as a collection.

Any subdivision of the set of physical objects (e.g. trees, plants, stones, rivers, etc.) involves some principle of active genesis. All these active creations become incorporated into the life of the active subject. Once the subject has made an active synthesis of its experience it will continue to see new experiences in this light. These accumulated active geneses will be part of the habitualities with which the subject confronts the present and the future; and as such they will be felt (if at all) as so much a part of the subject that the term 'active' might seem a misnomer. However, Husserl's point is that, in their origin (genesis), they were produced actively.

Where active genesis concerns the subject, passive genesis concerns what is presented. Husserl takes as an example a mere physical thing. This will be construed in experience as a table, as a hammer or whatever; but stripped of all these active construals one discovers that one is always presented with something physical, having one shape, having unitary aspects, etc. (see *CM*,

p. 79). The point is not just that in any perception one can strip that perception down into what is basically presented (e.g. 'object' as a substrate of predicates), and what might be said of those objects. Passive genesis concerns the history of the perceiving subject:

> It is owing to an essentially necessary genesis that I, the ego, can experience a physical thing and do so even at a glance. (*CM*, p. 79)

Three factors are involved here. First the genesis is seen as passive. What Husserl is trying to emphasize here is the fact that the awareness of physical things is something immediate or direct. One does not first have an awareness of various discrete sense-experiences, which one is then conscious of being united in the concept 'physical thing'. The sense-experiences can be properly described phenomenologically only in terms of the experience of the physical thing. They are intentionally related to each other by being part of the experience of the physical object.

Second, the ability to have passive awareness of physical things has its origins in one's experience in the past. This ability predates other modes of consciousness of physical things; and this is because the perception of the physical thing is prior (both logically and temporally) to any active generation of different ways physical things might be construed. One discovers that passive genesis is something one acquires very early. For, without it, no experience is possible. This connects with the third factor, namely that this immediate basic awareness, the passive genesis, is essentially necessary. Without it one would not be a transcendental Ego. This one discovers by the method of eidetic description. One cannot imagine a subject of experience making sense of its experiences unless it has the ability to synthesize, directly, what is presented in sense-experience as being a kind of object (physical, cultural, spatial, etc.). A subject's early history *must* include reference to this ability.

Parallel to this would be a kind of developmental psychology:

> With good reason it is said that in infancy we had to learn to see physical things, and that such modes of consciousness of them had to precede all others genetically. (*CM*, p. 79)

What the developmental psychologist discovers is a version of what can be discovered at the eidetic level. The difference, as we have noted before (Chapter Two, section 1), is one of 'nuance'. The eidetic description yields the claim that the priority of the passive genesis, both logical and temporal, is essential. The psychologist just records these sequences or facts, but as facts which have naturalistic ontological overtones.

Husserl makes a similar point in section 39 about the relationship between 'association' as the universal principle of passive genesis, and laws of association in the naturalistic framework of psychologists or philosophers such as David Hume. Hume's analysis of causation provides a useful example of this comparison.[5] Hume argued that one's experience of causal connections should be analysed in terms of the association (constant conjunction) of similar pairs of experiences in the past, built up so that one acquires habits of expectation (habitualities) that a particular type of event (labelled 'effect') will follow another type of event (labelled 'cause'). Husserl, likewise, thinks that there are laws of association that govern the habits of expectation (habitualities) that provide the basic passive syntheses. But the basis of Husserl's laws is different from that of Hume's. Husserl considers that Hume's laws of association are *empirical* discoveries of subjective necessity, whereas for Husserl these laws are 'eidetic'. They describe a *realm of the "innate"* Apriori, without which an ego as such is unthinkable' (*CM*, p. 81). The way the principles of association operate is not causally. They provide the basis for *all* experience, including experience of causal connections. Any appeal to experience on the basis of which one could discern causality in operation would be an appeal to experience which itself is structured by these principles of association. The recognition of succession, contingency and resemblance is itself only possible for a subject which already conforms to the principles of active and passive genesis.

4   Husserl's Transcendental Idealism

The full implication of the eidetic description of the Ego is that all experience, all knowledge, is seen as flowing from the transcendental Ego. The essential structures of the Ego, which have been discovered by the method of eidetic description, *are* the essential structures of knowledge and experience. 'Phenomenology is *eo ipso* "*transcendental idealism*"' (*CM*, p. 86). The structures of the world can only be those experienced by the subject. To claim any other structure for the world would be unintelligible. It is for this reason that Husserl's penultimate sentence in *CM* is:

> I must lose the world by epoché, in order to regain it by a universal self-examination. (*CM*, p. 157)

Understanding this quotation is crucial to an understanding of Husserl's transcendental idealism, for it raises a problem considered in *CM*, section 40, which is probably in the minds of most who read the *Cartesian Meditations*. This problem concerns the epoché (see Chapter One, section 3). At the beginning of the phenomenological project the meditating subject has suspended judgement about the existence of the world. The question which the reader may well ask is: when are the brackets going to be removed, so that we can regain a sense of reality? How does the phenomenologist re-establish contact with reality?

It is Husserl's aim to establish that there is something wrong in asking this question. He wants to say that, if one understands the transcendental theory of knowledge as it has evolved in these *Cartesian Meditations*, then one will realize that one already has a theory of knowledge, and it is one which renders certain kinds of questions in traditional theory of knowledge either inconsistent or inappropriate.

The attack on traditional theory of knowledge is something Husserl shares with Kant. Husserl says that the problem of traditional theory of knowledge is transcendence (*CM*, p. 81). What he means by this is that traditional epistemologists start off with a problem which has the form: 'How can I know, on the basis of my experience, the nature of the external world?' The external world is seen as one which transcends my experience. To begin with there seems to be a realist ontology presupposed in the question: that there is a world of things which exist independently of our experience of them. Husserl is very critical of this question because he has no sympathy with the idea of a transcendent realm. This would be a realm beyond experience:

> The attempt to conceive the universe of true being as something lying outside the universe of possible consciousness, possible knowledge, possible evidence, the two being related merely externally by a rigid law, is nonsensical. (*CM*, p. 84)

To ask how one could know this transcendent realm would be inappropriate. However, for Husserl, there is no need to posit an independent realm beyond all possible experience. Husserl has a different idea of what transcendence is. One has experiences of something 'out-there'. This 'out-there' is an aspect of the experience. One experiences, for example the die, with all its horizons, as something which is an object which goes beyond one's particular perception or experience of it. One has a sense of what is beyond particular experiences; but it is a sense which is explicated by describing all the other possible experiences which are implicit in the actual one. It is seen as transcendent because one can never have all the possible experiences of it. That is the sense in which the transcendent world 'goes beyond' experience. One has this *sense* of the transcendent; and for Husserl this is all we need. But in this sense a transcendent object is always an object-for-a-subject.

So the only kind of 'realism' that will make sense is one articulated from the point of view of the subject, the transcendental Ego. In this sense, one can ask whether knowledge of transcendent objects is possible; and, from this point of view, the answer to the question is 'yes'. Any other kind of realism rests on a mistake.

Husserl sees this mistake as common not only to realism but to many other previous reactions to the basic epistemological problem, including both (non-transcendental) idealism, such as Berkeley's, and scepticism, such as Hume's. The idealists have too naturalistic a view of how 'ideas' are to be described. Ideas are seen as existing: they are possible to investigate empirically, they are measurable, and they are discrete. All these features are questionable, according to Husserl, because of the intentional nature of sense-experience. It is not possible to describe sense-experience without reference to the objects of those experiences; and this, Husserl insists, involves the unfolding of the transcendental Ego. No proper description of sense-experience, or of consciousness, can be given without reference to the activity of the constituting subject.

Scepticism, the main alternative to idealism, claims that genuine knowledge of the external world is impossible because there will always be a logical gap between the appearances of the world in consciousness and the features and structures of the independent world. A virtue of scepticism is that it correctly argues that such an independent world could not be known. However, scepticism maintains that there is such a world, but it cannot be known. And so, it implicitly presupposes a realist standpoint. Having shown that such knowledge is impossible, it retreats to seeing the task of philosophy as that of giving causal or naturalistic explanations of how we think we know the external world. In so doing, it treats experience in a similar way to the idealists. It uses extensional descriptions of experience rather than intentional descriptions. It regards experiences as identifiable and describable without reference to other experiences, without reference to the world, and without reference to the subject.

Transcendental idealism is seen by Husserl as the solution (or dissolution) of all these problems. The naive assumptions of everyday life, of the positive sciences, and of traditional theory of knowledge are open to full investigation only by transcendental reflection. For whereas, in natural reflection, there is an acceptance that the objects one perceives exist or that the perceiver exists, in transcendental reflection these questions of existence are bracketed. Only by transcendental reflection can one recognize the extent to which one's experience is of existent objects *for the subject*.

When the empirical ego is immersed in activity in the world, it is not aware of itself. When it is aware of itself as a possible *object*, it is not properly aware of its true nature; for its true nature is as a *subject*, and as such it cannot be the direct object of experience (reflection). This subject, the one which can only be discovered by transcendental reflection, is the transcendental Ego. About this Husserl says:

> Accordingly, not only in respect of particulars but also *universally*, the phenomenologically meditating Ego can become the "non-participant onlooker" at himself – including furthermore every Objectivity that "is" for him, and *as* it is for him. Obviously it can be said that, as an Ego in the natural attitude, I am

likewise and at all times a transcendental Ego, but that I know about this only by executing phenomenological reduction. (*CM*, p. 37)

This suggests two aspects of the transcendental Ego. First, the immersed subject is not aware that it is a transcendental Ego in the world. It has no notion of the transcendental Ego. This is only discovered when the philosophizing subject reflects upon experience and discovers that this experience is that of a single subject. Second, the reflecting Ego discovers that there is an identity between the I which is reflecting and the I reflected upon. Both the experiences reflected upon and the experience of reflection-upon-experience are experienced as being by the same subject. The experience reflected upon belongs to the reflecting subject. The systematic unfolding of this experience, through the two stages of phenomenological analysis, yields:

> the *universal logos of all conceivable being*. In other words: As developed systematically and fully, transcendental phenomenology would be *ipso facto* the true and *genuine universal ontology.* ... This universal *concrete* ontology ... would therefore be the intrinsically first *universe of science* grounded on an absolute foundation. (*CM*, p. 155)

All the distinctions one needs to make to have experience of the world, to develop systematic enquiry into the world, are seen as emanating from the transcendental subject. The full eidetic description of the transcendental Ego, with all its experiential content, yields the concrete universe. It is this idea to which Husserl is referring when he ends the *Cartesian Meditations* with:

> "*Noli foras ire*," says Augustine, "*in te redi, in interiore homine habitat veritas*". (Do not wish to go out; go back into yourself. Truth dwells in the inner man – *De vera religione*, 39. n. 72).[6] (*CM*, p. 157)

A similar idea is put forward by Kant in his transcendental idealism, with its emphasis on the a priori aspects of the activity of the constituting subject. So we shall now conclude this chapter by comparing Husserl's transcendental idealism with that of Kant.

5   Kant and Husserl

Husserl himself invites comparision between his own transcendental idealism and Kant's. He notes (*CM*, p. 86) two distinguishing features between the two types of transcendental idealism. First, Kant retains the idea of a transcendent realm: this is Kant's world of things in themselves (noumena). Belief in such a world, for Kant, is intelligible despite its being impossible to know such a world. Husserl rejects this idea of a transcendent realm. For Husserl the only meaningful idea of transcendence is that seen from the point of view of the subject. Any other idea of transcendence is to be eliminated from philosophy.

The second distinguishing feature which Husserl notes is that Kant's transcendental idealism is the 'product of sportive argumentations, a prize to be won in the dialectical contest with "realisms"' (*CM*, p. 86). Husserl is here indicating a fundamental difference between his descriptive mode of philosophy, and Kant's mode of transcendental argument, where the aim is to *justify* the possibility of knowledge. This philosophical aim is, Husserl believes, what led Kant into giving a wrong analysis of our experience, and into retaining the wrong idea of transcendence. Husserl concedes that Kant, in his 'transcendental' turn, goes a long way along the right philosophical road in that he is, in effect, making the same move as the bracketing procedure; seeing that epistemological claims about objective reality must be understood from the point of view of the subject. But what, according to Husserl, Kant did not see was that ontological claims about what there is should also be subject to the same considerations. Transcendental idealism, properly understood as the

> explication of my ego as subject of every possible cognition, and indeed with respect to every sense of what exists, wherewith the latter might be able to *have* a sense for me, the ego (*CM*, p. 86),

renders any idea of the transcendent as a noumenal realm unintelligible.

The contrast between Kant and Husserl is illuminating because of the broad similarities between their philosophies. Both philosophies are to be understood, as we have just noted, in contrast to those governed by the spectre of transcendence. Kant, like Husserl, has the idea of a subject being both the source of the structure of experience, and ultimately bound up with the idea of an object. Both philosophers see the danger of conceiving the pure subject of consciousness as a possible object of consciousness; and they are united in thinking this a crucial mistake made by Descartes.[7] However, despite these similarities there are important differences which stem from the difference between transcendental phenomenology as a method and Kant's transcendental mode of reasoning. We shall now discuss the two points of divergence already outlined and some more detailed differences between the two philosophers. This will involve giving a brief outline of Kant's transcendental idealism.[8]

The starting point of Kant's arguments is everyday experience and knowledge of the objective world. The aim is to show how that experience and that knowledge are possible; and therefore to resist sceptical suggestions that claims to have such knowledge are not justifiable. Kant is anxious to prove that, if one conceives of the world in a particular way (transcendental realism), then knowledge of that world is impossible. This point is similar to Husserl's contrast between his transcendental idealism and traditional epistemology's conception of transcendence (see section 4, above). Moreover, Kant's move towards transcendental idealism in the epistemological sphere, according to which what is *known* is always subject to the limits of the transcendental subject, is similar, in its *effect*, to Husserl's bracketing of the realist ontological assumptions. But Kant does not, from the start, question the nature of ordinary experience. He assumes that knowledge is possible, a clear case of this knowledge being Newtonian science. His aim is to show on what presupposition *that* knowledge is possible. There is no questioning of the claim that there is a world of things which exist independently of perception of them, and which exist in causal relations with one another.

The sense in which Kant accepts this claim will become clear later in this section. But it is vital to see that, for Kant, this unquestioned claim is not to be understood as a philosophical one, for this would be to accept what Kant calls 'transcendental realism': the view that the world and its properties are ontologically independent of the subject of knowledge, and of that subject's experience. If one adopts this as a *philosophical* standpoint, then, Kant argues, knowledge of such objects is impossible. The descriptions of the world given by Newtonian science would not be justified as *knowledge* if that world were considered in a transcendental realist manner. For Kant, transcendental realism has sceptical implications which make it an unacceptable philosophical position.

At the philosophical level, the world of objects known must not be independent of the subject of experience: there must be, for Kant, some degree of dependence. Kant's transcendental idealism is an account of how the subject must contribute to knowledge. His distinctive solution is to look for some a priori elements, imposed on the world of objects by the subject. These elements, because they are necessary and universal (Kant's criteria of a priori), will guarantee the possibility of knowledge of the external world. They will be the ones which give the appropriate sense to 'external' such that, given *that* sense, it is possible to know the external world. The condition of the possibility of sense-experience yielding knowledge of the external world is that it involves some such a priori element. Kant identifies two. The first concerns the 'intuitions': what is presented in sense-experiences. The second concerns 'concepts': how these intuitions are described. We shall explain these notions in turn.

First, passively received sense-experiences, 'intuitions', have, according to Kant, two a priori features: time and space. These are the forms of intuitions. All one's sense-experience occurs in a single temporal sequence. This is not a feature which corresponds to anything real or independent of one's experience (i.e. there is nothing called 'time'); but it is an essential feature of one's sense-experience. Similarly, space does not exist outside one's experience; but one's experience of objects is such that one must perceive those objects as located in space. Space, like time, is a universal and essential, and so an a priori, aspect of sense-experience.

Second, these experiences, in order to be recognized as coherent, have to be brought under certain a priori concepts (the so-called categories). Without our experience being subject to concepts of substance, causality, measurability, existence, etc., there would be no possibility of experience. These concepts must be a priori if knowledge is to be shown to be possible. If they were based on the transcendent world or on sense-experience, formed for instance by abstraction, then they would be empirical concepts. And if they were empirical, and not a priori, they would not guarantee the possibility of knowledge. The only possible candidate for the basis of these required a priori concepts is the mind (the 'understanding'). This is why Kant considers that they are mind-imposed.

We shall give a very brief outline of the structure of Kant's complex argument, and then present it in a little more detail. The model Kant is using here is one where a series of passively received representations of the external world have first of all to be seen as representing a spatio-temporal world, and where all these representations occur in time (i.e. they are successive or simultaneous); but in order to make sense of this series of representations, the subject has to synthesize them, classify them, group them into being representations of different kinds – tables, chairs, memories, identifications, etc. For Kant, perception of any object demands judgement. It demands that one is in a position to judge that *what* is perceived satisfies a description which one could give if asked. Kant thus sees perception on the model of judgement.

The argument for a list of basic a priori concepts (categories) is partially concerned with the idea that all attempts to classify sense-representations will involve certain basic principles of classification, without which no kind of classification would be possible. So to be able to recognize two intuitions (passively received, but as yet unidentified, representations) as the same, despite the fact that they occur at different times, Kant claims that the subject has to have at its disposal certain ordering principles that make this comparison possible. For example, an intuition of a chair is possible only if one can compare this intuition with past intuitions of chairs, in order to be able to classify these intuitions as being of the same type. One would not be able to make *this* comparison unless one could operate a principle of classification which involved focusing on some features of objects, e.g. their shape and hardness, and not others (e.g. their colour). One could not do this without being able to operate the concept of negation. Hence, being able to make negative judgements, or having the concept of negation, is a necessary condition of the classification of intuitions. This concept is a priori because it could not have been acquired by experience, since having the appropriate experience (experiencing the chair) requires that one already possesses the concept in question.

So the *basic* ordering of perceptions is an active process. It is something the subject of experience imposes on the experience itself. This basic ordering provides a framework for all experience. The framework of the way the subject experiences the world is provided by the mind (or by the transcendental subject). In contrast, the *contents* of the framework have an empirical basis. For Kant, as for Husserl, this subject is not a possible object of experience, it is exclusively a subject. Knowledge of objects requires that experience be that of a single self-conscious subject. Kant says:

> It must be possible for the 'I think' to accompany all my representations; for otherwise something would be represented in me which could not be thought at all, and that is equivalent to saying that the representation would be impossible, or at least would be nothing to me. (B131–2, *KS*,⁹ pp. 152–3)

> The unity of this apperception I likewise entitle the *transcendental* unity of self-consciousness, in order to indicate the possibility of *a priori* knowledge arising from it. For the manifold representations, which are given in an intuition, would not be one and all *my* representations, if they did not all belong to one self-consciousness. (B132, *KS*, p. 152)

The reason for this necessary appeal to the 'I think' – to this transcendental self-consciousness – is that a minimal condition of being able to make sense of a series of experiences is that the subject must be able to recognize those experiences as its own. A condition of the possibility of this self-consciousness is that the subject imposes on the discrete perceptions some objective order, i.e. the subject must impose the categorical scheme for it to be possible to classify the sense representations. In this way Kant arrives at the idea of the transcendental unity of consciousness, an idea which is similar in some respects to Husserl's eidetic ego. For Kant, certain essential concepts (the categories) are imposed by the subject in order for that subject to make sense of its unified experience. The categories are the basic concepts which any subject of experience *must* have in order for its experiences to be intelligible to itself. This is similar to the description of the eidos ego, which lays down the essential universalities for the transcendental Ego (in Husserl's concrete-monadic sense).

We are now in a position to elaborate on the differences between Kant and Husserl outlined at the beginning of this section. First, Kant arrives at his a priori elements by *arguments*, which attempt to show how a certain kind of knowledge is possible. So, for instance, causality is necessary because without it one *could not* understand the distinction between the experience of successive events, and the successive experience of cotemporaneous states of affairs. To take one of Kant's rare examples, one is only able to distinguish the successive series of perception of a ship sailing downstream from the successive series of perceptions of a house if, in the first case, the order of perceptions has a specific relation (one can't see the ship downstream before one sees it upstream if one is seeing a ship sail downstream), and, in the second case, the order of perception is more variable (one can see the chimney before the back door, or vice versa: the order of perceptions is indifferent). Kant argues in the 'Second Analogy of Experience' (*CPR*,[10] pp. A189/B232–A211/B256) that one is not able to detect this difference between the case where the order of perception is necessary (the ship case) and the case where the order of perceptions is indifferent (the house case) unless one imposes the concept of causality on the experiences.

In some ways, Kant's method of transcendental argumentation, which involves appeal to 'what is not conceivable otherwise' (e.g. certain kinds of experiences are not conceivable without the category of causation), might appear to be the same as Husserl's method of eidetic description, with its appeal to 'imaginative variation'. However, the difference, in part, lies in the work that the results of the two methods are asked to perform. For Kant this method is used in the project of justifying knowledge (described in a particular way). For Husserl it is used to identify the essential elements involved in experience. He is not trying to show how that experience is possible, but, having described that experience, he notices that there are implicit in it certain a priori principles, including those of active and passive genesis, which govern the experiences of transcendental Egos. The emphasis is not on an *argument*, that without the principles of active and passive genesis transcendental Egos would not be possible (though of course this would be true); it is rather on the fact that we *discover* that all transcendental Egos are subject to these principles. This difference in emphasis reflects the differing philosophical aims of Kant and Husserl.

The other difference between Kant and Husserl concerns the nature of the world that is structured by their transcendental subjects. Kant, in his attempt to justify knowledge of the world, arrives at a set of twelve a priori principles which structure knowledge. These are different from the a priori principles which we have seen Husserl discover. For Kant, these basic twelve are fixed and unchanging. What Kant tries to show is that, though one must not start off with the idea of an independent reality which one is trying to know – for this way leads to scepticism – one ends up imposing on one's own experience of the world a realist structure: one sees the experiences as experiences of things which continue to exist when unperceived, and which exist in causal relationship to one another. But this aspect of experience is not something one discovers as being true of some independent reality; it is something that we, as subjects, impose on our experience. This is Kant's transcendental idealism – 'transcendental' because Kant is saying that the character of the world as it must be known (as opposed to how it is in itself) is necessarily the result of the mind imposing a certain structure on its experience.

As a result of imposing this structure the subject will experience the world as if it existed independently of the subject of perception. This Kant calls 'empirical realism'. From the point of view of the subject, the world does transcend our experience: it is real, and there are causal relations between the objects in that world. This empirical realism is justified only if one's philosophical position is that of transcendental idealism. But, because Kant's transcendental idealism thus entails an objectivist empirical realism, it is different from Husserl's. Husserl's transcendental idealism, with its a priori principles, does not yield *these* objectivist concepts. We have seen, for example, how Husserl eschewed the word 'causal' when talking of his eidetic principles of passive genesis. And this difference between the nature of their respective a priori principles relates to another fundamental disagreement between Husserl and Kant: this concerns Husserl's rejection of Kant's distinction between 'phenomena' and 'noumena'. (Here we return to the first distinguishing feature Husserl identified between himself and Kant, which we noted at the outset of this section.) To understand this rejection, it is first necessary to understand that Kant and Husserl use the term 'phenomena' in different ways.

For Kant, the basic concepts (categories) determine how the world of possible experience must be conceived, in order for experience or knowledge of the objective world to be possible. The possible objects of knowledge Kant terms 'phenomena'. A 'phenomenon' is an *object* of experience conceived of in accordance with the fixed list of basic categories. So we can already see that there are two basic differences between Kant's use of 'phenomena' and Husserl's. First, Kant's notion only concerns the noematic element of Husserl's notion. Second, Husserl wants to give a more flexible analysis of the concepts we discover to be applicable to the noematic element of 'phenomena'.

But a more important distinction concerns Kant's related concept of 'noumena'. The concept of 'noumena', or of 'things in themselves', refers to a world beyond sense-experience, a world which exists independently of any perceiver – a world which realists consider has properties independent of any knowing subject. This world is a 'transcendental' world. It cannot, according to Kant, be known. Sometimes Kant utilizes this idea of 'noumena' as a limiting concept: it refers to that which cannot be known. In this use it is helpful as a diagnostic term, to describe what it is that some metaphysicians mistakenly attempt to show that we can know. In this sense, for example, the beginning of the universe, an event which in principle it is impossible to have any experience of, would be a noumenal event. If we try to achieve knowledge of this event then we are bound to fail: for knowledge is possible only if it is possible to relate concepts to experience. Concepts which do not relate to experience are transcendent concepts, e.g. God, or the soul; and they refer to noumena.

Husserl objects to this division between a world which can be known and a world which cannot be known. Like Kant, Husserl rejects the idea of what transcends *all* experience as a possible object of knowledge, because it is impossible to experience; but, unlike Kant, he wants to eliminate such a concept from having any role to play in knowledge. For Kant, however, the idea of a transcendent realm does have a number of important roles. First, it makes some sense to say that it is that place from which our sensations come: so our sense representations, passively received, 'represent' this noumenal world. As we have seen, no adequate representation of this noumenal world can be given, only of a world conceived of in terms of the categories. But the categories provide only the basic framework of experience: the content of that framework might come from without, though a 'without' which we cannot describe. Second, the idea of there being an independent world beyond our sense-experience might serve as a stimulus to get nearer and nearer to a more adequate representation of the way the world really is – always subject to the proviso that any knowledge claim accepts the basic transcendental idealist thesis that the knowing subject makes a fundamental contribution to how the world is experienced. Human beings are constantly striving to gain knowledge of the world as it is. Kant says that this project is impossible to achieve, since what can be known is subject to the limitations of what it is possible to think. But there is no incoherence in trying to advance knowledge as far as possible, even though one knows that the ultimate aim is impossible to achieve. The search for universal laws in science would be an example here: one can never know that one has discovered such laws, but it serves science well to behave as if it were possible to try to formulate them.[11] And third, Kant requires this transcendent realm for morality. The freedom presupposed by morality is a property of noumenal selves, a property we cannot know, but can believe.

Husserl, by contrast, totally rejects the idea of a transcendent realm. His idea of transcendence is internal to experience, and one does not require any other idea of what is transcendent. So although Kant and Husserl share a belief that the transcendental Ego has an all-important role in grounding knowledge, their specific claims about this role and its implications differ significantly. These differences follow from their respectively different aims and methods. Kant is seeking to *justify* the possibility of knowledge (and of morality). Husserl is seeking to provide a secure foundation for philosophy by *describing* experience. According to Husserl, Kant is led to wrong conclusions about the essential features of that Ego; and he wrongly postulates the possible realm of noumena, which it is impossible to know. From Husserl's phenomenological standpoint, one discovers that all the crucial distinctions within our experience are those made from the standpoint of the transcendental Ego. For Husserl, the transcendental Ego is the source of sense, and from this source Kant's noumenal world does not make sense. Once one realizes this, one does not have to postulate the existence of anything outside this world of experience:

As developed systematically and fully, transcendental phenomenology would be *ipso facto* the true and *genuine universal ontology.* (*CM*, p. 155)

However, phenomenology does not necessarily rest with this pronouncement. Sartre and Merleau-Ponty both disagree with many of the claims of Husserl's transcendental phenomenology, and *ipso facto* with Husserl's 'genuine universal ontology', whilst nonetheless regarding themselves as 'phenomenologists'. It is to these disagreements and developments within phenomenology that we now turn.

4

Existentialism and Phenomenology

Sartre and Merleau-Ponty can both be called existential phenomenologists.[1] They follow Husserl's method of description, his phenomenology; but they reject the conclusions he reached via this method, his transcendental idealism. They select for description 'concrete' instances of 'man-in-the-world', focusing on action rather than experience. Sartre and Merleau-Ponty's ensuing descriptions of the subject and the world differ from each other; but they agree in rejecting Husserl's description of a transcendental subject experiencing a world of objects which are entirely 'constituted' by that subject. Existential phenomenology offers accounts of the subject and the world which are neither idealist nor realist. In this chapter, we shall explore Sartre's attempt to steer a course between these two positions. Chapters Five, Six and Seven are devoted to Merleau-Ponty's brand of existential phenomenology.

1 The Subject-in-the-World

Existential phenomenology rejects two central tenets of Husserl's transcendental idealism. It rejects the transcendental Ego: the standpoint, outside the natural world, of the philosophizing subject; and it rejects Husserl's account of the objective world as a world of 'sense'.[2] The existential phenomenologists find that phenomenological description reveals a different subject and a different world.

The existentialist aim is to characterize the ordinary experience of human beings living in the world. What existentialism holds to be distinctive about human existence is that it is, first and foremost, active, it acts in the world. By acting, it develops its own character and it interprets the world. In order to reveal the character of the subject and the meaning of the world, phenomenology should begin by describing ordinary human activities in the world, and not thoughts, cognitions, or perceptions of that world, nor reflections upon ordinary activities.

According to existentialism, intentionality, properly understood, indicates the radical interdependence between the subject and the world. To exist as a subject is to interact with the world, but also to stand back from, to question or wonder at, that world. Similarly, to be an object in the world is to be acted upon by a subject; but also it is to stand away from, to be resistant to, that activity.

Existential phenomenology typically takes at the starting-point of its investigation activities, or as Sartre calls them 'conducts'.[3] These are concrete instances of 'man-in-the-world'. The hyphenated phrase indicates the existentialist conviction that the world of objects acted upon and the conscious active subjects are interdependent. Neither could exist without the other; and any 'conduct' presupposes the existence of both. The existence of the world is not, for the existential phenomenologist, a prejudice to be 'bracketed' or put out of play in order to produce pure descriptions. The philosophical task is not one of finding foundations of knowledge; it is the task of enquiring into the respective characters of existent objects and active subjects, given their evident interaction. Transcendental phenomenology, in contrast, begins with the Ego's experiences, from which the existence of the world of objects has been 'bracketed'. Its task is to discover what the Ego which has these experiences must be like, and how the Ego construes out of its experiences an existent world of objects.

Based on its use of the phenomenological method, existential phenomenology aims to characterize the phenomena in a way which avoids the ontologies of idealism and realism. The existential subject differs from the subject of transcendental idealism and from that of realism. The idealist subject is outside the natural world; the existentialist subject lives inescapably in the world. The realist subject is an integral part of the world, a natural object among other natural objects; the existentialist subject is distinctively different from all natural objects.

The existentialist conception of the natural world is similarly neither that of idealism nor that of realism. The world is not, as idealism has it, reducible to appearances or meanings; the world must be there to be interpreted and interacted with. But neither is the existentialist world as the realist believes the world to be, having determinate, intelligible features which human perception and enquiry can aim to discover. For the existentialist, all that is determinate and intelligible in the world is so solely in virtue of human action upon it.

We recounted in our Introduction Sartre's first reaction to the philosophy of Husserl. His enthusiasm there seemed to be primarily for Husserl's method: producing philosophy by describing concrete objects. In a short article published in 1939 entitled 'Intentionality: A Fundamental Idea of Husserl's Philosophy',[4] Sartre again expressed his enthusiasm for Husserl's phenomenology.

From this article, we can identify five points which Sartre takes to be points of agreement between himself and Husserl. He begins by applauding what he sees as Husserl's attempt to steer a course between realism and idealism:

> against all 'psychologism', Husserl persistently affirmed that one cannot dissolve things into consciousness. (*I*,⁵ p. 4)

> But Husserl is not a realist: this tree on its bit of parched earth is not an absolute which would subsequently enter into communication with us. (*I*, p. 4)

Second, Sartre outlines what he calls 'the illusion common to both realism and idealism' and commends Husserl for rejecting it. This 'illusion' is a model of the mind as having 'contents' which enable it to interact with, particularly to know, the world. To have knowledge is to have 'taken in', or 'digested', parts of the world. The difference between idealism and realism lies in the different status they accord to this world: for the idealist, it is a projection of the mind and so dependent upon the mind's activities, whilst for the realist it is taken in by the mind and exists independently. Sartre uses the image of a spider digesting its prey to depict the idealist use of this model of the mind and knowledge. But the model itself he takes to be common to realism and idealism:⁶

> to know is to eat, … we have all believed that the spidery mind trapped things in its web, covered them with a white spit and slowly swallowed them, reducing them to its own substance. What is a table, a rock, a house? A certain assemblage of 'contents of consciousness', a class of such contents. O digestive philosophy! (*I*, p. 4)

Sartre agrees with Husserl's opposition to this philosophical position both in the philosophy of mind and in the theory of knowledge, and with Husserl's claim that it has been very pervasive, underlying both Berkeleyan idealism and realism.

Third, Sartre agrees with the view of consciousness which Husserl opposes to the 'contents' view: that consciousness is intentional. He praises Husserl for this insight which gives the proper view of the nature of the object, the nature of consciousness, and the relation between them:

> the tree escapes me and repulses me, and I can no more lose myself in the tree than it can dissolve itself in me. I'm beyond it; it's beyond me. (*I*, p. 4)

Fourth, Sartre sees Husserl as correcting an over-emphasis on knowledge in French philosophy:

But for Husserl and the phenomenologists our consciousness of things is by no means limited to knowledge of them. Knowledge, or pure 'representation', is only one of the possible forms of my consciousness 'of' this tree; I can also love it, fear it, hate it. (*I*, p. 5)

Sartre goes on to claim that this allows the phenomenologist to recognize a richer world. Not only knowledge but also love, fear, hate, etc., can reveal objective features of the world:

So it is that all at once hatred, love, fear, sympathy – all these famous 'subjective' reactions which were floating in the malodorous brine of the mind – are pulled out. They are merely ways of discovering the world. It is things which abruptly unveil themselves to us as hateful, sympathetic, horrible, lovable. (*I*, p. 5)

Husserl has restored to things their horror and their charm (*I*, p. 5).

Finally Sartre applauds Husserl's view of self-awareness or self-discovery:

Outside, in the world, among others. It is not in some hiding-place that we will discover ourselves, it is on the road, in the town, in the midst of the crowd, a thing among things, a man among men. (*I*, p. 5)

This fifth view is one which Sartre, in *The Transcendence of the Ego*,[7] explicitly claims that Husserl had given up by the time he wrote the *Cartesian Meditations*.

In this 'Intentionality' article, Sartre presents a somewhat existentialist interpretation of Husserl's phenomenology. He has, it seems, appropriated that part of Husserl's philosophy with which he is in agreement, while omitting all reference to the methodological constraints of the epoché, or bracketing, and the consequent transcendental idealist ontology comprising the transcendental Ego and its meanings. At all events, this article contains no hint of the criticisms of Husserl's philosophy raised by Sartre in his earlier publication *The Transcendence of the Ego*, and later in *Being and Nothingness*. We shall look at these criticisms in sections 2 and 3 below. Overall, Sartre's view seems to have been that, on close inspection, Husserl's developed theories, as expounded for example in the *Cartesian Meditations*, fail to keep faith with his initial insights as Sartre understood them – failed to lead Husserl to the philosophical position to which Sartre felt they ought to lead.

Sartre's discussions of Husserl in *The Transcendence of the Ego* and in *Being and Nothingness* consider his philosophical position in more detail. Husserl's application of his phenomenological method has led him to distinguish the transcendental Ego as subject and the meant object as object. On both counts Sartre accuses Husserl of having taken a wrong turn, the turn to transcendental idealism. Thus, in *The Transcendence of the Ego*, Sartre criticizes Husserl's conception of the subject of consciousness as transcendental Ego. Such an Ego is, according to Sartre, neither necessary to explain experience nor detectable in experience. In the Introduction to *Being and Nothingness*, Sartre argues for an alternative conception of consciousness as subjectless, unconstituted, and 'translucent'.

Also in the Introduction to *Being and Nothingness*, Sartre criticizes Husserl's conception of the objects of consciousness as being too idealist, too dependent upon the subject, reducing objects to their 'sense' or 'meaning' and ignoring their 'being'.[8] We shall examine Sartre's criticisms of Husserl in section 2 below.

The remaining sections of this chapter are devoted to an examination of Sartre's existential phenomenology as he presents it in Part I of *Being and Nothingness*. There Sartre, via his own application of the phenomenological method, offers a radical, existentialist revision of the traditional ontology which he has argued in his Introduction underlies realism and idealism. We shall look at how Sartre introduces 'non-being' and 'nothingness' in addition to 'being'; and how these feature in his phenomenological ontology which comprises two categories: being-for-itself or human subjects and being-in-itself or objects. We shall see in later chapters how Merleau-Ponty in the *Phenomenology of Perception* is in broad agreement with Sartre's existentialist and phenomenological aims but is critical of his ontology.

2 Translucent Consciousness and Transcendent Objects

In the first half of *The Transcendence of the Ego*, Sartre criticizes Husserl's conception of the transcendental Ego, on two counts. It lacks pheno-menological foundations (*TE*,[9] pp. 43–54); and it is philosophically redundant (*TE*, pp. 35–40). The second half of the work elaborates Sartre's own view of the ego.

In order to set Sartre's criticisms in context, let us recapitulate how Husserl introduces the transcendental Ego. In section 3 of Chapter One, we explored how, in the First Meditation, the Ego emerges when one performs the epoché. As we noted in section 2 of Chapter Two, in his Second Meditation, Husserl's phenomenological descriptions are of experiences; they are not intended to reveal the Ego. The noetic descriptions are concerned with *acts* of consciousness and not with the subject of those acts. The Ego is reintroduced as one part of the universal schema of phenomena: 'ego-cogito-cogitatum' (*CM*, p. 50). Finally, as we noted in section 1 of the previous chapter, in the Fourth Meditation Husserl claims that all phenomena involve experience of self, both empirical and transcendental, and that phenomenological descrip-tion can reveal this self:

I exist for myself and am continually given to myself, by experiental evidence, as '*I myself*'. This is true of the transcendental ego and, correspondingly, of the psychologically pure ego; it is true, moreover, with respect to any sense of the word ego. (*CM*, p. 68)

Sartre claims, against Husserl, that phenomenological description reveals no pure subject of experience. Sartre considers two kinds of case: unreflecting and reflecting conscious experience. We shall look at each of these in turn. In unreflecting consciousness, one is aware of no 'I', only of the *objects* of consciousness:

there is no *I* on the unreflected level. When I run after a streetcar, when I look at the time, when I am absorbed in contemplating a portrait, there is no *I*. There is consciousness *of the streetcar-having-to-be-overtaken* etc. (*TE*, pp. 48–9)

Sartre acknowledges that phenomenological description requires some reflecting upon, for example recollecting, the phenomena to be described. One will aim to describe not just the objects of consciousness but the unreflecting consciousness of those objects. But still no 'I' will emerge:

I was absorbed just now in my reading. I am going to try to remember the circumstances of my reading, my attitude, the lines that I was reading. I am thus going to revive not only those external details but a certain depth of unreflected consciousness, since the objects could only have been perceived *by* that consciousness and since they remain relative to it. . . . There is no doubt about the result: while I was reading, there was consciousness *of* the book, *of* the heroes of the novel, but the *I* was not inhabiting this consciousness. (*TE*, pp. 46–7)

These descriptions of the act of reading resemble Husserl's noetic descriptions: they include references to conscious acts, but not to the subject of those acts.

In the second half of *The Transcendence of the Ego*, Sartre considers a possible objection to his claim that descriptions of conscious acts do not reveal a subject. The objection is that such descriptions typically use the word 'I', and this surely refers to a subject. His response to this objection is twofold. First, he claims that, when one uses the word 'I' in describing unreflectively what one is doing, this 'I' does not refer to a personal subject, an ego, but is to be understood as indicating a public object, one's body.

If someone asks me 'what are you doing?' and I reply, all preoccupied, 'I am trying to hang this picture' or 'I am repairing the rear tyre,' these statements do not transport us to the level of reflection. I utter them without ceasing to work, without ceasing to envisage actions only as done or to be done – not insofar as I am doing them. (*TE*, p. 89)

Now *I* am breaking the wood, that is to say, the action is realized in the world, and the objective and empty support of this action is the *I-concept*. . . . The body there serves as a visible and tangible symbol for the *I*. (*TE*, p. 90)

In his second response to the criticism, Sartre considers reflective consciousness. When one uses the word 'I' in describing the results of reflecting on one's conscious experiences, the word 'I' still does not indicate a subject in Husserl's sense, a transcendental Ego. The 'I', or as Sartre later calls it, the 'Me', revealed by reflection is not Husserl's transcendental Ego but a person in the world. Sartre describes this self or ego as 'transcendent'. He means two things by this term. First, the Sartrean ego is *transcendent* as opposed to *transcendental*: that is to say, it is part of the world, not 'beyond' the world; second, it is *transcendent* as opposed to *immanent*: that is, it is not wholly 'in' the phenomena, it can have hidden facets, a past, a future, a character, about any of which one can be ignorant or mistaken. Sartre writes of this transcendent ego:

First, the *I* is an *existent*. It has a concrete type of existence, undoubtedly different from the existence of mathematical truths, of meanings, or of spatio-temporal beings, but no less real. The *I* gives itself as transcendent. Second, the *I* proffers itself to an intuition of a special kind which apprehends it, always inadequately, behind the reflected consciousness. (*TE*, pp. 52–3)

Sartre relates this point explicitly to Husserl:

But we know what a service Husserl has rendered to philosophy by distinguishing diverse kinds of evidence. Well, it is only too certain that the *I Think* is an object grasped with neither apodictic nor adequate evidence. The evidence is not apodictic, since by saying *I* we affirm far more than we know. It is not adequate for the *I* is presented as an opaque reality whose content would have to be unfolded. (*TE*, p. 51)

To sum up, what, according to Sartre, one discovers in the phenomena are conscious acts and a reflected object, 'me'; but the reflecting subject does not emerge. Phenomenological description reveals no trancendental Ego.

Sartre further claims that no such Ego is needed to explain the phenomena. We noted in section 3 of the previous chapter that the transcendental Ego in Husserl's system unifies experiences and constitutes objects. Sartre denies that it is needed to fulfil either of these roles.[10] We shall now look at each of these denials in turn.

First, Sartre claims that the transcendental Ego is not needed to explain the unity of experience either at a particular time or through time. The unity of experience or consciousness at a particular time is explained by the unity of the object of consciousness. For example (ours), the experiences of seeing, tasting, smelling and feeling one's cup of coffee are unified by all being experiences of the one cup of coffee. This, Sartre claims, follows from the intentionality of consciousness:

> Now, it is certain that phenomenology does not need to appeal to any such unifying and individualizing *I*. Indeed, consciousness is defined by intentionality.... The object is transcendent to the consciousnesses which grasp it, and it is in the object that the unity of consciousnesses is found. (*TE*, p. 38)

Sartre further denies the need for a transcendental Ego to account for the unity of consciousness through time. What unifies consciousness through time is not a single subject of consciousness, but certain kinds of conscious acts. For example, what unites one's consciousness now with one's past consciousness is one's present memory. Sartre claims that Husserl is in agreement with him on this point:

> Husserl ... never had recourse to a synthetic power of the *I*. It is consciousness which unifies itself, concretely, by a play of 'transversal' intentionalities which are concrete and real retentions of past consciousnesses.... In *Cartesianische Meditationen*, Husserl seems to have preserved intact this conception of consciousness unifying itself in time. (*TE*, p. 39)

Here, Sartre is seemingly alluding to Husserl's Second Meditation (section 18, p. 43). (We discussed the notion of synthesis which Husserl there employs in section 2 of Chapter Two.) However, in the Fourth Meditation, Husserl does see the transcendental Ego as unifying the synthesis of conscious acts. Sartre suggests later in *The Transcendence of the Ego* (pp. 72–5) that it is a misunderstanding of syntheses to suppose that they require any such unifying subject:

> an indissoluable synthetic totality which could support itself would have no need of a supporting X, provided of course that it were really and concretely unanalyzable. If we take a melody, for example, it is useless to presuppose an X which would serve as a support for the different notes. The unity here comes from the absolute indissolubility of the elements. (*TE*, p. 73)

In short, Sartre's claim is that, if intentionality and synthesis are properly understood, then no transcendental Ego is needed to account for the unity of consciousness.

The transcendental Ego is similarly not necessary, according to Sartre, as a constitutor; for what constitutes objects in the world is consciousness. The transcendent ego may have some role to play in this. But the transcendent ego is itself constituted by consciousness. There is no need for a transcendental

Ego as constitutor to explain the work of constitution. For example (ours), the way one perceives the world may depend on the sort of person one takes oneself to be; but both of these can be explained as the results of acts of consciousness and not as the work of a transcendental subject performing those acts in accordance with its own structure or constitution. More specifically, one might regard a particular rock face as a challenge; and this might be because one regards oneself as a climber. But this can be explained as the result of particular conscious choices. There is no need to introduce a choosing subject whose character is reflected in these choices. Sartre puts his criticism of Husserl as follows:

> For our part, we readily acknowledge the existence of a constituting consciousness. We find admirable all of Husserl's descriptions in which he shows transcendental consciousness constituting the world by imprisoning itself in empirical consciousness. Like Husserl, we are prepared that our psychic and psycho-physical *me* is a transcendent object which must fall before the εποχη. But we raise the following question: is not this psychic and psycho-physical *me* enough? Need one double it with a transcendental *I*, a structure of absolute consciousness? (*TE*, p. 36)

Sartre concludes his argument that the transcendental Ego is redundant with a sketch of his own view of consciousness:

> All is therefore clear and lucid in consciousness: the object with its characteristic opacity is before consciousness, but consciousness is purely and simply consciousness of being consciousness of that object. This is the law of its existence. (*TE*, p. 40)

This is Sartre's doctrine of the translucency of consciousness. A conscious state must be entirely translucent or transparent to itself; it cannot be hidden from itself and no further state can reveal it. This doctrine is presented in a more developed form in *Being and Nothingness*, where Sartre writes:

> Every conscious existence exists as consciousness of existing. (*BN*, p. xxx)

So, for example, the conscious act of pointing must be conscious of being the act of pointing. The difficulty in grasping this idea, as Sartre expresses it, derives from the oddness of ascribing consciousness to a conscious act rather than to a conscious subject, together with Sartre's evident desire not to introduce into his account a subject of consciousness whose phenomenological basis he has been at pains to challenge. An example might serve to provide an initial grasp of this central claim of Sartre's account of consciousness. Take the conscious act of pointing at a tree. There might be all manner of features of the tree which are in some way, at the time of pointing, obscured from the act of pointing: the birds in the tree, the hollow trunk, etc. These are features of the tree, but they are not being consciously pointed at. As one might more naturally say: in so far as one is simply conscious of pointing, one may not be aware of these features. In contrast, there can be no feature of the pointing, construed as a conscious act, which is similarly obscured from that act. A conscious act of pointing must be conscious of being that act. Again, it would be more natural to say: in so far as one is simply consciously pointing, one must be conscious of pointing: no further act is necessary to reveal one's pointing to oneself, and nothing of which one is not conscious is part of the conscious act. (These more natural descriptions may be misleading because they appear to make reference to a subject of consciousness.)

In section III of the Introduction to *Being and Nothingness*, Sartre further elaborates his conception of consciousness. His aim is to show that consciousness is translucent, that translucent consciousness is itself the subject of awareness, and that consciousness does not have a further subject with a determinate structure or 'constitution'. He first gives an argument to show that there must be some such subject. Then he produces a phenomenological description of an example of this subject.

The outline of his argument is as follows. He begins with the assumption that knowledge, by which he means awareness of objects rather than propositional knowledge, is possible. He argues first that knowledge presupposes a knowing subject; second, that this subject must be self-aware; and third, that this self-awareness cannot be construed as self-knowledge. He concludes that this self-awareness is a feature, not of a subject of consciousness, but of the act of consciousness itself.

We shall now present the details of the argument. Sartre begins by expressing agreement with Husserl that an account of knowledge must include an account of what Sartre calls the 'transphenomenal being of the subject'. What he means by this is that the subject must be more than a 'mere' phenomenon in the sense that its existence must not depend, as the existence of a phenomenon depends, on its being experienced by something other than itself. He also expresses agreement with Husserl that this subject must be conscious.

He then asks what this consciousness must be like if it is to have knowledge. His answer is that it must be conscious of knowing. If one knows, one must not be ignorant or mistaken about the fact that one knows. He bases this claim on his general principle that, for any conscious state, one can be in that state if and only if one is conscious of so being:

However, the necessary and sufficient condition for a knowing consciousness to be knowledge *of* its object, is that it be consciousness of itself as being that knowledge. This is a necessary condition, for if my consciousness were not consciousness of being consciousness of the table, it would then be consciousness of that table without consciousness of being so. In other words, it would be a consciousness ignorant of itself, an unconscious – which is absurd. This is a sufficient condition, for my being conscious of being conscious of that table suffices in fact for me to be conscious of it. (*BN*, p. xxviii)

Sartre offers here no *argument* for the absurdity of an unconscious, but it is a view which he maintains throughout *Being and Nothingness*, and which is an integral part of his conception of consciousness.[11]

Sartre next asks what this consciousness of knowing is, and rejects one widespread account of it as *knowledge* of knowing. Sartre has three related objections to this account. First, since knowledge is always a relation between a knowing subject and an object known, to construe consciousness of knowing as knowledge of knowing would be to split consciousness into a knowing consciousness and a known consciousness. Sartre objects to introducing this split or 'duality' into consciousness. He also objects to the opacity which this would introduce, since the known consciousness would be an object of knowledge and as such opaque to the knower. This objection depends on Sartre's general view that objects of knowledge are opaque – have features or aspects which are, at least potentially, hidden from the knower.

Sartre's second objection to the account of consciousness of knowing as knowledge of knowing is that it would render an incomplete account of knowledge. The original aim of the enquiry was to give an account of the subject of knowledge. Having divided that subject into knower and known, one gets an account of the known subject, but one still lacks an account of the knowing subject – the subject now of self-knowledge.

Third, Sartre argues that to require of the knowing consciousness that it knows itself is to set up an infinite regress: if all knowledge requires that one knows that one knows it, then that condition will apply also to one's knowledge that one knows; and so infinitely many states of knowledge will be required. For example, in order to know that there is a table in front of one, one must know that one knows that, and know that one knows that one knows that there is a table in front of one, and so on. Sartre takes this to be a *reductio ad absurdum* of the view that the kind of self-consciousness required by a knower is self-knowledge. All these three objections are raised in the following passage:

The reduction of consciousness to knowledge in fact involves our introducing into consciousness the subject–object dualism which is typical of knowledge [1st objection]. But if we accept the law of the knower–known dyad, then a third term will be necessary in order for the knower to become known in turn, and we will be faced with this dilemma: Either we stop at any one term of the series – the known, the knower known, the knower known by the knower, etc. In this case the totality of the phenomenon fall into the unknown; that is, we always bump up against a non-self-conscious reflection and a final term [2nd objection].

Or else we affirm the necessity of an infinite regress (idea ideae ideae etc.), which is absurd [3rd objection]. (*BN*, p. xxviii)

Having claimed absurdity both for the view that knowing consciousness is ignorant of itself and for the view that knowing consciousness knows itself, Sartre proceeds to describe the sort of 'immediate non-cognitive' (*BN*, p. xxix) self-awareness which consciousness has.

Sartre first allows that there are cases of consciousness knowing itself. These are cases of reflective consciousness where one turns one's attention towards oneself. Sartre calls these 'positional' or 'thetic' self-consciousness. By 'positional', Sartre means that reflective consciousness 'posits' a self as object, a 'me' as he called it in *The Transcendence of the Ego*. By 'thetic', he means that reflective consciousness interprets this 'me' as having a certain sort of character or 'structure'. This sort of reflective self-awareness is not what Sartre is aiming to describe. It is self-knowledge of the sort that we have just shown Sartre to dismiss as failing to account for the self-awareness of the subject. The same criticisms apply. Reflective consciousness is a relation between a subject and an object. The subject and object are different, so the relation cannot be one of self-awareness. The object reflected upon is not itself self-aware. The reflecting subject may be self-aware, but not in virtue of reflecting on itself as object. So its self-awareness remains unexplained.

Self-awareness, for Sartre, does not involve reflection on oneself; rather it is the sort of consciousness one has when one is acting with awareness but not actually thinking about oneself or one's actions or thought processes. The example of self-awareness Sartre describes is the act of counting – chosen, one may speculate (though Sartre does not say so explicitly), because it is one way of getting knowledge, one way of becoming a knowing consciousness. He describes the sort of example where one discovers how many cigarettes are in a case, and where one could say, if asked, *what* one was doing. While counting, the conscious activity is not an object of consciousness, not something one reflects on or has knowledge of; but one is aware of what one is doing. This is the sort of immediate self-awareness which Sartre believes to be the defining characteristic of consciousness:

If I count the cigarettes which are in that case, I have the impression of disclosing an objective property of this collection of cigarettes: *they are a dozen.* ... It is very possible that I have no positional consciousness of counting them. Then I do not know myself as counting. ... Yet at the moment when these cigarettes are revealed to me as a dozen, I have a non-thetic consciousness of my adding activity. If anyone questioned me, indeed, if anyone should ask, 'What are you doing there?' I should reply at once, 'I am counting.' This reply aims not only at the instantaneous consciousness which I can achieve by reflection but at those fleeting consciousnesses which have passed without being reflected-on, those which are forever not-reflected-on in my immediate past. (*BN*, p. xxix)

This example, in Sartre's view, reveals the fundamental nature of consciousness. Consciousness is nothing more than self-awareness. Hence, it must be as it appears to itself to be: that is to say, it must be translucent. Any conscious act has the characteristics it has only by being aware of them, so it can have no hidden characteristics: it cannot be opaque.

> Consciousness has nothing substantial, it is pure 'appearance' in the sense that it exists only to the degree to which it appears ... it is total emptiness (since the entire world is outside it).... (*BN*, p. xxxii)

One might later reflect on a previous conscious state and seem to discover in it previously unnoticed features. But, Sartre would say, this later reflection might be inaccurate, the 'discovery' might be illusory. What decides whether it is accurate or not is whether it matches one's immediate awareness at the time. The immediate awareness cannot be mistaken; the later reflection might be.

We noted earlier Sartre's requirement that the subject should be 'transphenomenal': that is, it should not be 'mere' phenomenon, for then its existence would depend on its appearing to something other than itself. There are two ways of satisfying this condition of independence. One is to be 'transcendent', to be more than an appearance; the other is to appear to oneself. Objects are transphenomenal in the first way; conscious states in the second way.

To sum up Sartre's view, phenomenology reveals no subject of consciousness, only translucent consciousness itself. We can now elaborate further on how Sartre's existentialist conception of consciousness differs both from that of transcendental idealism and from that of realism. The idealist subject, the transcendental Ego, as well as being a standpoint outside the world, is also a subject with a structure or constitution. This constitution is an enduring feature of the subject, carrying implications for its past and future. This opens up the possibility that, at any given time, the subject may be unaware of features of itself. For Sartre, the subject can have no such hidden features, so it can have no such structure or constitution.

Sartre rejects the realist conception of the subject on similar grounds. The realist subject, as a natural object in the natural world, is construed as having dispositions, potentials, as operating according to natural laws. Any such feature carries implications for the past and the future of the subject. Hence it is possible that, at any one time, a subject could be unaware of the laws governing it, or of its potentials or dispositions. The realist subject is opaque; Sartre's subject cannot be opaque, and so cannot be a natural object.

We shall explore, in Chapter Nine, Sartre's belief that human freedom requires that consciousness is unconstituted. We shall also discuss there how Merleau-Ponty's conceptions of the subject and of freedom differ from those of Sartre.

In section V of the Introduction to *Being and Nothingness*, Sartre challenges Husserl's account of objects. As we explained in section 3 of Chapter Two, Husserl accounts for the existence of objects in terms of their being 'constituted' as 'going beyond' any actual experience of them. When one perceives an object there are, implicit in one's actual experience of it, expectations of other possible appearances of the same object: 'horizons', which form a series whose totality one can never experience.

Sartre rejects Husserl's account on the grounds that it involves only absences of some appearances of the object and the presence of states (impressions and expectations) of the subject. Sartre then claims that what is to be accounted for, the presence to consciousness of transcendent objects, cannot be explained in terms of what is absent and what is purely subjective.

> It is true that things give themselves in profile; that is, simply by appearances. And it is true that each appearance refers to other appearances. But each of them is already in itself alone a *transcendent being*, not a subjective material of impressions – a *plenitude of being*, not a lack – a *presence*, not an absence. It is futile by a sleight of hand to attempt to found the *reality* of the object on the subjective plenitude of impressions and its *objectivity* on non-being; the objective will never come out of the subjective nor the transcendent from immanence, nor being from non-being. (*BN*, p. xxxvii)

Sartre bases his case against Husserl on a disagreement between them about the intentionality of consciousness. He believes that Husserl has misconstrued this central feature of consciousness. Sartre considers two interpretations:

> All consciousness is consciousness *of* something. This definition of consciousness can be taken in two very distinct senses: either we understand by this that consciousness is constitutive of the being of its object, or it means that consciousness in its inmost nature is a relation to a transcendent being. (*BN*, p. xxxvi)

The second interpretation, claims Sartre, is the correct one and it is this interpretation which Sartre in his 1939 article 'Intentionality' attributed to Husserl. But Husserl's transcendental idealism in effect involves the first interpretation:

> Husserl defines consciousness precisely as a transcendence. In truth he does. This is what he posits. This is his essential discovery. But from the moment that

he makes of the *noema* an *unreal*, a correlate *of* the *noesis*, a noema whose *esse* is *percipi*, he is totally unfaithful to his principle. (*BN*, p. xxxvii)

Sartre's positive claim, based on the second interpretation of intentionality, is that consciousness requires as its object a being other than itself.

To say that consciousness is consciousness of something is to say that it must produce itself as a revealed-revelation of a being which is not it and which gives itself as already existing when consciousness reveals it. (*BN*, p. xxxviii)

This is what Sartre calls the 'being of the existent' or the 'being of the phenomenon'. This, like the subject, must be 'transphenomenal'. It is independent of consciousness and not constituted by consciousness. It is not itself a phenomenon, but nor is it something distinct from phenomena – not an independent reality lying behind phenomena:

We must understand that this being is no other than the transphenomenal being of phenomena and not a noumenal being which is hidden behind them. It is the being of this table, of this package of tobacco, of the lamp, more generally the being of the world which is implied by consciousness. It requires simply that the being of that which *appears* does not exist *only* in so far as it appears. (*BN*, p. xxxviii)

In section VI of the Introduction to *Being and Nothingness*, Sartre sets out to say something about the kind of existence or 'being' that objects have. He calls this 'the being of the phenomena'. This task, he claims, can only be approached indirectly, via describing the phenomenon or appearance of the kind of existence objects have. He calls this 'the phenomenon of being'. But this phenomenon is not to be identified with the existence of objects; it merely indicates the sort of existence they have. He characterizes this phenomenon thus:

Being will be disclosed to us by some kind of immediate access – boredom, nausea, etc., and ontology will be the description of the phenomenon of being as it manifests itself; that is, without intermediary. (*BN*, p. xxiv)

Sartre's novel *Nausea* provides many descriptions of this 'phenomenon of being'. The best way of focusing on what Sartre means is by imagining a process of 'stripping away' meaning or interpretation from normal experience. The most famous example in *Nausea* is the experience of seeing a tree root.[12] Roquentin, the hero, encounters the tree root, but not *as* anything. He sees it neither as a tree root, nor as a pump supplying the tree with nutrition, nor as anchoring the tree to the ground, nor as anything else. His seeing is entirely unconceptualized: he neither projects onto the tree root, nor detects in it, any structure or meaning.

It is a necessary condition of having such an experience that the subject itself has no essential structure or meaning: no interests, purposes or intentions. These too must be 'stripped away' from the normal condition. For, if one had interests or purposes, the tree root would gain meaning either as an obstacle or as an aid to those purposes, or it would not be the object of one's attention. For Sartre, as for Husserl, the structure one detects in the world is the result of one's constituting acts, and not of how the world is in itself. For Sartre, however, it is one's elected goals, purposes, desires or projects which determine that structure. Roquentin is an example of a person who temporarily has no such projects, so he projects no meaning onto the objects of his consciousness. This, however, does not have the effect that consciousness ceases; rather, one confronts the phenomenon of bare, unconstituted being. This phenomenon is the appearance of the world as it exists independently of any sense a subject might make of it. The failure to acknowledge this phenomenon is, according to Sartre, a further deficiency in Husserl's account of the objects as wholly constituted by consciousness.

At the end of the Introduction to *Being and Nothingness* (pp. xl–xlii), Sartre attempts to characterize being by describing this phenomenon of being which he has called 'nausea'. He warns (p. xxxix) that, as a characterization of the existence of objects, this is only provisional; and that it may need to be revised in the light of the project of giving a non-realist and non-idealist account of how conscious subjects and objects relate to each other. He also reminds the reader that the account applies only to the being of objects or 'being-in-itself', and not to the being of consciousness or 'being-for-itself', which Sartre terms a different 'region' of being.[13]

Sartre takes his task to be one of describing the objective world stripped of all meaning, all conceptualization, all differentiation, that is to say, of all features or characteristics which a description might hope to pick out. Clearly, then, no literal, positive characterization of being is possible. Much of Sartre's description must be regarded as metaphorical.

Sartre first draws attention to some important concepts which do not apply to being: activity and passivity, temporality and change, possibility and necessity. Being, he says, is 'beyond' all these. It is not accurate to say even that being lacks these features, for that would involve applying a concept, the concept of negation, to being. Being is also 'beyond' affirmation and negation. It cannot be said of being either that it acts or that it is acted upon, that it changes or that it remains the same, that it must be or might not be.

A second strand in Sartre's characterization is to present being as the complete opposite of consciousness. Consciousness is translucent, it has no hidden feature; being, in contrast, is 'opaque', 'solid', 'filled with itself'. Consciousness involves a kind of 'distancing' or 'withdrawal' from itself – for example, to be consciously motivated is to be capable of assessing or questioning the strength of the motive. Being, in contrast, is described as lacking any such 'distance': it is 'compressed', 'glued to itself'.

Third, where consciousness can have purposes or reasons for what it does, can justify itself or envisage alternative possibilities for itself, being is 'without reason', 'contingent', 'superfluous', '*de trop*':

> Uncreated, without reason for being, without any connection with another being, being-in-itself is *de trop* for eternity. (*BN*, p. xlii)

A metaphor which springs naturally to mind is of consciousness as a light source illuminating itself and its phenomena but failing to reach the being of the phenomena, which remains dark, dense, impenetrable, unintelligible.

Sartre's conception of objects thus differs from those of both idealists and realists. It differs from that of the idealist in including the unconstituted being as well as the constituted meaning of objects; and from that of the realist in regarding any determinate, intelligible structure or constitution in objects as the result of interaction between those objects and a subject.

3 Sartre's Existential Phenomenology

The Introduction to *Being and Nothingness* opens with the claim that philosophy has made progress in rejecting the view of appearance and reality according to which reality lies hidden behind appearances:

> Modern thought has realized considerable progress by reducing the existent to the series of appearances which manifest it. (*BN*, p. xxi)

> the dualism of being and appearance is no longer entitled to any legal status within philosophy. The appearance refers to the total series of appearances and not to a hidden reality.... (*BN*, p. xxi)

This dualism, Sartre claims, has been replaced by 'the monism of the phenomenon'. The rest of the Introduction is spent demonstrating the inadequacy of this monism. One central theme is that, if we are to avoid idealism, which can give no adequate account of our knowledge of the world, we must recognize, as well as phenomena, two kinds of being: conscious being or being-for-itself, and the world of objects or being-in-itself. The Introduction ends with a series of questions:

> Thus we have left 'appearances' and have been led progressively to posit two types of being, the in-itself and the for-itself, concerning which we have as yet

only superficial and incomplete information. A multitude of questions remain unanswered: What is the ultimate meaning of these two types of being? For what reasons do they both belong to *being* in general? What is the meaning of that being which includes within itself these two radically separated regions of being? If idealism and realism both fail to explain the relations which *in fact* unite these regions which *in theory* are without communication, what other solution can we find for this problem? (*BN*, p. xliii)

Part One of *Being and Nothingness* begins with this last question about the connection between the two regions of being. Since, in his Introduction, Sartre was led to define being-in-itself as incapable of standing in any relation at all, and since he clearly believes that conscious being and the world are related, the attempt to give a satisfactory account of this relation will involve major revisions to the entire way of thinking of the Introduction:

> But we have been brought to an impasse since we have not been able to establish the connection between the two regions of being which we have discovered. No doubt this is because we have chosen an unfortunate approach. (*BM*, p. 3)

Sartre goes on to say that this 'unfortunate' approach involves the method of 'abstraction':

> an abstraction is made when something not capable of existing in isolation is thought of as in an isolated state. The concrete by contrast is a totality which can exist by itself alone. (*BN*, p. 3)

He then illustrates this general claim with the two central topics of his Introduction:

> consciousness is an abstraction since it conceals within itself an ontological source in the region of the in-itself, and conversely the phenomenon is likewise an abstraction since it must 'appear' to consciousness. (*BN*, p. 3)

> The concrete is man within the world in that specific union of man with the world which Heidegger, for example, calls 'being-in-the-world'. (*BN*, p. 3)

He also warns us of the likely dangers of abstraction:

> it is not profitable first to separate the two terms of a relation in order to try to join them together again later. (*BN*, p. 3)

It is important, in order to understand Part I of *Being and Nothingness* and how it relates to the Introduction, to see what Sartre's objection to abstraction is. Abstraction starts when one notices certain differences between kinds of things – in this case, between human beings and the rest of the world of objects. One then describes these different categories by picking out what is essential to, distinctive of, instances of each category: that is, features which instances of the other category do not have. What is distinctive of human beings is that they are conscious; and consciousness, when considered apart from its intentional connection with its objects, is translucent, consciousness of being conscious. What is distinctive of objects in the world, stripped of all human projections of meaning upon them, is their solidity, density, what Sartre calls their 'full positivity'. The error in abstraction comes with the supposition that there are actual existents which have only these essential featues, for then there seems to be an insoluble problem as to how any two existents of such essentially different kinds could possibly interact. The process of abstraction has precisely stripped actual subjects and objects of everything which renders interaction possible:

> Consequently the *results* of analysis can not be covered over again by the *moments* of this synthesis. (*BN*, p. 3)

Sartre recommends a different, more concrete method. Since consciousousness is never found without an object of which it is conscious, and since no object in the world is ever encountered without a consciousness to encounter it, one should begin the explanation of how consciousness and objects relate to each other by describing concrete instances of such relations. On the basis of these descriptions, one can re-define the categories of being-for-itself, and being-in-itself, describing them not in terms of what is peculiar to each, but in terms of how each must be, given that it is related to the other.

> It is enough now to open our eyes and question ingenuously this totality which is man-in-the-world. . . . What must man and the world be in order for a relation between them to be possible? (*BN*, p. 4)

Sartre begins with what he calls 'conducts'. These are events which are concrete – they can exist independently; and they are instances of *relations* between consciousness and the world, rather than instances of the items so related. The conduct which Sartre first submits to phenomenological description is the conduct of questioning. His description of this conduct reveals the phenomenon of 'non-being' in the world. The world which one looks to for answers to one's questions sometimes gives the answer 'no', and hence comprises not only being but also non-being.

One of Sartre's examples is the conduct of entering a café expecting to meet a friend named Pierre (*BN*, pp. 9, 10). The question is: 'Is Pierre in the café?' The answer to this question is: 'No'. Sartre describes the phenomenon of experiencing Pierre's absence, experiencing the café as devoid of Pierre. He stresses the difference between this sort of phenomenon, and making a negative judgement concerning the absence form the café of someone one did not expect to see there, someone whom one therefore does not see the café as lacking. The non-being of Pierre in the café is not simply an 'element of a negative judgement'; it is directly experienced as a feature of the world. What one experiences in such a case, the object of one's consciousness, is not being-in-itself, as described in the Introduction, as dense and inpenetrable, but an absence, a lack, a gap. The café is experienced as a backdrop for the absence, or 'non-being', of Pierre – as the place where Pierre should be, is expected to be, but is not.

Sartre gives other examples of non-being in the world: destruction (*BN*, pp. 8, 9), his lack of 200 francs which he believed to be in his wallet (*BN*, p. 11), the non-functioning of a car (*BN*, p. 7), the distance between two points (*BN*, p. 24). These are obvious examples where the lack, or non-being, is the focus of attention. But non-being is a feature of any experience, except only for the phenomenon of being, or 'nausea'. Whenever one makes sense of the world, identifies objects in it, this involves the phenomenon of non-being. When one notices an object, for example, a table, the table stands out from its background which is *not* the table, and one experiences the background as the non-being of the table. Experiencing the table depends on picking it out from its background which is *not* the table.[14] Non-being is what one must strip from ordinary experience in order to get to the bare phenomenon of being. The rarity of the phenomenon of being, or nausea, indicates the prevalence of the experience of non-being.

Sartre argues that non-being is an objective feature of reality and not merely a figment of a subject's imagination or a creation of consciousness.[15] One important aspect of the objectivity of non-being is its potential to resist. Pierre's absence can resist, can frustrate one's desires with as much force as his presence could. Sartre also argues that the phenomenon of non-being 'grounds' the concept of negation. If one did not experience non-being one would neither possess nor be able to apply the concept of negation; one would not be able to make or understand any negative judgement about the world.

This discovery of the phenomenon of non-being as a feature of the objective world makes necessary a revision of the provisional account of being-in-itself which Sartre gave at the end of his Introduction and which we sketched above. There, the being of objects, being-in-itself, was described as 'beyond' affirmation and negation, and hence beyond all characterization as possible, necessary, active, passive, changing, unchanging – beyond, in effect, our comprehension. It was defined, that is, as unintelligible. Further, it was defined as completely opaque, dense, impenetrable, and as fully determined. 'It is what it is': nothing more can be said about it.

Sartre's phenomenological description, of revealing non-being in the world, aims to show that the world which one encounters is quite unlike this.

It is an intelligible world of objects encountered variously as present or absent, negative or positive, active or passive, changing or remaining the same, having certain possibilities and lacking others. Also, the world is not wholly opaque. It has hidden features, but one can work to uncover them. Nor is the world dense and impenetrable. One's questions penetrate the world, uncover 'gaps' of non-being in its density. Hence, the world one discovers is not a closed system: it is a world upon which one can act, a world which contains room for change and for changes that one can make.

One feature of being-in-itself as defined in the Introduction, which is retained in the revised account in Part I, is that it obeys the Law of Identity. Each item which one discovers in world, negative and positive, is what it is and not some other thing:

> this inkwell *is* an inkwell, or the glass is a glass. (*BN*, p. 59)

In this respect, as Sartre indicated in his Introduction, being-in-itself differs from being-for-itself. Being-for-itself, as we shall explain in the next section, is not governed by the Law of Indentity.

4   Being-for-Itself

How does this revised account of being-in-itself as involving both being and non-being demonstrate its connection with being-for-itself, the other region of being mentioned in Sartre's Introduction? We have already noted two aspects of the relation between being-in-itself and conscious, human being. Being-in-itself resists conscious, human being; and it reveals itself only to an interested, questioning, expectant consciousness. But Sartre has a more complex account of this relationship, and it is one which leads to a revised account of the other 'region' of being, being-for-itself, and to an account of how conscious being can act freely in the world.

His discussion can be divided into three stages. He first argues that the existence of non-being in the world presupposes an 'originator' of that non-being. Second, he gives a phenomenological description of certain human conducts which reveal human being to be the originator of non-being in the world. Third, he draws conclusions based on this phenomenology about the ontological character or 'structure' of being-for-itself.

Sartre's argument is clearest when expressed in terms of freedom and causal determination. He sees non-being in the world as that in virture of which the world is not completely causally determined, not 'full positivity'. He argues that, since this is so, non-being must not itself be causally determined, but must have some origin other than a causal one. We noted (see section 3, above) that non-being originates from acts of questioning. Sartre now claims that these acts, in order to qualify as non-causal origins of non-being, must themselves not be causally determined by events in the world. He then describes what such acts must involve: they involve standing back, withdrawing from the world, questioning some part of it and thereby introducing the possibility that it might be otherwise. This he calls an act of 'nihilating':

in so far as the questioner must be able to effect in relation to the questioned a kind of nihilating withdrawal, he is not subject to the causal order of the world; he detaches himself from Being. (*BN*, p. 23)

Sartre then enquires into the character of a being capable of performing these acts of 'nihilating', of standing back to enquire about the world. He argues that one can do this only if one is able to stand back and enquire about oneself, and thus to 'nihilate' oneself as one 'nihilates' the world. In terms of freedom and causation, Sartre's point is that an act of questioning can break the causal chain of events only if it is itself not causally determined even by previous events in the life of the questioner; that is, it must itself be free. But since, for Sartre, any uncaused event requires that some questioner stand back, withdraw from what is questioned, the original source of such events must be something capable of withdrawing from itself, questioning its own activities. This demand for a self-questioner is satisfied by human beings. They are beings who can question, stand back from their own lives: who are, that is to say, free:

What first appears evident is that human reality can detach itself from the world – in questioning, in systematic doubt, in sceptical doubt, in the εποχη, etc. – only if by nature it has the possiblitity of self-detachment. (*BN*, p. 25)

Sartre also presents his argument in terms of the concepts of 'being' and 'nothingness'. He describes how being and nothingness combine: nothingness 'haunts' being (*BN*, pp. 11–16); it 'lies coiled in the heart of being – like a worm' (*BN*, p. 21). He describes the originator of non-being:

The Being by which Nothingness arrives in the world must nihilate Nothingness in its Being, ... [it] *must be its own Nothingness*. (*BN*, p. 23)

A discussion of Sartre's notion of nothingness would take us too far from our present concern, which is to explain how Sartre's phenomenological method leads to his existentialist ontology of being-in-itself and being-for-itself. We shall concentrate on his phenomenological descriptions of freedom, and on the characterization of being-for-itself which eventually issues from that.

Sartre's phenomenological descriptions of freedom fall into two groups.

The first involves descriptions of reflective consciousness of freedom, which Sartre claims is anguish. The second group involves descriptions of pre-reflective consciousness. The conduct which Sartre describes is that of flight from anguish, bad faith.

The conduct which exemplifies anguish, or reflective consciousness of freedom, is that of putting to oneself the question: 'What shall I do next?' What one discovers when one asks this question is a 'lack' or 'gap' in oneself, just as questioning the world can reveal a lack or non-being in the world. The lack revealed within oneself is a lack of anything which determines one's actions. Nothing in one's past or present, no character trait, reason, decision or promise, can actually force one to act in one way rather than another. One is, that is to say, free. An excellent literary example of this is the character Matthieu in Sartre's novel *The Age of Reason*. Matthieu wants to act on the basis of good reasons, justification, or at least overwhelming desire; but each time he questions whether such reasons or desires are sufficiently compelling, the very act of questioning reveals their lack of power over his future. Whenever he asks of a possible course of action whether this is something he must do, the fact that he has asked the question reveals that the answer is 'no', for the act of questioning presupposes that alternative courses of action are also possible for him.

In *Being and Nothingness*, Sartre describes two kinds of anguish. The first is anguish in the face of the future:

> in establishing a certain conduct as a possibility and precisely because it is *my* possibility, I am aware that *nothing* can compel me to adopt that conduct. Yet I am indeed already there in the future; it is for the sake of that being which I will be there at the turning of the path that I now exert all my strength, and in this sense there is already a relation between my future being and my present being. But a nothingness has slipped into the heart of this relation; I *am* not the self which I will be. (*BN*, p. 31)

The second is anguish in the face of the past:

> It is that of the gambler who has freely and sincerely decided not to gamble any more and who when he approaches the gaming table, suddenly sees all his resolutions melt away.... The resolution is still *me* to the extent that I realize constantly my identity with myself across the temporal flux, but it is no longer *me* – due to the fact that it has become an object *for* my consciousness. I am not subject to it, it fails in the mission which I have given it. The resolution is there still, I *am* it in the mode of not-being. (*BN*, pp. 32–3)

In both these descriptions, Sartre moves from describing anguish as the reflective awareness that nothing compels human action, to describing human beings as composed of an 'I' subject which reflects and a 'me' object which is reflected upon. He then describes the relation between these two as failing to conform to the principle of identity.

We have already explored Sartre's view of the self as object for consciousness when discussing *The Transcendence of the Ego* (see section 2, above). The self, or 'me', is also called by Sartre one's ego, essence or presence to the world: it includes one's past, one's body, how one appears to others, and it is that in virtue of which one is 'situated' in the world. Sartre's conception of the reflected 'me' is developed throughout *Being and Nothingness*. In Part I, Sartre's main focus is on the self as one's past or essence:

> This *self* with its *a priori* and historical content is the *essence* of man. . . . Essence is what has been. . . . Essence is all that human reality apprehends in itself as *having been*. . . . The overflow of our consciousness progressively constitutes that nature, but it remains always behind us and it dwells in us as the permanent object of our retrospective comprehension. (*BN*, p. 35)

This is how we are to understand what is often cited as a characteristically existentialist dictum, 'existence precedes essence'. Human beings act, produce a past, and can later review this past as their essence; but this essence is, or can always become, an object of consciousness. One can stand back from, review, one's essence and so one is free from its causal influence. One's essence cannot causally determine one's actions as, for example, the essence of a fragile vase, its fragility, could determine it to shatter when dropped. The existence of the human being consists in its not being bound by its essence, its past, and thus in its having a variety of possibilities left open to it, whatever the facts of its past may be.

Sartre expresses this relation between consciousness, and the self upon which it reflects, in somewhat paradoxical terms:

> Consciousness confronts its past and its future as facing a self which it is in the mode of not-being. (*BN*, p. 34)

This is part of what Sartre means when he claims that the principle of identity applies only to being-in-itself and not to human being. The relation between a conscious subject and an essence as they together make up a human being is not adequately captured either by an affirmation or by a denial of identity between them, as long as identity is understood in the sense in which it applies to being-in-itself, to objects in the world. What makes it oneself that one reflects on is a specially intimate concern which one has for the past and future of that self, for it is one's own; but, in reflecting upon it, one makes it an object of one's consciousness. It is not a subject, not consciousness. It is a 'me' and not an 'I'. The two are not identical. One is *not* any longer one's past self and *not* yet one's future self.

Sartre's description of a paederast encapsulates this thesis:

> He would be right actually if he understood the phrase, 'I am not a paederast' in the sense of 'I am not what I am.' That is, if he declared to himself, 'To the extent that a pattern of conduct is defined as the conduct of a paederast and to the extent that I have adopted this conduct, I am a paederast. But to the extent that human reality can not be finally defined by patterns of conduct, I am not one.' (*BN*, p. 64)

We noted earlier that Sartre expressed his aim to find, as the originator of non-being, a being which 'must be its own nothingness'. In these terms, what the phenomenology of anguish has revealed is that human being has nothingness within it.

> Anguish as the manifestation of freedom in the face of self means that man is always separated by a nothingness from his essence. (*BN*, p. 35)

Sartre does not, however, see his quest for the origin of non-being as complete yet. For this he must find nothingness also within pre-reflective consciousness:

> in the pure subjectivity of the instantaneous *cogito* we must discover the original act by which man is to himself his own nothingness. What must be the nature of consciousness in order that man in consciousness and in terms of consciousness should arise in the world as the being who is his own nothingness and by whom nothingness comes into the world? (*BN*, pp. 44–5)

Sartre thus turns to his second group of descriptions of freedom – descriptions of pre-reflective consciousness. The pre-reflective conduct which Sartre selects and submits to phenomenological description is the conduct of bad faith.[16] Sartre devotes an entire chapter (*BN*, Part I, chapter 2) to this issue. His discussion is extremely complex; we aim only to reveal the form of his overall argument about bad faith and the content of his conclusion concerning the 'structure' of human being.

We noted, in our discussion of reflective consciousness, that Sartre aimed to show what human action was not causally determined by its past. His discussion of pre-reflective consciousness can be seen as an attempt to show that human action is free in a more positive sense: it is freely chosen, there are genuine alternative choices available, and nothing determines which alternative is chosen. What this involves, according to Sartre, is that, whatever one's present state, whatever obligations, habits, desires, aims or motives one has, these never determine what one will do next, because one is always able to choose either to act on the basis of those states or to resist them. This constitutes a crucial difference between human beings and objects. The future of an object is entirely determined by its present states and potentials and by what will happen to it in the future. It has no capacity to resist its own nature, and hence is not free.

The basis of this difference lies in consciousness. It is because human beings are conscious that they can question, and so endorse or resist, their present states, and act towards a future state which is envisaged in advance as neither determined by the present nor the effect of external happenings. This is what Sartre means by his claim that the Law of Identity does not apply, is not the 'constitutive structure' of human being. One is not identical with the set of one's present states, since one can choose to resist them; but nor is one entirely different from them, since they are the states which one must take into consideration in one's choice: they are one's own states. A human being, then, 'is his present, in the mode of not being what he is'. This Sartre terms one's 'facticity'. He contrasts it with one's 'transcendence'. This is not now either the transcendence of the world, nor of the Ego. What Sartre means here by 'transcendence' is the capacity of a human being to choose, to 'go beyond' any present state towards a future envisaged state.

Sartre's discussion of bad faith is intended to establish that human being is not governed by the Law of Identity. Sartre's argument takes the form of exposing the conduct of bad faith, or self-deception, as having the (unachievable) aim of becoming a being-in-itself. This shows that human being is not being-in-itself, since to have something as an aim presupposes that one has not already achieved that aim. Only something which is not a being-in-itself can strive to become one.

Bad faith, Sartre claims, is a flight from anguish. Anguish is the awareness that one is both free and responsible. In bad faith, one flees from both these realizations. One flees from freedom by aiming at and identifying with some of one's present states, regarding them as determining one's future: hence one cannot avoid that future and so cannot be held responsible for it. At the same time one aims to dissociate oneself from, disown, other features of one's present, so that any future results of these features will be things which happen to one rather than things one does. This would enable one to evade responsibility since one cannot be held responsible for what one suffers as a passive victim.

Sartre's first example of the conduct of bad faith, and the one we shall discuss, is that of a young woman:

> Take the example of a woman who has consented to go out with a particular man for the first time. She knows very well the intentions which the man who is speaking to her cherishes regarding her. She knows also that it will be necessary sooner or later for her to make a decision. But she does not want to realize the urgency; she concerns herself only with what is respectful and discreet in the attitude of her companion. (*BN*, p. 55)

What the woman is deceiving herself about is her companion. She is pretending that he doesn't desire her while knowing that he does. Her aim is to enjoy his desire while not being humiliated by it:

> She is profoundly aware of the desire which she inspires, but the desire cruel and naked would humiliate and horrify her, yet she would find no charm in a respect which would be only respect. (*BN*, p. 55)

When he takes her hand, thereby making it urgent for her to make a choice, Sartre continues:

> We know what happens next; the young woman leaves her hand there, but she *does not notice* that she is leaving it. She does not notice because it happens by chance that she is at this moment all intellect. (*BN*, pp. 55–6)

What she does is to identify with that aspect of herself which is the object of his respect, her intellect; while disowning her body, the object of his desire. Hence she can enjoy his desire without being humiliated by it because it can reach her only as intellect and not as body. She can enjoy his attention as respect, while escaping it as desire.

She disowns her body by behaving as if it was a mere passive receiver of happenings, no part of her *self*, and so not her responsibility. She is responsible only for what she – her intellect – does. She identifies with her intellect by behaving as if it, and it alone, constitutes her present potentials and determines her future responses. She acts as if her intellect causes her actions as the fragility of a vase causes it to break. But this is to act as if she were a thing – albeit an intellectual one – a being-in-itself. It is to act as if the Laws of Identity governed her. Her motive for so acting is to become that being-in-itself. But the very fact that she needs to act in order to become it proves that she is not being-in-itself, not self-identical, not 'all intellect' and 'no body'.

> To posit as an ideal the being of things, is this not to assert by the same stroke that this being does not belong to human reality and that the principle of identity, far from being a universal axiom universally applied, is only a synthetic principle enjoying a merely regional universality? (*BN*, p. 58)

Sartre's discussions of anguish and bad faith aim to reveal that human being, whether reflectively or pre-reflectively conscious, does not 'coincide' with itself, does not conform to the principle of identity. Because it is conscious of itself, it is the originator of non-being in itself and hence is the right sort of being to be the originator of non-being in the world. As Sartre puts it, it is 'a Being which is its own Nothingness'.

Being-for-itself, then, is not pure consciousness, not simply the power to question and 'nihilate' being. It has something in common with being, in that one of the beings it can question is its own being. But it is not pure being, not a thing, because it can give negative answers to any question it asks about itself. Hence it cannot just be that self. This is the revision to the concept of being-for-itself which Sartre promised in the Introduction to *Being and Nothingness*.

Having revised the concepts of being-in-itself and being-for-itself, Sartre believes there is no longer any problem about how the two kinds of being can interact. They can be seen to interact in all manner of concrete situations. The task of the phenomenologist is to describe these situations. In Parts III and IV of *Being and Nothingness*, Sartre undertakes this task. We shall discuss some of Sartre's descriptions in Chapters Eight and Nine below.

Part I of *Being and Nothingness* ends with an indication of the next move in Sartre's enquiry:

> we can now approach the ontological study of consciousness, not as the totality of human being, but as the instantaneous nucleus of this being. (*BN*, p. 70)

Part II of *Being and Nothingness* can be seen as an attempt to supply a principle which would stand to being-for-itself as the principle of identity stands to being-in-itself. An object (being-in-itself) obeys the principle of identity: it is just the set of its properties.[17] A human being (being-for-itself), in contrast, because it is conscious of its properties, can dissociate itself from any of those properties. Being-for-itself obeys what Sartre calls the principle of 'presence to itself':

> The law of being of the *for-itself*, as the ontological foundation of consciousness, is to be itself in the form of presence to itself. (*BN*, p. 77)

We can see why the name 'being-for-itself' is appropriate. My self is the being which is present to me as a self for my consciousness, a self for me to be.

The whole of Part II of *Being and Nothingness* is concerned with this notion of 'presence to itself' as the law of being-for-itself. We shall confine our attention to three important aspects of this notion. The first is the translucency of consciousness. If one is present to oneself, one can scarcely be ignorant of oneself. Human beings are, according to Sartre, first and foremost, conscious subjects; and, as conscious subjects, they must be translucently aware of their own activities. There must be no feature of human thought or conduct, no feature of subjectivity, which is opaque or hidden from consciousness. Anything which appears hidden must be explained either as not really hidden or not really a feature of subjectivity.

The second feature of 'presence to itself' is that being-for-itself is undetermined, that it has and can acquire no fixed characteristics or nature. It is aware of its self, but it is not to be identified with that self to which it is present. So, there can be no sad consciousness but only consciousness of sadness, no desiring consciousness but only consciousness of desire. Consciousness can be situated only by being conscious of its situation, and its only essence is an essence which it is conscious of having. That the subject of consciousness should be undetermined in this way is, Sartre believes, a necessary condition for its being free. For if one had a fixed character, disposition or nature, that would close off future possibilities: that disposition or that character would cause one to act in one way or another. Sartre believes that, in order to be free from causal determination, the subject must be free from all determination. The free subject must have no fixed properties, no properties it cannot change.

The third feature of 'presence to itself' is that it goes hand in hand with the ability to withdraw from oneself. For Sartre, what is central to human reality is not its involvement in the world and its own activities, but its capacity to detach itself, to witness itself and the world. Sartre's aim was to characterize being-for-itself in a way which made it possible to explain interaction between it and the world. His solution is a being which can interact with the world only because it can detach itself from that part of itself which is capable of interacting with the world.

Most of the rest of *Being and Nothingness* is concerned to show how the nucleus of a human being, consciousness, is 'situated', as it always is, in concrete situations:

> The concrete consciousness arises in situation, and it is a unique, individualized consciousness *of* this situation, and (of)[18] itself in situation. It is to this concrete consciousness that the self is present.... (*BN*, p. 91)

However, a question naturally arises as to how far Sartre's conception of concrete human beings is influenced by his presentation of them as made up of pure consciousness, with a self which is present to but not identical with that consciousness.

5   Sartre's Presuppositions

We are now able to review Sartre's philosophical position and to ask, in particular, how far his conceptions of the world and of the conscious subject are existentialist, and how far his existentialism is grounded in his phenomenological method. We claimed in the first section of this chapter that one central aim of existential phenomenology was to avoid both realist and idealist conceptions of the world and the conscious subject. It has emerged now that Sartre's conception of objects in the world is not realist, since non-being is a feature of the world, and this non-being is not wholly independent of the conscious subject whose activities reveal it. Moreover it is the individual subject to whom non-being is revealed, so that the real world of objects, in Sartre's view, is not necessarily an inter-subjective one. But Sartre's conception of the world is not idealist, for it involves being as its basis. Being is what the conscious subject questions, and it is independent of that subject. This independent being, though, is not enough to make Sartre's a realist conception of the world; for being, in Sartre's view, lacks all determinate character.

Sartre's conception of the subject is similarly neither that of the realist nor that of the idealist. It is not realist because the Sartrean subject, being-for-itself, is entirely different from all natural objects. Being-for-itself is governed by the law of presence to itself and not by the law of identity. It has what Sartre calls a different 'structure', a different 'ontological foundation'. But nor is it an idealist subject for, though radically different from objects in the world, it is necessarily situated in the world. Its only standpoint is a standpoint in the world, and it is this standpoint which gives it its individuality.

So far, our exegesis of Sartre's work has emphasized the role of his phenomenological descriptions in grounding his existentialist conclusions. We shall now raise some queries about the 'presuppositionlessness' of those descriptions with respect to his conclusions both about objects and about subjects. The claim that Sartre's conception of objects is entirely based on presuppositionless phenomenological description might be challenged in two ways. First, the conduct Sartre selects for phenomenological description is that of the individual subject questioning the world. From this, he develops his individualistic conception of non-being in the world. We are offered at this stage no justification for this selection in favour of more 'collective' questioning of the world such as, for example, a crowd of partisan football supporters questioning a referee's decision.[19] Sartre could, hence, be accused of presupposing that the cases which he selects are the primary or central ones.

Second, the descriptions he gives of these conducts might be thought to involve a presupposition. Sartre insists that all questions can be formulated in such a way as to get a definite answer 'yes' or a definite answer 'no' from the world. From this issues his conception of objects in the world as determinate. Sartre might here be criticized for presupposing determinacy, and describing the phenomena in accordance with that presupposition. A conduct close to one which Sartre himself considers, namely asking the question 'Have I fixed it?' of a used car with an intermittent fault, might seem to be an example where pure presuppositionless description might not very obviously reveal a determinate answer.

The claim that Sartre's conception of the subject of consciousness is phenomenologically grounded can be criticized in similar ways. First, he selects, as examples of free conduct, anguish and bad faith – conducts in which the subject feels his freedom as respectively a burden and something from which to escape. From his description of these cases issues Sartre's conception of the subject of consciousness as lacking something, as undetermined, as distanced from self and prone to the perpetual risk of bad faith. Again, Sartre offers no justification for his selection of these cases rather than, for example, such phenomena as the feeling of freedom and release from everyday cares as one sets out on a touring holiday; the chronically anxious or depressed person who may find no 'space' between himself and his anxiety or depression; or the virtuoso cellist for whom there may seem to be no distance between her consciousness and her concentration on the music. Sartre's selection of examples might seem to involve the presupposition that his examples are the primary or central ones.[20]

Second, the description of these conducts of anguish and bad faith may also seem to involve a presupposition, namely that consciousness is translucent. One crucial role which this conviction plays in Sartre's conception of being-for-itself is that it is only because one must be aware of all one's subjective states that one can stand back to question them and hence be free of determination by them. But even Sartre's own examples of bad faith scarcely seem to invite a description which presents the subjects as completely lucid and aware of their own states of consciousness. These descriptions might seem to presuppose rather than reveal this translucency.

We shall explore in the next three chapters how Merleau-Ponty's phenomenological investigation leads him to different conceptions of the subject, and of the world. Merleau-Ponty shares Sartre's concern to avoid both realist and idealist conceptions; but, as we shall see, he challenges the sharpness of Sartre's contrast between determinate objects governed by the principle of identity and undetermined subjects governed by the law of presence to self and situated in the world in virtue of this self.

5

The Critique of Objective Thought

1 Merleau-Ponty's Critical Strategy

A work of existential phenomenology, Merleau-Ponty's *Phenomenology of Perception* shares with *Being and Nothingness* a number of features which set both of them apart from the transcendental phenomenology of Husserl's *Cartesian Meditations*: a rejection of the transcendental ego, and of the account of objects as what are 'meant' by this ego; an insistence upon the character of human 'being-in-the-world' as the primary focus of phenomenological enquiry; and an attempt, in general terms, to steer a course between realism and idealism. But there are also a number of important disagreements between Merleau-Ponty and Sartre. In Particular, Merleau-Ponty objects to the radical dichotomy between the for-itself and the in-itself articulated by Sartre, and argues that no satisfactory account of human existence can be given which relies upon this dichotomy (see Chapter Nine, section 3).

A striking feature of the *Phenomenology of Perception* is that its philosophical arguments are conducted largely through the detailed examination of substantive theories about human action and perception; and that consequently the writings of psychologists and physiologists are given equal prominence to those of philosophers. More specifically, Merleau-Ponty engages in a sustained critique of two distinctive approaches to the understanding of human beings, which he terms *empiricism* and *intellectualism*. In this chapter we shall explore what he means by these, and how his objections to them function in his overall critical strategy. To do so we shall start by looking briefly at the Preface which is more obviously and exclusively philosophical in character than much of the text which follows it.

Merleau-Ponty begins by addressing the question 'What is phenomenology?'. His answer to this proceeds in two main stages. First, he puts forward his own view of what is fundamental to phenomenology, by means of a contrast between *description*, on the one hand, and both *explanation* and *analysis*, on the other. Second, he goes on to propose certain interpretations for the concepts of 'reduction', 'essence' and 'intentionality' which, as we saw in earlier chapters, figure centrally in Husserl's phenomenology. We shall for the moment leave aside this second stage and concentrate upon the first.[1]

The hallmark of a genuinely phenomenological enquiry, says Merleau-Ponty, is that it regards its task as 'a matter of describing, not explaining or analysing' (*PP*, p. viii). Let us consider each of the latter pair in turn. The kind of explanation to which he is referring is *scientific*: the causal explanations which the various empirical sciences, such as physics, biology, psychology and sociology, attempt to provide. Phenomenology, then, involves describing things rather than explaining them; and Merleau-Ponty here, as often, cites Husserl in support of this view:

> Husserl's first directive to phenomenology ... to return to the 'things themselves', is from the start a foreswearing of science. (*PP*, p. viii)

It may at first seem strange to contrast phenomenology with other philosophical standpoints in this particular way: after all, few if any conceptions of philosophy straightforwardly identify it with the empirical sciences, or characterize its basic aim or method as that of scientific explanation. But what Merleau-Ponty has in mind is a distinction between phenomenology and those philosophical positions which depend upon the possibility of such scientific explanations. More specifically, although he does not use the term at this point, he is counter-posing phenomenology to a certain kind of *realism*.

We have, so far, talked of realism mainly in a fairly general form, as the view that the nature and existence of the world is independent of one's knowledge of it, and that human beings are just as much part of that world as anything else. We can now add to this the claim that it is by means of the empirical sciences that this knowledge of the world can be obtained. Hence human beings, along with the rest of the world, are legitimate 'objects' of scientific investigation and explanation. In particular, it should be possible to provide scientific explanations of how it is that humans *perceive* things, by investigating the causal processes through which external physical stimuli affect their sense-organs and give rise to perceptual experience. Similarly for human *action*: the behaviour of human beings, like any other events taking place in the world, has causal determinants which can be discovered by the normal methods of empirical science.

This 'scientific' realism, then, shares in realism's denial of any radical distinction between the 'subject' and 'object' of knowledge, whilst also ascribing to the empirical sciences a privileged position with respect to such knowledge. Hence the sciences of physiology, psychology, and so on, can explain both how humans perceive the world (including, of course, one another) and how they behave in it. Merleau-Ponty is thoroughly opposed to this view. In the

Preface he briefly makes two objections. The first is directed against its misunderstanding of the nature of scientific concepts and their relationship to the world one experiences in everyday life. We shall return to this in the next chapter. The second concerns its view of the human subject as an object of scientific knowledge. 'I am not', he declares,

> the outcome or the meeting-point of numerous causal agencies which determine my bodily make-up. I cannot conceive myself as nothing but a bit of the world, a mere object of biological, psychological, or sociological investigation. I cannot shut myself up within the realm of science. (*PP*, p. viii)

And likewise:

> Scientific points of view, according to which my existence is a moment of the world's, are always both naive and at the same time dishonest, because they take for granted, without explicitly mentioning it, the other point of view, namely that of consciousness, through which from the outset a world forms itself around me and begins to exist for me. (*PP*, p. ix)

But Merleau-Ponty is eager to correct a misunderstanding that might otherwise be generated by these claims. To oppose the 'scientific point of view' in such terms may seem to commit him to some form of transcendental idealism, according to which the world investigated by the empirical sciences is itself constituted, at least in its basic characteristics, by a conscious subject which is not itself a part of that world, but rather is presupposed by it. Yet this, says Merleau-Ponty, is not his position, nor that of a genuine phenomenology. Such idealism, he claims – and it is mainly Kant's that he has in mind, though his comments here might also be applicable to Husserl's position in the *Cartesian Meditations* – depends upon the procedure of analysis, or, as he often calls it, 'analytical reflection': and the descriptive procedure of phenomenology is as much at odds with this as it is with scientific explanation. Phenomenology's adoption of the 'point of view of consciousness', he declares,

> is absolutely distinct from the idealist return to consciousness, and the demand for a pure description excludes equally the procedure of analytical reflection on the one hand, and that of scientific explanation on the other. (*PP*, p. ix)

The procedure of analytical reflection consists in identifying the basic rules or concepts which supposedly underlie the way that the world is experienced, and which hence can be said to make this possible: for instance, the Kantian categories of substance, causality, and so on (see Chapter Three, section 5). The idealist then ascribes these rules and concepts to a transcendental subject which is, as it were, blessed with world-constitutive cognitive powers:

Analytical reflection starts from our experience of the world and goes back to the subject as to a condition of possibility distinct from that experience, revealing the all-embracing synthesis [in which the subject's cognitive powers are exercised] as that without which there would be no world. To this extent it ceases to remain part of our experience and offers, in place of an account [i.e. a phenomenological 'description'], a reconstruction. (*PP*, pp. ix–x)

Merleau-Ponty rejects this idealist conception of the subject, just as he also rejects the kind of realism to which he has counterposed it: the *Phenomenology of Perception* is devoted to showing what is wrong with both. However, he does not engage in a head-on confrontation with either: he does not 'trade philosophical arguments' with the proponents of realism and idealism. Instead, he tries to show that the specific procedures upon which each of them depends, namely scientific explanation and analytical reconstruction, cannot in fact succeed. It is here that the concepts of *empiricism* and *intellectualism* come into play. For these two distinctive approaches to the understanding of human perception and action are defined, in effect, by their respective employment of the two procedures just noted. The programme of empiricism is to provide scientifically validated causal explanations for these phenomena; whilst that of intellectualism is to provide analytical reconstructions, by identifying the rules which make them possible.

What Merleau-Ponty argues is that, in practice, neither of these programmes can actually achieve the goals set for them; and that, consequently, neither realism nor idealism is defensible. It is because of this overall strategy that so much of the *Phenomenology of Perception* consists in the detailed criticism of specific causal and reconstructive accounts that have been proposed by empiricists and intellectualists. But, as we shall now see, there is an additional and important element to this strategy, which involves the introduction of a further central concept, that of *objective thought*.

So far empiricism and intellectualism, and their related philosophical standpoints of realism and idealism, have been presented as entirely at odds with one another. But Merleau-Ponty claims also that there is something very important which they have in common, namely a certain view of *what the world is like* – what kinds of items it contains, and what kinds of relationships obtain between them. It is this view which he calls 'objective thought' (e.g. *PP*, p. 71). According to this, the world consists of clearly identifiable objects – such as houses, trees, stones, etc. – each of which has a definite location at any given time in a single spatial framework. Every object has a set of determinately specifiable properties – for example, a particular size, shape, weight, colour, and so on – which can be described independently of one another. These objects can interact causally with each other; and all their properties are open, in principle, to a complete description and causal explanation. The world conceived in this way Merleau-Ponty often calls 'the universe' (e.g. *PP*, p. 71).

Broadly speaking, then, objective thought characterizes the world in a way that makes it a suitable candidate for scientific treatment. But objective thought is indifferent, as such, to the rival philosophical claims of realists and idealists as to whether this world exists 'in its own right', or is somehow constituted by a transcendental subject. It is a view of what the world is like, and not of its ontological status. (Hence, Merleau-Ponty would regard Kant's combination of 'empirical realism' with 'transcendental idealism' – see Chapter Three, section 5 – as nonetheless displaying objective thought.) Further, says Merleau-Ponty, objective thought is assumed not only in the various empirical sciences, but also in what he often calls 'dogmatic common sense', or sometimes just 'common sense' (e.g. *PP*, pp. xi, 71).

The fact that both empiricists and intellectualists share this objectivist view of the world has important consequences for their respective attempts to understand perception and action, he argues. For example, in the case of perception, the empiricist tries to provide causal explanations for what is perceived, whilst the intellectualist tries to reconstruct what is perceived by reference to the subject's exercise of its cognitive powers. But both take it for granted that their task is to understand how humans manage to perceive the world as characterized by objective thought; and in doing so, he argues, they make a fundamental error.

For the world which humans actually perceive is *not* like this: it is not 'objective'. Instead it consists of 'objects' whose properties are not fully specifiable or determinate, but inherently non-determinate and even ambiguous; between these objects there obtain relationships of meaning and reciprocal expression, not of causal determination; they are not uniquely located in a single spatial framework, but varyingly situated in relation to the human agent's specific field of action; and so on. Merleau-Ponty sometimes refers to this world of everyday experience as 'the lived-through world' (e.g. *PP*, p. 71): for convenience we shall term it 'the lived world'.

'Nothing', says Merleau-Ponty, 'is more difficult to know than precisely *what we see*' (*PP*, p. 58). Both empiricists and intellectualists *misdescribe* the lived world: their descriptions are systematically distorted by the 'prejudice' of objective thought. So, however successfully they account for perception of an objective 'universe' – and Merleau-Ponty thinks intellectualism fares better than empiricism in this respect – they will have failed to understand what is in fact perceived. Furthermore, he argues, once one has arrived at a correct description of the lived world, one can show that its character is such as to defy both scientific explanation and analytical reconstruction.

Thus the prejudice of objective thought vitiates both empiricism and intellectualism, despite the radical divergence between realist and idealist views about the ontological status of this objective universe. As Merleau-Ponty puts it:

Empiricism retained an absolute [realist] belief in the world as the totality of spatio-temporal events, and treated consciousness as a province of this world. Analytical reflection, it is true, breaks with the world in itself, since it constitutes it through the working of consciousness, but this constituting consciousness ... is built up in such a way as to make possible the idea of an absolute determinate being. It [the constituting consciousness] is the correlative of a universe. (*PP*, p. 40)

But in other respects this divergence between the two is of major importance. For the realist, everything belongs to the universe of objective thought, including human consciousness. For the idealist, this universe is itself made possible by a constituting subject, which does not conform to objective thought. Correspondingly, therefore, intellectualism differs from empiricism in regarding human action and perception as the exercise of their subjects' distinctive, and non-objective, cognitive powers. Thus 'reasoning', 'judgement', 'decision' and other such acts of the subject are constantly invoked by intellectualists in carrying out their programme of analytical reconstruction.

Merleau-Ponty regards intellectualism as clearly superior to empiricism in recognizing the special status of the human subject. But he does not accept its specific characterization of this subject. The intellectualist, he argues, misdescribes what is actually involved in perceiving the world and in performing actions, and hence also misrepresents the nature of this subject and its relationship to the world. Amongst other things, he rejects the 'disembodied', purely 'mentalistic' character of the intellectualists' subject: and he proposes instead that the true subject of action and perception is an essentially 'bodily' one.

Returning now to Merleau-Ponty's espousal of the method or procedure of description, as against those of explanation and analysis, it can be seen that this method is not merely what distinguishes phenomenology from the competing philosophical standpoints of realism and idealism, but is also the crucial means by which their respective failings are to be demonstrated. It is not just a preferred alternative to the procedures they rely upon, but the basis for their criticism. Furthermore, he maintains, what is revealed by unprejudiced description is the distinctive character of human existence as 'being-in-the-world' (*PP*, p. xiv); and he goes on to argue that phenomenology should employ a method which consists in 'correctly reading phenomena, in grasping their meaning, that is, in treating them as modalities and variations of the subject's total being' (*PP*, p. 108).

In the final section of this chapter we shall develop further this initial account of Merleau-Ponty's overall critical strategy in the *Phenomenology of*

Perception, and of the positive views for which he argues.[2] But first we shall look more closely, in the following two sections, at his conception of objective thought, and of empiricism and intellectualism.

2   Objective Thought vs. the Lived World

Objective thought, as we have noted, is a view of what the world is like: what sorts of entities it contains, and what sorts of relationships hold between them. Merleau-Ponty's main objection to it is that it misrepresents the nature of the world one actually experiences; and since both empiricists and intellectualists accept this view, they are guilty of prejudiced description. To support these claims, Merleau-Ponty frequently invokes two central contrasts: between the *determinate* and the *non-determinate* character of 'objects' in, respectively, the objectivist's universe and the lived world; and between the *externality* and the *internality* of the relationships which obtain within them. We shall examine each of these in some detail, and then consider more briefly some further aspects of objective thought.

According to the objectivist, says Merleau-Ponty, every object is fully determinate (French *'determiné'*). This term comes from the Latin *'determinare'*, meaning literally 'to put boundaries upon', 'to set limits to', and, somewhat more generally, 'to fix, to make precise or distinct'. So something is determinate if it has fixed or precise limits or boundaries – if, as it were, it starts 'just here' and stops 'just there', and is thus distinct from everything else.

In denying that what one actually perceives is determinate, Merleau-Ponty sometimes means, in a relatively straightforward way, that is has no clear-cut boundaries. For instance, he says that one's visual field – the full extent of what one can see at any particular time – can never be precisely specified. There is always an imprecise area at the perimeter, where various items are at best only indistinctly perceived: there occurs here 'an *indeterminate vision*, a *vision of something or other*' (*PP*, p. 6). However, more often and more significantly, his claims about the non-determinacy of objects in the lived world concern the character of their *properties*. We can identify three separate points here, though Merleau-Ponty himself tends not to distinguish them.

The first is this. Objective thought maintains that one can in principle give a *complete* description of objects – comprising, in effect, a fully specified list of the properties which each object possesses. Merleau-Ponty denies that this is possible. The objects one actually encounters in the lived world have a richness and complexity which inevitably defies any such finite enumeration of their properties. They are therefore not, in this sense, determinate.

The second point concerns the 'determinacy' or 'definiteness' with which any particular property is possessed by an object. For the objectivist, says

Merleau-Ponty, every property must be such that, for any object, there is always a definite answer to the question whether the object possesses that property or not. In other words, for any object 'O', and any property 'P', the question 'does O possess P?' can always be answered either 'yes' or 'no'.

Merleau-Ponty claims that this is not so in the world one actually experiences. Instead one often finds that an object neither quite has, nor does not have, a particular property. An example he gives is this:

> The two straight lines in Müller-Lyer's optical illusion ... are neither of equal nor unequal length, it is only in the objective world that this question arises. (*PP*, p. 6)

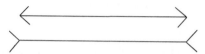

Merleau-Ponty thus denies a basic assumption of psychologists' discussions of this phenomenon: that the lines are really equal but are perceived as unequal.[3] Rather, he claims, the perceived lines are neither equal nor unequal; and he also rejects the objectivist's belief that 'at least in reality' they must be one or the other.

It may be helpful to compare Merleau-Ponty's disagreement with objective thought on this score with a partly analogous issue in the philosophy of language, about what sorts of definitions can or should be given to descriptive terms – the terms by which one ascribes properties to things. Two opposing views about this issue may be adopted. The first is that, ideally, every descriptive term should be given a definition which identifies the (jointly) necessary and sufficient conditions for its correct application. In this way, the meanings of all such terms are to be fully specified, so that one knows precisely what is meant in applying them, and hence exactly what would count as a correct or incorrect application.

But according to the second, opposing, view, such clear-cut definitions are not possible – or, at least, there is no good reason to regard them as especially desirable. Rather, it is said, most or all descriptive concepts are inherently 'open-ended'. One cannot fully specify their meanings: they are always somewhat imprecise, though not in an objectionable way. So although there will be many cases in which the applicability of a certain term is clear enough, there will be others in which it is not. As a result of this, there will often be situations in which there is no definite answer to the question whether or not an object possesses a particular property: one will be unable to say either that it does or that it does not. (It may be conceded that in the sciences, unlike ordinary language, precise definitions are required; but this, it is maintained, does not show the superiority of the former over the latter, only a difference in what is appropriate to each kind of language.)[4]

Drawing upon this analogy, one could say that, for Merleau-Ponty, the nature of the lived world is such that it cannot be adequately described by the 'determinate' concepts of the first of these views, but only by the 'non-determinate' concepts of the second. But it must be emphasized that, for him, non-determinacy is primarily a characteristic of what is actually experienced in the world, and only derivatively of the concepts employed to describe this. As a phenomenologist, he is concerned not with the analysis of concepts but with the description of experience; and, to the extent that the *Phenomenology of Perception* contains any clear view about the relationship between language and experience, it seems often to involve the tacit assumption that the former must properly 'represent' the latter. Hence, in particular, a language with determinately defined concepts will be unsuitable for the description of an actually non-determinate experienced world.

The final point about determinacy is the following. Merleau-Ponty often says that objects in the lived world, far from being determinate, are instead 'ambiguous', or 'equivocal' (e.g. *PP*, p. 6). Sometimes he means by this only that they have the kind of non-determinacy we have just considered. But at other times something more than this is being claimed, namely that they have two or more mutually conflicting or contradictory properties. So if something is ambiguous, in this sense, it is not so much that it neither has nor does not have a particular property; rather, there are positive grounds for saying both that it has that property and, either that it does not have that property, or that it has another which is incompatible with it.[5]

Ambiguity, then, is not for Merleau-Ponty a feature of *words* – namely their being used, or being able to be used, in a number of distinct (and sometimes quite unrelated) senses. Instead it is a feature of the lived world itself – that its objects often display mutually incompatible properties. In claiming this, what he has in mind is quite close to the way in which one commonly talks of certain human situations or relationships as 'ambiguous'. For example (ours, not his), a personal relationship between two people might be described as 'sexually ambiguous', in that it could equally well be interpreted as sexual or as non-sexual. The point here would be, not that it was somehow on the borderline between one and the other, but rather that it displayed characteristics typical of both. It would be 'open to both interpretations', not because one had failed to discover which was the correct one, but because of the co-existence of (and indeed the tension between) both 'meanings'. But Merleau-Ponty departs from this relatively familiar use of the concept by extending its potential application to everything that one experiences in the lived world: not just to human and social situations, but also to both organic and inorganic nature (e.g. *PP*, p. 24). As he puts it at one point: 'The visual world is that strange zone in which contradictory notions jostle each other' (*PP*, p. 6).

The determinacy of the objectivist's universe, then, is in all these respects at odds with the non-determinacy of the lived world; and if objective thought is taken straightforwardly to describe what one actually experiences, it is thus guilty of misdescription. But Merleau-Ponty recognizes that the advocate of objective thought may respond to this by trying to distinguish between 'the world as it really is' and 'the world as it appears', in one's perception or knowledge of it; and by then claiming that non-determinacy applies only to the latter and not to the former. For instance, in the case of perception, the objectivist may claim that

> In the world taken in itself, everything is determinate. There are many unclear sights, as for example a landscape on a misty day, but then we [as objectivists] always say that no real landscape is in itself unclear. It is so only for us. The object, psychologists would assert, is never ambiguous, but becomes so only through our inattention. (*PP*, p. 6 trans. adjusted)

And likewise in the case of knowledge:

> what is not determinate for me could become determinate for a more complete knowledge, which is as it were realized in advance in the [determinate] thing, or rather which is the thing itself. (*PP*, p. 54)

Merleau-Ponty will not accept these kinds of response, nor the radical distinction between 'appearance' and 'reality' which they necessarily rely upon. But his reasons for not doing so emerge mainly in the course of his more specific objections to empiricism and intellectualism which, because of their commitment to objective thought, are forced either directly to misrepresent what is experienced, or to try somehow to account for its non-determinate character by reference to the determinate concepts used in their explanatory or reconstructive procedures. As we shall see later, he argues that neither can succeed.

We turn now to the second main contrast noted earlier, between the externality of relationships in the universe and the internality of those in the lived world. A relationship is external if the related items can be identified without reference to one another. Conversely, items are internally related if they cannot thus be independently identified (cf. Chapter Two, section 1, above). One kind of relationship with which Merleau-Ponty is concerned is that which obtains between the various properties possessed by particular objects – their size, shape, colour, texture, and suchlike. For the objectivist, such relationships are external. Merleau-Ponty denies that this is so. For example, he says about the red colour of a carpet that 'this red would literally not be the same if it were not the "woolly red" of a carpet' (*PP*, pp. 4–5). Its colour and texture cannot altogether be distinguished from each other: they are not separately identifiable properties, externally related.

But his main interest, in discussing externality, is in *causal* relationships, or, somewhat more generally, in the relationships involved in the laws that are postulated by the empirical sciences. Objective thought, says Merleau-Ponty, recognizes between objects

> only external and mechanical relationships, whether in the narrow sense of motion received and transmitted [e.g. in classical mechanics], or in the wider sense of the relation of function and variable. (*PP*, p. 73)

Let us take as an example the ideal gas law, $PV = kT$. Here the variables are the pressure, volume and temperature of a gas, denoted by 'P', 'V' and 'T' ('k' denotes a constant, which can be ignored here). The law specifies a functional relationship between these variables, so that the values of any two determine that of the third. Thus one can calculate the temperature of any gas by multiplying its pressure by its volume; its pressure, by dividing its temperature by its volume; and so on. One may also regard this equation as representing various causal relationships: for example, an increase in the temperature of a given volume of gas may be said to cause an increase in its pressure.

The externality of such relationships can best be seen by considering how the truth or falsity of claims about them can be assessed. For instance, to test empirically the ideal gas law, it must be possible to measure independently the pressure, volume and temperature of a gas: and this requires that each variable be definable without reference to the others. Likewise, and more generally, to test any claim that one item or event is the cause of another, one must be able to identify the presence or absence of each independently of the other – otherwise, for instance, one would not be able to devise experimental procedures to discover whether or not they regularly accompany each other.

Thus in denying that relationships in the lived world are external, Merleau-Ponty is denying that they are causal or functional. Rather, he says, they are internal relationships of a 'meaningful' or 'expressive' nature, in which the related items cannot be specified independently of one another. To see what he means by this, consider a particular example which he provides in the following passage:

> In ordinary experience we find a fittingness and a meaningful relationship between the gesture, the smile, and the tone of a speaker. But this reciprocal relationship of expression which presents the human body as the outward manifestation of a certain manner of being-in-the-world, had, for mechanistic physiology, to be resolved into a series of causal relationships. (*PP*, p. 55)

Suppose, for instance, that someone is greeting a friend. There will be, one may imagine, a smile on their face, a warmth to their tone of voice and a welcoming gesture – say, a wave of the arm. What will be experienced, according to Merleau-Ponty, is a meaningful configuration of facial expression, sound and movement, in which each element is perceived as 'appropriate' to the others, as 'suitably' conjoined, and indeed as not altogether distinguishable from them. Further, he says, each element is itself an expression of 'a certain manner of being-in-the-world'. Leaving aside the philosophical niceties of this concept, let us say that it consists here of a certain 'attitude', a 'friendly' one. Then the smile, gesture and tone of voice can all be said to be experienced as expressions of this attitude.

But, says Merleau-Ponty, the relationship between an expression and what is expressed is not external, and hence not causal. Being friendly cannot be specified independently of its expressions, such as these; nor can they be identified independently of 'it'. Further, each of these expressions is internally related to the others, partly at least by virtue of their 'sharing' the attitude which they express. It might also be noted (though Merleau-Ponty does not do so here) that similarly 'meaningful' relationships would obtain even if no single or consistent attitude were being expressed. Suppose, for example, that one saw a smile and a welcoming gesture, but heard a cold or hostile tone of voice. There would then be a tension or dissonance within the overall configuration: and one might experience the person concerned as ambivalent, as expressing two conflicting attitudes. The smile and the hostile tone would be experienced as inappropriate to one another – but this is just as 'meaningful' a relationship as appropriateness is.

By contrast, says Merleau-Ponty, the proponent of objective thought – in this case, an empiricist – will try to provide a causal explanation for the person's gesture, smile and tone of voice: for example, by claiming that these are the effects of various physiological processes. Thus the meaningful configuration that is actually experienced will have to be de-composed into supposedly discrete, independently identifiable (and determinately describable) elements, to each of which a physiological cause is ascribed. The only relationship which could then be said to obtain between these elements would be that of co-occurrence, itself possibly to be explained by further external, causal relationships between the various physiological processes that have been postulated in each case. But, claims Merleau-Ponty, in adopting this approach the objectivist effectively destroys the phenomenon: what is actually experienced is necessarily misrepresented when forced into the framework of objective thought.

It should also be noted that nothing would be gained, in Merleau-Ponty's view, were the physiological explanation to be replaced or supplemented by a psychological one which referred, say, to a desire to be welcoming, or to a feeling of warmth or friendliness, as possible causes. For this would still require one to conceive of the various relationships as external, and thereby to misrepresent the meaningful, reciprocally expressive nature of what is in fact perceived. Thus objective thought is not, for Merleau-Ponty, exclusively materialist or physicalist in character; and, as we shall see, he regards the implicit acceptance by many empiricist psychologists of some version of Cartesian dualism – of supposedly interacting psycho-physical processes – as itself an influential form of objective thought.

One further point must be emphasized here. Although the example we have been considering is one involving the attitudes of humans to one another, Merleau-Ponty does not restrict his view of the internality of relationships to this domain: much the same is true of all relationships in the lived world, including those involving both organic and inorganic entities. There are, admittedly, important differences between human being-in-the-world and the (non-human) world in which humans 'exist'. But the latter is not the universe of objective thought; for the relationships which hold within it, too, are internal and meaningful.

Thus Merleau-Ponty's position here differs significantly from that of certain analytical philosophers, who have likewise denied that causal explanations can be given for human action and asserted that what are instead involved are internal relations of meaning.[6] For in claiming this they have typically contrasted human action with the causal character of non-human phenomena. Furthermore, their 'internal relations of meaning' have been regarded as primarily linguistic or conceptual in nature, holding between the concepts employed in describing actions, desires, beliefs, and so on. For Merleau-Ponty, by contrast, any such conceptual relations in the language of action could only be secondary: due, as it were, to the relations of non-linguistic meaning experienced in the lived world itself (cf. Chapter Two, section 4, above).

The contrasts which we have been exploring between objective thought and the lived world are encapsulated in the following passage, where Merleau-Ponty declares that

> the notion of a *universe*, that is to say, a completed and explicit totality, in which the relationships are those of reciprocal determination, exceeds [i.e. illicitly 'goes beyond'] that of a world, or an open and indefinite multiplicity of relationships which are of reciprocal implication. (*PP*, p. 71)

Indeed, as his use of the phrase 'reciprocal determination' suggests, there is an important connection between the concepts of externality and determinacy. It is no accident that the terms often used to denote causal relationships – 'determine', 'determination', and so on – are so closely related to 'determinacy' and 'determinate'. For it might well be argued that relationships of causal determination can hold only between items which are themselves determinate. This, at least, seems to be Merleau-Ponty's view; and hence his claims about the non-determinacy of the lived world may be seen as giving additional weight to his rejection of objectivism's external relationships.

To conclude this account of objective thought we shall consider briefly two further characteristics which Merleau-Ponty ascribes to it. The first concerns its conception of spatiality. According to this, every object has, at any given time, a determinate location in a unified spatial framework which is, as Merleau-Ponty puts it, 'indifferent to its contents' (*PP*, p. 54). The basic idea here is that the nature of an object is taken to be in no way affected by its position in space, including its position relative both to observers and to other objects. One implication of this view is that an object remains exactly the same whatever its spatial 'orientation' – whether it is, for example, 'upright', or 'on its side', or 'upside down'.

But, claims Merleau-Ponty, this is not true of one's actual experience of things in the lived world. Rather, he says,

> I have only to look at a landscape upside down to recognize nothing in it. Now 'top' and 'bottom' have only a relative meaning for the understanding [i.e. for a Kantian version of objective thought], which can hardly regard the orientation of a landscape as an absolute obstacle [to its recognition]. For the understanding a square is always a square, whether it stands on its side or at an angle. For perception it is in the second case hardly recognizable. (*PP*, p. 46)

Furthermore, he argues, neither does one's perception of the spatial relationships which obtain between different objects conform to objective thought. For example, in everyday experience one discriminates between the relationships denoted by the terms 'on', 'under' and 'beside', despite the fact that the relative positions of the objects concerned may well be exactly the same in 'objective' space (*PP*, pp. 100–1). What must be recognized, then, is that in the lived world one is dealing not with 'a *spatiality of position*, but a *spatiality of situation*' (*PP*, p. 101) – and hence with objects that are 'situated', always in relation to specific human actions, whether actual or projected.[7]

The final aspect of objective thought to be considered here is rather more difficult to specify. It concerns the objectivist's tendency to make a radical distinction between the kinds of properties which objects genuinely possess, and those which they only appear to the perceiver as possessing. Just where this distinction is drawn varies between different versions of objective thought. But Merleau-Ponty is especially concerned with those which use such a distinction to criticize a supposed human tendency to anthropomorphize nature – wrongly to ascribe to it characteristics which belong, if at all, only to humans themselves, and even then perhaps only to their 'inner experiences'.

For example, he says, according to one such view:

> There is nothing in the appearance of a landscape, an object, or a body whereby it is predestined to look 'gay' or 'sad', 'lively' or 'dreary', 'elegant' or 'coarse'. (*PP*, p. 23)

Instead, it is argued, such ascriptions should be regarded as projections onto the world of what are in fact only the effects of its real characteristics upon the perceiver: the genuine, non-human properties of things in the natural world give rise to various human experiences, the characteristics of which are then mistakenly attributed by the perceiver to their external causal origins (*PP*, p. 24).

But this philosophical view, says Merleau-Ponty, is quite wrong. There is no more reason for denying the reality of these kinds of perceived properties than there is for any others. Nor will he accept the closely related view that such statements as 'the landscape is dreary', 'the sea boiled angrily' or 'the clouds are threatening' (the latter examples ours) are at best to be regarded as purely metaphorical – that taken literally they are strictly false, and based merely on various associations and projections on the part of the perceiver. Rather, says Merleau-Ponty,

> [once] we admit that all these 'projections', all these 'associations', all these 'transferences' are based on some intrinsic characteristic of the object, the 'human world' ceases to be a metaphor and becomes once more what it really is, the seat and as it were the *homeland* of our thoughts. (*PP*, p. 24)

Here, as elsewhere, Merleau-Ponty is inclined to insist that what objective thought regards as metaphorical should instead be taken as literally true of the lived world; and to deny that it is only what the objectivist deems literal that can be truly ascribed to it. Indeed the reader of the *Phenomenology of Perception* is bound to be struck by the frequency with which, as in the passage just quoted, crucial philosophical claims are themselves presented by Merleau-Ponty in what would generally be seen as metaphorical language. His defence of this practice might be that it is the only way in which they can be appropriately expressed.

However, objective thought's willingness to deny the reality of various kinds of (merely) apparent properties may itself seem to pose a problem for Merleau-Ponty. His main aim, in criticizing objective thought, is to demonstrate how it systematically misrepresents the character of the lived world. But the advocate of objective thought might reply to this in the following way. To the extent that the character of the experienced world differs from that of the universe, this should be taken to indicate the inadequacy of perceptual experience as a straightforward guide to the nature of the real world. The 'lived' world is, after all, only the world *as experienced*; and one should not assume that human perception, taken 'at face value', gives one direct and unchallengeable access to reality. Rather, one must be aware of the possibility of systematic misperception, as displayed in the tendency towards various kinds of anthropomorphism, projection, and so on. In other words, objective thought need not present itself as providing a description of how one in fact experiences the world, but 'only' of what its character actually is; and hence it cannot be directly criticized in the way that Merleau-Ponty apparently thinks legitimate.

Merleau-Ponty does not explicitly address this possible response. But he would no doubt argue that the objectivist, in thus relying upon a distinction between the world as perceived and the world as it is, is thereby obliged to provide some (explanatory or reconstructive) account of the former, and of how it is that this supposedly distorted perception of the world occurs. But no such account can, in Merleau-Ponty's view, be given; and one may regard his criticisms of empiricist and intellectualist approaches to perception as, at least implicitly, intended also to meet this objectivist response.[8]

3 Empiricism and Intellectualism

The account we have given of Merleau-Ponty's conception of objective thought draws mainly on the substantial Introduction to the *Phenomenology of Perception*, 'Traditional Prejudices and the Return to the Phenomena'. Here Merleau-Ponty criticizes empiricist and intellectualist approaches to perception, both because of their shared acceptance of objective thought, and for reasons peculiar to each of them. He returns to this critical task more extensively in Part Two, 'The World as Perceived'; and we shall discuss this in Chapter Seven below. But we shall now look briefly at his specific criticisms of empiricism and intellectualism in the Introduction, to provide a fuller sense than has so far been given of how he conceives of these two approaches.

The empiricist account of perception, says Merleau-Ponty, has two main elements. First, it takes as the basic unit of perceptual experience what it calls the 'sensation'.[9] Second, it identifies various mechanisms through which these sensations are combined so as to generate one's actual perception of the world. In the opening two chapters of the Introduction, he criticizes each in turn. Noting that several different definitions of 'sensation' have been employed by empiricists, he focuses mainly on those according to which the experience of particular colours, shapes and sounds are typical cases. Each such sensation is regarded as corresponding to, and indeed as being produced by, the specific physical stimuli or sets of stimuli through which external objects impinge upon the sense-organs. For example, the pattern of retinal stimulation caused by light of a certain wave-length being reflected from an object might be said to produce the 'sensation' of redness. That there is always some such regular causal relationship between external stimuli and sensations Merleau-Ponty calls 'the constancy hypothesis' (*PP*, pp. 7–8).

Merleau-Ponty's main objection to this concept of sensation is that, if one examines one's actual experience, it will be found that one never in fact encounters anything that could be correctly described in this way. For example (*PP*, pp. 4–5) one might see a red patch on the carpet; but this does not involve the experiencing of any pure sensation of redness. Rather, the colour is seen as a feature of (that part of) the carpet, as one aspect of a total configuration which includes the play of light and shadows, the size and shape of the patch, the texture of the carpet, and so on.

Furthermore, says Merleau-Ponty, the empiricist cannot reply to this by saying that what is going on here is the simultaneous experiencing of a number of distinct sensations, including the colour amongst others. For what is perceived is a 'whole' which is not thus decomposable into discrete parts. Instead, he claims, these parts are not fully separable from one another. The specific character of each is influenced at least to some extent by its relations with the others in constituting this particular whole. So, for example, 'this red would literally not be the same if it were not the "woolly red" of the carpet' (*PP*, p. 5): its colour and texture are not altogether distinguishable from one other.

Merleau-Ponty goes on to argue that the empiricist cannot explain how it is that, in perceiving a particular object – such as a tree or a bicycle – one sees its various features as 'belonging together', as forming a unity which makes the object distinct from its background, including other objects (*PP*, pp. 15–16). This cannot be due to any corresponding 'grouping' of the various external stimuli supposedly operating at the time one is perceiving the object – i.e. the relative physical proximity to one another of those stimuli (or their sources) responsible for seeing the objects, as distinct from those responsible for seeing its background. For there will often be features of an object which are less close to one another than they are to features of its background – of what is not seen as 'belonging' to it.

The empiricist, according to Merleau-Ponty, must try to deal with this problem by invoking, in addition, the effects of one's past experience. This introduces the second main element of the empiricist account, its theory of 'associations' between sensations, and of the 'projection of memories'. For example, says Merleau-Ponty, the empiricist may try to explain the perceived unity of an object's features by claiming that this object, or another of the same kind, has often in the past been seen in motion. Whilst moving, its various features 'kept together', unlike its non-moving background, and thereby became associated with one another. When the object is now perceived stationary, the memory of this past association is recalled, and 'projected' onto the present situation.

But, argues Merleau-Ponty, such explanations inevitably beg the question. For how is the perceiver to 'know' *which* are the relevant memories or associations to rely upon? To perceive, for example, the unity of a mountain – an object which is, in any case, itself always stationary – it must somehow remind one of similar objects whose features were previously seen to stay together. This would require one to recognize the mountain as the same (kind of) thing as that which displayed such unity in the past. However, if such recognition is possible, the recourse to past associations is redundant; for one must already be able to perceive those features as belonging to an object of that kind. If, on the other hand, such recognition is not possible, then there is no guarantee that the past associations would be the 'right' ones, that is, ones whose projected memory will cause one to see the object's unity: to summon up the appropriate memory would be quite fortuitous.

As Merleau-Ponty acknowledges, these kinds of objections to empiricism have often been made by intellectualists. Having implicitly endorsed these objections, however, he goes on in the second two chapters of the Introduction to criticize the intellectualists' positive account of perception. Like its empiricist rival, this has two main elements. The first is the concept of sensation; but the intellectualist claims, in opposition to empiricism, that sensations are never themselves directly experienced. Instead, it is argued, what is actually perceived is always the outcome of an interpretive process, in which various rules or principles are applied to the raw material provided by sensations. More specifically, perception is said necessarily to involve some act of *judgement* on the part of the perceiving subject; and it is this idea of judgement which forms the second main element of the intellectualist account of perception.

By 'judgement', says Merleau-Ponty, the intellectualist means something akin to a process of reasoning. As such it requires both premisses, which are provided by the sensations, and rules or principles of inference, which are provided by the cognitive equipment of the perceiving subject. The conclusion of this process of reasoning is the act of perception itself. Hence, for example, the intellectualist will account for one's perception of a (unitary) object, with its properties 'belonging' to it, as the outcome of an exercise of judgement, in which various pre-established rules or conceptual schemata defining the unity of objects are applied to the interpretation of bare sensations.

Merleau-Ponty regards this intellectualist approach as in many respects superior to empiricism. It rightly emphasizes the active role of the perceiving subject; and it succeeds, at least in its own terms, in accounting for the unitary character of perceived objects, which empiricism was unable to do. But intellectualism is nonetheless unsatisfactory. Its view of the part played by judgement misrepresents what it is actually like to perceive something. And it shares with empiricism the objectivist misdescription of the perceived world, an error which also affects adversely its conception of the subject. Let us consider these criticisms in more detail.

Merleau-Ponty begins by noting how the function ascribed by intellectualism to judgement is essentially defined by its complementary relationship to sensation. 'Judgement', as he puts it, 'is often introduced as *what sensation lacks to make perception possible*' (*PP*, p. 32). But since the concept of sensation is itself, in Merleau-Ponty's view, entirely without foundation, there is no such 'gap' between sensation and perception needing to be filled by judgement. Thus, although intellectualism is to be applauded for recognizing that perception is never a matter of pure sensation, it remains 'haunted' by this empiricist concept – a prejudice that should be removed altogether, and not merely compensated by the introduction of another.

By assimilating perception to judgement, says Merleau-Ponty, the intellectualist conflates what are, in fact, two quite distinct activities:

> ordinary experience draws a clear distinction between sense experience [i.e. perception] and judgment. It sees judgment as the taking of a stand, as an effort to know something which shall be valid for every moment of my life, and equally for other actual or potential minds; sense experience on the contrary, is taking appearance at its face value, without trying to possess it and learn its truth. This distinction disappears in intellectualism, because judgment is everywhere where pure sensation is not – that is, absolutely everywhere. (*PP*, p. 34)

Perception and judgement, says Merleau-Ponty, are clearly distinguishable kinds of activity: to see something in front of one, for example, is quite different from making the judgement that it is there. In the latter case, one is making a claim about the object's existence and location, at least potentially supportable by reasons that will justify its validity to others. In the former case, one simply experiences the object as there, as visually present: one 'takes its appearance at face value'. Thus the intellectualist misrepresents what it is like to perceive something.

However, Merleau-Ponty concedes that this objection may hold only against a philosophically unsophisticated form of intellectualism, which conceives of judgement as an actual mental operation performed by the human perceiver (*PP*, pp. 36–8).[10] But intellectualism need not take this 'psychologistic' form. Instead it may regard its primary task as the identification of a set of formally specifiable rules which 'make perception possible' in that they enable one to reconstruct the basic character of the objects perceived. These rules, or knowledge of them, are then ascribed to a transcendental consciousness which can thus be thought of as possessing object-constitutive powers. There is no implication here that human perceivers literally *apply* such rules, and *make* judgements, either consciously or unconsciously: no attempt is being made to provide a psychological description of what is involved in the experience of perceiving something.

But, says Merleau-Ponty, this form of intellectualism suffers from the fact that, like empiricism, it accepts an objectivist view of what the world is like; and this, as we have already seen, in his view misrepresents the nature of what is actually experienced. Thus intellectualism succeeds only in reconstructing the 'wrong' world, the universe of objective thought. As Merleau-Ponty puts it, commenting on the transition from empiricist to intellectualist accounts of perception,

We started from a world in itself which acted upon our eyes so as to cause us to see it, and we now have consciousness of or thought about the world, but the nature of this world remains unchanged: it is still defined by the absolute mutual exteriority of its parts, and is merely duplicated throughout its extent by a thought which sustains it. We pass from absolute objectivity to absolute subjectivity, but this second idea is no better than the first, and is upheld only against it, which means by it. (*PP*, p. 39)

Furthermore, he argues, this prejudice of objective thought also affects adversely intellectualism's conception of the subject. For the nature of the perceived world is such that it cannot be fully and explicitly articulated. Analytical reconstruction of this world is impossible: its character cannot be understood by reference to any formally specifiable set of rules. Correspondingly, therefore, any account of the subject which defines it in terms of such rules – and attempts thereby to explain how knowledge or consciousness of 'the world' is possible – must be seriously flawed (*PP*, p. 60).

We can now go on to consider in more general terms how Merleau-Ponty conceives of empiricism and intellectualism. Let us start with the former. In the opening section of this chapter we initially defined the empiricist approach as one that sought to discover scientific, causal explanations for human action and perception. But it can now be seen that, at least in the case of perception, Merleau-Ponty's conception of empiricism is more restricted than this might lead one to expect, since it involves a quite limited range of possible explanations which refer only to external (physical) stimuli, their effects upon the sense-organs, sensations, the mechanisms of association and memory, and suchlike.

The empiricist account of perception, then, presents it as a relatively passive and mechanical affair, in which the mental processes involved are of a somewhat primitive variety. It is, perhaps, most obviously recognizable as the kind of account provided by philosophers who have traditionally been called 'empiricists', such as Locke, Hume and Mill. But Merleau-Ponty does not primarily mean by 'empiricism' the epistemological thesis that all human knowledge is based upon, or derived from, sensory perception. Rather he uses this term to refer to the account of perception which has, on the whole, been espoused by these philosophers, and which has also been a major influence in the history of psychology. Indeed, most of the 'empiricist' writers cited in the *Phenomenology of Perception* are psychologists or physiologists, not philosophers; nor are they committed, at least explicitly, to specific philosophical standpoints, epistemological or otherwise.[11]

But empiricism is not confined in scope to the explanation of human perception. It also, for Merleau-Ponty, involves an analogous approach to the understanding of human *action*. Here the paradigmatic examples of empiricism are the various forms of behaviourist psychology – with their theories of learning based on the concepts of stimulus, response, conditioning, and so on – together with the correspondingly 'mechanistic' traditions of physiology and neurophysiology. Empiricist explanations of human action are not, however, exclusively materialist in character: some role may often be ascribed to distinctively 'mental' events and processes. But, as with the empiricist approach to perception, these psychological items will typically be of a fairly simple kind: sensations of heat or cold, feelings of pain or pleasure, desires for food or sexual gratification, emotions of fear or anger, and the like.[12]

By contrast with empiricism, the intellectualist regards both perception and action as the work of a human subject endowed with a wide range of cognitive powers. We have already noted how the intellectualist ascribes to the perceiver various rules or principles which enable bare sensations to be transformed into the perception of unitary objects through the exercise of judgement. Analogously, in the case of action, the intellectualist will try to identify the various plans, rules and purposes of the human agent. Thus reference will be made to processes of planning and deliberation, to the following of various rules and principles, to the adoption of specific aims and goals, to acts of choice and decision, and so on. Human action is above all 'intelligent' action; and intelligent action, like perception, is an achievement involving the exercise of sophisticated cognitive abilities. Correspondingly, therefore, the aim of an intellectualist analysis is to reconstruct these achievements, to show how they are possible, by identifying the conceptual resources of the subject and their specific modes of employment.

It may also be helpful to note, in explicating what Merleau-Ponty means by 'intellectualism', that he sometimes uses instead the term 'rationalism', and draws upon the work of philosophers traditionally described as rationalists – such as Descartes, Leibniz and Spinoza, as well as Kant – to provide examples of intellectualist analyses. However, as with empiricism, his primary interest in rationalism is not in its epistemological thesis that there is a priori, non-empirical knowledge of the world, but rather in the ways that rationalist philosophers have characterized the various cognitive processes supposedly involved in human activity. Relatedly, many of the writers he cites as intellectualists are not philosophers, but psychologists of a broadly 'cognitivist' orientation – including Piaget – whose work has been directly or indirectly influenced by the rationalist tradition in philosophy.[13]

To conclude this discussion of Merleau-Ponty's conceptions of empiricism and intellectualism we shall note certain problems about the distinctions between them, and about their respective relationships to realism and idealism. The first such problem is raised by the rather limited and simplistic character of the kinds of explanations which he attributes to empiricism. For it might be argued that, even if Merleau-Ponty succeeds in showing that 'the empiricist' cannot satisfactorily explain human action and perception, it would not follow that *no* kind of scientific, causal explanation can be provided for these. Perhaps there are others, of a more sophisticated theoretical nature than those he allows to the empiricist? Such possibilities are presumably important if Merleau-Ponty's aim, in criticizing empiricism, is to demonstrate what is wrong with any 'scientific' form of realism.

Merleau-Ponty might respond to this by saying that these supposedly more sophisticated 'explanations' would probably involve reference to the kinds of mental processes identified by those whom he presents as intellectualists; and that his criticisms of intellectualist 'reconstructions' would still apply, even if they were instead regarded as belonging to a more sophisticated form of 'scientific' empiricism. (Indeed, many of the intellectualist psychologists he discusses may well have seen their work as strictly scientific, as attempting to provide genuinely causal explanations for human perception and action.)

However, this response may indicate a further problem. If intellectualist psychology is 'scientific', how can Merleau-Ponty make use of its supposed failings so as to demonstrate the untenability of transcendental idealism, as he apparently wishes to do (see section 1, above)? For, according to the idealist, the mental processes of human beings are themselves part of the world which is constituted as such by a non-worldly transcendental subject. And it might seem odd to believe that a philosophical theory about the transcendental subject can be defeated by revealing the shortcomings of merely psychological theories about (worldly) human subjects. But Merleau-Ponty clearly does not think so. In his view, any deficiencies in a psychological theory of the human subject 'carry over' to its transcendental counterpart; and hence the critique of intellectualist psychology would indeed entail a corresponding critique of transcendental idealism.[14]

4   The Dialectical Critique of Realism and Idealism

In the opening section of this chapter we described how the concepts of empiricism, intellectualism and objective thought function in Merleau-Ponty's overall critical strategy. Having examined these concepts in more detail, we can now elaborate our initial account of this. We will begin by noting a basic pattern to which most of the *Phenomenology of Perception*'s individual chapters, or sequence of chapters, conform. This pattern, as will be seen, is by no means a matter of mere presentation. It also indicates the 'dialectical' character of Merleau-Ponty's mode of argument; and by attending to this we can identify in outline the existential phenomenological position for which he is arguing.

Merleau-Ponty typically starts by presenting a possible empiricist explanation for some phenomenon involving human perception or action, often taken from the work of psychologists or physiologists. He then argues that this scientific hypothesis fails to meet the empiricist's own criteria for explanatory adequacy; and in doing so he sometimes makes use of objections which have been advanced by intellectualist critics of empiricism. Next, he outlines an intellectualist alternative, which is in turn criticized on the grounds that the proposed reconstruction does not deal with the actual character of the phenomenon, and that it misrepresents the role of the human subject. He concludes by proposing his own, existential-phenomenological analysis of the phenomenon, which is informed by the nature of his objections to the empiricist's and intellectualist's rival accounts.

This basic pattern also displays a number of additional features. The first concerns objective thought. Both empiricism and intellectualism are criticized for their objectivist misdescriptions of the phenomena. But Merleau-Ponty is inclined to argue that, whilst empiricist explanations would fail even for an objective universe, intellectualist reconstructions might well succeed. The victory is, of course, a hollow one; and he maintains that neither can account for the phenomena correctly described. Further, he often suggests that the difficulties actually encountered by the empiricist in attempting to explain the phenomena are due precisely to their non-objective character which, whilst not acknowledged because of the prejudice of objective thought, nonetheless makes its presence felt to the empiricist in this unwelcome manner.

Second, Merleau-Ponty rarely if ever claims to have provided a strictly conclusive refutation of either empiricist or intellectualist accounts of any phenomenon. Indeed at times he implies that this would not be possible (e.g. *PP*, p. 8, note 5). Instead he tries to show the difficulties which every particular application of either approach seems constantly to encounter; and how each attempt to modify these to deal with a specific problem seems always to generate yet more problems of its own. It is partly for this reason that Merleau-Ponty's arguments in the *Phenomenology of Perception* may often appear to be repetitive – similar objections and criticisms are made time and again. But this is because such 'repetition' is, in his view, the only way in which the failure of empiricism and intellectualism can be shown. Thus, borrowing the terminology more recently introduced in the philosophy of science by Imre Lakatos, one could say that, for Merleau-Ponty, empiricism and intellectualism are two competing 'research programmes' for understanding human perception and action; and whilst neither can be conclusively refuted, both are clearly 'degenerating' rather than 'progressing'. To retain their respective 'hard cores' in the face of counter-evidence, they become increasingly complex and unwieldy, and thereby unpersuasive.[15]

The third feature is this. Whilst Merleau-Ponty is critical of both empiricism and intellectualism, he does not wish to reject either of them altogether. Each has something positive to offer, which is therefore to be preserved, albeit in a significantly modified form, by existential phenomenology. This is more obviously so in the case of intellectualism. For example, Merleau-Ponty is sympathetic to its emphasis upon the active role of the human subject in perception, though not to the kind of consciousness ascribed to it; and he likewise agrees with the intellectualist's view of the purposive, intentional nature of human action, whilst rejecting its unduly cognitive, deliberative characterization. But it is also true, though to a lesser extent, in the case of empiricism. For example, he regards it as a virtue of empiricist approaches to perception that they emphasize the distinctive contributions made by each of the human senses, despite their objectivist prejudices concerning these; and he argues that empiricist explanations of action at least have the merit of recognizing its dependence on the agent's bodily organization, despite misinterpreting the nature of this dependence.

Thus Merleau-Ponty's attitude towards the mutually opposing programmes of empiricism and intellectualism is by no means wholly negative. Rather, he might be said to proceed in a manner that resembles the 'dialectical' character of a Hegelian critique.[16] Existential phenomenology 'overcomes' (or 'transcends') the opposition between the two. In doing so it rejects certain elements of each, whilst preserving others which are then reintegrated in a way that partly alters their previous nature. Admittedly, Merleau-Ponty never declares his allegiance to this mode of critique. But we shall implicitly take it as a model in now outlining some of the main elements in the positive position for which he argues.

Merleau-Ponty's strategy, we have claimed, is to show that neither realism nor idealism are defensible, by demonstrating the inadequacies of both empiricist explanations and intellectualist reconstructions. So let us now focus more specifically on the competing philosophical standpoints of realism and idealism themselves. The fundamental disagreement between them concerns the ontological status of 'the real world'. The idealist claims that this is somehow constituted as such by a transcendental subject; whilst the realist denies this, maintaining instead that this world exists in its own right, independently of one's knowledge of it, and including within it those beings who are able to acquire such knowledge. This disagreement may be represented, as it often has been, by saying that, whereas for the idealist there is a radical dichotomy between the 'subject' and 'object' of knowledge, no such dichotomy is accepted by the realist, for whom, as it were, everything belongs to the category of 'object'.

In the terms of this admittedly crude formulation, we can express Merleau-Ponty's own position in the following way. He accepts that there is some significant differentiation between subject and object – between, as he sometimes puts it, the 'for-itself' and the 'in-itself'; but he rejects the idealist understanding of the distinction. This is partly because the world, for Merleau-Ponty, is less 'object-like' than either realists or idealists maintain: it is not the universe of objective thought. But it is also because he denies the transcendental status of the idealist's subject. The 'true' subject is a *human* subject; and whilst this subject cannot be regarded simply as belonging to the world along with other objects, as realism claims, neither can it be seen as wholly prior to, as somehow the source or origin of, the world of objects.[17] The human subject cannot be conceived of independently of its relationships to the world, nor vice versa: it is, in that much used existentialist phrase, a 'being-in-the-world'. Furthermore, for Merleau-Ponty the primary mode of such 'being-in' is a *practical* one: it is not a cognitive relationship of 'thinking of' or 'being conscious of' the world.

Merleau-Ponty indicates his commitment to a position of this kind at several points in the Preface. For example, in the following passage he refers to Augustine's famous dictum (which had been quoted approvingly by Husserl at the very end of the *Cartesian Meditations*) – 'Go back into yourself; truth inhabits ['dwells in'] the inner man' – and claims that this is not the correct alternative to realism:

> Truth does not 'inhabit' only 'the inner man', or more accurately, there is no inner man, man is in the world, and only in the world does he know himself. When I return to myself from an excursion into the realm of dogmatic common sense or of science, I find, not a source of intrinsic truth, but a subject destined to the world [*voue au monde*]. (*PP*, p. xi)

And a little later on, discussing Husserl's view of philosophical reflection (the '*Cogito*') and its relationship to Descartes' concept of 'meditation', he rejects the idea that this leads one to recognize a transcendental, conscious subject:

> The true *Cogito* does not define the subject's existence in terms of the thought he has of existing, and furthermore does not convert the indubitability of the world into the indubitability of thought about the world, nor finally does it replace the world itself by the world as meaning. On the contrary it recognizes my thought itself as an inalienable fact, and does away with any kind of idealism in revealing me as 'being-in-the world' [*être au monde*]. (*PP*, p. xiii)

Both these passages raise, amongst others, important questions about Merleau-Ponty's relationship to Husserl. But before commenting on this, some further content can be given to this rather bare description of Merleau-Ponty's existential phenomenology by introducing what is arguably its central and philosophically most striking component, its conception of the *human body*. In Part One of the *Phenomenology of Perception*, 'The Body', he argues not only that this is not an 'object' (as defined by objective thought, and as both empiricists and intellectualists assume), but that it should instead be understood as a 'subject': more specifically, as the subject of action ('in-the-world'). But its subjectivity is not of the kind envisaged by intellectualists or idealists. In particular, although like the intellectualist's subject it possesses both knowledge and intentionality, it does so in an essentially practical and 'pre-conscious' form.[18]

We shall discuss these claims in the following chapter. In chapter Seven we go on to consider Part Two of the *Phenomenonology of Perception*, 'The World as Perceived', in which Merleau-Ponty returns to the question of perception, initially addressed in the Introduction. He attends both to the nature of what is perceived, insisting upon its non-objective character, and also to that of the perceiving subject. Here too the body is ascribed a central role; and intellectualism is criticized for being unable, amongst other things, to account for the 'fact' that one perceives with one's eyes, ears and other sense-organs. Further, Merleau-Ponty develops here a view of the 'strictly bilateral' character of the relationship between the subject and object of perception, as an alternative both to realism and to idealism.

Thus one can begin to see how the concept of the 'body-subject' operates in the *Phenomenology of Perception* as the means by which, as we put it earlier, the opposition between realism and idealism can be 'overcome' – 'transcended', in the Hegelian sense. And, on the face of it, this view of the subject involves a major departure from Husserl's conception of phenomenology, at least in the *Cartesian Meditations*. But Merleau-Ponty's relationship to Husserl is more complex than this would suggest, for at least two reasons. First, there is Merleau-Ponty's tendency always to present himself as a 'true Husserlian', as working within the 'spirit' of Husserl's phenomenology. This is expressed, amongst other ways, in his attempt to interpret the key concepts of reduction, essence and intentionality in a manner that minimizes any apparent disagreement with Husserl.

Second, and more importantly, there is the fact that Merleau-Ponty's view of Husserl's phenomenology was strongly influenced by his reading of the material later published as *The Crisis*, where a number of significantly new elements were introduced into Husserl's work. Amongst these was the rejection of 'scientific', objectivist, conceptions of the human body. So in the next chapter, before examining Merleau-Ponty's own account of the body, we shall look first at *The Crisis* and at its philosophical relationship to the *Phenomenology of Perception*.

6

The Body as Subject

1 Galilean Science and the Life-World

In Part I of *The Crisis*, as we noted in section 3 of our Introduction, Husserl considers the nature of what he took to be a (then) contemporary cultural crisis: the collapse of faith in the sciences, and the flight into various forms of irrationalism. He offers a diagnosis for this crisis by sketching its origins in the historical development of philosophy and its relationship to the empirical sciences.

At the time of the Renaissance, claims Husserl, there had re-emerged in Europe an ancient Greek ideal of philosophy as a universal science, which was based on a view of humans as rational and autonomous beings, and according to which

> Sciences in the plural, all those sciences ever to be established or already under construction, are but dependent branches of the One Philosophy. (*CES*, p. 8)

But this ideal was never to be realized. Instead, says Husserl, the concept of science – of genuine, rationally grounded human knowledge – came increasingly to be identified only with the empirical sciences: with physics, chemistry, psychology, sociology, and so on.[1] These 'positive' sciences restrict themselves to 'establishing what the world, the physical as well as the spiritual world, is in fact'; and

> their rigorous scientific character requires, we are told, that the scholar carefully exclude all valuative positions, all questions of the reason or unreason of their human subject matter and its cultural configurations. (*CES*, p. 6)

Yet these normative, evaluative questions still demand answers. The empirical sciences could not provide them. So, given the identification of rational human knowledge with these sciences, recourse could be had only to irrationalist solutions – hence, the cultural crisis.

According to Husserl, the first and crucial episode in this historical failure of the Renaissance ideal of a universal philosophy was the emergence of 'modern', Galilean science – or rather, the philosophical misunderstanding of the implications of this science, a misunderstanding to which Galileo himself, and then Descartes, significantly contributed. It is this thesis which Husserl is concerned to establish in Part II of *The Crisis*. Galileo's great achievement, he says, was both to conceive and to implement 'the completely new idea of *mathematical natural science*' (*CES*, pp. 22–3). Such a science aims to discover laws of nature which can be expressed in the form of mathematically specified functional relationships between measurable variables – such as the laws for pendular motion and the free fall of bodies. But Galileo's equally great mistake, argues Husserl, was to claim that the only real properties of objects were those which could be directly represented by those variables, namely shape, size, position, and so on. All other properties, such as colour, taste and smell, were only apparent: they were the subjective effects of the real properties of things acting upon the perceiver's senses.

Husserl rejects this identification of the 'real' world with the mathematized nature of Galilean science, and the consequent relegation of what he calls the 'life-world' ('*Lebenswelt*' – the world as it is experienced in everyday, pre-scientific, life) to the status of mere subjective appearance.[2] He argues that the main reason for Galileo's philosophical error here – which was soon to be reproduced and amplified in Descartes' dualism of body and mind – was his failure to recognize that the concepts employed in the new science were themselves formed through abstraction and idealization from the life-world. As such, in Husserl's view, they should properly be regarded only as conceptual devices, by means of which more refined and successful predictions about that world can be made. Instead, Galileo both reified these conceptual contructs, and subjectivized the life-world. Husserl describes this error as involving

> the surreptitious substitution of the mathematically substructed world of idealities for the only real world, the one that is actually given through perception, that is ever experienced and experienceable – our everyday life-world. (*CES*, pp. 48–9)

In thus affirming the 'reality' of the life-world, however, and its ontological primacy with respect to the scientific world, Husserl is not abandoning the transcendental standpoint of his earliest work. He is not, that is, defending some form of common-sense realism against scientific realism. That this is so becomes clear in Part III, where Husserl provides an extensive introduction to transcendental phenomenology, including reference to its eidetic stage (cf. Chapter Three, sections 2 and 3). But in the light of his preceding criticisms of the philosophical misinterpretation on Galilean science, he is especially concerned to ensure that, before performing the transcendental reduction, one has arrived first at a proper characterization of the life-world. In particular, one must carefully avoid the assumption that the concepts of the empirical sciences describe it correctly: for example, those of orthodox psychology with its prejudices of Cartesian dualism. Only when the scientific conceptualization of the world has, in a certain sense, been 'suspended', and its origins through abstraction from the life-world identified, can the transcendental reduction of the latter proceed (see especially *CES*, sections 34–41).

We shall now examine in more detail Husserl's discussion of Galilean science in Part II of *The Crisis*. In constructing the new mathematical physics, says Husserl, Galileo took over from the Greeks their development of a 'pure geometry of shapes': 'pure' in the sense that it dealt, not with the actual, concrete shapes of things which one encounters in the everyday world, but rather with various idealized forms of these – 'perfectly' straight lines, circles, squares, and so on (*CES*, pp. 22–8). Further, this pure geometry was soon to be greatly extended in scope with the development of analytical geometry. In this, algebraic equations could be formulated to specify all possible pure geometrical shapes, unlike the pre-algebraic geometry, which could deal only with a small subset of these.

What Galileo ignored, argues Husserl, was that the concepts of this pure geometry had themselves been initially constructed by a process of idealization from the shapes experienced in the life-world. One never actually encounters, for example, a 'perfect' or 'ideal' circle, but only objects which are, as it were, more or less circular. Galileo likewise ignored the fact that this pure geometry, with its idealized shapes, had itself been developed in specific practical contexts: in particular, as an aid to such activities as building and surveying. This pure geometry provided a set of conceptual techniques and methods for dealing more effectively with the everyday world: its idealized concepts had an exclusively instrumental status. Yet Galileo failed to recognize this, and instead believed that nature itself was characterized by these pure, mathematically representable properties.

But a more significant mistake was to come, says Husserl. The objects encountered in the life-world possess not only the properties of (impure) shape, the so-called primary properties, with respect to which the pure shapes of geometry are idealizations; but also the 'secondary' properties, such as colour, sound, taste, warmth, coldness, and so on. Husserl refers to these as the 'specific sense-qualities' (e.g. *CES*, p. 54). The latter properties could not, it seemed to Galileo, be *directly* mathematized. In the case, for instance, of colours, there was no equivalent to the geometry of pure shapes which could stand in the same relationship to 'impure colours' as geometry stood in relation to impure shapes. Nonetheless, suggested Galileo, these properties could be indirectly mathematized, by hypothesizing that they are in some way systematically related to the primary properties:

everything which manifests itself as real through the specific sense-qualities [secondary properties] must have its *mathematical index* in events belonging to the sphere of shapes [primary properties] – which is, of course, already thought of as idealized. (*CES*, p. 37)

What Galileo proposed, then, according to Husserl, was the existence of systematic relationships between primary and secondary properties, such that the latter could be explained by reference to the former, and hence by a mathematical physics which was itself couched exclusively in terms of the geometrical properties of pure shapes. The actual nature of these relationships was not yet known: their discovery was to form part of science's future programme. But Galileo did not doubt that success would be forthcoming; and in a certain way, says Husserl, he was right. For one now accepts quite easily such claims as the following:

What we experienced, in pre-scientific life, as colours, tones, warmth and weight belonging to the things themselves ... indicates in terms of physics, of course, tone-vibrations, warmth-vibrations, i.e. pure events in the world of shapes. (*CES*, p. 36)

Husserl has no objection to such scientific hypotheses, provided that their philosophical status and implications are properly understood. He would not wish to deny, for example (ours, not his), that it may be possible to 'explain' colour-perception by reference to the mathematically specifiable properties of light waves. But he insists that any such explanation must only be regarded as providing a conceptual technique or method for making predictions about the perception of colour; and hence that such explanations provide no grounds for denying the reality of colour itself as a feature of objects in the life-world.

Husserl, in effect, adopts here what is often called an 'instrumentalist' view of the status of science's theoretical concepts and laws, and criticizes Galileo for failing to do so.[3] Instead, Galileo not only ascribed reality to the idealized geometrical concepts of pure shape, but maintained that the only properties which genuinely belonged to nature were those represented by the laws of mathematical physics. Hence, as we noted earlier, Husserl accuses Galileo of substituting 'the mathematically substructed world of idealities for the only real world' (*CES*, pp. 48–9); and he characterizes this error as one in which

we take for *true being* what is actually a *method* – a method which is designed for the purpose of progressively improving, *in infinitum*, through 'scientific' predictions, those rough predictions which are the only ones originally possible within the sphere of what is actually experienced and experienceable in the life-world. (*CES*, pp. 51–2)

Having denied the reality of secondary properties on the grounds that they do not belong to the mathematized view of nature in his new science, says Husserl, Galileo was forced to give them an alternative philosophical status. He did so by relocating them within the mind of the human perceiver: colour, taste, and so on, were merely subjective experiences, the effects in the perceiver's mind of the real world of physical bodies operating upon the human sense-organs. But it was soon realized by other philosophers, continues Husserl, that there was no good reason to restrict this subjectivization to the secondary properties alone. Rather, it could easily be extended in the form of a more general dichotomy between 'inner experience' – including all perceptual experience, whether of primary or secondary properties – and the 'outer world' of material objects, as depicted by the physical sciences.[4]

What resulted, then, from this Galilean trajectory was a duality of subjective experience and objective nature, the empirical sciences having a privileged position in identifying the character of the latter, which could then be used to explain the former. The reality of the life-world was thus displaced by that of the scientific world, and transformed into a dependent realm of psychological experience, of mere 'phenomena' or 'appearances'. According to this view, says Husserl:

> The phenomena are only in the subjects: they are there only as causal results of events taking place in true nature, which events exist only with mathematical properties. If the intuited world of our life is merely subjective, then all the truths of pre- and extrascientific life which have to do with its factual being are deprived of value. They have meaning only insofar as they, while themselves false, vaguely indicate an in-itself which lies behind this world of possible experience and is transcendent in respect to it. (*CES*, p. 54)

Thus:

> The world splits, as it were, into two worlds: nature and the psychic world, although the latter, because of the way in which it is related to nature [i.e. exclusively as its effect], does not achieve the status of an independent world. (*CES*, p. 60)

This split between nature and the psychic world, says Husserl, found a particularly clear and historically influential expression in Descartes' philosophy. The dichotomy between *res cogitans* and *res extensa* served both to separate humans, as conscious beings, from the rest of the world, and to provide a dualistic picture of each human being as a union of mind and body. In the following section we shall compare Husserl's view of Descartes in *The Crisis*, with his earlier view of him in the *Cartesian Meditations* (see Chapter One, section 4). This will then enable us to explore the significance of *The Crisis* for Merleau-Ponty's relationship to Husserl.

2   Cartesian Dualism and the Galilean Body

In the *Cartesian Meditations*, Descartes is criticized primarily for his realism: for failing to follow through the supposedly transcendentalist implications of his self-reflective philosophical method, and instead identifying the meditating Ego with the 'worldly' *res cogitans*. In *The Crisis*, this criticism of Descartes is repeated in much the same terms (*CES*, sections 17–19). What is distinctive about Husserl's later treatment of Descartes is not that his previous objections disappear, but that there is now an additional set of objections, not to be found in the *Cartesian Meditations*. In effect, this further criticism is addressed to the specific form of Descartes' supposed realism, namely as (Galilean) *scientific* realism; and in Husserl's view this gives rise, amongst other things, to a mischaracterization of the human body. Descartes, he argues, wrongly assumed that this is the physical 'body' of Galilean science. But the human body belongs to the life-world, which for Husserl differs significantly from the scientific 'world'.

Let us consider this additional line of criticism in more detail. In the *Cartesian Meditations*, Husserl implicitly accepts that both the empirical sciences and everyday life relate directly to one and the same world (*CM*, section 7: see Chapter One, section 3, above). Thus the phenomenological epoché suspends 'at a single stroke' the existence-assumptions of both, since they are taken to be the same. In *The Crisis*, by contrast, the relationship between the life-world and the scientific 'world' becomes problematized; and the phenomenological epoché comes into operation upon the life-world only after a preceding stage of analysis in which it has been rescued from scientific misrepresentation.

Descartes' dualistic ontology, argues Husserl, was based not on a proper description of the life-world, but rather on a philosophically illicit endorsement of the conception of nature provided by modern science. Thus, in identifying the reflecting Ego with the *res cogitans*, a double error was committed. Not only was the Ego's transcendental status denied; but it was also assigned to an ontological category – that of the mental – which had been constructed partly to accommodate what had wrongly been removed from the life-world. Correspondingly, the body with which this mind was said to be united was not the body as actually experienced in everyday life, but the 'scientific' body of Galileo's mathematized nature.

The 'bodies' which one encounters in the life-world, says Husserl, are of a number of different kinds. They include, for example (ours, not his), inorganic entities such as rocks or stones; human artefacts such as buildings or tools; and the bodies of various organic entities, such as animals and human beings. Whilst all such bodies may have in common the properties of Galilean bodies (albeit, as noted earlier, in an 'impure' form), their full range of properties consists by no means exclusively of these. Furthermore, he argues, each human being has an especially significant and distinctive acquaintance with their *own* body, which displays features entirely ignored in Descartes' assumption that the human body is, like any other, Galilean.

Husserl marks the distinction between the physical-geometrical body and the body of an animal or human by his respective use of the two terms '*Körper*' and '*Leib*' (the latter related to '*Leben*', to live). This distinction is initially alluded to in Part II (*CES*, p. 50), and then explored more fully in Part III (especially sections 28 and 62). In particular, he attends to the kinds of experience one has of one's own body, and its significant role in one's engagement with the life-world. Amongst many claims here, the following may be noted.

First, Husserl says that, in perceiving things by sight, hearing, touch, and so on, one's body is essentially involved not merely by virtue of using one's eyes, ears, hands, and so on, but also through the so-called kinesthetic experiences one has of its own 'motility': the sense of one's body's position, movement, weight, muscular tension, and suchlike (*CES*, pp. 106–7). Second, he says that, in explicating the various kinds of 'habituality' that are always implicitly involved in one's experience of the world, consideration must be given to those which concern one's body and its kinesthetic activities. Thus he talks of the ego, through its 'kinesthetically functioning living body', as operating with 'a peculiar sort of activity and habituality' (*CES*, pp. 106–7). In effect, Husserl adds here a bodily dimension to the account of passive synthesis in the *Cartesian Meditations* (see Chapter Three, section 3).

Third, Husserl emphasizes the importance of bodily movements, and their accompanying kinesthetic experiences, in the various practical activities of everyday life. In such activities, he says, one's body 'holds sway' ('*walten*') over the objects of the life-world:

> Through bodily 'holding-sway' in the form of striking, lifting, resisting, and the like, I act as ego across distances, primarily on the corporeal aspects of objects in the world. (*CES*, p. 217)

Finally, he maintains that there is some process of 'analogizing apperception' through which one can understand that there are other egos who, like oneself, have bodies which are distinctively 'their own'.[5] Thus:

> Only through my own originally experienced holding-sway, which is the sole original experience of living-bodiliness as such, can I understand another physical body in which another 'I' is embodied and holds sway. (*CES*, p. 217)

As will be seen later in this chapter, there are important continuities between these claims about the human body in *The Crisis* and Merleau-Ponty's account in Part One of the *Phenomenology of Perception*. But for the moment we shall focus upon the more general relationship between these two works, and their respective conceptions of phenomenology. We shall do this by considering Merleau-Ponty's attitude towards Husserl's position in *The Crisis*. He endorses Husserl's view of the primacy of the life-world with respect to that of the empirical sciences; the insistence upon careful, detailed description of the former; and the concern to avoid its misrepresentation through scientific prejudices. But Merleau-Ponty does not accept the second and equally significant stage in the programme for phenomenology in *The Crisis*, the transcendental reduction of the life-world. This, he believes, has too much in common with Kant's transcendental idealism, despite Husserl's attempts – which he partly accepts – to distinguish the two (see Chapter Three, section 5).

We can now examine these points of agreement and disagreement in more detail. In the Preface to the *Phenomenology of Perception*, one finds Merleau-Ponty echoing Husserl's view of the relationship between empirical science and the life-world. For example:

> The whole universe of science is built upon the world as directly experienced, and if we want to subject science itself to rigorous scrutiny and arrive at a precise assessment of its meaning and scope, we must begin by re-awakening the basic experience of the world of which science is the second-order expression. (*PP*, p. viii)

And likewise:

> To return to things themselves is to return to that world which precedes knowledge, of which knowledge always *speaks*, and in relation to which every scientific schematization is an abstract and derivative sign-language, as is geography in relation to the countryside in which we have learnt beforehand what a forest, a prairie or a river is. (*PP*, p. ix)

There are also a number of parallels between Husserl's characterization of the 'world' of modern science and Merleau-Ponty's conception of the 'universe' of objective thought; and both writers are equally concerned to deny these any straightforward, let alone privileged, ontological status. Nonetheless there are also certain differences here, which make Merleau-Ponty's critique of the 'universe' of objective thought in some respects more wide-ranging in its implications than Husserl's of the scientific 'world'. This is partly because, as we noted in the previous chapter, Merleau-Ponty does not restrict the concept of objectivism to distinctively scientific theories of what the world is like: he includes also (dogmatic) 'common-sense'. But it is also because the central features of the objectivist's universe are more broadly defined than those of Husserl's mathematized nature. For Merleau-Ponty, what is wrong with objective thought is not just the idealized 'purity' of the primary properties and the absence of the secondary ones. It is also the assumed determinacy of all properties and objects, and the supposed externality of the relations between them (see Chapter Five, section 2).

Furthermore, Merleau-Ponty denies the possibility of a transcendental reduction of the life-world which, as we have seen, is still advocated by Husserl in *The Crisis*, and which marks the essential continuity of this work with the *Cartesian Meditations*. As the full title of *The Crisis* indicates, it is transcendental phenomenology which is somehow to resolve 'the crisis of European sciences'; and Husserl makes it clear that, as in the *Cartesian Meditations*, there is to be an eidetic stage of the reduction, which will give to phenomenology the status of a genuine (though of course non-empirical) science:

> the full concrete facticity of universal transcendental subjectivity can nevertheless be scientifically grasped in another good sense [i.e. not in the sense of empirical science], precisely because, truly through an eidetic method, the great task can and must be undertaken of investigating the essential form of the transcendental accomplishments in all their types of individual and intersubjective accomplishments. (*CES*, p. 178)

Phenomenology aims, then, as Husserl often puts it in *The Crisis*, to explicate 'the a priori of the life-world' (see, e.g. *CES*, section 36). This a priori will differ from Kant's, not only for the reasons adduced in the *Cartesian Meditations* (see Chapter Three, section 5, above), but also because Kant failed to understand the relationship between the life-world and the scientific 'world'. This additional criticism of Kant, in *The Crisis* (see sections 26–32), parallels the additional criticism of Descartes which we have already noted. Kant is congratulated for his transcendentalism, for having pursued, unlike Descartes, what Husserl terms 'the motif of inquiring back into the ultimate source of all the formations of knowledge', namely the 'I', the 'ego' (*CES*, pp. 97–8). But he is criticized for having ignored the life-world, and for instead concentrating his attention upon the conditions for the possibility of knowing the world as depicted by modern science.

For Merleau-Ponty, by contrast, no form of transcendental idealism is acceptable, whether it addresses the scientific 'world' or the life-world. And although he is always keen to emphasize his allegiance to Husserl, he does at times acknowledge Husserl's continued commitment to the programme of transcendental phenomenology, and his own rejection of it. For example, in the following passage he presents an account of what is recognizably Husserl's conception of phenomenology in *The Crisis*:

> The process of making explicit, which had laid bare the 'lived-through' world which is prior to the objective one, is put into operation upon the 'lived-

through' world itself, thus revealing, prior to the phenomenal field, the
transcendental field. The system 'self-others-world' [i.e. the basic structure of
the lived world] is in its turn taken as an object of analysis and it is now a matter
of awakening the thoughts which constitute other people, myself as an individual subject and the world as the pole of my perception. This new 'reduction'
would then recognize only one true subject, the thinking Ego.... Such is the
ordinary perspective of a transcendental philosophy, and also, to all appearances
at least, the programme of a transcendental phenomenology. (*PP*, p. 60)

And in a footnote he adds: 'it is set forth in these terms in most of Husserl's
work, even in those published during his last period' (*PP*, p. 60).[6]

But, Merleau-Ponty argues, the lived world is such that it cannot be fully
explicated and reconstructed in the manner required by a transcendental
reduction: the intellectualist project, and with it any form of transcendental
idealism, is rendered impossible by – amongst other things – the non-
determinacy of the lived world. Further, he claims, the 'true subject' which
emerges from phenomenological description is not 'the thinking Ego', but a
body-subject which is 'always already in-the-world'. So we turn now to his
discussion of bodily action in Part One of the *Phenomenology of Perception*.

3   The Peculiarities of One's Own Body

Merleau-Ponty's discussion of the human body in Part One of the *Phenomenology of Perception* has three main aims. The first is to show that the body
is not an 'object' in the sense given to this term by objective thought (see
Chapter Five, section 2). Its properties are not determinate; its activities defy
the empiricist attempt to provide causal explanations which depend upon
scientifically testable claims about external relationships; and its spatiality
is that of situation, rather than location. The second is to undermine the idealist's conception of the subject, by criticizing the intellectualist account of purposive bodily action to which, according to Merleau-Ponty, the idealist is
committed. The third is to establish that it is the body that is the subject of
action, a claim which is central to his overall project of replacing the idealist's
subject by the body-subject. (This project is continued in Part Two, where he
argues that the body is likewise the subject of perception: see Chapter Seven,
below.) But in ascribing this new status to the body, Merleau-Ponty is also
revising and reinterpreting the nature of the powers traditionally ascribed to
the subject by idealists. In particular, he argues that, whilst 'knowledge' and
'intentionality' are possessed by the body-subject, these must be understood as
essentially practical and pre-conscious in character, unlike their idealist
counterparts.

At the outset of Part One, Merleau-Ponty announces that he will take objective thought on its own terms and not ask it any questions which it does not ask itself.... Let us consider it then at work in the constitution of our body as an object, since this is a crucial moment in the genesis of the objective world. It will be seen that one's own body evades, even within science itself, the treatment to which it is intended to subject it. (*PP*, p. 72)

Adopting this procedure, whose rationale we explored at the end of the previous chapter, he examines in some detail a wide range of scientific literature, and criticizes both empiricist and intellectualist approaches, with their shared objectivist conception of the body. We shall concentrate on what is arguably the central (third) chapter of Part One, 'The Spatiality of One's Own Body and Motility'. This consists largely of an extended analysis of the case of a brain-damaged veteran of the First World War, named Schneider. But first we shall look briefly at the two preceding chapters, to get some initial idea of what Merleau-Ponty means by 'one's own body' ('*le corps propre*'), and of how it 'evades' objective thought.[7]

In the first of these he considers a number of accounts offered for the apparently strange medical condition known as the 'phantom limb'. Patients who have suffered the loss of one of their limbs, either through accident or surgery, may sometimes continue to experience sensations such as pain 'in' the missing limb, and to act in ways that apparently indicate a continuing sense of the limb's presence – for example, trying to walk with a missing leg, or to scratch a missing arm. From the standpoint of objective thought, says Merleau-Ponty, it is clearly the case that the limb *is* missing, that it is no longer a part of the patient's real body. The problem, therefore, is taken to be that of trying to account for the essentially illusory sensations and mental images which nonetheless clearly do occur.[8]

Merleau-Ponty starts by criticizing various theories advanced by empiricist pyschologists and physiologists in attempting to explain these phenomena. He argues that none of these causal explanations, whether couched in exclusively psychological or physiological terms, or in some combination of the two, actually succeed in meeting empiricism's own requirements for a satisfactory scientific explanation. We shall not discuss his specific arguments here, since we shall later be examining the equivalent arguments in the case of Schneider. Merleau-Ponty then goes on to consider the intellectualist alternative to these empiricist theories, which, instead of trying to identify causal determinants, attributes the phenomena to some specific project of decision on the part of the subject concerned. For example, he says, it may be claimed that what is basically involved here is a 'refusal of the mutilation': a decision not to accept what has happened to the limb, and to continue living as if it were still there.

Merleau-Ponty regards this intellectualist analysis as a distinct improvement on empiricism, but argues that it needs to be revised so as to remove its depiction of the subject as a conscious and disembodied decision-maker.

Taking the case of the phantom limb along with the similar phenomenon of *anosognosia*, in which someone with a diseased or injured limb 'attempts to ignore it', he comments as follows:

> The refusal of mutilation in the case of the phantom limb, or the refusal of disablement in anosognosia are not deliberate decisions, and do not take place at the level of positing consciousness which takes up its position explicitly after considering various possibilities. The will to have a sound body or the rejection of an infirm one are not formulated for themselves; and the awareness of the amputated arm as present or of the disabled arm as absent is not of the kind: 'I think that . . . ' (*PP*, p. 81)

But if 'the refusal of mutilation' is not like this, what exactly is it? Merleau-Ponty's answer is that it is primarily a matter of the person's continuing to maintain the repertoire of bodily actions that was in operation before the loss of the limb; and that, whilst this repertoire must itself be described in intentional, purposive terms, this does not involve the ascription to the agent of consciously formulated plans or decisions.[9] Thus, as he puts it:

> To have a phantom arm is to remain open to all the actions of which the arm alone is capable; it is to retain the practical field which one enjoyed before mutilation. The body is the vehicle of being in the world, and having a body is, for a living creature, to be interested in a definite environment, to identify oneself with certain projects and be continually committed to them. (*PP*, pp. 81–2)

Hence to have a phantom limb is to continue to act in a certain way: or rather, to attempt to do so, since, for example, when someone with a phantom leg tries to walk, they will fall. What this means, says Merleau-Ponty, is that, for the person concerned, this limb is both present *and* absent. That is, it is not a matter of the limb *really* being absent, but being *imagined* to be present, i.e. some kind of illusion. Rather, there is a genuine ambiguity in the situation; and one cannot, as the objectivist requires, give a determinate answer to the question 'is the limb present of absent?' (cf. Chapter Five, section 2). It is, as it were, both and neither:

> The consciousness of the phantom limb remains, then, itself unclear. The man with one leg feels the missing limb in the same way that I feel keenly the existence of a friend who is, nonetheless, not before my eyes; he has not lost it because he continues to allow for it. . . . The phantom arm is not a representation of the arm [i.e. an illusory representation], but the ambivalent presence of an arm. (*PP*, p. 81)

Thus Merleau-Ponty's discussion of the phantom limb is intended to show how 'one's own body' cannot be described in the categories of objective thought, shared by empiricists and intellectualists; and also to indicate what is wrong with the intellectualist's conception of the subject as a disembodied consciousness. One might be tempted to respond to this by doubting whether any such general conclusions could be drawn from so bizarre and abnormal an example. We shall consider Merleau-Ponty's rationale for using such cases later on in this chapter. But certainly he wishes to argue that this particular example does indeed illustrate a characteristic and mistaken tendency on the part of advocates of objective thought: faced with any apparent divergence between features of 'one's own body' and the body as conceived by objective thought, the problematic features are 'psychologized' – that is, reinterpreted as purely mental phenomena, such as sensations, images, representations, and so on. The phantom limb can then be regarded as no more than an illusory mental representation.

It is this general tendency to 'psychologize' any non-objective features of the body which Merleau-Ponty criticizes in the second chapter of Part One. Psychologists, he says, have often drawn attention to a number of 'peculiarities' of one's own body, including various ways in which one's experience of it differs from one's experience of other bodies, whether animate of inanimate. They have noted, for example, that, when touching a part of one's body with another part, one experiences what they call 'double sensations', i.e. in both the touching and the touched parts; and that, whereas one is aware of the movement of other bodies only through 'external' perception, the movement of one's own is indicated also by what they term 'internal' perception, including kinesthetic sensations.

But, claims Merleau-Ponty, these psychologistic characterizations of the peculiarities of one's own body can be shown to be inadequate. We shall not examine Merleau-Ponty's specific arguments here, but merely note how, in a manner which parallels Husserl's in *The Crisis*, he criticizes empiricist psychologists for invoking a form of Cartesian dualism so as to enable them to retain their commitment to an objectivist conception of the body. Thus:

> For the living subject his own body might well be different from all external objects; the fact remains that for the unsituated thought of the psychologist the experience of the living subject became itself an object and, far from requiring a fresh definition of being, took its place in universal being [i.e. the 'universe' of objective thought]. It was the life of the 'psyche' which stood in opposition to the real, but which was treated as a second reality, as an object of scientific investigation to be brought under a set of laws. (*PP*, p. 94)

What objective thought thereby fails to recognize, says Merleau-Ponty, is the active, purposive nature of one's own body, its practical orientation towards various tasks and goals, its 'attitude' towards the world. It is to these features that one must attend, if one is to provide an adequate phenomenological description of 'one's own body'. We can best see what this involves by turning now to Merleau-Ponty's analysis of Schneider's case in Chapter 3 of Part One. We will first present an outline of the main stages in this rather complex discussion, before examining them in detail in the following sections.

After some opening remarks about the ways in which the concept of a 'body-image' has been interpreted by empiricists and intellectualists, and the respective defects of these (pp. 98–102), Merleau-Ponty presents the main features of this case, which had been investigated and analysed by the neuropsychologists Kurt Goldstein and Adhemar Gelb (pp. 103–112).[10] Schneider, a veteran of the First World War, had suffered a brain injury from a shell-splinter penetrating the back of his skull (the occipital region). This had caused damage to the visual cortex, an area of the brain within which the processing of visual data is generally believed to take place; and consequently his sight was defective, in ways which we shall describe later.[11]

But Merleau-Ponty's main interest is in the defective character of Schneider's repertoire of bodily movements and sense of body-location, which obtained despite the fact that there had been no apparent damage to the tactile-motor area of the cortex, generally regarded as (amongst other things) controlling movement. Adopting the terminology used by Goldstein and Gelb, Merleau-Ponty says that Schneider, whilst reasonably well able to perform *concrete* movements, has considerable difficulties in performing *abstract* movements. Concrete movements are those involved in the immediate practical tasks of everyday life. For example, Schneider is employed in a workshop making leather wallets by hand-sewing, and he is able to deal quite successfully with the materials and implements involved in this – his production rate is about 75 per cent of the average worker's. He can likewise perform such tasks as removing a handkerchief from his pocket to blow his nose, taking a match from its box to light a lamp, or scratching the place on his leg where he has just been bitten by a mosquito.

By contrast, abstract movements require one to detach oneself from these immediate practical tasks so that it is one's body itself, the movements and positions of its various parts, that become the main focus. Thus, for example, when Schneider is asked simply to point to his nose, he cannot do so – the best that he can eventually manage is to take hold of it as if to blow it; and when asked to identify the place on his body where he has been touched by a ruler, he is unable to do this. Similarly, he has great difficulty in answering questions about the overall spatial arrangement of his limbs – for instance, whether or not his arm is horizontal to the ground, or whether he is lying down or standing up. And he finds it very hard to perform, upon request, actions such as tracing out a specified shape with his hand, or making a particular gesture such as a military salute – he can manage this only after a lengthy process in which he self-consciously adjusts his whole body so that it conforms to his mental picture of a military posture.

Similarly self-conscious and abnormal means are used by Schneider in attempting to perform other such abstract movements. For example:

> If the subject is asked to trace a square or a circle in the air, he first 'finds ' his arm, then lifts it in front of him as normal subject would to find a wall in the dark and finally he makes a few rough movements in a straight line or describing various curves, and if one of these happens to be circular he promptly completes the circle. (*PP*, p. 110)

Again, when Schneider is asked whether his arm is extended horizontally to the ground, he engages in:

> a set of pendular movements which convey to him the arm position in relation to the trunk, that of the forearm to the rest of the arm, and that of the trunk in relation to the vertical;

and from this process he eventually manages to infer the correct answer (*PP*, p. 107). He likewise, when asked, arrives at the conclusion that he is lying down by deducing this from the pressure of the mattress on his back; or, that he is standing upright, from the pressure of the ground on the soles of his feet.

This abnormal reliance upon consciously performed inferences is also displayed in the particular character of Schneider's visual disorders. His eyes themselves were undamaged, but he suffers from what is termed 'psychological blindness' (*PP*, p. 119): only the separate qualities or features of things are directly perceived, and the complete objects to which they 'belong' are arrived at only by a series of inferential conjectures. For instance:

> If a fountain pen is shown to the patient, in such a way that the clip is not seen, the phases of recognition are as follows: 'It is black, blue and shiny', says the patient. 'There is a white patch on it, and it is rather long; it has the shape of a stick. It may be some sort of instrument. It shines and reflects light. It could also be coloured glass.' The pen is then brought closer and the clip is turned towards the patient. He goes on: 'It must be a pencil or a fountain pen'. (*PP*, p. 131; cf. p. 112, note 2)

Having presented this picture of Schneider's difficulties, Merleau-Ponty goes on to consider empiricist and intellectualist approaches to understanding them. The empiricist (pp. 112–20) will try to provide a causal explanation of Schneider's defective motility – for example, by reference to his defective vision. But Merleau-Ponty argues that no such explanation can be either verified or refuted. The intellectualist, by contrast (pp. 120–30), will tend to regard Schneider as having effectively lost the basic powers of a human subject: he lacks understanding of the overall system of objective spatial relationships, he is unable to name or identify things correctly, and so on. On

this view, says Merleau-Ponty, Schneider's continued ability to perform concrete movements must be seen as a merely mechanical, object-like capacity.
But, he argues, on such radical distinction between abstract and concrete
movement, which maps it on to that between subject and object, is defensible.
There is indeed a difference between the two kinds of movement; but this,
he claims, can be understood only from an existential-phenomenological
perspective.

So Merleau-Ponty completes his discussion of Schneider by providing an
alternative, positive account, which preserves those features of intellectualism
which make it superior to empiricism, whilst avoiding its distinction between
the conscious subject and the body as mere object (pp. 130–9); and in doing
so he elaborates upon certain ideas introduced earlier in the chapter (pp.
108–12). Schneider's difficulties in performing abstract movements, says
Merleau-Ponty, can best be seen as indicating an inability to project himself
into possible or imaginary situations, as distinct from actual ones. He lacks,
that is, the 'power of projection' possessed by normal agents; and because of
this, he lacks 'concrete liberty' (p. 135). Merleau-Ponty insists, however, that
this projective power must not be understood as a purely cognitive one, as
'thought' which is divorced from bodily action. Intellectualism typically
makes this error. But Schneider's abnormality consists partly in just such a
reliance upon conscious thought in the performance of abstract movements.
He is, indeed, a caricature of the intellectualist's subject, a parodic refutation
of its disembodied conception of intelligent action.

Merleau-Ponty concludes the chapter (pp. 137–47) by drawing out the
implications of the preceding discussion for a proper account of knowledge,
understanding and intentionality. He emphasizes their intrinsically practical
and bodily character; and he illustrates his claims by reference to various
examples of the acquisition and exercise of motor skills, such as using a type-
writer and playing a musical instrument. These quite normal activities, he
argues, are no more open to empiricist or intellectualist analyses than is the
abnormal case of Schneider.

4   Schneider as the Refutation of Empiricism and Intellectualism

We can now consider Merleau-Ponty's arguments in more detail. His main
aim is to show that, in attempting to account for Schneider's case, both
empiricism and intellectualism encounter insuperable problems which cannot
be resolved in their own terms; and that their failure here reveals their more
general deficiencies. For empiricism, with which he begins, he argues that
these problems have the following character: any specific causal hypothesis
that might be proposed to explain Schneider's difficulties will turn out to be

incapable of conclusive confirmation or refutation; and alternative hypotheses will always be available that are equally plausible in relation to the relevant data. Merleau-Ponty then offers a diagnosis for this state of affairs: what the empiricist regards (in accordance with objective thought) as externally related variables or causal factors are in fact internally related, and hence not susceptible to the procedures of scientific theory-testing.

Merleau-Ponty starts by considering a particular hypothesis that had been advanced in the scientific literature on Schneider: that his difficulties in performing abstract movements were caused by the disorder of his visual sense – by his 'psychological blindness', itself resulting from the occipital brain injury. Schneider, then, was forced to rely purely on his tactile experience; and this implies that, whilst the tactile sense by itself is a sufficient basis for concrete movements, which Schneider can still perform, it is not so for abstract movement. Additional support for this hypothesis is apparently provided by the fact that Schneider's occasional, and partially successful, attempts at abstract movements usually required him to employ his limited visual capacity in monitoring these movements as they developed (*PP*, p. 113).

However, says Merleau-Ponty (still couching his discussion within the empiricist framework), against this hypothesis the following objection might be raised (*PP*, p. 116): normal people are able to perform abstract movements with their eyes shut, presumably relying on their tactile sense alone; and so it cannot be the case that Schneider's difficulties are caused by his visual disability. But a defender of the initial hypothesis could reply that the tactile experience of normal people has been in some way modified by past experience, in which visual and tactile data have become associated with one another – the so-called education of the senses (*PP*, p. 116). Thus it could still be maintained that Schneider's difficulties are due to relying on tactile experience alone, unaided by vision. But this reply immediately encounters a further objection: that even those who are totally blind, and thus cannot have had their tactile experience modified by sight, are nonetheless able to perform abstract movements. Yet to this it may be responded that, in the case of blind people, their sense of touch has instead been 'educated' by their kinaesthetic sense; and that, anyway, their attempts abstract movement do display some degree of abnormality, namely the use of 'preparatory movements' similar to Schneider's (*PP*, p. 117).

Hence the initial hypothesis remains unrefuted. Nonetheless, says Merleau-Ponty, there is also an alternative causal hypothesis available for the empiricist, which is equally consistent with the relevant data: that Schneider's difficulties are due, not to visual disorders, but to some primary disorder of his tactile sense (*PP*, p. 117). In other words, Schneider's problem is not that, because of his visual defects, he has to rely on his tactile sense – which differs from that of normal people only in being unaided by vision, or from blind people in being unaided by kinaesthesis. Rather, it is his tactile sense itself which is disordered, and it is this, and not his visual defects, that is the cause of his difficulties with abstract movement. Hence, for example, when Schneider makes use of his limited vision to perform, albeit imperfectly, abstract movements, what he is doing is compensating for his defective sense of touch by relying instead upon vision.

Merleau-Ponty then considers some additional evidence that might be used by an empiricist to support this latter hypothesis; and how a defender of the former hypothesis might then counter this by interpreting the new evidence in a different way. What becomes clear, he says, is 'that the facts are ambiguous, that no experiment is decisive, and no explanation final' (*PP*, p. 116); and although he has argued this only in the case of two hypotheses, he believes that the some could be shown for any others. For the 'ambiguity' displayed here, he maintains, does not indicate defects in the specific hypotheses: it is, rather, a genuine feature of the actual phenomena (cf. Chapter Five, section 2).

However, Merleau-Ponty accepts that a defender of empiricism might point to similar situations in the natural sciences, where the testing of theories is likewise often inconclusive; and that one should thus be careful, in discussing the implications for empiricism of Schneider's case, not to assume an unduly simplistic model of science, in which there are decisive experimental results and direct relationships between causal hypothesis and empirical data – the model implicit, for example, in Mill's methods of induction (*PP*, p. 115). For in the natural sciences, theories are often proposed which, since their concepts are not limited to observationally definable ones, can be neither conclusively verified nor conclusively refuted.[12]

Nonetheless, says Merleau-Ponty, it is still possible in such cases to compare competing theories in terms of their degree of probability, to determine how well supported they are by the data, and hence to assess, albeit inconclusively, their relative merits (*PP*, p. 118). What he has to show, therefore, is that even this is impossible in the case of Schneider where, as Merleau-Ponty puts it:

> Not only do we never arrive at an exclusive interpretation (deficiency of sense of potential touch or deficiency of visual world), but, what is more, we necessarily have to do with *equally probable* interpretations. (*PP*, p. 118)

The reason for this, says Merleau-Ponty, is that, in order to assess the relative merits of hypotheses relating abstract movement to either vision or touch, it must be possible to define each of these three variables independently of the others. If this is not possible, however, what might seem to be empirically supported correlations between, for example, movement and vision, will always turn out to be equally well interpretable as correlations between movement and touch. For if vision and touch cannot be defined independently of one another, anything that appears to be correlated with the former will necessarily appear also to be correlated with the latter, since what counts as vision will necessarily refer also to touch, and vice versa. Furthermore, if one cannot define either vision or touch without reference to movement, one will be bound to discover apparent 'correlations' between all three of them; but since these 'correlations' are due to the internality of the relationships, they cannot be taken to support claims of causal determination.

That these relationships are indeed internal is asserted by Merleau-Ponty in the following passage:

> Tactile experience is not a condition apart which might be kept constant while the 'visual' experience was varied with a view to pinning on to each its own causality, nor is behaviour a function of these variables. It [i.e. behaviour, for instance abstract movement] is on the contrary presupposed in defining them just as each is presupposed in defining the other. (*PP*, p. 119)

At least two reasons are given to support this claim. The first is that there are, in Merleau-Ponty's view, no such phenomena as 'purely visual' or 'purely tactile' experiences (*PP*, p. 114). The second is that (normal) vision, touch and movement all involve the 'power of projection', and this makes it impossible to define any one of them without some implicit reference to the others:

> Visual representations, tactile data and motility are three phenomena which stand out sharply within the unity of behaviour. When, by reason of the fact that they show correlated variations, we try to explain one in terms of the other, we forget, for example, that the act of visual representation ... already presupposes the same power of projection as is seen in abstract movement ... and thus we beg the question. (*PP*, pp. 119–20)

As we noted earlier, Merleau-Ponty thinks that Schneider's difficulties in performing abstract movements are best understood in terms of a loss of this 'projective power' of the normal person. Hence it can be expected that his visual and tactile capacities will be likewise diminished, since each presupposes the same more basic capacity for projection:

> Psychological blindness, deficiency of sense of touch and motor disturbances are three *expressions* of a more fundamental disturbance through which they can be understood and not three component factors of morbid behaviour. (*PP*, p. 119)

This 'expressive' relationship between the fundamental disturbance of Schneider's power of projection and the defects of vision, touch and movement is not a causal one, since it is internal rather than external (see Chapter Five, section 2). Furthermore, claims Merleau-Ponty, the identification of this disturbance requires a quite different kind of analysis to that employed in an empiricist, scientific investigation. What is required instead is another kind of thought, that which grasps its object as it comes into being and as it appears to the person experiencing it with the atmosphere of meaning thus surrounding it, and which tries to infiltrate into that atmosphere in order to discover, behind scattered facts and symptoms, the subject's whole being, when he is normal, or the basic disturbance, when he is a patient. (*PP*, p. 120)

But before considering what this 'other kind of thought' – i.e. an existential-phenomenological analysis – reveals about Schneider, we will first examine Merleau-Ponty's criticisms of the intellectualist alternative to empiricism.

The intellectualist, says Merleau-Ponty, will be inclined to regard Schneider's difficulties as indicating that he is no longer a true subject: that he has lost those central capacities which distinguish the conscious subject from the world of mere objects (*PP*, pp. 120–2). First, he lacks understanding of the objective system of spatial relationships obtaining between the various parts of the body, and between these and other objects. Second, his inability to perform abstract movements shows that he is unable sufficiently to detach himself from his immediate environment so as to act in accordance with freely adopted goals, which refer to imagined, as yet non-existent, states of affairs. Third, in no longer being able to point ('*zeigen*') to things, including the parts of his own body, as distinct from being able to grasp ('*greifen*') them, he shows a loss of the subject's fundamental ability to distance itself from the world so as to adopt a 'categorical attitude' towards it – to name things, to apply identifying concepts to them, and so on:

> In exactly the same way as the act of naming, the act of pointing out presupposes that the object, instead of being approached, grasped and absorbed by the body, is kept at a distance and stands as a picture in front of the patient.... If the patient is no longer able to point to some part of his body which is touched, it is because he is no longer a subject face to face with an objective world, and can no longer take up 'a categorical attitude'. (*PP*, pp. 120–1)

Hence Schneider, according to the intellectualist, has relapsed into the condition of 'a thing':

> the thing being precisely what does not know, what slumbers in absolute ignorance of itself and the world, what consequently is not a true 'self', i.e. a 'for-itself' and has only a spatio-temporal form of individuation, existence in itself. (*PP*, p. 121)

But, says Merleau-Ponty, since Schneider is still able to perform concrete movements, and to grasp things, the intellectualist must regard these activities as susceptible to mechanistic, causal explanations, just like anything else that occurs in the objective world. Thus, for the intellectualist:

The distinction between concrete and abstract movement, between *Greifen* and *Zeigen*, comes down to that between the physiological and the psychic, existence in itself and existence for itself. (*PP*, p. 122)

This view of the difference between these two kinds of movement differs markedly, of course, from the empiricist's view, according to which:

the distinction between concrete and abstract movement, like that between *Greifen* and *Zeigen*, is reducible to the traditional distinction between tactile and visual. (*PP*, p. 113)

For the empiricist, that is, the distinction is a matter of the different causal processes, operating through the two different senses, by reference to which each kind of movement can be explained. For the intellectualist, by contrast, it is between movement which can be causally explained and movement which cannot, and which is instead to be understood as the exercise by a conscious subject of its cognitive powers. The failure of the empiricist account, according to Merleau-Ponty, showed that the human body is no mere object; whilst the failure of the intellectualist account will show that the human subject is not separable from its body, and will thereby undermine the dichotomy between subject and object, the for-itself and the in-itself.

The problems facing the intellectualist's view of the difference between concrete and abstract movement, says Merleau-Ponty, are as follows. If one is prepared to accept causal explanations of the former – say, by reference to physiologically based reflex patterns, whether conditioned or unconditioned – it would be entirely arbitrary to refuse such explanations for the latter also. This is because, from the standpoint of physiological explanation, there is insufficient difference between the external stimuli, muscular contractions and physically describable behaviour which are involved in the two kinds of movement. For example:

Between the mosquito which pricks the skin and the ruler which the doctor presses on the same spot, the physical difference is not great enough to explain why the grasping movement is possible, but the act of pointing impossible. (*PP*, p. 123)

And likewise:

Does not the patient who, in doing his job, moves his hand towards a tool lying on the table, displace the segments of his arm exactly as he would have to do to perform the abstract movement of extending it [on request]? (*PP*, p. 123)

Thus, says Merleau-Ponty, 'it is impossible to set limits to physiological explanation' (*PP*, p. 123) in this way since, within the scientific framework of objective thought, there is no criterion by which one could appropriately distinguish the two kinds of movement. But, conversely, once one has assigned abstract movement to the powers of a conscious subject, there is no basis for refusing to regard concrete movement in the same manner. If, for example, the ability to point to the various parts of one's body is taken to indicate that one has knowledge of the overall structure of their spatial relationships, there is no good reason to deny that precisely the same knowledge is being applied when one grasps those parts in performing concrete movements.

So the intellectualist analysis of Schneider's difficulties cannot succeed. It requires that a radical distinction be made between concrete and abstract movement. But the concepts it employs to do this are such that they inevitably fail to preserve the very distinction they were intended to characterize, and the two kinds of movement are instead unwittingly assimilated:

> Any physiological explanation becomes generalized into mechanistic physiology, and any achievement of self-awareness into intellectualist psychology, and mechanistic physiology or intellectualist psychology bring behaviour down to the same uniform level and wipe out the distinction between abstract and concrete movement, between *Zeigen* and *Greifen*. (*PP*, p. 124)

A similar difficulty arises for the intellectualist in attempting to characterize Schneider's knowledge of the location of his body and its parts. It would be wrong, says Merleau-Ponty, to deny altogether that Schneider has any such knowledge. For example, he can legitimately be said to know where a mosquito has bitten him, when it is a matter of scratching the bitten area, and to know where his nose is, when it is a matter of blowing it. That Schneider does not know where these are, when asked to point to them or to give an identifying description of them, shows only that 'knowledge of where something is can be understood in a number of different ways' (*PP*, p. 104). But intellectualism is unable to recognize such differentiation, because it accepts the objectivist conception of a determinate, unified structure of spatial relationships and positions.

Thus, for the intellectualist, Schneider must be said either to know where his nose is, or not to know this, since there is 'in reality' only a single, objectively specifiable location to be known. In Merleau-Ponty's view, however, one should instead say that Schneider's nose is differently *situated* with respect to the different practical contexts in which the question of where it actually arises for him. Hence one can only understand Schneider's difficulties in pointing at things, and in performing abstract movements, by an existential-phenomenological analysis which attempts to identify what these different kinds of movement and spatiality mean to Schneider himself, and the basic attitudes towards the world which they can be taken to express. As Merleau-Ponty puts it, one needs to recognize' the *Greifen* and the *Zeigen* as two ways of relating to the object and two types of being in the world' (*PP*, p. 123). Schneider's problems, then, reside basically in his 'loss' of one of these. Unlike Schneider, says Merleau-Ponty, the normal person

> enjoys the use of his body not only in so far as it is involved in a concrete setting, he is in a situation not only in relation to the tasks imposed by a particular job, he is not open merely to real situations; for, over and above all this, his body is correlated with pure stimuli devoid of any practical bearing; he is open to those verbal and imaginary situations which he can choose for himself or which may be suggested to him in the course of an experiment. (*PP*, p. 108)

In abstract movement, that is, one detaches oneself from the immediate situation, in relation to the demands of which concrete movements are performed. One's body becomes the potential vehicle of actions which are addressed, not to the actual, but to the possible or the imaginary. In order to do so it must have what Merleau-Ponty calls a capacity for 'projection':

> The normal function which makes abstract movement possible is one of 'projection' whereby the subject of movement keeps in front of him an area of free space in which what does not naturally exist takes on a semblance of existing. (*PP*, p. 111)

It is this capacity which Schneider has lost; and consequently he now lacks 'that concrete liberty which comprises the general power of putting oneself in a situation' (*PP*, p. 135).

But this projective power must not, says Merleau-Ponty, be understood as a primarily cognitive one, as a capacity for thought and conscious deliberation which is separable from bodily action. This is how it would be regarded by intellectualism. Yet Schneider in fact *has* this capacity, in its intellectualist interpretation; and it is precisely in this that his abnormality is so clearly displayed. As noted earlier, Schneider does eventually manage to perform abstract movements, but by strikingly abnormal means. For example, he traces shapes in the air with his arm by forming a mental picture of the desired shape, and consciously monitoring his arm's movements to check their conformity to this picture; and he works out the position of his limbs in relation to the ground by a series of consciously performed inferences. Merleau-Ponty suggests that, from an intellectualist standpoint, the only abnormality involved is that these procedures are operating more slowly and clumsily than usual; whereas in fact it is the very use of such procedures which is abnormal:

> Nothing would be more misleading than to suppose the normal person adopting similar procedures, differing merely in being shortened by constant use. (*PP*, p. 108)

For, he says, one must recognize that:

> Illness, like childhood and 'primitive mentality', is a complete form of existence and the procedures it employs to replace normal functions which have been destroyed are equally pathological phenomena. (*PP*, p. 107)

Schneider, then, represents in effect a parody of intellectualism's conception of the human agent. The intellectualist, in Merleau-Ponty's view, inevitably views intelligent, purposive action as the application or exercise by agents of the various cognitive capacities which define them as being genuine subjects; and these capacities are regarded as existing independently of the various bodily performances based upon them. They are capacities of the subject; and the subject is not itself a body, but rather a consciousness which guides its body's activities in the light of its knowledge, aims, and so on. But this is just what Schneider does, albeit in a somewhat inferior manner. For Merleau-Ponty, it is precisely this divorce between 'thought' and 'action' which characterizes Schneider's abnormality.

When, for example, Schneider is asked to trace a circle in the air with his hand, he clearly understands what is required, and can judge whether or not he has succeeded. But, says Merleau-Ponty,

> although the order has an *intellectual significance* for him, it does not have a *motor* one, it does not communicate anything to him as a mobile subject.... What he lacks is neither motility nor thought, and we are brought to the recognition of something between movement as a third person process and thought as a representation of movement ... a motor intentionality in the absence of which the order remains a dead letter. (*PP*, p. 110 trans. adjusted)

The basic error of intellectualism, then, is to abstract the thought and knowledge of the agent from the bodily practices through which they are supposedly displayed:

> The intellectualist analysis, here as elsewhere, is less false than abstract. It is true that the 'symbolic function' or the 'representative function' underlies our movement, but it is not a final term for analysis. It too rests on a certain groundwork. The mistake of intellectualism is to make it self-sufficient, to remove it from the stuff in which it is realized. (*PP*, p. 124)

This 'stuff' consists in bodily action, and the sensory and motor 'equipment' which it relies upon. Indeed, says Merleau-Ponty, if this is not recognized then there is a further feature of Schneider's case that cannot be understood: that he was, after all, the victim of an injury to his brain, and more specifically to the visual cortex. The intellectualist, by abstracting the subject's cognitive capacities from the realm of bodily existence, is unable to account for the effects of that injury upon them:

> Schneider's trouble was not initially metaphysical, for it was a shell splinter which wounded him at the back of his head. The damage to his sight was serious, but it would be ridiculous, as we have said, to explain all the other deficiencies in terms of the visual one as their cause; but no less ridiculous to think that the shell splinter directly struck symbolic consciousness. It was through his sight that mind in him was impired. (*PP*, p. 126)

So although the empiricist is mistaken in attempting to provide causal explanations for Schneider's difficulties, there is at least one important virtue of the empiricist position: it emphasizes the essential contingency of human powers, their dependence upon the specific character and organization of the human body, and hence their vulnerability to damage and disorders of various kinds. For the intellectualist, by contrast, it is as if the subject could possess any kind of body, or none at all, and its powers not be diminished by the loss of sensory faculties or limbs.[13]

5 Habit, Practical Knowledge and Intentionality

Having completed his lengthy discussion of Schneider, Merleau-Ponty goes on to develop, in the concluding pages of the chapter, a more positive account of the kinds of knowledge, understanding and intentionality which are possessed by the human body as the subject of action (*PP*, pp. 136–49). Turning his attention to various motor skills such as typing, driving or playing a musical instrument, he begins by arguing that empiricism and intellectualism fare no better in accounting for these normal, habitual activities than they did for the abnormal case of Schneider.

For the empiricist, he argues, the acquisition of such skills has to be explained by a process of learning, through which certain 'stimuli' come to be associated with certain bodily 'responses', both of these being physicalistically defined. Hence the skill that is acquired must be capable, in principle, of being specified in terms of a determinate repertoire of behaviour that takes place in a similarly specifiable set of circumstances. Against this Merleau-Ponty presents the following objection. Any such 'mechanistic' theory, he says,

> runs up against the fact that the learning process is systematic: the subject does not weld together the individual movements and individual stimuli but acquires the power to respond with a certain type of solution to situations of a certain general form. The situations may vary widely from case to case [i.e. when their identity or difference is characterized physicalistically], and the response movements may be entrusted sometimes to one operative organ, sometimes to

another, both situations and responses in the various cases having in common not so much a partial identity of elements as a shared meaning. (*PP*, p. 142)

Merleau-Ponty's main illustration of these claims concerns the playing of a musical instrument. He cites the study of an organist who needed only an hour's practice to be able to perform successfully his musical programme on an unfamiliar instrument, the physical arrangement of whose stops and pedals was very different to the one that he was used to playing on (*PP*, p. 145). Thus the physical movements required to play the new instrument were radically different from those which, on an empiricist account, he could be thought of as having previously acquired; yet, within so brief a period of time, it is inconceivable that a quite new set of conditioned responses could have been learnt. To enable this rapid transfer to take place, therefore, what must have been acquired from the outset was the ability to 'respond with a certain type of solution' to a situation of 'a certain general form'; and he argues that both situation and solution are specifiable ultimately only in relation to their musical significance for the organist.

Merleau-Ponty also claims that the way in which the organ player familiarizes himself with the new instrument shows what is wrong with an intellectualist account of bodily skills. According to this, one would expect him to proceed by examining carefully the unfamiliar instrument, noting the positions of its various parts, and drawing up a new mental map or plan of their arrangement, which he would then apply in practice. But what in fact he does is this:

> He sits on the seat, works on the pedals, pulls out the stops, gets the measure of the instrument with his body, incorporates within himself the relevant directions and dimensions, settles into the organ as one settles into a house. He does not learn objective spatial positions for stop and pedal, nor does he commit them to memory. (*PP*, p. 145)

However, notes Merleau-Ponty, it might be objected that the acquisition of new bodily skills, as distinct from the modification of already habituated ones, is perhaps more susceptible to an intellectualist analysis. For example,

> is it not the case that forming the habit of dancing is discovering, by analysis, the formula of the movement in question, and then reconstructing it on the basis of the ideal outline by the use of previously acquired movements, those of walking and running? (*PP*, p. 142)

Presumably the idea here is this: faced with learning, say, a new dance movement, one might proceed by first watching it being executed by someone; then breaking it down, mentally, into its sequential elements; and finally, utilizing one's already acquired repertoire of movements, attempting to apply this 'formula', monitoring one's attempt to do so by reference to a mental picture of what one is aiming to achieve.

Merleau-Ponty's reply to this objection is as follows:

> But before the formula of the new dance can incorporate certain elements of general motility [i.e. the already acquired ability to walk, run etc.], it must first have had, as it were, the stamp of movement set upon it. As had often been said, it is the body which 'catches' (*kapiert*) and 'comprehends' movement. The acquisition of a habit is indeed the grasping of a significance, but it is the motor grasping of a motor significance. (*PP*, pp. 142–3)

What he seems to be saying is this. It may well be that, in acquiring this new skill, a certain amount of conscious analysis and mental imagery is involved. But there is also an irreducibly bodily element of 'understanding', without which the crucial transition from the established to the new movement cannot occur. However carefully one analyses the new movement, and pictures its relationship to already acquired forms, it is ultimately one's body which has to 'grasp' this relationship, to 'sense' how this transformation can be executed, to 'feel' incipiently what the new movement would be like, and so on. There is a point at which one's body 'knows what to do', and 'knows how to do it'; and without this practical knowledge on *its* part, a purely intellectual grasp will be of no avail. Hence, says Merleau-Ponty, one must accept that:

> it is the body which 'understands' in the acquisition of habit. This way of putting it will appear absurd, if understanding is [as the intellectualist maintains] subsuming a sense-datum under an idea, and if the body is [regarded as] an object. But the phenomenon of habit is just what prompts us to revise our notion of 'understand' and our notion of the body. (*PP*, p. 144)

Further, in revising one's concept of understanding so that it is no longer regarded as an act performed by a disembodied subject, and is instead directly attributable to the (non-objective) body, one needs also to revise one's concept of knowledge. One's body 'knows' the world upon which it operates, and 'knows how' to deal with it successfully, in a way that does not require any explicitly formulable thought or beliefs on the part of a conscious subject:

> Our bodily experience of movement ... provides us with a way of access to the world and the object, with a 'praktognosia' [practical knowledge], which has to be recognized as *original* and perhaps as *primary*. My body has its world, or understands its world, without having to make use of any 'symbolic' or 'objectifying function', (*PP*, pp. 140–1; our italics)

Interpreting the terms translated here as 'original' (*'originale'*) and 'primary' (*'originaire'*) in the following way, one can take Merleau-Ponty to be making two distinguishable claims about the body's practical knowledge.[14] The first is that is *irreducible*: 'original' in the sense that it cannot be analysed further by reference to more basic concepts. In particular, it is not susceptible to an intellectualist analysis as, in effect, the practical application or exercise of the subject's cognitive abilities. The second is that this practical knowledge possessed by the body provides the *foundation* for other forms of knowledge: that it is, in this sense, 'primary'. Hence, for example, although humans can articulate the knowledge of spatial relationships involved in abstract movement in the form of explicitly stated propositions, one should regard this cognitive 'representation' of spatiality as rooted in, and derivative from, the practical knowledge displayed in the actual ability to perform such movement.

Furthermore, argues Merleau-Ponty, and perhaps most fundamentally, one needs also to revise the intellectualist conception of *intentionality*:

> These elucidations enable us clearly to understand motility as basic [*originale*] intentionality. Consciousness is in the first place [*originairement*] not a matter of 'I think that' but of 'I can' (*PP*, p. 137)

In other words, the irreducible and foundational form of intentionality is that which is involved in one's ability to act on the world. In such action it is one's body which is 'directed towards' that world. Hence, for example:

> In the action of the hand which is raised towards an object is contained a reference to the object, not as an object represented, but as that highly specific thing towards which we project ourselves, near which we are, in anticipation, and which we haunt. (*PP*, p. 138)

The hand, as it were, seeks out its object; it aims to reach this object; and its movements are organized so as to achieve this aim. In performing such actions, one's body is not to be seen as guided by an intentional consciousness which exists independently of it: the intentionality instead belongs to the body itself, and provides the basic 'connection' between humans and the world, without any need for intervening (mental) 'representations' of it.

Clearly, this conception of intentionality differs radically from the one employed by Husserl in the *Cartesian Meditations*. As we noted in earlier chapters (especially Chapter Two, section 1), intentionality is taken there to characterize the relationship between acts of consciousness and their objects. The former are said to be 'directed at', to 'intend' or 'mean', the latter; whilst the latter are said to be 'intended' or 'meant' by the former. This account of intentionality locates it within what it is, for Husserl, the basic unit of analysis for the purposes of phenomenological investigation: the cogitatio, the particular conscious act, which always displays the same underlying structure, ego–cogito–cogitatum. From this perspective, there can be no question of the *body* occupying anything other than the position of an object intended by the conscious acts of the non-bodily subject, the ego.[15]

Corresponding to this difference in the conception of intentionality, there is an equally radical difference in the way that phenomenological description is understood and practised. For Husserl, at least in the *Cartesian Meditations*, this is an essentially first-person, self-reflective process, in which each philosophizing 'I' reflects upon its own cogitationes. Phenomenological description of 'one's own body' would thus consist in explicating this particular kind of object of one's conscious acts. But this is far from what is involved in Merleau-Ponty's phenomenological descriptions of 'one's own body'. The reader is not, for example, presented with an account of Merleau-Ponty's experience of his own body as an object of his consciousness; nor in the discussion of Schneider, with an equivalent account of Schneider's experience of *his*. Instead, Merleau-Ponty describes the nature of Schneider's 'body-in-action'; articulates the mode of 'existence' it expresses; characterizes Schneider's bodily 'attitude' towards the world; and so on. And it remains (perhaps deliberately) unclear, throughout these descriptions, from whose standpoint they are being provided.

These differing conceptions of phenomenological description are related to differing interpretations of what is involved in the phenomenological reduction. We shall consider this issue more fully in section 1 of the Conclusion. But there is one point that can be made here, since it concerns the use made by Merleau-Ponty of Schneider's case. Why, after all, is so much attention given to this example of pathological bodily action? One reason has already been noted: it enables Merleau-Ponty to present what he takes to be a caricature of the intellectualist's subject of action. But a second reason is this. Schneider's difficulties in performing abstract movements, and the abnormal means by which he attempts to do so, are intended by Merleau-Ponty to draw one's attention, in a dramatic way, to everyday abilities with which one is so familiar that it is easy not to notice them at all. The pathological case operates as a heuristic device that shocks one into awareness of what is taken for granted. It is a means of gaining distance from the familiar, so that one is better able to explicate it; and this, in Merleau-Ponty's view, is the basic nature of the phenomenological reduction.[16] As he puts it in the Preface:

It is because we are through and through compounded of relationships with the world that for us the only way to become aware of the fact is to suspend the resultant activity, to refuse it our complicity ..., to put it 'out of play'. Not because we reject the certainties of common sense and a natural attitude to things – they are, on the contrary, the constant theme of philosophy – but because, being the presupposed basis of any thought, they are taken for granted, and go unnoticed, and because in order to arouse them and bring them into view, we have to suspend for a moment our recognition of them. (*PP*, p. xiii)

7

The Perception of Objects

In Part Two of the *Phenomenology of Perception*, 'The World as Perceived', Merleau-Ponty returns to the task of giving a phenomenologically adequate account of perception, which he had begun in the Introduction (see Chapter Five, section 3). In this chapter we shall focus on the third chapter of Part Two, 'The Thing and the Natural World'. Our purpose in doing so is three-fold: first, to illustrate and develop our earlier account of Merleau-Ponty's critique of objective thought, and of its assumption by both empiricists and intellectualists; second, to provide more evidence of the dialectical character of Merleau-Ponty's mode of argument (see Chapter Five, section 4); and third, and most importantly, to show how Merleau-Ponty attempts to transcend the dichotomy between realism and idealism. This requires him to give a positive account of perception which integrates elements both from empiricism (its view of the necessary role of the body and its sense organs) and from intellectualism (its view of the subject imposing structures on its experience of the world), though in a way that partly alters how these elements had previously been conceived.

Each section of this chapter will focus on Merleau-Ponty's treatment of a particular aspect of perceptual experience. Section 1 will examine the perception of size and shape, and section 2 the perception of colours; in section 3 the focus will be on the transcendent character of things; and in section 4 we will briefly examine Merleau-Ponty's account of hallucinations.

1   The Perception of Size and Shape

In the first third of chapter 3 of Part Two (*PP*, pp. 299–317), Merleau-Ponty considers two types of properties of things which might be thought to be con-stant properties of the object itself, rather than of any appearance of it. The first type includes what Galileo and others would regard as primary qualities (see Chapter Six, section 1). Merleau-Ponty considers a thing's shape and its size. A thing can apparently be understood as having its shape and size independently of any particular experience of these. A thing of a particular determinate size may appear big, if seen close by, or small, if seen at a distance; but it itself nonetheless has the size that it has, as identified by the objective procedures of science. Thus there are two features of this type of property. First, there is some *real* size and shape of the object; and second, this size or shape is determinate.

The second type of property that Merleau-Ponty considers has, as its chief example, colour. This is a property which those who subscribe to the distinction between primary and secondary qualities would normally regard as secondary. Although Merleau-Ponty does not explicitly present shape and size as examples of primary qualities, nor colour as an example of secondary qualities, it is probably not accidental that he considers examples of each type. For if his account of these is correct, it would follow that the distinction cannot be maintained. Colour, he maintains, is just as 'real' a property of things as shape or size. In this section we focus on Merleau-Ponty's account of size and shape (*PP*, pp. 299–304).

Merleau-Ponty begins the chapter with a question:

> A thing has 'characteristics' or 'properties' which are stable, even if they do not entirely serve to define it, and we propose to approach the phenomenon of reality by studying perceptual constants. A thing has in the first place *its* size and *its* shape throughout variations of perspective which are merely apparent. We do not attribute these appearances to the object itself, but regard them as an accidental feature of our relations with it, and not as being of it. What do we mean by this, and on what basis do we judge that form or size are the form and size *of the object*? (*PP*, p. 299)

Merleau-Ponty first considers the answer given to this question by 'the psychologist'. (From the context, it seems that this refers to the empiricist.) This answer is that there is no 'true' size or shape of things. Rather, what is regarded as the 'true' size or shape is one particular size or shape chosen conventionally from a range of possible sizes and shapes seen from different perspectives:

> it is conventional to regard as true the size which the object has when within reach, or the shape which it assumes when it is in a plane parallel to the frontal elevation. (*PP*, p. 299)

What the psychologist does is to explain how one particular determinate shape or size is chosen as representing what will be regarded as the thing's objective shape or size. What is chosen is the most 'typical' one; and the body provides an important point of reference here. What is most commonly perceived as the size of an object, e.g. when it is within reach, is deemed to be the norm; and other perceptions of the same thing, seen at a closer distance or further away, will be regarded as deviations from this norm. The norm is explained by reference to what is conventionally expected.[1]

Merleau-Ponty's criticism of the psychologist's explanation is that it assumes precisely what is sets out to prove:

> namely a gamut of *determinate* sizes and shapes from which it is sufficient to select one as the real size or shape. (*PP*, p. 299)

But as we saw in Chapter Five, section 3, Merleau-Ponty rejects the empiricist view that sensations are determinate. Thus he thinks that the empiricist should answer the following question:

> how a determinate shape or size – true or even apparent – can come to light before me. (*PP*, p. 300)

Unless there is an answer to this question, empiricists have no basis for their objective judgements. But to answer the question of how one determines *any* shape or size by reference to a choice *between* determinate sizes or shapes is clearly to beg the question. Furthermore, says Merleau-Ponty, the phenomenon that is most in need of explanation is that one tends in fact to see something as having 'the same size', despite the fact that when it is close it 'ought' to look bigger, and when distant it 'ought' to look smaller. The conventionalist psychologist not only makes the mistake of thinking that these sizes are determinate, but also makes the mistake of thinking that what 'ought' to be the case about the object's perceived size actually is the case.

One way of avoiding this second error is considered by Merleau-Ponty in discussing a possible attempt to evade the question of how a determinate shape or size of an object can be given to the perceiver. This attempted evasion consists in saying that

> it is in fact never the case that size and shape are perceived as attributes of a single object, and that they are simply names for the relations between the parts of the phenomenal field. (*PP*, p. 300)

On this view, one's perception of objects as having the same size, despite a wide variation in perspective, is not due to those objects *having* a particular size; it is due to the existence of a set of relations between the visual appearance of the object and the distance it is from the perceiver. Thus:

> the constancy of the real size or shape which is maintained through varying perspectives is merely the constancy in the relations between the phenomenon and the conditions accompanying its presentation. (*PP*, p. 300)

For example, small things such as pens will still appear small when seen at close quarters; and large things such as mountains will still appear big when seen at a distance, because the conditions in which they are perceived (in these cases, the distances of the objects from the perceiver) are known by the perceiver. Pens will only appear big, or mountains small, if the perceiver is not aware how near or how far away these objects are.

Merleau-Ponty is critical of this explanation. His first criticism is that the knowledge supposedly incorporated into the perceiver's perceptual apparatus consists of laws governing variations between determinate appearances and determinate distances. So, once again, determinacy is being assumed rather than explained:

> When it is said that the true size or shape are no more than the constant law according to which the appearance, the distance and the orientation vary, it is assumed that they can be treated as variables or measurable sizes, and therefore that they are already determinate, when what we are concerned with is precisely how they become so. (*PP*, p. 301)

Merleau-Ponty's second criticism concerns *how* these laws of constancy are supposed to operate in perception. These laws construe the size of objects as a function of visual appearance in relation to apparent distance. What becomes clear in Merleau-Ponty's account of this proposed explanation is that the laws are considered to be a priori, and to be posited by the subject. In other words, Merleau-Ponty is now considering an intellectualist explanation. On this view any postulation of objective size and shape presupposes that there is a system of interrelated variables. It is this system which makes possible the determination of the objective size of objects. The laws governing this system cannot be empirical, for this would involve correlating experiences (e.g. of the size of the visual image) that are only made possible by the laws. So they must be a priori.

The Kantian flavour to this does not go unnoticed by Merleau-Ponty:

> In all its appearances the object retains invariable characteristics, remains itself invariable and is an object because all the possible values in relation to size and shape which it can assume are bound up in advance in the formula of its relations with the context.... In following out the logic of objective size and shape, we should, with Kant, see that it refers to the positing of a world as a rigorously interrelated system, that we are never enclosed within appearance. (*PP*, p. 301)

For Merleau-Ponty, both the idea that there is an important relationship between the subject and its experiences of things in the world, and that there is a complex set of relationships between parts of the phenomenal field, are important. But what he objects to, here, is the implication that these relationships should be seen as a priori. For this, according to Merleau-Ponty, means that the subject 'thinks [or judges] rather than perceives his perception' (*PP*, p. 301).

If the subject imposes a priori laws of constancy governing the relations between size, distance and orientation, and it is this which enables the subject to recognize objective qualities, then the subject knows in advance that any perception is to fit into an organized body of laws. The element of 'thought' in perception consists in knowledge of these laws. This knowledge is, on this intellectualist account, imposed in any perceptual experience. But it is here that Merleau-Ponty disagrees. His objections involve both of the two criticisms of intellectualism we discussed in Chapter Five, section 3. First, perception of size and shape is not judgement: one simply *perceives* them. Indeed this is the phenomenon one is trying to explain. To say that perception is possible only if perception is judgement is to alter the nature of what was to be explained. And this leads to the second criticism: that the intellectualist wrongly assumes that there is an objective world, with determinate properties.

The intellectualist argument is that knowledge of this objective world with its determinate properties is only possible if that 'objective' world is conceived as the construction of the intellect. The mind imposes certain laws (the Categories or Principles in Kant; the laws of constancy in intellectualist psychology), which make possible the determination of particular properties. On this kind of account, things as known are not conceived as having some independent ontological status; for as such they cannot be known. Rather, these things are known only as 'appearances' (see Chapter Three, section 5). Only by conceiving objects as part of an inter-related system imposed by the intellect can intellectualists explain how determinate judgements about the world are possible. Any particular experience of an appearance is always related to the system of appearances. But, according to Merleau-Ponty (*PP*, p. 301), this means that intellectualism cannot comprehend appearance *as* appearance; for it has the wrong idea of how things appear.

Merleau-Ponty is thus arguing that the intellectualist does not throw off the objectivist presupposition, shared with empiricism, about the nature of our experience of the world. The intellectualist is trying to lay down the conditions for making determinate judgements of a thing's particular size, shape, colour, etc. But Merleau-Ponty wants to draw attention to the fact that not all perceptions of the appearance of things are in fact determinate:

> The variations in appearance are not so many increases or decreases in size, or real distortions. It is simply that sometimes the parts mingle and become confused, at others they link up into a clearly articulated whole, and reveal their wealth of detail. (*PP*, p. 302)

On the intellectualist account, any fuzzy or confused perception is a failure of knowledge – of the requisite conditions of perception, of the appropriate law governing the variations of distance, and so on. On Merleau-Ponty's account, by contrast, whether perception is fuzzy or clear depends more on how the body is situated in the world; and it is not a matter of how well one *thinks* about the world.

Despite this criticism of intellectualism, and of Kant in particular, Merleau-Ponty does commend Kant for claiming that 'internal' experience is possible only against the background of 'external' experience (*PP*, p. 303), and hence that one cannot explain the latter in terms of the former, as the empiricist tries to do. Merleau-Ponty agrees. To attempt to explain external experience (the perception of a things's definite shape and size) in terms of laws relating distance, orientation and internal experience (its apparent size) is to misunderstand the relationship. Instead, the understanding of the constancy laws is itself parasitic on the perception of things with their shape and size:

> it is because I perceive the table with its definite shape and size that I presume, for every change of distance or orientation, a corresponding change of shape and size, and not the reverse. (*PP*, p. 302)

Thus the problem with which Merleau-Ponty began remains unresolved: how the perception of a thing with its definite shape and size comes about. He has ruled out the empiricist answer to this question on the grounds that it begs the question. He has ruled out the intellectualist answer on the grounds that it does not explain the perception either of definite or of indefinite shape, and that it conceives of perception as involving thought. Merleau-Ponty's own answer to the question incorporates elements of both the empiricist answer and the intellectualist answer. From empiricism he takes the crucial role of the body in the perception of definite shape and size. (This was the basis for the conventionalist psychologist's account discussed earlier.) But empiricism, as we saw in section 4 of Chapter Six, cannot give a proper account of the role of the body in experience because it regards the body as an object, whereas for Merleau-Ponty the body cannot be conceived in objectivist terms. So Merleau-Ponty needs to describe how the body-subject does operate in perception of things. From intellectualism he takes the idea that there is an imposed network of relationships between the subject and the world, and between the things perceived and the conditions of their perception. But intellectualism, with its emphasis on thought, is led to regard the subject as a disembodied, timeless consciousness. This misleads intellectualism into giving the wrong account of both the body and the thing (see *PP*, p. 303).

How, then, does Merleau-Ponty try to ground the perception of a thing's shape and size in the activity of the body-subject? He returns to a description of the lived experience of things. Knowledge of things' sizes and shapes is grounded in the activity of the body. The framework of the experience of things, with their definite shape and size, is given by the body. This is confirmed by considering the fact that there is an optimum distance for perceiving things. When a thing is too far away to be seen in detail or to be touched, or when a thing is too close, the subject *feels* a tension, a lack of balance. The balance is restored when the thing comes back into proper focus. Its definite shape and size (and other properties) are discerned when the subject is in an 'optimum attitude' with respect to the thing. Any variation in distance or orientation is then perceived as variation from perception in the optimal situation. So a pen is still seen as small, though not in such clear outline, when seen at close quarters; and a mountain is still seen as large, though without all the detail of its rugged shape, when seen at a distance. But at an optimum distance one would see, for instance, that the mountain is both rugged and large.

Merleau-Ponty considers the example of looking at pictures in an art gallery (*PP*, p. 302). For each picture one adjusts the position from which to view it. One's perception can be blurred through being too close or too far away. The body is aware of this, and acts so as to achieve the optimum attitude for seeing the picture in greater detail. Similarly for other objects: if a tension or imbalance is felt, the body moves to take up a better position from which to view that particular thing with its particular properties.

Two related phenomena are being emphasized in Merleau-Ponty's account. First, one does not discover properties of things independently of the identification of things. The clearest identification of the properties of a thing is when that thing is itself identified (as a mountain, a pen, etc.) in the optimum attitude.[2] Secondly, this identification of things and their properties takes place within a framework provided by the body. So the reason, Merleau-Ponty suggests, why one might draw an object closer to one, or turn it around in one's fingers, 'to see it better', is that:

> my body is permanently stationed before things in order to perceive them and, conversely, appearances are always enveloped for me in a certain bodily attitude. In so far, therefore, as I know the relation of appearances to the kinaesthetic situation, this is not in virtue of any law or in terms of any formula, but to the extent that I have a body, and that through that body I am at grips with the world. (*PP*, p. 303)[3]

This central relationship between the body and the world is not recognized by intellectualism, and is misrepresented by empiricism. The former, in its account of perception, takes up some God-like spectator position, from which it surveys all experiences of appearances of things. What will be missing from this spectator's account is the fact that the subject is not in fact a spectator, but is *involved* in perception. The experience of things in the world is lived from a certain point of view: the body's. It is this point of view which makes possible

both the finiteness of my perception and its opening out upon the complete
world as a horizon of every perception. (*PP*, p. 304)

How this complete world unfolds will be the subject of section 3 of this
chapter, where we look at Merleau-Ponty's account of what he calls the
'transcendence' of things and the natural world.

The empiricist misrepresentation of the relationship between the body and
the world is to construe the body in objectivist terms, and to think of how the
body is used in perceptual experience in causal terms. For example, the body
is considered as being affected by external stimuli, or as being caused to
respond in certain ways by various internal and external factors. By contrast,
Merleau-Ponty thinks that how the subject incorporates the requisite foundation for each finite perception is explained by the body's comprehensive
hold on the world.

To understand this claim it is helpful to look at the opening chapter of Part
Two, 'Sense Experience' (*PP*, pp. 207–42). There Merleau-Ponty talks of the
body-subject having a pre-logical form of knowledge or synthesis (which is
another reason why he is critical of the intellectualist account of perception as
judgement):

> My act of perception, in its unsophisticated form,... takes advantage of work
> already done, of a general synthesis constituted once and for all, and this is what
> I mean when I say that I perceive with my body or my senses, since my body
> and my senses are precisely that familiarity with the world born of habit, that
> implicit or sedimentary body of knowledge. (*PP*, p. 238)

Here we can see Merleau-Ponty's emphasis on the body as the subject of perception. This is one aspect of bodily intentionality. In section 5 of Chapter Six
we saw that Merleau-Ponty regards the body as knowing how to act: it
displays intentionality in action. Now we can see him claiming that the body
knows how to perceive. But just how the body knows how to perceive is
important.

Merleau-Ponty says that the body is 'primed' to experience the world in a
certain way. There is a 'sedimented' stock of knowledge. This stock of knowledge is not an innate structure: it accumulates with experience. Any body-
subject experiencing the world has a history of prior experiences of things
in the world. This history is literally embodied. The subject accumulates
habitual knowledge of things.[4] An example of this (ours) would be when one's
sedimented behaviour is 'shaken up' by moving to a new environment. Then
one notices how habitual one's awareness of things is. Because one has to *think*
where things are, in the new situation, one becomes aware that one's knowledge of their previous location did not involve this level of conscious thought.

It is important to note that, for Merleau-Ponty, the habits which make perception possible are not to be seen as *causes*. This would be an example of the empiricist misrepresentation of the role of the body, which Merleau-Ponty criticizes. The empiricist might try to explain the perception of, say, a thing's size, by reference to the causal power of certain habits of expectation of the body. This would entail (on a commonly accepted view of causation) that these habits, *qua* causes, could be specified independently of their supposed effect, the perception. But Merleau-Ponty thinks that the ways of perceiving things are themselves the expression of these habits. So the empiricist, according to Merleau-Ponty, presupposes in his description of what is to be explained precisely what is its supposed explanation. What is presupposed is this habitual knowledge of things; so this cannot properly be seen as *causing* the perception of a thing's size, or of any other property.

This argument depends upon Merleau-Ponty's claim that there is an internal relation between bodily habits and the perception of things with their constant properties, so that they cannot be causally related to one another (see Chapter Five, section 2). But he accepts that it is easy to be mistaken here, and to think that one *can* independently describe the habits and the perception, and thus regard them as externally related. The mistake is easy to make since there are considerable difficulties in *describing* habits. Because they are so engrained in behaviour it is not easy to notice them. And there is always a gap between an act of perception and the act of describing it. At the time when one experiences a thing, one is unable to experience oneself experiencing it. So when one tries to describe the initial experience, one has to step back from it so as to discern it. In this stepping back, a gap develops between the experience and its description, and it is thus always possible for the description to be wrong. (In Sartre's terminology, the consciousness of perception is not translucent: see Chapter Four, section 2.)

This lack of clarity in one's pre-logical bodily awareness of things, in normal cases, partly explains why Merleau-Ponty so often approaches his explication of what is going on when one experiences things in the world via the discussion of abnormal cases (see Chapter Six, section 5). It also explains, in Merleau-Ponty's view, why it is easy to think one has independently described elements of bodily habits and perception which are not really independent.

2   The Perception of Colours

Merleau-Ponty's arguments about the perception of colour constancy (*PP*, pp. 304–13) have a similar structure to his arguments about the perception of size and shape. Their interest – apart from their treating a 'secondary' quality in the same way as 'primary' qualities – lies in the fact that Merleau-Ponty here makes more explicit the idea that there is a systematic unity in one's perception of a thing's properties. In particular, the various attributes of a thing, and the background against which this is seen, are to be conceived as internally connected – a point that was only implicit in his earlier discussion of the imposed network of relations that is involved in the perception of size and shape.

Merleau-Ponty starts by saying that the phenomenon that requires explanation is how one has access to a thing's real colour:

> The table is, and remains, brown throughout the varied play of natural or artificial lighting. Now what, to begin with, is this real colour, and how have we access to it? (*PP*, p. 304)

The first explanation that Merleau-Ponty considers, the empiricist one, is that the 'real' colour of the object is that perceived in 'normal conditions' – in daylight, not too far away, in its usual context, etc. On this view, when these conditions are not met, as when the lighting has a colour of its own, one makes an appropriate adjustment. One remembers the most frequently perceived 'colour', and substitutes this for the perceived colour. The colour perceived in standard conditions is thus deemed to be the (real) constant colour; and one would explain not perceiving this colour by reference to deviant conditions.

But Merleau-Ponty argues that this view rests on an artificial reconstruction, for it assumes that the true colour of the thing presented is identical with the remembered colour:

> it cannot be said that the brown of the table presents itself in all kinds of light as the same brown, the same quality actually given by memory. A piece of white paper seen in shadow and recognized for what it is, is not purely and simply white. (*PP*, p. 304)

What Merleau-Ponty is claiming here is that, when one experiences colours in non-standard conditions, one does not in fact adjust one's perception to account for these conditions. One *sees* a different colour from that which one would perceive in different conditions. One does not *see* that the true colour of the thing is identical with the colour one would see in the standard conditions. Thus the empiricist is misreporting the experience of colours. To suggest that the brown of the table is identical with one particular set of appearances of brown is to misrepresent what is experienced in perception.

The intellectualist answer fares no better. According to Merleau-Ponty, the intellectualist will try to explain colour constancy by reference to a judgement of an 'ideal constancy'. So, rather than the ideal constancy being the function of commonly received experiences, it is the function of judgement. This judgement would involve separating out elements of the perceptual experience, so that the subject could identify the true colour. This would involve recognizing the role of the different lighting conditions, etc. But this is to make the same mistakes as the empiricist, namely to assume that the true colour of the thing *is* identical through all the different circumstances.

The accusation against both the empiricist and the intellectualist is that they make this mistake because of a more basic error:

> their refusing to recognize any colours other than those fixed qualities which make their appearance in a reflective attitude, whereas colour in living perception is a way into the thing. (*PP*, p. 305)

This error, according to Merleau-Ponty, is due to their construing colour as an abstraction from individual experiences of things. But no such abstraction refers to any colour as it is actually perceived.

Two related considerations are used to support this claim. First, in discussing Maori perception of colour, Merleau-Ponty says:

> The Maoris have 3,000 names of colours, not because they perceive a great many, but, on the contrary, because they fail to identify them when they belong to objects structurally different from each other. (*PP*, p. 305)

So if one were, as an objectivist, to argue that a number of Maori colours were what is called 'red' in another culture, one would be abstracting from Maori experience, and saying that there is something in common to a particular set of experiences to which the name 'red' can be given. But Merleau-Ponty would not accept that the colour that has been named in this way is the colour that is perceived by any particular subject whose experiences form part of the set from which the abstraction was made. One reason for this is that the perception of colour is so intimately linked with the thing perceived. Merleau-Ponty gives as an example:

> I say that my fountain-pen is black, and I see it as black under the sun's rays. But this blackness is less the sensible quality of blackness than a sombre power which radiates from the object. (*PP*, p. 305)

This 'blackness' one might not experience in any other thing; and it is certainly not the blackness picked out by any concept 'black' formed by the process of abstraction.

Similarly – and this introduces the second consideration – any perception of colour is linked to the other qualities a thing might have. The gloss, glow, brightness, size and texture of the surface are relevant to what colour is perceived. For example (ours), the problems involved in choosing which colour paint to use when painting a wall are not due solely to the limited size of the coloured area on a paint colour-chart. As any painter or decorator knows, the nature of the surface is important too. The colour-chart colour will appear flat when compared with the richer texture of the paint whose colour is supposed to match the colour on the chart.

This argument about the inter-connectedness of colour and other properties is quite general. Merleau-Ponty thinks that colours are differently perceived when conjoined with different other properties. So, for example, a blue metallic surface will display a different blue from a blue woollen surface:

> the blue of a carpet would never be the same blue were it not a woolly blue. (*PP*, p. 313)

Furthermore, Merleau-Ponty thinks that other senses can affect our visual perception. For example:

> it is impossible completely to describe the colour of the carpet without saying that it *is* a carpet, made of wool, and without implying in this colour a certain tactile value, a certain weight and a certain resistance to sound. (*PP*, p. 323)

And he cites favourably Cézanne's claim that a picture contains within itself even the smell of the landscape (*PP*, p. 318).

To add to one's understanding of Merleau-Ponty's position here, let us consider an objection that might be made to it by an advocate of objective thought (cf. Chapter Five, section 2). It might be accepted that the objectivist account of 'real colour' does not provide an account of colours as they are experienced: for instance, that the abstraction 'red' does not name any of the reds actually perceived. But it might nonetheless be argued that one can explain the perceived colour by reference to some real, objective colour – e.g. to the 'red' corresponding to the abstraction – which, when taken with a description of the conditions of perception, would explain why one does not perceive the colour as it really is. But Merleau-Ponty could reply to this by using the same form of argument we noted earlier, in section 1: that what are being proposed as the explanatory factors will turn out to assume what is to be explained, and hence are not genuinely explanatory.

Consider, for example, an empiricist version of this objectivist response to Merleau-Ponty. The empiricist would try to explain colour perception in terms of variables such as lighting and the organization of the perceptual field (what is in the foreground, what is in the background, etc.). In this way one would understand colour perception in terms of a functional or causal relation between these variables, so that for any particular value of each variable one could predict, on the basis of law-like regularities, what colour would be perceived. But this would require that each element of the process could be considered as an independently specifiable variable, and hence as identifiable prior to the identification of the colour whose perception one is trying to explain. Against this, Merleau-Ponty argues that each element is only discovered via the actual process of perceiving the colour of things: the identification of the elements is parasitic on having the kind of experience one is trying to make sense of, by appeal to the laws supposedly relating these elements to one another.

To support his argument that the 'variables' involved in perception are not independently specifiable, Merleau-Ponty considers the role of lighting in colour perception. Lighting appears as part of the essential background to visual perception. For the most part its presence is taken for granted; but its presence is noticed in abnormal situations. For example: when watching a film, a beam of torch light can appear solid; or immediately upon leaving daylight, electric lighting can appear yellow (*PP*, p. 311). When the presence of light is noticed, it is different from the way it is normally perceived. In the case of the torch light, if the light is the object of one's perception one does not see the objects picked out by the torch beam as one would if one were focusing the torch light on the objects for oneself. In the case of electric lighting, Merleau-Ponty notes that it soon ceases to have any definite colour. So lighting is normally background; and if it becomes identified it becomes foreground, and as such has different features from those it possesses when it functions as background. Thus if any supposedly independent identification of lighting is used in explaining how lighting contributes to colour perception, it will misrepresent the role of lighting.

According to Merleau-Ponty, one cannot determine the role of lighting without taking into consideration the other coexistent features of perception. For example, a cone of light might initially appear solid; but if one then introduces an object, such as a piece of paper, this will transform the cone's appearance of solidity, and enable one to see the cone as light. *What* one sees depends upon various configurations of lighting, what is in the visual field, how these things stand in relation to each other, and so on. If one tries separately to identify these factors, and to treat them as independently specifiable variables, then they are different from how they would be as constituents of ordinary perception.

In his discussion of the inter-related roles of lighting and visual field, Merleau-Ponty develops his positive views about colour perception. As with size and shape, he notes especially the importance of the body's role:

> Lighting and the constancy of the thing illuminated, which is its correlative, are directly dependent on our bodily situation. If, in a brightly lit room, we observe a white disc placed in a shady corner, the constancy of the white is imperfect. It improves when we approach the shady zone containing the disc. It becomes perfect when we actually enter it. (*PP*, pp. 310–11)

The ways one perceives things, the ways one allows lighting to enable colours to be seen, the ways one can focus on foreground or background, the way one looks, are all dependent upon the body's activities. For:

my body is my general power of inhabiting all the environments which the world contains. (*PP*, p. 311)

Furthermore, Merleau-Ponty claims, colour perception, like size and shape perception, is dependent on the perception of things. The activity of the body-subject provides the access to the inter-sensory unity of the thing, and hence to the thing's shape, size, colour, etc. What is perceived by the body, with its sedimentary structure, is presented as an inter-sensory unity. Sense-experience is thus to be seen as involving

certain kinds of symbiosis, certain ways the outside has of invading us and certain ways we have of meeting this invasion. (*PP*, p. 317)

He develops this claim in the following way:

what I call experience of the thing or of reality ... is my full co-existence with the phenomenon, at the moment when it is in every way at its maximum articulation, and the 'data of the different senses' are directed towards this one pole. (*PP*, p. 318)

This maximum articulation is the presentation to the perceiving subject of properties affecting different senses, in such a way that the subject perceives the thing with maximum clarity and richness. Here Merleau-Ponty is saying that the reality of a thing increases when it is perceived by more of the senses. If one perceives an object with only one sense, it may appear less real than if one could perceive that same object with more senses. The unity and the reality of the thing perceived are only fully appreciated when the senses are acting in unison.

Because Merleau-Ponty considers that the reality of the thing is experienced when the senses are operating together, he thinks that there can be no idea of an *it itself* that can be experienced. What is experienced is always experienced by the body in action. So, if one attempts to provide an objectivist account of the object of experience, in which one abstracts from the bodily experience of things and thereby omits reference to the activity of the body, one will not correctly describe anything which is experienced. Merleau-Ponty summarizes his position as follows:

The fact that this may not have been realized earlier is explained by the fact that any coming to awareness of the perceptual world was hampered by the prejudices arising from objective thinking. The function of the latter is to reduce all phenomena which bear witness to the union of subject and world, putting in their place the clear idea of the object as *in itself* and of the subject as pure consciousness. It therefore severs the links which unite the thing and the embodied subject. (*PP*, p. 320)

In this passage we can see Merleau-Ponty shifting from a criticism of objective thought's attempts to describe and explain the experience of the 'objective' (i.e. independent of the bodily subject) aspect of things, to a criticism more specifically directed at intellectualism. For it is intellectualism, and not empiricism, which would talk of the subject as 'pure consciousness'. Both empiricism and intellectualism are being criticized for their shared objectivism; but intellectualism is then being further criticized for its false idea of the subject, to which its objectivist presuppositions supposedly lead.

But, despite these criticisms, Merleau-Ponty thinks there are aspects of perceptual experience that each of the empiricist and the intellectualist goes some way towards capturing. Empiricists highlight the idea that colour perception is a function of lighting conditions, and of what else is in the field of vision. The intellectualist recognizes that the subject has an active role to play in perception. But both, according to Merleau-Ponty, misconstrue the experience. The empiricist has the wrong idea of the relations between colour, lighting and the organization of the field, thinking of these as externally related, connected in accordance with laws; whereas Merleau-Ponty thinks that they stand in internal relations. The intellectualist at least provides (an improvement on the empiricist) an account of the active subject; but this account involves a misunderstanding. Intellectualists think of the subject primarily as making judgements, whereas Merleau-Ponty emphasizes the pre-logical syntheses of the body-subject. So both empiricism and intellectualism have the wrong idea of both the object of experience and the subject of experience. These wrong ideas stem from their lack of recognition of the union of the bodily subject and the world.

But there is one further aspect of the empiricist account of perception that Merleau-Ponty thinks important, though he rejects the specific way in which empiricism interprets this, due to its commitment to realism. This is the idea that there *is* a world of things to be experienced, a world that is 'out there', the ground of one's experience of it. It is Merleau-Ponty's account of this feature of one's experience of the world (*PP*, pp. 322–34) which is the focus of the next section.

3   The Transcendence of Things and the Natural World

the fact remains that the thing presents itself to the person who perceives it as a thing in itself, and thus poses the problem of a genuine *in-itself-for-us*. (*PP*, p. 322)

Merleau-Ponty wants to say that there is an alien, silent, potentially hostile 'otherness' which remains aloof from experience. This can never be captured by a complete set of experiences. There is always something beyond one's present experience, something that remains opaque to the perceiver.

This feature of experience, that there is something which transcends it, is one which Merleau-Ponty thinks the intellectualist does not succeed in explaining.[5] We saw in Chapter Three how Husserl and Kant attempt to give a sense to the transcendence of the world, a sense consistent with their different versions of transcendental idealism.[6] But Merleau-Ponty argues that the intellectualist cannot escape idealism. For him, the intellectualist either *infers* the external world, as a presupposition of the possibility of experience, or has the subject *constituting* the external world. In either case the real world is a construct from the subject's experiences. According to Merleau-Ponty this means that, for the intellectualist, the thing (or its reality) can be fully grasped by thought (or judgement), whereas in fact:

> To 'live' a thing is not to coincide with it, nor fully to embrace it in thought. (*PP*, p. 325)

Earlier, in the chapter on sense-experience (*PP*, Part Two, chapter 1), Merleau-Ponty had commented on this intellectualist mistake:

> What makes the 'reality' of the thing is therefore precisely what snatches it from our grasp. The aseity [independent existence] of the thing, its unchallengeable presence and the perpetual absence into which it withdraws, are two inseparable aspects of transcendence. Intellectualism overlooks both. (*PP*, p. 233)

These two aspects of transcendence form the basis for what Merleau-Ponty says about the otherness of reality in the chapter we are considering here, 'The Thing and the Natural World'. He has four main claims to make about this. First, things have an unchallengeable presence. Secondly, these things are open to unending exploration. Thirdly, they are rooted in a background of nature, of the 'natural world'. Finally, this background of nature is also an unchallengeable presence, which transcends experience.

One important feature to be noted about Merleau-Ponty's discussion of these four claims is that he relates his account of the object of perception to the activity of the subject. He is trying to capture the germ of truth in the empiricist account of the reality of things: that there *is* something external. But his discussion is intended to show that whatever is externally real is nonetheless real-for-a-subject. So, although the focus for his discussion is the object of perception, Merleau-Ponty is drawn into stressing the germ of truth in the intellectualist account: the activity of the subject. But the intellectualist account is sharply criticized for having too 'pure' a view of this subject.

The first claim (see *PP*, pp. 322–4) about the otherness of reality is that things have an unchallengeable presence, which is associated with their always potentially 'hostile and alien' character (*PP*, p. 322). This aspect of things is not always obvious, especially when the subject is familiar with the things in its environment. But Merleau-Ponty thinks that closer inspection of the experience of things yields this presence of a hidden, non-human element. The reality of a thing, as we saw in the previous section, is intimately connected with a system of appearances. Things are perceived as having increasing reality the more senses are involved. Correspondingly, things lack reality (e.g. are imaginary) if the kind of experience of them is not linked to other possible experiences. In the perception of real things there is, according to Merleau-Ponty, a significance which 'permeates matter' (*PP*, p. 334), in a way that is absent in the case of imagination.

One might be tempted to think that this 'permeating significance' is nothing but the possibility of further experiences of a thing (a possibility one is aware of with familiar things). But Merleau-Ponty rejects this. In one's experience of real things, he claims, the thing *is* there in the world. For instance, when the subject sees a die (Merleau-Ponty, like Husserl, uses this example), the die is perceived as being there in the world (*PP*, p. 324). The subject, moving around it, sees the die – sees and feels the sides of the die (and not mere 'signs' of it). It is not projections of the die that are seen: it is the die itself, at one time from this side, at another time from another. What connects these perceptions is that they are perceptions of the same die. But this is not because the concept 'same die' has been imposed on the experience, but because the die *is* what is experienced. There is something there to be explored.

Merleau-Ponty's second claim (see *PP*, pp. 324–7) about the otherness of reality is that things lend themselves to unending exploration. For each experience one has, one becomes directly aware that the thing being perceived is being perceived in a particular way. A thing can be seen, at a certain distance, in a certain light. In any such experience the subject is aware that the thing could also be seen at different distances, in different lights, against the background of different objects, and so on. One also becomes aware that there are different possible modes of perception of the same object: one can touch it, move it around with one's fingers, smell it – perhaps one can hear it, etc. For each of these possible perceptions, one is also aware that there are further possible perceptions, with different variations of sensory mode and background. There seems to be no limit to the sequence of ways in which one might explore the thing that is the object of any particular perception.

What one is also aware of, in this unending perceptual exploration, is the background of nature which is the basis for it. This is the third point about the otherness of reality: that there is a background of nature that is experienced (see *PP*, pp. 327–30). This background includes what is beyond any particular experience. This 'beyond' is not thought, neither is it visualized; it is experienced as there in the infinite unfolding of different perspectives. This is the area of 'perpetual absence' that Merleau-Ponty mentions in the passage quoted above from the chapter on sense-experience (*PP*, p. 233). This direct awareness of what is absent, i.e. of what is beyond the thing one is experiencing, includes an awareness that what is thus 'beyond' is a world that is the same world, even though one only experiences part of it. This is what Merleau-Ponty calls the 'natural world'. The set of experiences of a thing are experienced as unified. This unity is not only the unity of the properties of the object (e.g. the size, shape, colour, material, texture of a single chair), but the unity of the world. All objects are experienced as being part of the same world:

> The world remains the same world throughout my life, because it is that permanent being within which I make all corrections to my knowledge, a world which in its unity remains unaffected by those corrections. (*PP*, pp. 327–8)

Thus Merleau-Ponty is claiming, as a fact revealed by phenomenological description, that when one experiences any particular thing, or aspect of a thing, one senses that thing, with its unchallengeable presence, as being related to a greater world which endures and remains forever beyond one's present experience (the perpetual absence). Other experiences of other parts of this world will likewise be experienced as being of one and the same world. And it is by reference to these possible experiences that one can correct one's perceptions of apparent properties, and so gain knowledge of a thing's real properties. Merleau-Ponty does not go into detail about *how* this process of correction takes place. But it is clear that he thinks the experienced existence of this natural world is the basis for knowledge of things.

The way that one perceives this natural world is said by Merleau-Ponty (*PP*, p. 327) to be analogous to the way that one perceives the style of a writer, or to the way that one recognizes an individual whom one has not seen for a while. One is able to do this without being able, consciously, to articulate the factors in virtue of which one does in fact recognize the style or the person. Similarly with the unitary nature of the natural world:

> I experience the unity of the world as I recognize a style. (*PP*, p. 327)

Merleau-Ponty suggests that there might be some variation over time in the 'style' the world presents to one, so that it may appear a different world at different times in one's life. But he maintains (*PP*, p. 327) that it is only *knowledge* of the world that thus varies. The world itself remains the same throughout one's life.

The last claim about the otherness of reality which Merleau-Ponty makes (see *PP*, pp. 330–4) concerns this natural world. Like things, this world is an unchallengeable, alien presence, which transcends all possible experience:

I have the impression that the world itself is a living self-subsistent entity outside me. (*PP*, p. 333) (trans. adjusted)

The reason why Merleau-Ponty thinks this is connected with his second claim
about the otherness of reality: the inexhaustible exploration of things. For any
set of experiences of a thing it is always possible to have further information.
One's experience is always incomplete. This means that for Merleau-Ponty it
is impossible to give a complete description of any object.

In order to provide a complete description one would have to know, in
advance, that there were no new types of experience relevant to the thing in
question. This Merleau-Ponty rules out; and in so doing he rules out the
discovery of any *essences* of things.[7] For any perception which occurs at a particular time, for a particular body-subject, there are always possible future
experiences to synthesize with one's present (and past) experiences, which
might change one's judgement of that (now past) perception. And for any
present perception, past perceptions which are also relevant for the identification or description of the thing might become recalcitrant to one's recollection.
This means that, for any object, there are both future and past experiences
that one cannot call on to enable one to 'fix' a thing with a determinate
property. For a thing to have a determinate property there would have to be
a completed synthesis, so that one would know that no more possible
experiences were relevant to one's perception of the thing's having this
particular determinate property.

But the temptation to search for the determinate qualities of things is seen
as almost inevitable by Merleau-Ponty; for he admits that there is the experience of seeing that 'this stone *is* white, hard and cool' (*PP*, p. 332), and that
this experience seems graspable because it seems to be an immediate,
instantaneous awareness. The experience seems to take no time: the object
with properties is right here in the present. So it appears a small step to take,
to think of all objects with their determinate properties as existing in similar
presents.

This might suggest, says Merleau-Ponty, that one way of avoiding the
impossibility of providing a complete, determinate description of things is to
try to escape from the temporal restrictions which apply to the subject. That
is, one might try to consider the perception of things as taking place from
some point of view outside time. This is a characteristic intellectualist move:
to consider the subject of experience as being a universal consciousness which
operates either outside time, or for all time (i.e. is eternal). But of such a subject Merleau-Ponty says:

If I am at all times . . . then I am at no time. (*PP*, p. 332)

Yet if one tries to solve the problem of the incompleteness of experience,
which makes determinacy impossible, in this way, then everything would be

transparent to consciousness. It is Merleau-Ponty's contention that not every-thing is thus transparent: there is the otherness of reality. So the intellectualist notion of a pure consciousness cannot do justice to the way one experiences the world. It is a crucial aspect of this experience that the subject is temporally situated in the world. For this temporal subject, the one which lives and operates in the world, Merleau-Ponty thinks that there is an ambiguity in its temporality:

> What needs to be understood is that for the same reason I am present here and now, and present elsewhere and always, and also absent from here and from now, and absent from every place and from every time. (*PP*, p. 332)

This feature of the subject is linked to the unchallengeable presence and perpetual absence which are the roots of the transcendence of reality. When the subject is aware of the presence of the thing, or of the natural world, the subject is in the present. When the subject has direct awareness of what is absent, or beyond its present experience, there is an awareness of the subject at a different time. At this different time the present experience would be in the past or in the future.[8] Thus ultimately, because of the temporality of one's experience, both this experience and the world are ambiguous: they are both indeterminate. This does not prevent one thinking that some things have determinate qualities, but these are always open to review. The objectivist mistake is to forget this qualification. Objectivists allow the thought that things have determinate qualities to distort their perception. They *think* one is perceiving things with determinate qualities when in fact one is not.

4 Hallucinations

The occurrence of hallucinations might seem to jeopardize Merleau-Ponty's account of transcendence. He himself says:

> Hallucination causes the real to disintegrate before our eyes, and puts a quasi-reality in its place. (*PP*, p. 334)

For if one cannot account for the difference between hallucinations and experience of the real, then there is always the possibility that all our perceptions are illusory: that there is no transcendent reality. However, Merleau-Ponty thinks that a proper description of hallucinations will in fact serve to confirm his account of the thing and the natural world (see *PP*, pp. 334–45).

An essential premiss of his argument is that most people who suffer from hallucinations – his evidence is derived from reports of psychiatric patients –

can discriminate between their hallucinations and their normal perceptions. He then goes on to argue that neither empiricists nor intellectualists can account for this fact. Their objectivist presuppositions lead them to give an account of hallucination which fails to do justice to how the subject experiences this.[9] But if one accepts the basic fact about hallucinatory experience, that the subject is aware of the difference between this experience and normal perception, then one has confirmation, even from this unusual case, of the transcendence of the thing and of the natural world.

The empiricist tries to explain hallucinations in terms of the effects of certain physiological causes (e.g. abnormalities of brain-processes due to drugs, lesions, alcohol, etc.) being the same as the effects upon the sensory apparatus of real objects. On this empiricist account there is no experienced difference between, for example, the feel of a real guinea pig, and the feel of the doctor's hand which is taken to be a guinea pig (*PP*, p. 334). There would be a difference in the objective conditions causing the two experiences, which would explain the (non-experienced) difference between hallucination and perception. But Merleau-Ponty thinks that the subject who has the hallucination can, when reporting it, tell the difference between the two kinds of experience. This difference in awareness is not explained by the empiricist account. For in the empiricist view, the subject is not aware that the experience is hallucinatory.

The intellectualist, says Merleau-Ponty, at least accepts that hallucinators know the nature of their experience. This is because all experience is transparent to the intellectualist's subject. On this account, hallucinations are regarded as false judgements, whilst perceptions are regarded as true judgements. Thus what has gone wrong in hallucination is that the subject *believes* that it sees or hears what it is hallucinating, but does not *really* see or hear them. But Merleau-Ponty believes that hallucination is not a matter of false judgement. Partly, this is because of his earlier and more general claim that perception is not judgement. But more specifically he argues that, at the level of judgement, people know the difference between hallucination and veridical perception. An example given (*PP*, p. 334) is of a patient suffering from hallucination who 'sees' someone outside, and is able to describe the person in detail. But when the doctor arranges for someone answering the patient's description to stand in the 'same' place, the patient knows the difference in character between this experience and the previous hallucinatory one.

This mistaken reality is difficult for the intellectualist to account for, says Merleau-Ponty. This is because, if all thoughts are clearly paraded before the pure subject of consciousness (the intellectualist subject), they should always be correct:

> if the hallucinated subject objectively *knows* or thinks of his hallucination as being what it is, how is hallucinatory deception possible? (*PP*, p. 336)

What the intellectualist fails to account for is how, when the subject is having the hallucinations, it is convinced of what it sees or hears. For there is no room, in the intellectualist account, for this mistake. So whereas the empiricist cannot explain how the subject knows (on the level of judgement) that it has been hallucinating, the intellectualist cannot explain how the subject, in pre-logical experience, can nonetheless be convinced that it is seeing and hearing things.

For Merleau-Ponty, of course, the common error is the shared objectivism of empiricism and intellectualism. They fail to examine the phenomena of hallucinations. What this examination shows is that there is an ambiguity in the hallucinator's experience. One both *is* deceived by the experiences and one is *not* deceived. When one is having the hallucinatory experience, one is deceived; but when one reflects on it one knows that it was a hallucination. How is this so?

To answer this question Merleau-Ponty draws on his themes of presence and absence in the transcendence of things and the natural world (see section 3, above). He also draws on his idea that the body-subject has a pre-logical form of knowledge (see section 1, above). All experiences have as a background a whole system of the subject's perceptions, which yields the natural world – which itself, as we have seen, is the basis for correcting perceptions. This background provides the basis for testing the reality of what is experienced in hallucinations. When the subject reports its hallucinatory experience, certain features can be noticed by the reporter which, despite the full force of reality experienced, support the lack of reality in the hallucinatory experience. During the hallucinatory experience itself, the subject is more fully focused on the presence of the thing experienced; and, because of the limited nature of its bodily experience, it fails to notice, at the time, the all important background, the absence.

But when the subject reflects on its experience it does notice this, and so becomes aware of the hallucination as such. The hallucinatory experience is less rich: there is a lack of contact with all the possible experiences of the 'thing' being experienced in the hallucination. An example of this is provided by dreams:

> The person who speaks to me in my dream has no sooner opened his mouth before his thought is conveyed miraculously to me; I know what the person is saying to me before he says anything at all. (*PP*, p. 339)

What Merleau-Ponty wishes to highlight in this case is that the subject is not engaged in the world as it would be in reality. There are two respects in which this is so. First, in the dream one does not have to hear what the other person is 'saying'. Secondly, the temporal order of experiences in the dream is different from normal: one knows what the other person is saying *before* he says anything. What this indicates is that the body lacks the usual connections with the system of interconnected experiences that form the basis for the transcendence of things.

Thus, in hallucinations, the subject's hold on the world lacks its usual fullness which, as we noted in section 2, is relevant to the reality of the thing perceived. A schizophrenic might *hear* voices, but never see the speaker; might *feel* the presence of someone, without seeing or hearing them. Further, the subject does not have the same temporal stance towards the world. It is almost as if there is only a continual present for the subject having the hallucinations: it lacks both a past and a future. And without these the connections with transcendence are curtailed. All this is realized from the perspective of the subject reflecting on its hallucinatory experience. So it is the same framework of the natural world, and of the things in it, that grounds both one's perception of things and one's recognition of hallucinations. It is the absence of this framework, or parts of it, that explain the hallucinatory experience.

We can summarize Merleau-Ponty's overall argument in this chapter as follows. First, one does not have experience of fixed determinate things. Second, the subject of perception is not a pure subject entirely conscious of its own activity. Third, there is range of phenomena (including constancy of size, constancy of colour, otherness of things, and hallucinations) which one cannot account for if one does not recognize both of the previous claims. The correct account of these phenomena yields an understanding of the subject of perception as a bodily subject, situated in time, and having a living engagement with a world of things which, whilst displaying systematic unity, has an irreducible opacity.

8

The Recognition of Other Selves

Phenomenology is often criticized for its adoption of an egocentric standpoint. One problem which then arises is that of solipsism – a scepticism about or a failure to account for knowledge of other people. Husserl raised this as a problem in his Second Meditation (see section 1 of Chapter Two, above). It is in the famous Fifth Meditation that he offers his solution.[1] In this chapter we shall explore this 'solution' along with the accounts of knowledge of other people given by Sartre and Merleau-Ponty.

1 The Traditional Problem of 'Other Minds'

The problem of other minds[2] as traditionally understood is that of justifying claims to know of the existence or the states of minds other than one's own. It arises as a problem because of two theses held by a great many philosophers since Descartes. The first of these is Cartesian Dualism.[3] This states that people are composed of two independent parts (substances, aspects, sets of properties), mind and body, and that these parts are logically distinct. One thing which is meant by 'distinct' is that no deductively valid inference can be made from statements about one such 'part' of a person to statements about the other. In particular, one cannot validly infer, on the basis of knowledge of a body, any conclusion about a mind.

The second thesis concerns the nature of knowledge. It is the basic thesis of empiricism that knowledge derives from the senses, and that knowledge claims are justified by being 'traced back' to sensory input.[4] A knowledge claim which cannot be so traced is, to that extent, suspect. The extreme version of empiricism claims that one can legitimately claim to know only propositions which describe sensory data and propositions which can be inferred from them. Weaker versions would require that what one claims to know be somehow 'answerable to' sensory data.

Putting together these two theses produces the problem of other minds.

One does not have direct sensory contact with other minds. Since persons comprise a union of mind and body, the natural place to look for sensory evidence of other minds is other bodies. Knowledge of other bodies does derive from the senses. But statements about other minds, it is claimed, cannot be validly inferred from, or in any other way legitimately based upon, claims about other bodies.

Add to this a further Cartesian claim that one's access to one's own mind is direct and gives indubitable knowledge, and an asymmetry emerges between self-knowledge and knowledge of others. The Cartesian view of self-knowledge provides an ideal of knowledge of minds. But one does not have knowledge of that kind of any other mind. Even if beliefs about other minds could in some way be justified, it would not satisfy this ideal of directness and incorrigibility.

Traditional responses to the other minds problem fall into two broad classes. The first retains in essence the two theses sketched above but seeks to show that there is a legitimate passage from sensory data about bodies to claims about minds.[5] The second involves rejection of one, or both, of the theses which together give rise to the problem.

Within the first class of 'solutions' there are two chief lines of defence of the claim that knowledge of other minds is possible: reasoning by analogy, and adopting the 'best explanatory hypothesis'. Arguing by analogy involves arguing from observed similarities to unobserved similarites. If two items have been found to have a great many features in common, and one of them has a further feature which one is not in a position to test in the other, one is justified in inferring that the second also has that feature.

Applied to the case of other minds, the argument would go thus: when one is in a certain physical state of behaving angrily – red-faced, stamping feet, clenched fists, shouting, etc. – one is also in a certain mental state of feeling angry. Another body is like one's own in all these observable respects. So, it is reasonable to conclude that the body 'houses' a mind which is, like one's own mind, angry.

The second attempt to justify claims concerning other minds, given that one experiences only other bodies, is that the hypothesis that there are other minds is the best explanation of the observable behaviour of other bodies. This kind of reasoning, like reasoning by analogy, is often used in fields other than that of other minds, e.g. in the natural sciences, and it often proves reliable and successful.

The second type of approach to the problem of other minds recognizes the certainty attaching to one's perceptions of other people and seeks to explain it. The task is not to *justify* beliefs, but to explore the *content* of those beliefs. Proponents of this sort of account include Wittgenstein, Ryle and Strawson.[6] They reject the narrowly egocentric standpoint of Descartes, and also the fundamental tenet of Cartesian dualism that minds and bodies are logically distinct. Egocentricity and the certainty of the cogito are challenged on the grounds that it is not an adequate source of the meanings of mental terms. One experiences, for example, one's own anger, but that experience does not explain one's acquisition of the concept 'anger'. One can be certain that one is angry only if one possesses the concept of anger, otherwise one could not be certain that what one felt was properly called 'anger'. Possession of a concept involves the ability to apply that concept. So, in the case of anger, one does not count as possessing the concept unless one can apply it to other people as well as to oneself. Mental concepts have second and third as well as first-person aspects. The first two aspects involve their being properly applied on the basis of observations of other bodies. So, mental concepts also have a physical aspect: minds and bodies are not fully separable.

To the first kind of treatment of the problem of other minds – the attempt to justify beliefs – the phenomenologists have two main responses. The first is that this strategy would give at best only a high degree of probability to claims that other minds exist. Husserl, Sartre and Merleau-Ponty all believe that this would be an inadequate solution to the problem: one's knowledge of other minds must be shown to be more secure than that, more than probable or even highly probable. This specific criticism is based on a deeper objection to the entire enterprise of justifying beliefs. The proper philosophical task is not, here or elsewhere, one of justification. For Husserl (see section 2, below), knowledge of other minds is foundational of all other knowledge. If he is to succeed in his aim of securely grounding scientific and other knowledge, knowledge of other minds must be more than probabilistic: it must have the kind of self-evidence which attaches to the Cartesian cogito, it must be inconceivable that other minds do not exist. There can be no question of *justifying* such knowledge, for there is nothing more secure in terms of which it might be justified.

Sartre and Merleau-Ponty also maintain the inadequacy of any thesis which claims only probabilistic knowledge of other minds. No such account, they believe, adequately captures the actual experience of interacting with other people. One is certain, one cannot doubt, that there are other people. Sartre refers to the experience of others as a 'second cogito'. One cannot doubt the existence of others any more than one can doubt one's own existence.

The phenomenologists' treatment of the problem of other minds has more in common with that of Wittgenstein, Ryle and Strawson. Both camps challenge the framework necessary to formulate the problem: Cartesian dualism. They argue that 'mind' and 'body' are abstractions, though they disagree about what they are abstractions from. For the analytic philosophers, they are abstractions from the more fundamental concept 'person'. Husserl and Sartre, in contrast, retain a robustly egocentric standpoint; for them, abstraction is from the subject-in-its-world. Merleau-Ponty, however, like the analytic philosophers, challenges this. His position is that experience is primarily inter-subjective; *personal* experience is the result of abstraction and hence lacks certainty. This has affinities with the view that acquisition of mental concepts, including their application to others, is a necessary condition of any application to oneself about which one might claim certainty.

2 Husserl's Fifth Meditation

As early as the Second Meditation, Husserl saw that his phenomenology, with its egocentric standpoint, looked inevitably solipsistic:

> Without doubt the sense of the transcendental reduction implies that, at the beginning, this science can posit nothing but the ego and what is included in the ego himself.... Without doubt ... it begins accordingly as a pure egology and as a science that apparently condemns us to a solipsism.... (*CM*, p. 30)

Any first-person centred philosophy will encounter problems in establishing that one ego can have knowledge of the existence of another ego. However, the problem which Husserl envisages is more acute. It is the problem that, from the standpoint he recommends, it will make no sense even to posit the existence of others:

> As yet it is quite impossible to foresee how, for me in the attitude of reduction, other egos – not as merely worldly phenomena but as other transcendental egos – can become positable as existing and thus become equally legitimate themes of a phenomenological egology. (*CM*, p. 30)

But Husserl is optimistic:

> Perhaps reduction to the transcendental ego only *seems* to entail a *permanently* solipsistic science; whereas the consequential elaboration of this science, in accordance with its own sense, leads over to a phenomenology of transcendental intersubjectivity.... But, at this point in our meditations, we can make no definite decision about this matter. (*CM*, pp. 30–1)

It is in the Fifth Meditation that the decision is to be made. The Meditation begins with a reminder of the problem. Husserl states it thus: when the meditating philosopher performs the phenomenological epoché, he precisely performs a reduction to his own ego and hence becomes the only ego:

> When I, the meditating I, reduce myself to my absolute transcendental ego by phenomenological epoché do I not become *solus ipse*...? (*CM*, p. 89)

The reduction is to the meditator's conscious processes and their constitution into unities:

> Transcendental reduction restricts me to the stream of my pure conscious processes and the unities constituted by their actualities and potentialities. (*CM*, p. 89)

But other egos are, by definition, not just processes and unities in the meditator's consciousness, but other consciousnesses:

> But what about other egos, who surely are not a mere intending and intended *in me*, merely synthetic unities of possible verification *in me*, but, according to their sense, precisely *others*? (*CM*, p. 89)

Hence, it would seem that Husserl's transcendental phenomenology can give no account of other egos, so understood. Other egos 'transcend', go beyond, are 'outside', independent of, the meditator's own ego; but the meditator can make sense only of what is 'inside' his ego. Husserl even goes so far as to suggest, in this respect, transcendental realism might seem superior. It can at least speak of other egos, and so sensibly enquire into the possibility of having knowledge of them; transcendental phenomenology, it now seems, cannot do even that:

> Accordingly can we avoid saying likewise: 'The very question of the possibility of actually transcendent knowledge – above all, that of the possibility of my going outside my ego and reaching other egos ... this question cannot be asked purely phenomenologically'? (*CM*, p. 90)

Husserl does not reply directly to the challenge he has presented, except by suggesting that there might be a flaw in the reasoning. His response is to offer a 'phenomenological explication' of 'alter [other] ego'. In section 43 he sketches the features of experience which such a phenomenological description will include. This is the purely descriptive stage which will provide the 'transcendental clues' to a theory of what is involved in constituting the experience of another subject. Husserl identifies three aspects of experiencing others. First, one experiences them as 'psycho-physical objects', as human beings, in the world; second, as subjects 'for' the world, experiencing the same world of objects as oneself; and third, as subjects who experience one as one experiences them.

But as well as these explicit experiences of others, Husserl claims, there is an implicit reference to other subjects in any experience of the objective world. To experience something as an object in the world includes, as a horizon, experiencing it as available to other subjects. One experiences the objective world *as* an inter-subjective world, a world for others, and which others can experience:

> The existence-sense of the world and of Nature in particular, as Objective Nature, includes after all, as we have already mentioned, thereness-for-every-one. This is always cointended wherever we speak of Objective actuality. (*CM*, p. 92)

An illustration of this (ours) would be a phenomenological description of perceiving a book. This would typically include, as horizons, references to other readers, to the author, to the way the book looked from an angle some-one else had on it, and more generally, to the fact that an objective world must stretch beyond an individual perceiver's personal powers to verify it – it must, for example, be capable of surviving that individual's death.

For the analysis of 'objective world' to be complete, then, it must include an analysis of 'other subject'. Husserl distinguishes here between the natural world and the social world; but he emphasizes that they are both 'there-for-everyone.' In experiencing the world, natural or social, as objectively existing, one is experiencing it as 'there-for-all', there for other subjects. This 'thereness-for-all' is part of the sense of 'objective', one of the 'horizons' of experience of the objective world.

Though this is presented by Husserl as the beginning of his solution to the problem of other minds, it also serves to show how important it is for Husserl to solve the problem. His original aim was to find firm foundations for one's knowledge of the objective world. But now, experience of such a world presupposes that there are or could be other subjects: one experiences it as an inter-subjective world. If, however, the phenomenologist can make no sense of the notion of another subject, then this unintelligibility must reflect back onto the notion the objective world, one's experience of it, and any knowledge one might claim to have of it.

Husserl's aim in the Fifth Meditation is to explore, in accordance with his phenomenological method, the 'existence-sense' of other subject, or other ego. This programme has four chief stages. The first stage, outlined in the first half of section 44, is the performance of the 'reduction to the sphere of ownness'. Husserl calls this a second epoché. Where the epoché of the First Meditation bracketed the assumption that objects exist, the second epoché involves a further bracketing of the assumption that other subjects exist. The next three stages are performed from this 'purely subjective' standpoint. The second stage (sections 44–6) explicates phenomenologically the sense of 'my self'; the third (sections 50–4) of 'other selves'; the fourth (sections 55–61) of 'com-munity' or 'inter-subjectivity'. Husserl concludes that his transcendental phenomenology can give an adequate account of the existence-sense of other self, and that knowledge of other selves is possible. Further, his transcendental phenomenology can give an adequate account of our inter-subjective experience of the objective world, and so his account of our knowledge of such a world is complete.

2(a)   Reduction to the Sphere of Ownness (*CM*, section 44)

The original epoché of the First Meditation involved bracketing all assumptions concerning the existence of objects in the world. This would include bracketing assumptions about the existence of human beings construed as objects in the world. The second epoché or 'reduction', which Husserl now proposes, goes beyond the first in that it involves bracketing assumptions which survived the first epoché. One must now bracket assumptions about the existence of other *subjects*, other co-experiencers of the natural and cultural worlds. But the existence of other subjects is implicit in one's experience of these worlds as inter-subjective, as 'there-for-all'. So one must now bracket the assumption that these worlds have this inter-subjective character. The phenomenologist must now adopt an entirely subjective standpoint, limiting attention to subjective experiences alone. From this standpoint, one can explore the sense or constitution of 'other subjectivity'. This is different from the standpoint, adopted following the first epoché, from which one could explicate the sense or constitution of 'objective world'.

Husserl distinguishes (*CM*, p. 93) this second epoché from simply imagining oneself alone in the world. This would be to imagine oneself in fact alone, but in a world which would be available to someone else, were anyone else there. Reduction to the sphere of ownness, in contrast, involves focusing on that aspect of one's experience which only one *can* have. Anything which presents itself as other than one must be construed now as, not really other, but as a feature of one's own subjective experience.

The reduction to the sphere of ownness Husserl also calls a reduction to one's 'monad' (*CM*, p. 94) (see Chapter Three, section 1). This allusion to Leibniz[7] is, of course, not to be understood as an endorsement of Leibniz's metaphysical view of monads as the ultimate constituents of reality. Husserl explicitly rejects that interpretation in section 62. Husserl is recommending a method, not a metaphysic. His point is that the sphere of ownness, like a Leibnizian monad, is insulated from anything other than itself, it 'has no windows'. Just as, for Leibniz, any apparent relation between monads is to be construed in terms of non-relational properties of essentially unrelated monads, so, for Husserl, in the sphere of ownness, one is to construe any apparent relation between oneself and anything else as solely a property of one's own subjective experience, a 'mirroring' of what is included in one's monad and not a perceiving of something outside. A second feature of monads which Husserl stresses is that monads are 'concrete'. One's monadic standpoint is one's own specific personal standpoint. Only from such a standpoint,

Husserl claims, can one explore, without presuppositions, the sense of 'other subjects'.

On page 96, Husserl remarks briefly that the reduction to the sphere of ownness leaves one with experience which is 'harmonious', a 'unitarily coherent stratum of the phenomenon world', and that this is a 'founding ' or 'primordial' stratum. This, Husserl tells us, is important, but he does not here elaborate on the claim. A comparison with the first epoché is enlightening. There, having performed the epoché, the first important discovery was that 'nothing had changed' (see Chapter Two, section 1). Experience was still coherent and structured, it was still the experience of objects. Futher, that it retained this structure was there cited by Husserl as a necessary condition of ever perceiving or having knowledge of the existing world. The task of phenomenology is to explicate this structure and thereby elucidate the 'existence-sense' of objective world. Similarly, here in the Fifth Meditation, the bracketing of the existence of other subjects does not render one's subjective experience incoherent. One still finds oneself in a 'stratum of continuing world-experience'. That this is so, Husserl claims, is a necessary condition for ever experiencing other subjects or an objective world:

> This unitary stratum, furthermore, is distinguished by being essentially the *founding* stratum – that is to say: I obviously cannot have the 'alien' or 'other' as experience, and therefore cannot have the sense 'Objective world' as an experiential sense, without having this stratum in actual experience; whereas the reverse is not the case. (*CM*, p. 96)

The phenomenological task now is to explicate the structures of this subjective or 'primordial' stratum, thereby elucidating the 'existence-sense' of 'other subject', and so complete the account of the existence-sense of 'objective world'.

2(b)   Explication of the Sense of 'My Own Self' (*CM*, sections 44–8)

The aim of these sections is to give an account of 'my self' from the standpoint of the sphere of ownness. What is crucially revealed is that the self includes, not only the constituting transcendental Ego, but also an empirical self which is experienced as an object in the natural world.

Husserl first notes that, from this new standpoint, one experiences 'Nature'. This is to be distinguished from objective nature experienced by other subjects and studied by natural scientists. It is 'nature for me', or ' "Nature" included in my ownness':

> Thus there is included in my ownness, as purified from every sense pertaining to other subjectivity, *a sense*, '*mere Nature*', that has lost precisely that [experienceable] 'by everyone'.... (*CM*, p. 96)

Second, Husserl notes that one experiences one's own body as being part of that 'nature'. This body differs from other bodies in 'mere nature' in that one feels sensations in it and one controls it. It is through this body that one can perceive and act upon 'nature'. One experiences one's body as an 'animate organism', as having a mind, or 'psyche', and as forming a psycho-physical unity with this psyche. This psycho-physical unity is one's personal worldly ego. In sum, following the reduction to the sphere of ownness, one finds that some of one's experiences are also experiences *of* one's self. Husserl characterizes this 'self' or 'ego' variously as 'natural', 'worldly', 'empirical' and 'concrete'. We shall mainly use the term 'empirical'. These experiences of one's empirical self have what Husserl calls a 'peculiar ownness'.

Next (section 45), Husserl explores how this empirical self, experienced as peculiarly one's own, relates to the transcendental Ego. His answer is that the transcendental Ego's role here, as elsewhere, is to constitute experiences into unities, into groups or syntheses of experiences which are all experiences of the same thing. When that thing is the empirical self, the role of the transcendental Ego is to perform what Husserl calls 'a mundanizing self-apperception'. The transcendental Ego, that is, 'apperceives' (literally, 'perceives itself') as having a 'mundane' (literally 'worldly') self.[8]

In section 46, Husserl sets out to explicate this self, to reveal what is essential to it. He notes that this self-explication involves just the same method used for explicating any object. One starts from groups of experiences of the same object, and via describing horizons one reveals the essence of the object. So with self-explication: one starts with experiences which are all of the same (one's own) empirical self; then, one looks for features without which they would not be experiences of that self. These reveal the essence of 'empirical self':

> In unqualifiedly apodictic evidence self-explication brings out only the all-embracing structural forms in which I exist as ego. (*CM*, p. 103)

Husserl gives a schematic account of this self-explication. He notes first that each self-perception is a perception of a self understood as already existing and continuing into the future. Next, he observes that experiences of oneself are not confined to perception in the normal sense, but include memories and intentions, which provide a very special access to, respectively, one's past and future self. The content of any of these experiences may be unclear, illusory or imperfect – one can misremember, or have vague intentions. What self-explication aims to bring out is not this content but the form or structure of one's experience of oneself.

One crucial structure is 'immanent temporality'. Husserl indicates that the heart of this notion is that a self persists through time, and changes through time. It also, at any given time, has a point of view on itself, and each such view is itself one of the experiences which make up the temporally extended self. The self, as it were, views itself 'from the inside'.[9] Husserl further notes that the self regards itself as a 'self constitutor': it can initiate change in its own life:

> They [the structural forms of the empirical ego] include (among others) the mode of existence in the form of a certain all-embracing life of some sort or other, that of existence in the form of the continuous self-constitution of that life's own processes, as temporal within an all-embracing time, and so forth. (*CM*, p. 103)

In revealing these essential structural forms of self-experience, self-explication uncovers the laws or structures of the transcendental Ego with respect to its own empirical, concrete existence:

> This fully determined content itself, with the sense of something firmly identifiable again and again, in respect of all its parts and moments, is an 'idea', valid a priori. (*CM*, p. 103)

To summarize, the relation between the transcendental Ego and the empirical ego is that the transcendental Ego has an 'idea' of itself which is exemplified by the empirical ego. The empirical ego is that in which the transcendental Ego lives its life in the world. It is crucially a temporal, changing, self-aware and self-directed life.

2(c)   Explication of the Sense of 'Other Self' (*CM*, sections 50–4)

In section 47, Husserl observes that complete self-explication will include uncovering the structures not only of those experiences which are of one's empirical ego, but also of those experiences which are of other objects. In section 48, he poses the problem with which the rest of the Fifth Meditation will deal, namely, what is involved in being aware of these objects:

> And now the *problem* is how we are to understand the fact that the ego has, and can always go on forming, in himself such intentionalities of a different kind, intentionalities with an existence-sense whereby *he wholly transcends his own being*. (*CM*, p. 105)

In short, Husserl needs to show first, that knowledge of other people is possible; and second, that all people experience the same world. The task, as he sees it, is to explicate the existence-sense of 'other self' , and to show that it is part of that existence-sense that other selves experience the same world one experiences. The standpoint for both these explications must be one's primordial sphere, one's sphere of ownness, in which one constitutes these existence-senses. The hope will be that, having clarified this existence sense, one's experience will confirm that others do indeed exist and share one's world.

In section 49, Husserl distinguishes four levels of constitution which the explication will reveal. Each successive level, he claims, presupposes earlier levels. First is the constitution of 'other Ego' (*CM*, sections 50–4). We shall discuss this level in the remainder of this section. Second is the constitution of the Ego-community, which must be a harmony of subjects. Third is the constitution of the objective world as a world for everyone, as a world experienced as transcendent by the community of Egos. Fourth is the constitution of people as objects in this objective world and as giving 'worldly' sense to transcendental Egos. We shall discuss these three levels (*CM*, sections 55–61) in section 2(d) below.

Husserl begins with the experience of 'other men', that is, other empirical egos. The aim is to explore their existence-sense. What is revealed in the course of the next four sections (50–4) is that some experiences are of empirical selves – they have the constitution described in sections 44–6; but these selves are not 'my self', hence they must be other selves or egos.

Husserl begins with experiences of bodies. As we noted, one experiences one's own body in a distinctive way. One also experience other bodies, not in this distinctive way, but as like one's own. The other body is actually presented but it is also 'meant' as being an animate organism. This kind of experience Husserl calls 'analogical apperception'. One perceives the other body as analogous to one's own. Husserl uses the word 'apperception', following Leibniz, to indicate an element of self-perception: the analogy is between one's perception of the other body and one's perception of one's own. 'Analogical apperception' involves a 'transfer of sense' from one's experience of one's own body (one's self-experience or '*ap*perception') to one's experience of the other body:

> the body over there, which is nevertheless apprehended as an animate organism, must have derived this sense by an *apperceptive transfer from my animate organism....* (*CM*, p. 110)

This 'analogical' perception, Husserl insists, does not involve inference: it is not an example of the argument from analogy. Nor is such perception, as opposed to apperception, peculiar to the perception of others. Analogical perception occurs whenever one perceives a familiar kind of object. His example is of a child learning what scissors are. The child has learnt what scissors are when it sees new scissors as analogous to scissors it has seen before. The later experience receives a 'transfer of sense' from the earlier ones:

> Thus *each everyday experience* involves an *analogizing transfer* of an originally instituted objective sense to a new case, with its anticipative apprehension of the object as having a similar sense. (*CM*, p. 111)

Section 51 opens with the claim that there are two distinctive features of the analogical apperception of other human bodies. These two features are discussed in sections 51 and 52. The first is the presence of 'pairing' in every experience of other human bodies. Pairing, like analogical perception, is, Husserl argues, a common feature of experience. It occurs whenever one experiences a pair (or group) of similar objects. One perceives them as similar, as being of the same kind. Pairing is, Husserl claims, always present when one perceives another human body. One is, he claims, constantly aware, if only peripherally, of one's own body as an animate organism. Hence, whenever one is also aware of the body of another, one is aware of a 'pair' of similar things. Further, since one first learnt what animate organisms are from perceiving one's own, it is natural to transfer that sense to a new case, to the other member of the pair.

The second distinctive feature of analogical apperception of other bodies as animate organisms is that it involves experiencing other bodies as like one's own. Hence, it has horizons, 'appresented aspects', which one can never directly experience. It is part of the existence-sense of *other* body, *other* animate organism, that one cannot directly experience the kinaesthetic sensations one apperceives it as having, nor the intentions one apperceives it as directing itself by. One can have such direct experience only of one's *own* animate organism:

what is *appresented* by virtue of the aforesaid analogizing can never attain actual presence, never become an object of perception proper. (*CM*, p. 112)

Hence, there is no possibility of directly verifying, making actual, these horizons of the other body apperceived as animate organism. One cannot directly verify that the other body is another animate organism.

However, as Husserl observes in section 52, one's apperceptions of other animate organisms have other horizons which can be verified. What one expects of an animate organism is that its behaviour is 'harmonious'. As long as one continues to apperceive the continuing movements of the body as harmonious behaviour, one verifies he original apperception of it as an animate organism:

Every experience points to further experiences that would fulfil and verify the appresented horizons, which include, in the form of non-intuitive anticipations, potentially verifiable syntheses of harmonious further experience. (*CM*, p. 114)

Husserl further observes:

The organism becomes experienced as a pseudo-organism, precisely if there is something discordant about its behaviour. (*CM*, p. 114)

One is put in mind of science fiction plays in which humanoid robots can 'give themselves away' by behaving in ways one would not expect of a human.

The sort of direct verification which one can have serves as indirect verification that the body of the other is an animate organism. This 'indirect' verification, Husserl remarks, is of the same kind as one has for one's memories construed as giving access to one's past experiences. One cannot *have* again the past experiences in order to compare them with one's memories of them. What serves instead as a 'verification' of a memory experience is that it coheres with the rest of one's memories.

In section 53, Husserl reveals a further horizon of the perception of other human bodies. This involves their spatial location. One experiences one's own body as 'here'; other human bodies as 'there'. But the location which one perceives human bodies to have involves more than simply occupying a region of space in the way, for example, a table does. One is 'oriented' in space. One's position in space is the one from which one views the rest of space, and one can change it by moving to another position:

> By free modification of my kinesthesias, particularly those of locomotion, I can change my position in such a manner that I convert any There into a Here – that is to say, I could occupy any spatial locus with my organism. (*CM*, p. 116)

This kind of orientation which one experiences in the case of one's own body is transferred, by analogical apperception, to other human bodies. One apperceives another human body as oriented 'there' as one experiences oneself as oriented 'here'. The other body is apperceived as occupying its space in the same way as one would occupy it if one were there. So, the other body is experienced as a point of view on the world, and one which can move, can change its point of view. All this, claims Husserl, adds up to apperceiving the other body as the body of a concrete ego.

But now, this concrete ego apperceived as 'there' cannot be *one's own* ego, for one is not there but here, and one cannot be in both places at the same time. The two locations are incompatible as simultaneous locations of one's own ego. They become compatible only if one apperceives the body 'there' as the body of an *other* ego:

> Therefore, an ego is *appresented*, as *other* than mine. That which is primordially incompatible, in simultaneous coexistence, becomes compatible. (*CM*, p. 119)

Husserl goes on to describe how one comes to ascribe 'contents' to this other ego, how its activities and psychic states are appresented. One 'reads' its behaviour, by 'pairing' with one's own, as the behaviour of an ego:

the understanding of the members as hands groping or functioning in pushing, as feet functioning in walking, as eyes functioning in seeing, and so forth. (*CM*, p. 119)

'Reading' such behaviour as expressing psychic states involves what Husserl calls 'empathizing', apperceiving the behaviour as that of an ego:

> Such contents too are indicated somatically and in the conduct of the organism toward the outside world – for example: as the outward conduct of someone who is angry or cheerful, which I easily understand from my own conduct in similar circumstances. (*CM*, p. 120)

In all these experiences, one apperceives an ego which is like one's own, but is not one's own: one apperceives, that is, another ego.

To summarize: one knows what an empirical ego is from one's own case. One recognizes other empirical egos as like oneself. One's experience confirms that they exist. Any feature of them which one cannot directly verify counts, not as a ground for doubting their existence, but as a confirming that they are *other* egos. In Husserl's terms, the explication of the existence-sense of 'other ego' indicates what one's experience must be like if others exist. Since one's experience satisfies these requirements, one does know that others exist.

Husserl still has to establish that knowledge of other transcendental Egos is possible. His method is just like the one he used to establish the possibility of knowledge of other empirical egos. One's experience of other empirical egos has horizons. One experiences the other concrete ego as a self-constitutor, as constituting its empirical self as part of nature, and as constituted from a primordial sphere. That is to say, one experiences the other empirical ego as the natural aspect of a transcendental Ego; but that transcendental Ego is not one's own, since one cannot have the experiences which these horizons indicate. One cannot experience the other's 'primordial sphere' or 'sphere of ownness'. This, however, indicates not that one is alone, but that the transcendental Egos are precisely *other* Egos.

2(d)   The Community of Egos (*CM*, sections 55ff)

The remainder of the Fifth Meditation (sections 55–61) is spent in establishing that this other Ego experiences the same world one experiences oneself, that it coexperiences the same inter-subjective world. This coexperience, Husserl claims, is implicit in one's experience of others and of the world, and so it can be revealed by phenomenological description.

Husserl first gives an account of how one shares the same natural (as opposed to cultural) world with the other Ego. When one perceives another body as the body of an other Ego, the other Ego is apperceived as just like one's own. It is apperceived as experiencing its body as part of nature, as having a perspective on nature, as having a primordial sphere from which it founds the natural world. It is apperceived as having a different body, a different perspective, a different primordial sphere from one's own; but the body is apperceived as part of the same nature, the perspective as a perspective on the same world, the primordial sphere as founding the same objective world that one experiences oneself. One apperceives the other as having a different perspective, but a perspective on the same world:

> It is implicit in the sense of my successful apperception of others that their world, the world belonging to their appearance-systems, must be experienced forthwith as the same as the world belonging to my appearance-systems; and this involves an identity of our appearance-systems. (*CM*, p. 125)

This apperception of another person as experiencing the same world as one's own Husserl calls 'presentation'. One experience 'presentiates' another experience when it presents itself as the experience of the same thing. Presentation, like analogical apperception and pairing, is not peculiar to the perception of other people. Presentation also occurs when one recollects a past experience. One cannot now have the past experience, for it is past; but it is 'presentiated' in one's present recollections as an experience with the same content as the present one. There is a connection between the present experience and the past 'presentiated' one: they are experiences of the same thing. In a similar way, one cannot have someone else's experiences; but they are presentiated in one's own experiences. One's own and the other's experiences are experiences of the same thing, the same world.

Husserl concludes his description of what he calls 'the first level of community' with the claim that one apperceives the other as having, like oneself, an 'immanent temporality'. The essential structure of the other's experiences is a temporal one. This temporality is presentiated as like one's own immanent temporality: they are both exemplifications of the very same form – the objective time in which concrete egos live and natural objects exist.

> In this connexion we see that the temporal community of the constitutively interrelated monads is indissoluble, because it is tied up essentially with the constitution of *a world and a world time*. (*CM*, p. 128)

To summarize: one apperceives other subjects as experiencing the same world as one experiences and as constituting their world and their experiences in essentially the same way one constitutes one's own. Furthermore, and this is something which Sartre applauds in Husserl's account (see section 3, below), Husserl observes that one experiences the world as a world which admits of other perspectives. This is all one needs in order for knowledge of the existence of an inter-subjective world to be possible.

The second level of community concerns one's experiencing others as experiencing one in turn:

> If, with my understanding of someone else, I penetrate more deeply into him, into his horizon of ownness, I shall soon run into the fact that, just as his animate bodily organism lies in my field of perception, so my animate organism lies in his field of perception and that, in general, he experiences me forthwith as an Other for him, just as I experience him as *my* Other. (*CM*, pp. 129–130)

In short, in perceiving something as another person, one perceives that person as perceiving one in return, as perceiving the objective aspect of oneself.

A further feature implicit in one's perception of other people is that one experiences others as having a culture. But, whereas to see someone as a person requires regarding them as sharing the same natural world, their cultural world may be experienced as differing from one's own.

> Everyone, as a matter of a priori necessity, lives in the same Nature. . . . But this, after all, does not exclude, either a priori or de facto, the truth that men belonging to one and the same world live in a loose cultural community – or even none at all – and accordingly constitute different surrounding worlds of culture, as concrete life-worlds. . . . (*CM*, p. 133)

This notion of 'life-worlds' is developed more fully by Husserl in *The Crisis* and adopted with enthusiasm by Merleau-Ponty (see Chapter Five, section 2, and Chapter Six, section 1, above). Two crucial features of it which Husserl cites here, in the *Cartesian Meditations*, are its historical character and its orientedness. Life-worlds are acquired in time and from a point of view. They must be *lived* by a person with a developing character and a body, and not simply understood intellectually. Life-worlds, cultures, are essentially shared. One could not have a culture without the capacity to perceive others as having the same culture; nor could one perceive others if one did not have an appreciation of a culture – one's own or another – of which the other might be a member.

All these features – the body of the other, the empirical ego, the transcendental Ego, the natural world and life-world of the other – have now been seen to be involved in the sense of 'other ego'. This is all constituted in one's sphere of ownness, for that was Husserl's starting-point. Nothing, Husserl claims, from outside that sphere has been imported to explain the sense which one attaches to 'other self'. Hence, contrary to Husserl's original worry (see the beginning of section 2, above), the transcendental phenomenologist can attach sense to the idea of 'other selves' or 'other Ego'. Questions such as: 'Do other Egos exist?' or 'Can one have knowledge of other

Egos?' are intelligible. And, as interpreted by Husserl, the answer to both questions, so understood, is 'Yes'. One's experience reveals, and constantly confirms, that there are other Egos and that they are coexperiencers with oneself of an objective world.

The work of the Fifth Meditation, Husserl believes, serves to dispel his two inter-connected worries: that his transcendental phenomenology entails solipsism, and that this would undermine his entire account of the objective world. Husserl regards himself as having achieved his aim of showing how transcendental phenomenology can give an adequate account of knowledge of other subjects and so can complete its account of knowledge of the objective world. It has emerged that Husserl's account takes the form, not of seeking to justify inferences to the conclusion that others exist, but of undertaking an investigation which he believes to be essentially prior to the possibility of justification: the investigation of the sense of any such claim. Once this sense has been properly explicated, one must, Husserl believes, accept that others exist and that one has knowledge of them. In this, his treatment of the problem of other minds falls within the second broad class of 'solution' outlined in section 1 above. The exploration he presents shares with this class of treatments a second feature: namely, the rejection of the Cartesian thesis that mind and body are logically distinct. Husserl's phenomenological descriptions of one's experience of one's own self and other selves have revealed the importance of the body of the subject as it lives in, acts upon and experiences the world.

3   The Existential Other

Predictably, Sartre's discussion of Husserl's account of knowledge of other subjects is continuous with his discussion of Husserl's account of subjects (see Chapter Four, section 2). Sartre begins by applauding Husserl's account of the relation between empirical egos. Husserl recognizes, Sartre claims, that one experiences others not only directly when one encounters them, but also implicitly in any experience of the objective world. As we noted at the beginning of section 2 above, it was precisely the inter-subjective character of the natural world which led Husserl to enquire into the experience of other subjects; and Husserl goes on to describe the world as one which admits of other perspectives (see section 2(d) above). Summarizing Husserl's account, Sartre writes:

> The Other is present in it [the world] not only as a particular concrete and empirical appearance but as a permanent condition of its unity and of its richness. (*BN*, p. 233)

it is *on* the table, *on* the wall that the Other is revealed to me as that to which the object under consideration is perpetually referred – as well as on the occasion of the concrete appearances of Pierre or Paul. (*BN*, p. 233)

Further, on Husserl's account, one's empirical self is as much a part of the objective world as are other empirical selves. Sartre sees this as having the desirable consequence, for Husserl, that one can have as secure knowledge of other empirical egos as one can of one's own:

> If I am to doubt the existence of my friend Pierre ... then ... I must of necess-
> ity doubt also my concrete being, my empirical reality as a professor having this
> or that tendency, these habits, this particular character. There is no privilege for
> *my* self: my empirical Ego and the Other's empirical Ego appear in the world at
> the same time. (*BN*, p. 233)

But, continues Sartre, this cannot be a complete solution to the problem of other minds for Husserl, because, according to Husserl, the subject is not only an empirical ego, but also a transcendental Ego which is 'referred to' by the empirical ego and, as the subject of experience, is 'beyond experience':

> the Other is *never* that empirical person who is encountered in my experience;
> he is the transcendental subject to whom this person by nature refers. Thus the
> true problem is that of the connection of transcendental subjects who are
> beyond experience. (*BN*, p. 234)

What Husserl gives us, according to Sartre, is an account of the *meaning* and not the *being* of other Egos. Husserl gives, that is to say, an account of the structures, grounded in one's own Ego, of the series of appearances which constitute the existence-sense of other Egos. He then claims that there can be no further question as to whether or not there are other transcendental Egos. Given that one's experience conforms to these structures, one has knowledge of others. Husserl is thus, claims Sartre, 'making knowledge the measure of being'.

We noted, in Chapter Four, section 1, that Sartre objects quite generally to Husserl's account of 'being' in terms of meaning and knowledge. Here, however, Sartre's objection is not this general one, but a specific objection to such an account of other transcendental Egos. Even if it were possible to give an adequate account of the being of most things, including empirical egos, in terms of knowledge of them, there would be a special difficulty in doing this for other transcendental Egos. This arises because the other is essentially a self-knower. Hence, in Sartre's terms, if any knowledge is the measure of the other's being, it must be the knowledge that the other has of itself. What is needed, therefore, to give access to the being of an other transcendental Ego, would be the knowledge that it has of its own empirical ego, and this is impossible for anyone else to have. It is actually unintelligible that one should have such knowledge of an *other* person, since if one had such knowledge one would *be* that person. So, Sartre, concludes, Husserl has not shown how his transcendental phenomenology can make sense of the hypothesis that there are other transcendental Egos:

> Now even admitting that knowledge in general measures being, the Other's being is measured in its reality by the knowledge which the Other has of himself, not by that which I have of him. What I must attain is the Other, not as I obtain knowledge of him, but as he obtains knowledge of himself – which is impossible. (*BN*, p. 234)

Sartre completes his attack on Husserl by saying that it is unclear how Husserl can move from the fact that one has an intuition of absence with respect to the transcendental Egos of others to any claim concerning the reality of anything except our own intuitions:

> But within Husserl's philosophy, at least, how can one have a full intuition of an absence? The Other is the object of empty intentions, the Other on principle refuses himself to us and flees. The only reality which remains is therefore that of *my* intention. (*BN*, pp. 234–5)

As we shall explore in section 4 below, Sartre believes that one has a distinctive direct experience of the *presence* of other people.

Sartre goes on to indicate the way in which he sees his own philosophical position as having a problem in avoiding solipsism. He has rejected Husserl's transcendental Ego (see Chapter Four, section 2), so Husserl's problems are not Sartre's. However, Sartre still acknowledges that there is more to people than their empirical selves. There are also what he calls 'transcendental fields of consciousness'. People, on Sartre's account (see Chapter Four, section 4), are not to be identified with their empirical selves. There is also the consciousness which can 'stand back' and question that self. Sartre still needs to explain the connection between different such consciousnesses:

> Even if outside the empirical Ego there is *nothing other* than the consciousness *of* that Ego – that is, a transcendental field without a subject – the fact remains that my affirmation of the Other demands and requires the existence beyond the world of a similar transcendental field. (*BN*, p. 235)

This connection, Sartre believes, must be, not as Husserl has it, a relation of knowledge, mediated by meaning, but a relation prior to both – a non-thetic, non-conceptualized, relation between beings. As such, Sartre adds, this relation will 'affect the being' of those so related:

> Consequently the only way to escape solipsism would be here again to prove that
> my transcendental consciousness is in its very being, affected by the extra-
> mundane existence of other consciousnesses of the same type. (*BN*, p. 235)

We must now look at Sartre's positive account to see what this demand
comes to and how it is to be met.

4   Being-for-Others, Shame and Conflict

Sartre begins Part III of *Being and Nothingness* by describing a kind of
experience which is neither a reflective experience of oneself as object, nor an
experience of one's being-for-itself. This experience, he claims, indicates a
new 'ontological structure' not so far introduced:

> This ontological structure is *mine*; it is in relation to myself as subject that I am
> concerned about myself, and yet this concern (for-my-self) reveals to me a being
> which is *my* being without being-for-me. (*BN*, p. 221)

What one experiences on certain occasions when another person is present is
oneself, but oneself as viewed from a standpoint other than one's own. One
experiences oneself 'before', in the eyes of, another person. Sartre gives as an
example of this experience, shame:

> By the mere appearance of the Other, I am put in the position of passing judge-
> ment on myself as on an object, for it is as an object that I appear to the Other.
> (*BN*, p. 222)

One experiences oneself as judged, as endowed with a significance, a meaning,
of which one is not the author. One is no longer a being-for-itself but a being-
for-the-other: the other dictates how one's behaviour is to be regarded,
interpreted:[10]

> The For-itself refers to the For-others. Therefore if we wish to grasp in its total-
> ity the relation of man's being to being-in-itself, we can not be satisfied with the
> descriptions outlined in the earlier chapters of this work. (*BN*, p. 222)

In *Being and Nothingness*, part 3, chapter 1, section IV, entitled 'The Look',
Sartre explores in more detail this phenomenon of being-for-others. He
describes two different kinds of experience and the relation between them.
Pages 252–6 contain a description of the experience of perceiving another person as a kind of object in the world. The remainder of the section contains a
description of the experience of being perceived by another subject, the
experience of being an object in someone else's world.

The section begins in a way which is very like Husserl's horizonal description of perceiving other human beings. One perceives another person as a purposive being interacting with his environment:

> this man sees the lawn, . . . in spite of the prohibiting sign he is preparing to walk on the grass, etc. (*BN*, p. 254)

In seeing something as a purposive being in the world, one also thereby perceives that world as having aspects which one does not experience. The aspects of the world which the other experiences 'escape' one, they are experienced as absent:

> This green turns toward the Other a face which escapes me. I apprehend the relation of the green to the Other as an objective relation, but I cannot apprehend the green *as* it appears to the Other. (*BN*, p. 255)

More generally, when one experiences another person, one experiences the world as containing a perspective which is not one's own – the world has in it an alternative viewpoint:

> The Other is first the permanent flight of things toward a goal which I apprehend as an object at a certain distance from me but which escapes me inasmuch as it unfolds about itself its own distances. (*BN*, p. 255)

So far, this account of perceiving other people is, Sartre repeatedly reminds us, an account of the experience of others as *objects* of consciousness:

> None of this enables us to leave the level on which the Other is an *object*. (*BN*, p. 256)

Perceiving other people, as so far described, never makes it more than highly probable that the bodies which one perceives as the bodies of other people are in fact other people with perceptions and purposes. They might be robots, or they might have quite different purposes from those one takes them to have:

> First, it is *probable* that this object is a man. Second, even granted that he is a man, it remains only probable that he *sees* the lawn at the moment that I perceive him; it is possible that he is dreaming of some project without exactly being aware of what is around him, or that he is blind, etc., etc. (*BN*, p. 254)

No account has yet been ventured of the experience of the other as a subject. Hence the true issue, as Sartre sees it, of characterizing a relation between subjects, has not yet been touched upon. What Sartre wants is an account of how one experiences the other as a subject.

As we noted in the course of examining Sartre's criticisms of Husserl, Sartre requires that the relation between subjects should be one of being and not knowledge, and also that this relation be one which does not leave one's own being unaffected. He has also stated earlier in his own account that he wants his account to explain the basis of one's certainty – a certainty which, like one's certainty of one's own existence, is beyond all intelligible doubt – that other subjects exist.

The next move in his account is to argue that, since our perceiving others as objects has 'horizons of absence' – that is, one perceives others as conscious but one does not experience their consciousness – these 'absences' 'refer to a presence', an experience one could have of the other's consciousness. Hence, Sartre believes, a solution to the other minds problem must involve finding some direct experience of the presence of another consciousness. Sartre then finds this experience in the phenomenon with which he began the chapter: one's being-for-others. Here he takes the example of being looked at:

> if the Other-as-object is defined in connection with the world as the object which *sees* what I see, then my fundamental connection with the Other-as-subject must be able to be referred back to my permanent possibility of *being seen by* the Other. (*BN*, p. 256)

He goes on to explore the 'meaning' of this experience. Sartre describes it graphically and at some length on pages 257–302, elaborating the description of being-for-others with which he began the chapter. Very briefly, he finds two things. First, it is the experience of oneself as object (pp. 257–68). It is oneself one experiences, just as the objective self one can reflect upon is oneself. But this objective self, one's being-for-others, is an object, not in one's own world, but in the world perceived by the other, the world as it 'escapes' one:

> Now, shame, as we noted at the beginning of this chapter, is shame of *self*; it is the *recognition* of the fact that I *am* indeed that object which the Other is looking at and judging. (*BN*, p. 261)

Second, (pp. 269–302), it is an experience of the other as subject:

> if I am wholly engulfed in my shame, the Other is the immense, invisible presence which supports this shame and embraces it on every side. (*BN*, p. 269)

That it is another subject who looks at one is apparent, Sartre claims, since the experience of being looked at is incompatible with looking at the other person. Indeed one employs precisely that looking at the other, turning the other into an object of one's perception, as a defence against one's being looked at. The possibility of success for this defensive strategy relies on the two experiences, of the other as subject and the other as object, being incompatible:

> The Other is in no way given to us as an object. The objectivation of the Other would be the collapse of his being-as-a-look. . . . In the phenomenon of the look, the Other is on principle that which can not be an object. (*BN*, p. 268)

Hence, this is the experience Sartre was seeking and which he thought Husserl's account deficient in not recognizing. In so far as one experiences oneself as object, one is not unaffected by the experience. In so far as one experiences the other as subject, the other is not related to one merely by knowledge. So, it is a relation of being in which one stands to the other. This experience of being looked at is the 'second cogito' which Sartre believes (see section 1, above) there must be if the existence of other people is to be certain and not merely a matter of probabilistic knowledge:

> If the Other's existence is not a vain conjecture, a pure fiction, this is because there is a sort of *cogito* concerning it. (*BN*, p. 251)

Given this experience, solipsism cannot be lived or thought; though, Sartre allows, it can still be stated, just as one can state that one doubts one's own existence.

What is distinctive about Sartre's account of the relations between subjects (and this is an element to which Sartre devotes the whole of chapter 3 of Part 3 of *Being and Nothingness*, entitled 'Concrete Relations with Others'), is that all relations with others are based on confrontation and conflict.[11] Whenever another human being is an object of one's consciousness, one's experience indicates that one can become an object of the other's consciousness. When this occurs, one experiences one's being-for-others. This experience in its turn indicates that one can reverse the situation by making the other an object of one's consciousness again. So, relations with others are essentially unstable in the sense that they are ever fluctuating between one's being an object to the other's subject and one's being a subject to the other's object. Sartre further presents this dynamic of human interaction as one which is experienced as threatening. It is, according to Sartre, a struggle for dominance which can never end nor be reconciled for, at each stage, one experiences the other as a threat to one as a conscious (and free) subject: other people not only 'affect' one's being but appear to endanger it. One experiences the other as a threat, and one can neutralize this threat only by threatening the other. It is this uneasy dynamic which, for Sartre, constitutes the certainty that others exist.

228 The Recognition of Other Selves

5 Communality and the Social World

There is agreement between Husserl, Sartre and Merleau-Ponty that the philosopher's task is to describe the phenomena which give rise to certainty that other subjects exist. Further, they agree that these phenomena, properly described, rob solipsism of any philosophical plausibility.

A crucial disagreement between the two existentialists is that Merleau-Ponty believes that Sartre has selected the wrong phenomena for the purposes of exploring the certainty that other people exist. Where Sartre believes conflict to lie at the heart of this certainty, Merleau-Ponty believes that the certainty first appears in experiences of communality; that these latter experiences are presupposed by phenomena of conflict; and that Sartrean conflict involves reflection on and withdrawal from communality. Merleau-Ponty makes the criticism with reference to Hegel,[12] but it would apply equally to Sartre:

> For the struggle ever to begin, and for each consciousness to be capable of suspecting the alien presences which it negates, all must necessarily have some common ground and be mindful of their peaceful co-existence in the world of childhood. (*PP*, p. 355)

In short, Merleau-Ponty's point is that, if one experiences another person's world as in competition with one's own world, or the other person as threatening, this can only be because of a more basic awareness of being similar and sharing a common world. We shall explore later Merleau-Ponty's descriptions of the phenomenon of communality.

There is a further difference between Sartre and Merleau-Ponty. They disagree about the role of the body in the experience of other subjects. For Sartre, as we noted in section 4 above, one perceives human bodies as objects. These perceptions play no essential role in one's experience of other subjects.[13] For Merleau-Ponty, as will emerge later in this section, one's experience of others' bodies is an integral part of one's experience of other subjects. In the Preface to the *Phenomenology of Perception*, Merleau-Ponty writes:

> I must be the exterior that I present to others, and the body of the other must be the other himself. (*PP*, p. xii)

In this emphasis on the significance of the body, Merleau-Ponty is in some measure of agreement with Husserl (see sections 2(b) and (c), above).

Merleau-Ponty's response to the problem of other minds and his account of relations between subjects is contained in Part Two, Chapter 4 of the *Phenomenology of Perception*, entitled 'Other Selves and the Human World'.[14]

The discussion divides into two parts. First (pp. 346–56), Merleau-Ponty offers his description of the cultural or human world and argues that objective thought[15] can give no adequate account of this world. Second (pp. 356–61), he argues that solipsistic conclusions cannot legitimately be drawn from premisses appealing to the individuality of personal experience since any such experience presupposes the cultural, social world where subjects, contrary to solipsistic claims, do inter-relate and communicate.

Merleau-Ponty begins by observing that, just as one finds oneself surrounded by the natural world, so one finds oneself also in a cultural world. This cultural or social world is shared by subjects in community with each other and is, like the natural world, experienced as self-evident, as beyond sceptical doubt. Objects in this world are artefacts, made by people for the use of people. Later in the chapter (pp. 352–4) he picks out for special attention two cultural objects: the human body, which he terms the 'first' cultural object, since it is the body which uses all other cultural objects; and language, the importance of which as a cultural object lies in its use in interpersonal communication.

Artefacts, he claims, result from natural objects being moulded to human use, and these human uses, the behaviour patterns involved in using the artefact, are visible in the artefact:

> Just as nature finds its way to the core of my personal life and becomes inextricably linked with it, so behaviour patterns settle into that nature, being deposited in the form of a cultural world. (*PP*, p. 347)

These behaviour patterns which are 'deposited' in cultural objects are not the behaviour patterns of any particular human being. Artefacts are not only for one's own use nor for the use of any other specified individual, but for the use of any human subject whatsoever. The subject of the cultural world is, Merleau-Ponty says, an 'anonymous' subject:

> In the cultural object, I feel the close presence of others beneath a veil of anonymity. *Someone* uses the pipe for smoking, the spoon for eating, the bell for summoning.... (*PP*, p. 348)

Merleau-Ponty then argues that objective thought, be it empiricist or intellectualist (for an account of what Merleau-Ponty means by these, see Chapter Five, section 3, above), can give no adequate account of the anonymous subject. Objective thought, he speculates, would typically claim that one comes to understand the anonymous subject, 'one' or 'they', by analogy from one's own case. For example, when one sees another person using an artefact, one understands the other's behaviour by analogy with one's own: the other is doing the same thing one does oneself when one uses that artefact. Hence one concludes that others, like oneself, have inner experiences 'directing' their actions. So, anyone using the object is, like oneself, a conscious subject. But this line of reasoning, Merleau-Ponty observes, does not explain how one comes to understand the anonymous subject, but rather presupposes that one already has that understanding. It is a premise of this argument from analogy that one does perceive others as doing the same thing one does oneself, that one perceives others as like oneself. But this 'analogical perception' involves using, and so already having, an understanding of the anonymous subject: to 'read' actions as the same whoever does them is precisely to experience the anonymous subject. So any argument from analogy used to explain one's awareness of anonymous subjects assumes what it is trying to prove.

Further, objective thought is unable to explain how one could possibly perceive others as analogous to oneself. Perceiving another as like oneself would have to involve one perceiving a body as displaying a state of consciousness, and a consciousness as visible in that body. But proponents of objective thought give accounts of the body and of consciousness which make this kind of perception paradoxical. Objective thought conceives of bodies as mechanisms which at best somehow, mysteriously, hide, but certainly cannot display, states of consciousness. The objectivist's conception of consciousness, in contrast, is of inner states and processes. So defined, consciousness has no outside, no capacity to be seen, and so cannot be perceived in the bodies of others:

> Other men, and myself, seen as empirical beings, are merely pieces of mechanism worked by springs, but the true subject is irrepeatable, for that consciousness which is hidden in so much flesh and blood is the least intelligible of occult qualities. (*PP*, p. 349)

To summarize, Merleau-Ponty's claim is not that one does not perceive others analogically. His claim is that objective thought cannot explain analogical perception of others and so cannot appeal to its occurrence to establish the existence, intelligibility or knowability of other subjects.

Merleau-Ponty then argues, more generally, that, in the framework of objective thought, the perception of one subject by another involves a contradiction. In so far as it is a subject, the perceived other person must be for-itself, a self constitutor; but as object of perception, the perceived other person must be in-itself, constituted. According to objective thought, nothing can be both for-itself and in-itself, both constitutor and constituted, and there is no third category. Hence one can never experience other subjects; the concept of an *other* subject or ego makes no sense, and so objective thought is inevitably solipsistic.

Merleau-Ponty next argues that the ill-fated project of objective thought to explain how one comes to recognize other egos by analogy with one's own case is radically misguided. It does not reflect the actual order of events. A child does not experience itself as an individual first and then notice that others are similar; the first experience is of similarity, and individuality is a development from that:

> The perception of other people and the intersubjective world is problematical only for adults. The child lives in a world which he unhesitatingly believes accessible to all around him. He has no awareness of himself or of others as private subjectivities.... (*PP*, p. 355)

Merleau-Ponty cites the work of Piaget in his support here.

This general claim that inter-subjective experience precedes personal experience is introduced via two examples involving respectively the body and language. These, as we noted above, Merleau-Ponty regards as cultural objects. The first example features the activity of a young baby:

> A baby of fifteen months opens its mouth if I playfully take one of its fingers between my teeth and pretend to bite it. (*PP*, p. 352)

Merleau-Ponty's point here is that the baby is aware of the activity of biting, and more generally of bodily activities, as the same whoever engages in them; and this awareness is evident before the child develops any sense of its own individual bodily acts. The baby, that is, is aware of a plurality of subjects doing the same thing before it becomes aware of individual subjects. This awareness of sameness cannot depend on analogical reasoning, since the baby responds to a bite by biting before it has seen its own face in a mirror, and so before it is in a position to have noticed similarities between its own appearance and the appearance of others.

Merleau-Ponty's second example is that of adults engaged in dialogue. In the course of a conversation, he claims, the use of language is a shared activity. There can emerge, in the interchange, thoughts whose authorship is joint, not personal:

> In the experience of dialogue, there is constituted between the other person and myself a common ground; my thought and his are inter-woven into a single fabric, my words and those of my interlocutor are called forth by the state of the discussion, and they are inserted into a shared operation of which neither of us is the creator. (*PP*, p. 354)

Only when one party later reflects on the dialogue does it appear as one's personal activity, and only then does it become questionable whether the other person was indeed a comprehending and contributing party to it.

It is only retrospectively, when I have withdrawn from the dialogue and am recalling it that I am able to reintegrate it into my life and make of it an episode in my private history, and that the other recedes into his absence, or, in so far as he remains present for me, is felt as a threat. (*PP*, pp. 354–5)

The general claim which this example is intended to support is that solipsistic doubts are the product of reflection. But reflection requires some pre-reflective activity upon which to reflect, and pre-reflective activity involves communication in the social world. The temporal development is from the social to the personal.

Hence, contrary to the claims implicit in objective thought, the notion of anonymous subjects doing the same thing, communicating and interacting, does not develop out of the notion of one's personal self; so there is no need to explain, by the use of the argument from analogy or in any other way, any such development. Similarly, there is no need to combat solipsism at the level of anonymous subjects: such subjects are first and foremost in communication with each other.

Merleau-Ponty introduces the second stage of his discussion (*PP*, pp. 356–61) by raising a possible criticism of what he has said so far.[16] It might be objected that his description of the anonymous subject in its social world cannot be a complete solution to the problem of other minds, since it has not explained how one ego can perceive another, but rather has eliminated the distinction between different egos:

But is it indeed other people that we arrive at in this way? What we do in effect is to iron out the I and the Thou in an experience shared by a plurality, thus introducing the impersonal into the heart of subjectivity and eliminating the individuality of perspectives. But have we not, in this general confusion, done away with the alter Ego as well as the Ego? (*PP*, pp. 355–6)

He then offers a description of this 'individuality of perspective' which he also calls 'the uniqueness of the cogito' and of 'subjectivity'. The way in which one experiences one's own conscious states is crucially different from the way one experiences those of another individual:

The grief and the anger of another have never quite the same significance for him as they have for me. For him these situations are lived through, for me they are displayed. (*PP*, p. 356)

However closely one interacts with others, one's own experiences of the joint activity is uniquely one's own and one can never have someone else's experience of that activity:

If, moreover, we undertake some project in common, this common project is not one single project, it does not appear in the selfsame light to both of us.... (*PP*, p. 356)

This individuality of experience, though a development out of anonymous activity, is nonetheless a genuine phenomenon. Though objective thought misconstrues this individuality, it does not invent it. Individuality gives rise to at least prime facie problems concerning how one perceives other people. How can one perceive this individuality of experience in others? Merleau-Ponty acknowledges these problems:

> The difficulties inherent in considering the perception of others did not all stem from objective thought, nor do they all dissolve with the discovery of behaviour, or rather objective thought and the uniqueness of the *cogito* which flows from it are not fictions, but firmly grounded phenomena.... (*PP*, p. 356)

Merleau-Ponty's response to this difficulty is to accept that, as an adult, one does experience in this individual and personal way. But he denies that such experience could serve as a support for any solipsistic conclusion. One argument he gives is that *presentation* of solipsist arguments is self-defeating since any such presentation involves using language, a cultural object, and assuming an audience to understand and be persuaded by the argument. It presupposes, that is, contrary to the conclusions of solipsism, that there is a cultural world, that people do communicate with each other:

> I can evolve a solipsist philosophy but, in doing so, I assume the existence of a community of men endowed with speech, and I address myself to it. (*PP*, p. 360)

Merleau-Ponty's chief line of reasoning against drawing solipsist conclusions from premises which appeal to the individuality of experience takes the form of arguing that individual experience presupposes inter-subjective interaction. The cultural world shared by anonymous subjects is not just temporally, as his earlier examples aimed to show, but logically prior to individual experience. Individual experience cannot be adequately characterized without reference to the social world which is implicit in it. Hence, any argument for solipsism which appeals to such individual experience for its premise will fail, since the premiss, properly understood, will contradict the conclusion.

Merleau-Ponty's claim that individual experience presupposes inter-subjectivity is presented on pages 360–1 of *Phenomenology of Perception*. He first claims quite generally that, though one is the unique subject of all one's experiences, one is also nonetheless a unique subject 'situated' in the social world:

> *I am given*, that is, I find myself already situated and involved in a physical and social world – *I am given to myself*, which means that this situation is never hidden from me.... (*PP*, p. 360)

Withdrawal from this social world is an option, but any such withdrawal is a response to and so a recognition of the social world. It is also a withdrawal into some other world, some other situation. One cannot withdraw entirely into one's individuality: it is an individual perspective and, as such, requires a world on which it is a perspective:

> Even the 'indefinite refusal to be anything at all' assumes something which is refused and in relation to which the subject holds himself apart. (*PP*, p. 360)

Merleau-Ponty then turns his attention to the kind of example on which Sartre bases his account of interpersonal relationships. As we noted earlier (section 4, above), these involve a fluctuation between objectifying and being objectified by the other. Merleau-Ponty's claim is that, so far from precluding the possibility of inter-subjective recognition, these cases actually presuppose such recognition in two ways. They involve withdrawal from, and so recognition of, the social world; they also involve perceiving the other person as having withdrawn from such a world into their own individuality. These are examples of *refusing* to communicate, and, as such, depend on the realization that communication is possible. Merleau-Ponty appears to endorse Sartre's view that one finds such situations 'unbearable' and 'embarrassing'; but cites these responses in support of his own interpretation:

> the objectification of each by the other's gaze is felt as unbearable only because it takes the place of possible communication. A dog's gaze directed towards me causes me no embarrassment. The refusal to communicate, however, is still a form of communication. (*PP*, p. 361)

Alternatively, withdrawal might take a philosophical form of 'retreat' to the standpoint of the transcendental ego. But this, Merleau-Ponty claims, still presupposes inter-subjectivity:

> The philosopher cannot fail to draw others with him into his reflective retreat, because in the uncertainty of the world, he has for ever learned to treat them as *consorts*.... (*PP*, p. 361)

Merleau-Ponty has claimed that one is situated in a social world which one shares with other subjects who are like oneself, and with whom one can communicate. At this level, there is no question that other people exist and that one is certain that they do. Questions and doubts can arise only if one 'withdraws' from this social world, but implicit in any such withdrawal is the recognition of the world from which one has withdrawn. Hence, to use such doubts to support solipsism is to deny what one recognizes, and hence to contradict oneself.

It is true that one cannot experience another person's individuality as one does one's own; but one can and does perceive and relate to other people as having such individuality: as implementing their projects by their actions, as being committed to those projects, and as being able to change those projects and adopt others without ceasing to be the same person:

> As soon as existence collects itself together and commits itself in some line of conduct, it falls beneath perception. Like every other perception, this one asserts more things than it grasps: ... when I say that I know and like someone, I aim, beyond his qualities, at an inexhaustible ground.... (*PP*, p. 361)

At the beginning of this chapter, we identified two distinct kinds of approach to the problem of other minds. The first approach saw the problem as one of justifying our beliefs that there are other subjects where such beliefs are construed as the conclusions of inferences. The second approach seeks to explore the meaning of such beliefs. Despite the differences in the accounts we have just discussed, it is clear that they share broad affinities with this second approach and fundamental disagreement with the first.

9

Freedom and its Limits

The final chapter of the *Phenomenology of Perception* (Part Three, chapter 3) is devoted to a discussion of freedom. There never seems to be any doubt in Merleau-Ponty's mind that human freedom is possible. His discussion draws upon the main themes of the rest of the book in order to show how freedom is properly to be understood. For Merleau-Ponty, actions of the body subject in an indeterminate world are the basis of freedom. His strategy here as elsewhere is to introduce his positive account of the topic via his criticisms of objectivist accounts.[1] His chief target is intellectualism, a position which, despite the differences between them, Kant and Sartre, in Merleau-Ponty's view, both exemplify. We shall first explore Merleau-Ponty's criticisms of objectivist views, then, via comparison with Kant and with Sartre, his positive account of freedom.

Merleau-Ponty's discussion of freedom as embodied action in the world proceeds in three stages. First, there is an attack on those who would deny freedom: the proponents of empiricism. Merleau-Ponty wants to resist those who argue that human activity is causally determined by 'objective' features of the world, such as biological or environmental ones. He does not spend much time dismissing this position. The foundations have already been laid in his earlier attack on the objectivist view that the world has determinate qualities (see Chapter Seven, sections 1 and 2, above).

Second, there is an attack on what he regards as false conceptions of freedom. The principal target here is the intellectualist response to determinism: the claim that there is absolute freedom. This absolute freedom, the unrestricted power to initiate new actions in the world despite any causal processes that happen to be around, is seen by its advocates either as a fundamental feature of all human beings (Sartre), or as a condition of the possibility of any kind of moral evaluation (Kant). Part of Merleau-Ponty's criticism of this view of freedom is that it is dominated by the spectre of objective thought in the form of the dilemma: either human action is completely causally determined, or it is absolutely free. It is this dilemma which Merleau-Ponty thinks is false. The denial of determinism does not entail that humans have absolute freedom. Instead, a proper understanding of the ways in which human activity is (non-causally) determined yields a proper understanding of how it is also free. In Merleau-Ponty's view, freedom is relative, there can be degrees of freedom: some actions and some people are more free than others.

The third stage of the argument is Merleau-Ponty's positive characterization of freedom as embodied action in the world. The full force of his criticisms of empiricism and intellectualism and their shared objectivism can be appreciated only when this third stage is presented, for it is part of the criticism of the empiricist and the intellectualist that they misrepresent the actual experience of freedom. When this experience is properly described, these errors will no longer be made.

1 The Empiricist Account of Freedom

In the opening sentence of the chapter on freedom, Merleau-Ponty declares:

> Again, it is clear that no causal relationship is conceivable between the subject and his body, his world or his society. (*PP*, p. 434)

It is important to remember that the thesis of determinism which Merleau-Ponty wishes to attack is the one associated with objective thought. This is the thesis that all human actions are causally determined: that there are objectively identifiable phenomena (causal conditions) standing in law-like regularities with other objectively identifiable phenomena (including all aspects of human activity). It is an essential presupposition of this thesis of causal determination that it is possible to provide independent and determinate descriptions of both cause and effect. We have already explored in Chapters Five, Six and Seven how Merleau-Ponty denies this possibility. This denial is implicit in the particular arguments he uses to attack determinism. We shall now look more fully at his denials, as he presents them in the *Phenomenology of Perception*, Part Three, chapter 3. In outline he claims that causal explanations of human actions misrepresent the actions, the alleged causes, and hence the relation between the two.

Merleau-Ponty argues first (*PP*, pp. 434–5) that causal explanations of actions misrepresent those actions. To construe the relationship between the subject and the world or society as a causal one is to adopt a third person (external) point of view of the subject; and this will involve misrepresenting how the person concerned experiences their own activity. If one takes as an example (ours) jealous behaviour, and tries to explain this causally by reference to some prior states of the person whose jealous behaviour one is trying to explain, then one will give a description of that behaviour in terms of kinds of objectively observable patterns of responses. But this kind of description would not typically be given by the jealous person.

> For myself I am neither 'jealous', nor 'inquisitive', nor 'hunchbacked' nor 'a civil servant'. (*PP*, p. 434)

It is typically the case that, if one is a jealous person, one does not see oneself as jealous. It is possible for one to stop and reflect on one's behaviour: to see that it exhibits a certain pattern, and that this pattern of behavioural responses towards another person – wanting to be with them, not liking their absence, hating the other person being with others – *is* jealousy. But when one is undergoing these feelings and conducting oneself in this way one does not experience oneself as jealous. This is usually something which has to be pointed out by some third party, or by taking an 'objective' look at oneself. So a causal explanation of jealous behaviour will not be an explanation of the behaviour as experienced unreflectingly by the subject. And an explanation of the behaviour *as experienced* will not be an explanation of jealous behaviour.

Further, says Merleau-Ponty:

> In order to be determined ... by an external factor, it is necessary that I should be a thing. (*PP*, p. 434)

Causal explanations misrepresent the factors they take to be causes. They give an account of these alleged causes which ignores the subject's experiences of them. To do this is to treat the subject as a thing. Treating someone as a thing involves precisely ignoring those aspects of them and their circumstances which are seen only from their own point of view. A causal explanation presents factors in one's environment or in one's background as external; whereas Merleau-Ponty wants to emphasize that such factors stand in a special 'intentional' relationship to the subject. This relationship can be seen only by considering just those aspects of intentionality overlooked by taking the objective or external point of view.

A supporting argument which Merleau-Ponty offers here focuses on the candidate causal conditions, in order to show that these, taken by themselves and conceived of as external, cannot produce any meaningful human behaviour. The conscious activity of a body-subject is not produced in this way. Class consciousness is an example given by Merleau-Ponty:

> it is never the case that my objective position in the production process is sufficient to awaken class consciousness. There was exploitation long before there were revolutionaries. (*PP*, p. 443)

What makes me a proletarian is not the economic system or society considered
as systems of impersonal forces, but these institutions as I carry them within me
and experience them. (*PP*, p. 443)

What the second quotation adds to the first is the consideration that any
factor which already exists as a possible determining factor of one's activity
can determine that activity only by being experienced. So a causal analysis
which isolates objective conditions from how these are experienced is bound to
result in a failure to explain the phenomenon in question – in this case, class
consciousness.

Furthermore, a causal analysis which treats these experiences as themselves
'internal' causal conditions of the activity to be explained objectifies both the
experiences and the activity in a way which fails to capture the phenomena.

Merleau-Ponty offers another example of an explanation in terms of internal causal factors on p. 442. This is the case of a person who has built their life
upon an inferiority complex which has been operative for twenty years. The
way an empiricist might consider this case would be to take the term 'inferiority complex' as referring to a set of causal determinants which enable one to
predict that in certain kinds of situation the person who has this complex will,
or will tend to, exhibit patterns of behaviour which fall short of some ideal,
usually that held by the person in question. The determinants will usually be
items in the person's history: e.g. the relationship with parent(s), or a continuous programme of failure which has built up the expectation of failure. By
knowing these facts about the person's past, one can either provide a causal
explanation of the person's behaviour, or one can predict their 'inferior'
behaviour. Such would be the kind of picture a causal determinist might wish
to paint of the person with the inferiority complex.[2]

Merleau-Ponty is against any characterization of external reality, or of any
internal psychological process, which is independent of the activities of the
body-subject. Any such characterization is an abstraction from the reality,
discovered by phenomenological reflection, of how the person acts in the
world of perceptual objects. A correct description of the nature of the objects
which one perceives, with which one interacts, etc., and a correct description
of the role of the body in these interactions will be such that one discerns the
nature of the intentional relationships between the subject (body) and object.
In terms of this kind of relationship it is not possible to define any 'object'
without some reference to the role of some body-subject. Likewise, the
characterization of the body-subject will be in terms of the world around
which and through which this subject 'moves'. Given this, no *causal* interaction between world and subject is possible. So the psychological factors,
which might be seen by the empiricist as causally determining the behaviour
of the person with the inferiority complex, can in fact be seen only in terms

of that behaviour. And that behaviour can be seen only against the background of the person with their own specific history.

2   The Intellectualist Account of Freedom

We have already noted (in Chapter Five, section 3) that Merleau-Ponty is sympathetic to the intellectualist emphasis upon the active role of the human subject in perception, and with its view of human action as purposive and intentional. We have also observed that Merleau-Ponty nonetheless rejects what he regards as the unduly cognitive, deliberative characterization which the intellectualist gives of that activity. The same combination of attitudes is displayed in his discussion of the intellectualist account of freedom. Intellectualists are seen as claiming both that there is freedom (contra empiricism) and that this freedom is absolute. Merleau-Ponty agrees with the first claim whilst rejecting the second.

The intellectualist view of freedom is that human action is free because it results from acts of 'constituting' consciousness – intentions or acts of will. Merleau-Ponty claims further that the intellectualist believes that the rejection of causal determinism of human activity entails that all human activity is instead to be seen as resulting entirely from constituting consciousness, as being exactly what that consciousness takes it to be. It is a short move, he says, from 'the Kantian idea of a consciousness which "finds in things only what it has put into them"' to 'defining ourselves as a universal power of *Sinn-Gebung* [literally 'sense-giving']' (*PP*, p. 439). This suggests that we make of ourselves *whatever* meaning or interpretation *we* impose. So, for example (ours), if we see ourselves as working class, or as clever, or as inferior, then this is how we are.

Merleau-Ponty regards this intellectualist position as asserting an absolute freedom:

> The choice would seem to lie between scientism's conception of causality, which is incompatible with the consciousness which we have of ourselves, and the assertion of an absolute freedom divorced from the outside. (*PP*, p. 436)

In this view, either all our actions are free or none are. Strictly speaking, this position is to be distinguished from one which holds that only specific sorts of actions (e.g. those with moral significance) are free. But the target for Merleau-Ponty's attack is a concept of freedom *shared* by the universal freedom thesis and the more restricted thesis: a concept of absolute freedom. When an action is free, it is absolutely free; and when a subject performs free actions, whether these are all its actions or only some of them, that subject is absolutely free. There are no limitations on freedom: human freedom is not dependent on, and so not limited by, any state of the world. Freedom admits of no degree: human subjects cannot be more or less free.

The believer in absolute freedom may argue in something like the following way.[3] The human subject, which is responsible for making sense of the world, is such that the thesis of determinism cannot apply to it. This is partly for the reasons given in the previous section in discussing empiricist views about freedom, viz, that determinism would be incompatible with the consciousness one has of oneself as a subject. But there is also a further argument for absolute freedom, especially for those philosophers committed to some form of transcendental idealism. Since any causal relations in the objective world are the result of the activity of the constituting subject rather than the other way round, it would not make sense for those activities to be themselves causally determined. So, the sense-giving activities of the subject cannot be subject to *any* causal determination: partial causal determination of an action is to be rejected along with universal causal determinism. And, pursuing this line of argument further, it may also be claimed that *all* human actions are free. For a free subject is one who makes sense of the world. That activity is not dependent on any state of the world. So the subject is not dependent on anything other than itself. Hence its freedom cannot be limited by anything outside itself, which is to say that its freedom is unlimited. Against this intellectualist account of absolute freedom, Merleau-Ponty argues that, since this alleged kind of freedom is guaranteed by being necessarily already possessed by any human subject, it in fact would follow that there *cannot* be free action. The subject is already free, on this absolute freedom thesis, prior to any action. Given this, Merleau-Ponty argues, there is no possibility of an unfree action, and therefore no possibility of a free one. We shall explore this claim further. Merleau-Ponty writes:

> If indeed it is the case that our freedom is the same in all our actions, and even in our passions, if it is not to be measured in terms of our conduct, and if the slave displays freedom as much by living in fear as by breaking his chains, then it cannot be held that there is such a thing as *free action*. (*PP*, pp. 436–7)

To explain Merleau-Ponty's argument here, we shall return to the example we discussed earlier of the person with the 'inferiority complex'. The believer in absolute freedom must maintain two claims: first, that whether one acts in accordance with the complex, or in ways that involve change, either way one is equally free. Either form of activity would be the result of one's sense-giving choice. Second, if one tries to stop being 'inferior', then, whether or not one succeeds, one would still be free. If one fails, this is not because of any impossibility of doing otherwise, which would mean that one was unfree; it is because one has in fact chosen to continue with the inferiority complex. One must have made this choice because one is acting in accordance with it, and all action is the result of choice. Merleau-Ponty finds both these claims implausible.

He wants to claim that in such cases one is free only if it is actually possible for one to cease to be inferior. On the intellectualist account, this possibility is dependent on the conscious deliberative activity of the subject. So freedom is dependent on deliberation: one has only to change one's view of oneself and one changes oneself.

According to Merleau-Ponty, however, two things are wrong with this view. First, although one can make decisions about how one is to change one-self, one cannot guarantee their success. (Many an alcoholic and many a person desirous of giving up smoking cigarettes is witness to this fact.) So, the absolute freedom the intellectualist is characterizing can only be freedom of intention and not freedom of action. Merleau-Ponty stresses how different these two are:

> There are merely intentions immediately followed by their effects, and we are very near to the Kantian idea of an intention which is tantamount to the act, which Scheler countered with the argument that the cripple who would like to be able to save a drowning man and the good swimmer who actually saves him do not have the same experience of autonomy. (*PP*, p. 437)

So the first mistake the believer in deliberative intentions as the source of free-dom makes is to have no account of the relevance of action, or lack of it, to whether or not the subject is free to perform any particular kind of action. *Action* is not considered relevant for the believer in absolute freedom; and, in Merleau-Ponty's view, it is in action that freedom must be displayed.

> The very notion of freedom demands that our decision should plunge into the future, that something should have been *done* by it. (*PP*, p. 437)

Merleau-Ponty's second criticism of this emphasis on intention and deliber-ation is that, when changes in behaviour patterns, ways of life, modes of being in the world, etc., do actually occur, they very rarely do so as a result of con-scious deliberation. It is not usually the case that one first deliberates about change, then decides to change, and finally changes. Rather, one discovers that one has 'decided' *through* having changed; and then one deliberates about this change:

> What misleads us..., is that we often look for freedom in the voluntary deliber-ation which examines one motive after another and seems to opt for the weightiest or most convincing. In reality the deliberation follows the decision. (*PP*, p. 435)

Indeed:

> That is why it so often happens that after giving up a plan I experience a feeling of relief: 'After all, I wasn't all that involved'; the debate was purely a matter of form, and the deliberation a mere parody, for I had decided against from the start. (*PP*, p. 436)

About the role of deliberation in change of behaviour, or indeed in any practical action, Merleau-Ponty is making two points. The first is one familiar to philosophers within the analytical tradition: that not all intentional actions are preceded by a prior intention.[4] One can ride a bicycle intentionally without constantly formulating intentions or making a series of conscious choices. The second point is also one which has a long philosophical history: rational deliberation is not the most potent force for change.[5] Here there are resonances of Hume's claim that reason alone cannot move us to action; but there are also resonances of Nietzsche: that when we are deliberating or making noises about our deliberations we are hiding the fact that the real choice lies elsewhere. The reasoning is often a disguise. In Merleau-Ponty's view, it is not so much that the reasoning is an attempt to disguise what is really going on, but rather that if one focuses attention on the reasoning then one is more likely to misdescribe the project or the change of project.

But there is also a deeper error in the intellectualist's belief in absolute freedom. This error arises because the intellectualist is often under the spell of two philosophical doctrines. One is objectivism: the world is considered to be subject to universal causal determinism, and it is thought that the only way to protect any freedom is to insist on absolute freedom. But if one found fault with objectivism, as Merleau-Ponty does, one would not need recourse to such a problematic concept of freedom. The other doctrine which influences the intellectualist is specifically Kantian. One may be led to a mistaken view of freedom if one is engaged in a Kantian project of *justification*. The project is to justify knowledge claims, and also moral judgements. This latter aim, Merleau-Ponty believes, lies behind the intellectualist's error about freedom. What is thought to justify moral judgements is the possibility of freedom. And, if one considers freedom in this way, as a necessary condition of the possibility of morality, one may well be led to think of freedom in absolutist terms. As Merleau-Ponty puts it:

> By defining ourselves as a universal power of *Sinn-Gebung*, we have reverted to the method of the 'thing without which' ... which seeks the conditions of possibility without concerning itself with the conditions of reality. (*PP*, p. 439)

Kant is the obvious example of a philosopher who does pursue this method.[6] He was interested in the conditions of the possibility of morality; and what he says about freedom in *The Critique of Pure Reason* and *The Critique of Practical Reason* is very much geared to this philosophical project. Merleau-Ponty's general criticism of Kant is that Kant's concern for justifying morality blinds him to the reality both of perceptual experience and of the experience of freedom. Although Merleau-Ponty does not deal systematically with Kant in his discussion of absolute freedom, we shall now provide a brief account of Kant's view of freedom, since it can serve to illustrate some of the points Merleau-Ponty considers typical of intellectualist conceptions of freedom.

Kant's account of freedom has three features which it shares with intellectualism. First, he accepts causal determinism (objectivism); second, he thinks of freedom as unconditional (absolute); and third, he sees freedom as being the autonomous rational determination of human action. We shall consider these in turn.

Kant cannot deny that the thesis of causal determinism is true, since it forms part of his programme of justifying knowledge of the empirical world (see Chapter Three, section 5). So he is faced with a problem about morality. For it seems that the making of moral judgements requires that moral acts are regarded as free from causal determination. If an agent were subject to causal determination, so that for any action one performed it would not have been possible for one to have chosen successfully to act otherwise, then it might be considered unfair to hold the agent responsible for the action performed. The possibility of conceiving human wills to be free is a prerequisite of the possibility of morality, according to Kant.

This possibility of human freedom is established in *The Critique of Pure Reason*, where Kant roots it in an alternative standpoint to the phenomenal world, to the world subject to causal determinism. This alternative standpoint is that of the noumenal world. Individuals, *qua* phenomena, are causally determined. But agents, *qua* noumena, are free. This possibility of freedom is developed further in *The Critique of Practical Reason* and in the *Groundwork of the Metaphysic of Morals*, where more is said about the alternative, absolute standpoint required to make morality possible. Kant searches for a basis for acting in accordance with moral principles, which for him are universally applicable and unconditional, where such a basis has to be different from anything provided by the phenomenal world. Only one genuine candidate suggests itself to Kant: reason. Only if it is possible to act in accordance with reason is freedom, and hence morality, possible. This freedom is a property of all human beings (or at least those capable of reasoning). Nothing can affect this reason: it is absolute.

For Kant the only way practical freedom is possible is for us to conceive of free-will as noumenal, and therefore beyond causal determination. If we consider human beings as noumena, then we accept them as possible subjects for morality. Humans, *qua* noumena, are not subject to causal determination and are therefore free. As noumena, they are purely rational beings. However, there remains a problem. If the subject is only phenomenal, it cannot be moral; but if the subject is only noumenal, then it cannot help being moral – it would be what Kant calls a 'holy will'. Kant's solution is to claim that, as a moral being, the subject has to be both noumenal and phenomenal. Morality is rooted in the struggle between these two selves:

> The moral 'I ought' is thus an 'I will' for man as a member of the intelligible [noumenal] world; and it is conceived by him as an 'I ought' only in so far as he considers himself at the same time to be a member of the sensible [phenomenal] world.[7]

A human action considered from the empirical (phenomenal) point of view is determined or predictable. The same action, such as Kant's example of the malicious lie,[8] considered from the noumenal point of view, is free. The freedom which will allow the possibility of praise and blame, etc., is the freedom of noumenal agents. Through no cause in the world can one cease to be a freely acting being; and thus one can be held responsible for one's actions. It is the noumenal self which makes the decision, e.g. to tell a deliberate lie. If the lie is told, it would always have been possible, according to Kant, for the agent to have decided and done otherwise.

This is not the place to discuss the view of morality which requires this unconditional freedom as its basis; but we can now identify the objections Merleau-Ponty has to the three features of the position which we have just outlined. First, as we noted (Chapter Seven, section 2), Merleau-Ponty does not accept Kant's arguments for causal determinism, so he is bound to be critical of Kant's attempts to preserve the possibility of freedom by ascribing causal relations to the phenomenal world, and of his stipulation that freedom is possible only if we postulate a noumenal world. If Kant were wrong about causal determinism, then, even if he were correct in his view of morality as being unconditionally demanding on everyone, he would not need to postulate the idea of a *noumenal* realm as the basis for the freedom which makes morality possible. Take away the threat of causal determinism, and alternative bases for morality become possible.

Second, the retreat from the spectre of causal determinism forces Kant to adopt a view of freedom as absolute; and hence, according to Merleau-Ponty, to regard freedom as attaching to intentions rather than actions. It is intentions that are free, for it is intentions that are judged, irrespective of whether they issue in action. From the phenomenal point of view, the action might not be free – one might even be able to predict it; but, from the noumenal point of view, it can still be free, for it is freely intended. Such a view of freedom represents, in Merleau-Ponty's view, a retreat from the world of action.

Third, Kant's emphasis on reason as the crucial feature of moral action is wrong. For Merleau-Ponty, phenomenological descriptions of human action do not support the claim that reason is a determining factor in action. To this, Kant would no doubt reply that the facts here are irrelevant. He knows that people, *in fact*, do not act in accordance with reason. His point is that they *ought* to do so; and this 'ought' makes sense only if the agent *can* act in accordance with reason. This possibility is supported by the appeal to the noumenal realm. But this appeal Merleau-Ponty finds unacceptable. Noumenal determination of action does not make sense. This is because the noumenal world is outside space and time. Thus noumenal decisions do not occur in time. Merleau-Ponty finds noumenal determination difficult to accept, because it is at odds with his positive characterization of freedom in action, according to which the basis of human freedom lies in the fact that human beings – as bodily, and as social beings – are temporally situated:

> As my living present opens upon a past which I nevertheless am no longer living through, and on a future which I do not yet live, and perhaps never shall, it can also open on to temporalities outside my living experience and acquire a social horizon, with the result that my world is expanded to the dimensions of that collective history which my private existence takes up and carries forward. (*PP*, p. 433)

Kant's atemporal self is such that it is difficult to make sense of how a subject relates to its social existence, or to its past, or its future. This is to neglect an important aspect of human activity. It is also, for Merleau-Ponty, to deny the basis for freedom.

3   Merleau-Ponty and Sartre

In this section we will examine some of Merleau-Ponty's criticisms of Sartre's account of freedom; and this will provide a link between Merleau-Ponty's criticisms of empiricist and intellectualist accounts of freedom, and his positive account of freedom. There are similarities between Sartre and Merleau-Ponty; but there are also important differences. Two important similarities concern their shared antipathy to certain aspects of intellectualism. Both think that the project of providing a transcendental grounding for morality (or for knowledge, or reality) should not be the concern of philosophy; and Merleau-Ponty's resistance to the intellectualist emphasis on deliberation and intention, rather than on action, parallels Sartre's discussion of free action in Part IV of *Being and Nothingness*. However, Sartre can also be seen as a target for some of Merleau-Ponty's criticisms of intellectualism because of his insistence on absolute freedom, which, according to Merleau-Ponty, is rooted in his distinction between being-for-itself and being-in-itself.[9]

We noted in Chapter Four, section 3, that Sartre objects to regarding the two categories of being – being-for-itself and being-in-itself – as distinct from each other, as abstractions; and that later on, in *Being and Nothingness*, he thus offers characterizations of the two that differ from those initially presented in his Introduction (where translucency of consciousness defines the former; and solidity, density and full positivity define the latter) (see Chapter Four, section 2, above). However, although Sartre maintains the stance throughout *Being and Nothingness* of presenting being-for-itself and being-in-itself only in inter-relationship with one another, Merleau-Ponty claims that an element of abstraction nonetheless remains. The world of being-in-itself is, in Sartre's view, deterministic. His central concern in *Being and Nothingness* is to explain how freedom is possible in such a world. He sees this as a problem; and his answer to it is that freedom is possible only if one can stand back from the world, thereby introducing the possibility that it might be otherwise (see Chapter Four, section 3). This, he then claims, is something which human beings can always do. Merleau-Ponty regards this as essentially an example of the intellectualist strategy of positing absolute freedom in order to maintain the possibility of any freedom in a world where there seems no room for it. Merleau-Ponty argues that Sartre remains trapped in a dualism of being-for-itself and being-in-itself, and is therefore unable to discern the true nature of freedom.

Further, Merleau-Ponty argues, Sartre's account of human beings is that they are made up of two elements: consciousness and the self, the 'me' of which it is conscious. So, one has a past, present and future only by being conscious of them. Merleau-Ponty takes issue with Sartre on this view of how human beings are temporally situated, and with the conception of the human beings which gives rise to it.

In relation to a tendency like the inferiority complex, discussed earlier in this chapter, Sartre would be committed to the view that, to believe that one could not change (that one was trapped by one's past) would be to treat oneself as a being-in-itself, something with fixed properties, a disposition which determines what one will do next; whereas in reality one is also a being-for-itself and in virtue of this one can change. To act as if one is a being-in-itself is, for Sartre, a sign of bad faith. But it is also bad faith to act as if one's dispositions, one's past patterns of behaviour, are of no relevance to one's present choices. What does Sartre take their relevance to be? What they cannot do, according to Sartre, is lessen or curtail one's freedom in any way. Sartre's construal of someone with an inferiority complex who wants to change would be as follows (see *BN*, part 4, chapter 1, section II). First, so far from preventing the envisaged change, one's complex is a necessary condition of that change. One cannot lose a complex one does not have. Second, it is only because one has chosen to change that the complex presents itself as 'something to be changed'. It appears as a constraint on one's freedom, if it does, only because one has chosen a project which puts it in this light. But this, Sartre believes, is tantamount to having chosen the constraint; and a *chosen* constraint is not a constraint on *freedom*.[10]

Quite generally, Sartre's view is that one's own past, and one's own present – one's habits, desires, intentions, and so on – cannot affect or lessen one's freedom. They are a necessary condition for action, since to act is precisely to change one's present condition; and they have the significance they have only because, in choosing to act, one has oneself endowed them with that significance. So, if they seem to lessen one's freedom, that is not because they do, but because one has chosen to see them in that light.

In Merleau-Ponty's view, Sartre takes this (mistaken) view of freedom because of his (mistaken) view of human beings as composed of pure consciousness and a 'self' which is an object of that consciousness. Freedom, for Sartre, cannot be curtailed because it is a property of pure consciousness. Anything which seems to threaten freedom is, for Sartre, only an object of consciousness – albeit an object which is one's *self*. Consciousness can always choose to 'distance' itself from its objects, and so those objects cannot lessen one's freedom to choose. Being-for-itself is 'situated', spatially and temporally; but one is situated by being conscious of one's situation. Merleau-Ponty rejects this account of human beings and how they are 'situated', that is, how they relate to their past, their present, and, indeed, their external surroundings.

For Sartre, then, the relationship with one's past is like that portrayed by Merleau-Ponty in his comments on what he calls 'the rationalist's dilemma' (here 'rationalist' can be treated as synonymous with 'intellectualist'):

> The rationalist's dilemma: either the free act is possible, or it is not – either the event originates in me or is imposed on me from outside, does not apply to our relations with the world and with our past. (*PP*, p. 442)

Sartre, in Merleau-Ponty's view, can be seen as accepting the first horn of this dilemma. The past is something which does not impose itself from outside, for it is something which originates in oneself. But Merleau-Ponty wants to say that this dilemma does not apply: one's relationship with one's past is neither one nor the other. The past is indeed part of one's situation; but the situation is neither something totally created by the subject, nor totally determining it.

We can see how Sartre may well seem to be intellectualist in this respect by considering in more detail how he treats change. Like Merleau-Ponty, Sartre does not believe that the possibility of change, e.g. in the case of the inferiority complex, is a matter of deliberation. He too sees the choice as exhibited in a mode of action (a project); and he also accepts that this new project, not to be inferior, might have too high a cost for the individual. So what Sartre is saying is this: for any project, being inferior, climbing a mountain, etc., it is always possible to engage in another project which is such as to render the old project otiose. Indeed the only guarantee that one has ceased to be living the life of someone suffering from an inferiority complex is that one is living instead the life of someone who 'succeeds'. But this possibility might not be realized. If it is not, this is because the new project often demands so much by way of adjustment, so much by way of loss of aspects of life one found valuable in the old project, that one does not count as having *chosen* the new project.

A famous example of this is Sartre's tired mountain walker (*BN*, pp. 454–5). Sartre says that it is possible for the fatigue not to be given into, and hence that a causal explanation of stopping walking due to irresistible tiredness is ruled out. But at what cost? The cost is the adoption of a completely different attitude to 'nature', to the activity of walking, to gradually being taken over by fatigue itself. All this is possible; but it is also possible that one 'chooses' not to engage in this new project. This choice, which is not the result of deliberation, will be manifest in the continuance of the old project. Giving in to the fatigue is a manifestation of this choice. The giving in is not gratuitous.

Sartre's point is that changing and remaining the same both involve a choice, both are an exercise of freedom. No matter what one does, one is exhibiting freedom; and it would be bad faith to deny this. So in the walking example it is bad faith to blame the tiredness, 'I couldn't walk a step further'; for the giving in is in fact an exercise of one's freedom. One elects not to undertake the costly project which would involve a different response to the fatigue. If one is not the kind of walker who welcomes tiredness, who gets a kind of physical glow from aching limbs, then, at the point of the fatigue being noticed, it is difficult to do otherwise than to give in. But such a walker has to recognize that they have chosen to live life like this; so that giving in is part of their own choice.

If one succeeds in adopting a new project, one's past is seen in a new light: it has a different significance. But one cannot alter the fact that one had *that* past. So, for example, if one ceases to be a religious believer then it remains true of one that one used to believe. The old beliefs *now* no longer have the significance for one that they used to have; but they still have significance as the beliefs one has *rejected*. Likewise if one maintains a project, e.g. keeping to a marriage contract, one's present projects, fidelity, etc., come to illuminate the past marriage vow and confer on it its actual and continuing value (*BN*, p. 499). And, for Sartre, since it is also possible to *change* the significance of those marriage vows by adopting a different project, their significance as binding is always something one chooses. Thus any way of acting in the world can be seen as free because of the role of the for-itself in choosing that project.

The judgement that human beings have freedom is a basic ontological claim. It follows from the analysis of questioning in Part I of *Being and Nothingness* (see Chapter Four, section 4); and is linked to Sartre's distinction between being-for-itself and being-in-itself. For it is in terms of these ontological categories that bad faith, the attempted running away from freedom (or from the anguish of recognizing freedom) is seen. So what Sartre seems to be saying is that, despite appearances to the contrary, if one goes deeply enough into the description of human conduct, one finds that one is always and absolutely free. For any project there is a dual sense of freedom. There is always a theoretical possibility that one could engage in an alternative project; and, even in those projects which are so much a part of one that it seems unlikely that one would change, one can nonetheless be seen to be choosing to maintain them and so to be free. The reason why one is free, even in those cases where one does not change, is that one is accepting, now, that past projects are to continue. One *makes* one's past one's own; it does not influence one causally. The past is overcome or accepted by the sense-conferring aspect of the subject. For Sartre this is being-for-itself.

There are aspects of this account that Merleau-Ponty agrees with. In particular that, although there are projects which are difficult to change, even in these one is free – though, for Merleau-Ponty, perhaps less free than in other projects. But Merleau-Ponty has a different view about the role of the past. The crucial difference between him and Sartre centres on what Merleau-Ponty calls 'sedimentation'. Whereas for Sartre the past becomes the subject's by the sense-conferring activity of that subject, for Merleau-Ponty the past is already part of the subject. Merleau-Ponty's subject has sedimentation; and this different view of the subject and its past entails a different account of freedom from Sartre's:

> we must recognise a sort of sedimentation of our life: an attitude towards the world, when it has received frequent confirmation, acquires a favoured status for us ... having built our life upon an inferiority complex which has been operative for twenty years, it is not *probable* that we shall change. (*PP*, pp. 441–2)

It is by virtue of what Merleau-Ponty calls 'sedimentation' or 'our habitual being-in-the-world' that the judgement is made that it is not *probable* that the person with the inferiority complex will change. Merleau-Ponty is at pains to point out (*PP*, p. 442) that this judgement about probabilities is not an objective statistical judgement, but is a judgement which has a phenomenological basis. He says of the claim that 'it is improbable' that one should at this moment destroy a twenty-year-old inferiority complex:

> That means that I have committed myself to inferiority, that I have made it my abode, that this past, though not a fate, has at least a specific weight and is not a set of events over there, at a distance from me, but the atmosphere of my present. (*PP*, p. 442)

The 'I have committed myself to inferiority' has echoes of Sartre's sense of freedom; but Merleau-Ponty puts more weight on the phenomenology of the 'feel' of sedimentation. So, although one's habitual patterns of behaviour may be chosen, they are felt *as part of oneself* in such a way that they are unlikely to change. In fact these habitualities are usually so much a part of one's way of being in the world that one does not notice them. It is only when one is placed in a new environment, or when one tries to alter one's habits, that the nature and weight of that sedimentation become clear to one. One notices one's habits (both good and bad) when confronted by a new situation: for example (ours) when one looks after someone else's home, both their and one's own domestic habits soon become evident.

For both Sartre and Merleau-Ponty sedimentation (which is part of what Sartre calls the 'situation') is necessary for the exercise of freedom. But whereas for Sartre what Merleau-Ponty calls 'sedimentation' is seen as an object of one's consciousness, for Merleau-Ponty it is seen as a feature of the subject. So Merleau-Ponty's concept of the subject of action is different from Sartre's. According to Merleau-Ponty, Sartre is too trapped, even in his account of the human subject, by the dichotomy of the subject – consciousness – and the object of consciousness; and this prevents him from seeing that sedimentation is an integral part of the subject.

A further way in which the Sartrean dichotomy between subject and object gives rise to different understandings of 'the situation' by Sartre and Merleau-Ponty concerns the fact that 'other subjects' are often part of the situation in which one acts. Sartre's dichotomy is seen most clearly in his analysis of the relationship between subjects. As we have noted in section 4 of Chapter Eight, Sartre regards this as a battle against becoming the object of someone else's consciousness. If one is an object of another's consciousness, one becomes merely a part of their situation, subject to their freedom. This is experienced as threatening. The only recourse is to make them into an object of one's own consciousness, subject to one's own freedom. Merleau-Ponty (see Chapter Eight, section 5, above) does not see the relationship between selves like this:

> Another person is not necessarily, is not even ever quite an object for me. . . .
> The-other-as-object is nothing but an insincere modality of others, just as absol-
> ute subjectivity is nothing but an abstract notion of myself. (*PP*, p. 448)

So not only does Merleau-Ponty think that one does not see the other as an object; he also thinks that the subject is more than pure consciousness. It is a subject exhibiting bodily intentionality, a subject with a history, a subject with sedimentation – where all these qualities are qualities of the subject and not, as Sartre would say, qualities of the self seen as an object by a reflective consciousness, i.e. as qualities of *me*.

One particular quality of the self, and of other selves, which Merleau-Ponty wishes to highlight, is 'a kind of halo of generality or a kind of atmosphere of

"sociality"' (*PP*, p. 448). By this Merleau-Ponty means that each person's life
has a meaning or significance which is not constituted by that person. One has
an awareness of oneself as being more than just how one constitutes oneself.
One is male or female, bourgeois or working class, clever or dim, etc., where
these are properties which, initially at least, one cannot escape having ascribed
to one. One is constituted as an individual by others. One is born into, and
develops, a social milieu – an inter-subjectivity – so that everyone has a dual
aspect. One is what one is for oneself; and one is what one is for others. But
these others are not seen as alien objects; but as fellow subjects, and as a part
of the source of one's own experienced significance. If this were not so, one
could not come to see oneself as male, Jewish, bourgeois, etc., for these are not
properties that one can just decide whether or not to possess or exhibit.
Merleau-Ponty says:

> We are not asserting that history from end to end has only one meaning, any
> more than has an individual life. We mean simply that in any case freedom
> modifies it only by taking up the meaning which history *was offering* at the
> moment in question, and by a kind of unobtrusive assimilation. (*PP*, p. 450)

For example, there are extra-individual facts in virtue of which one can
choose to accept or reject that one is bourgeois. One cannot make oneself
bourgeois by an absolutely free conscious choice. One already exists in a historically located social role which confers meaning on one's activity, and on
the basis of which one can act further. Thus Merleau-Ponty wishes to steer a
line between saying that a social phenomenon such as class-consciousness
is objectively determined, and saying that it consists purely in a state of
awareness:

> Objective thought derives class consciousness from the objective condition of
> the proletariat. Idealist [intellectualist] reflection reduces the proletarian con-
> dition to the awareness of it, which the proletarian arrives at. The former traces
> class-consciousness to the class defined in terms of objective characteristics, the
> latter on the other hand reduces 'being a workman' to the consciousness of being
> one. . . . If we approach the question afresh with the idea of discovering, not the
> causes of the act of becoming aware, for there is no cause which can act from
> outside upon a consciousness – nor the conditions of its possibility, for we need
> to know the conditions which actually produce it – but class-consciousness itself
> . . . what do we find? I am not conscious of being working class or middle class
> simply because, as a matter of fact, I sell my labour or, equally as a matter of
> fact, because my interests are bound up with capitalism, nor do I become one or
> the other on the day on which I elect to view history in the light of the class
> struggle: what happens is that 'I exist as working class' or 'I exist as middle
> class' in the first place, and it is this mode of dealing with the world and society
> which provides both the motives for my revolutionary or conservative projects
> and my explicit judgements of the type: 'I am working class' or 'I am middle

class', without its being possible to deduce the former from the latter, or *vice versa*. (*PP*, p. 443)

In the first half of this passage we find simply the reiteration of the anti-objectivist and anti-intellectualist lines of argument. But in the second half, with its emphasis on 'I exist as working class', or 'I exist as middle class *in the first place*', one has the beginnings of Merleau-Ponty's more positive view (see section 4 below).

This takes as its base a particular way of being in the world – a way which is public, which is seen by others in a certain light and which can become something of which one is oneself aware. What Merleau-Ponty insists that one cannot deny is that one experiences some aspects of one's social significance as coming from outside oneself. Hence, there has to be a socio-historical situation which is part of the required background for action. So, for example, a revolutionary action (at least one which is not doomed to failure) requires a certain situation (rising food prices, shortage of food, recognition of corruption of officials, etc.). Without this structure, Merleau-Ponty states, somewhat ironically, 'A social revolution would be equally possible at any moment' (*PP*, p. 449).

The situation in which one acts is pregnant with meaning. And, contra Sartre, this meaning does not come solely from the actor. But, despite this external source of meaning, the historical or social situation is not seen as detached from the agent's viewpoint, and therefore it is not seen or felt as operating on the agent in a causal fashion. It is a situation which is lived through; and one aspect of this living through it is that one has a generalized, anonymous existence as a social individual, or as a historical subject. One cannot help being already defined as a particular kind of individual, e.g. as a member of a social group or class (parent, aristocrat, man, intellectual, etc). This is the 'halo of generality'. Opposed to this generality is the individual subject, which Merleau-Ponty thinks is not pure consciousness.

The concrete subject, for Merleau-Ponty, is not the pure consciousness in a situation that is external to it – which is how Merleau-Ponty sees Sartre's portrayal of the subject. For Merleau-Ponty, the subject has a structure of two elements. There is presence to oneself as mediated by others and by the world; and there is the consciousness of being open to different possibilities. This first element is genuinely a part of the subject. So if, as (according to Merleau-Ponty) Sartre does, one treats the situation, which includes this social determination of the subject, as external to it, one is abstracting from the subject-in-its-situation. And if one does that, one thereby takes the wrong view of the subject, as an absolutely free, pure consciousness. But if, instead, one accepts that the situation forms part of the subject's sedimentation, then one is more likely to discern that the correct description of the subject will include reference to the social individual.

Merleau-Ponty's account of freedom stresses both these aspects of the concrete subject, whereas it is arguable that Sartre, by putting the social aspects and the habitualities onto the 'object' side of the intentional relationship between consciousness and its 'self', gives undue emphasis to the pure consciousness in virtue of which one can, in principle, be a 'general refusal to be anything' (*PP*, p. 452).

Merleau-Ponty adds:

> We must not say that I continually choose myself, on the excuse that I *might* continually refuse what I am. Not to refuse is not the same thing as to choose. (*PP*, p. 452)

For Merleau-Ponty one can only refuse to be something one has been by being something else, i.e. not by remaining nothing. He expresses the point thus:

> By taking up a present, I draw together and transform my past, altering its significance, freeing and detaching myself from it. But I do so only by committing myself somewhere else. (*PP*, p. 455)

This much Sartre and Merleau-Ponty agree on; but, as we have seen, Sartre is insistent on the claim that, if one continues to engage in a project, then one has chosen to do so. Merleau-Ponty on the other hand denies this. Habit, sedimentation, inertia, are all features of the subject's action in the world; but to see these as actively chosen by the individual is to deny those extra-individual features of oneself which are already part of the subject. The pure consciousness has to be embodied, has to find itself partially defined by others and has to have a history, lasting through a period of time and geared towards the future. Merleau-Ponty says:

> I am from the start outside myself and open to the world. (*PP*, p. 456)

And:

> A consciousness for which the world 'can be taken for granted', which finds it 'already constituted' and present even in consciousness itself, does not *absolutely* choose either its being or its manner of being. (*PP*, p. 453)

The emphasis for Merleau-Ponty is on the subject both being acted upon, and being open to different possibilities, *at once*. In virtue of the latter, and also of the intentionality of others' definitions of oneself, causal determinism is not true. And in virtue of the world, including oneself, already being constituted by others, absolute choice is impossible. Thus:

I am never a thing and never bare consciousness. (*PP*, p. 453)

As a thing one would be subject to causal determination; and as a pure consciousness one would never be already constituted, and so would be absolutely free. In fact, says Merleau-Ponty, one is neither; and hence Sartre is wrong in his espousal of absolute freedom, because he is wrong in his characterization of the subject.

4 Merleau-Ponty's Positive Characterization of Freedom

To draw out some of the implications of this discussion of Merleau-Ponty's attitude towards Sartre, and to illustrate what Merleau-Ponty means by 'a mode of existing in the world', which forms the basis for his account of freedom, we shall now examine what Merleau-Ponty says about 'being an intellectual'. An intellectual is someone who lives life as if intellectualism were true. The intellectual's way of being in the world is one which emphasizes the role of judgement, decision, choice, thought, etc. Merleau-Ponty emphasizes that this is indeed a possible way of being:

> Even the decision to become a revolutionary ... by an act of pure freedom would express a certain way of being in the natural and social world, which is typically that of the intellectual. He 'throws in his lot with the working class' from the starting point of his situation as an intellectual.... (and this is why even fideism, in his case, remains rightly suspect). (*PP*, p. 447)

In other words it is possible to try to be a living instantiation of the intellectualist position, or even of the Sartrean position, of absolute freedom. It is possible to be someone who believes that problems, both theoretical and practical, should be solved on an intellectual or reflective level, and then imposed upon the life one has reflected on.[11] So in epistemology, for example, one *first* works out how the world *should* be (e.g. conforming to the Kantian categories) and then, lo and behold, this is how the world *is* seen. Likewise in practical matters one might have abstract ideas of justice, equality, love, etc., which one *then* imposes on social reality. A Utopian idealist would be an example of this position. The deliberating intellectual revolutionary, the subject of the above quotation, is another example. The decision to become a revolutionary is based on and rooted in the life of the intellectual: so, for example, it might be based on an idea of justice which is the result of many hours of thought. The intellectual's decision is *rooted*; but in the intellect. By contrast, there are revolutionaries whose decision to revolt is rooted in their experience of their position in relation to those they wish to overthrow.

Merleau-Ponty does not deny that the intellectual exemplifies a possible way
of living in the world: it can be a practical life too. But he does cast doubts on
this as a basis for most forms of life, in saying, for example, that the fideism of
the intellectual revolutionary is 'rightly suspect'.

The reason for this is that

> with the worker it is *a fortiori* the case that his decision is elaborated in the
> course of his life . . . for the worker revolution is a more immediate possibility,
> and one closer to his own interests than for the intellectual, since he is at grips
> with the economic system in his very life. (*PP*, p. 447)

As an intellectual, one is not rooted in the class that one wishes to help. One
tends to treat oneself as an individual thinking about class, thinking about
those in a particular social environment. But about this Merleau-Ponty says:

> at the outset, I am not an individual beyond class, I am situated in a social
> environment, and my freedom, though it may have the power to commit me
> elsewhere, has not the power to transform me instantaneously into what I decide
> to be. (*PP*, p. 447)

The intellectual is true to his or her thoughts; the worker is true to his or
her involvement in economic life. The former can only become like the latter
by 'transcending' the distinction between intellectual and worker (as, for
example, Merleau-Ponty thought Lenin did (*PP*, p. 447). But this is rarely
possible.

What Merleau-Ponty is principally against is the view that the intellectual's
mode of being in the world is the paradigmatic case for all ways of being in the
world. This is the view taken by the upholder of intellectualism. Merleau-
Ponty has two criticisms of intellectualism on this point. First, although there
are cases of deliberation, decision, course of action and modes of being which
exemplify the intellectualist account of the subject, *most* cases are not like this.
Second, and more importantly, the intellectualist analysis of even the intellectual's mode of being is wrong. The set of features (sedimentation, sociality,
history, etc.) which is the basis for freedom include more than pure
consciousness or pure intellect, even for the intellectual. As we have noted, for
Merleau-Ponty, understanding the intellectual's decisions involves understanding both what the social situation of the intellectual is and what it is not.
What it *is* concerns the fact that being an intellectual is this individual's
characteristic way of being. What it is *not* concerns the fact that the intellectual's history is not, usually, a worker's:

> I am a psychological and historical structure, and have received, with existence,
> a manner of existing, a style. All my actions and thoughts stand in a relationship

to this structure.... The fact remains that I am free, not in spite of, or on the hither side of, these motivations, but by means of them. For this significant life, this certain significance of nature and history which I am, does not limit my access to the world, but on the contrary is my means of entering into communication with it. It is by being unrestrictedly and unreservedly what I am at present that I have a chance of moving forward.... I can miss being free only if I try to bypass my natural and social situation. (*PP*, pp. 455–6)

We have already explored how Merleau-Ponty emphasizes the natural and social situation as part of the subject's being in the world. But here Merleau-Ponty links these features of being in the world to the possibility of freedom. How does this work?

At one level of analysis, Merleau-Ponty can say that all human beings are free to the extent to which they are open to different possibilities. We have noted (Chapter Seven, section 3) that this is true in human perception in so far as things are not perceived as entirely fixed and determinate. It is always possible to adopt a different stance with respect to the world and thereby perceive different aspects of the world. There is the same ambiguity in the existential project,

> which is the polarization of a life towards a goal which is both determinate and indeterminate, which, to the person concerned, is entirely unrepresented, and which is recognized only on being attained. (*PP*, p. 446)

There is an openness in any existential project. The project cannot be fixed in advance; and indeed the only way a project can be fixed is retrospectively, when one has achieved the goal or abandoned the project. To think otherwise is to abandon the future-orientated nature of projects.

This much is Sartrean, and it suggests that freedom is a capacity of any being capable of projects or capable of perception. All body-subjects are free in virtue of their capacity to structure their world. However, Merleau-Ponty differs from Sartre in regarding this openness to possibilities as being manifested differently in the various modes of being in the world. Sedimentation is both the root and route of freedom; as was clear in the case of the intellectual. But it is also a factor which makes some people less free than others. Some people are more weighed down by their sedimentation than others. Merleau-Ponty says of freedom that

> it shrinks without ever disappearing altogether in direct proportion to the lessening of the *tolerance* allowed by the bodily and institutional data of our lives. (*PP*, p. 454)

People who live a very sedimented life, who find it very difficult to 'shake up' their sediment, are nonetheless free to the extent that they act in and perceive the world. So Schneider, whom we discussed in Chapter Six, section 4, with his brain injury, is not able to change his basic way of being in the world; but given this mode of being he is free to the extent that he is open to different actions and perceptual experiences. Likewise the person with the inferiority complex may be unlikely to undergo a conversion experience; but the project of inferiority still has aspects of openness. The inferiority is experienced as a weight to struggle against and as a way of making one's activities under-standable. But what counts as fitting into this pattern is open-ended; and there is always the slim possibility that one will change the project.

Some people may be better able than others to change their manner of being in the world. This, as we have noted, itself presupposes a certain way of existing, which is then modified and developed into a new way of existing. Merleau-Ponty refers to this (*PP*, p. 439) as 'a conversion involving our whole existence': a new tradition is founded. Such people are more free than people like Schneider, in so far as they can overcome the power of a particular habi-tual way of acting. The way that this may happen is that one's life pattern, which expresses certain intentional relationships to the world, can bring such despair or dissatisfaction that one comes to realize that one has, in effect, already dropped one's previous commitments. For example (ours), there may be cases of people trapped in a particular lifestyle, or in a marriage, or in an occupation, where their feelings and actions may seem to indicate that they wish their previous commitments were no longer binding. But what the feelings and actions in fact indicate is that these commitments *are* no longer binding. Indeed, people in most despair may often be those who have not fully recognized that they are no longer committed to a particular way of being: they therefore 'pretend' that they are still committed, and so fail to enact any other commitment.

According to Merleau-Ponty it is only with the adoption of a new project, e.g. taking up a different lifestyle or occupation, that one sees how the old project really was. Sometimes, prior to the change, the dissatisfaction is some-thing one does not want to voice, and one tries to reason that one is doing the right thing by not changing (staying in a certain personal relationship might be a good example of this). But the moment one does change (e.g. by commit-ting oneself elsewhere), it becomes obvious to one that previously one was not really holding onto the old commitment; and one realizes that all the deliberations in defence of the old project were really rationalizations. Merleau-Ponty provides the example of psychoanalysis:

> Psychoanalytical treatment does not bring about its cure by producing direct awareness of the past, but in the first place by binding the subject to his doctor through new existential relationships. It is not a matter of giving scientific assent to the psychoanalytical interpretation, and discovering a notional significance for the past; it is a matter of reliving this or that as significant, and this the patient succeeds in doing only by seeing his past in the perspective of his co-existence with the doctor. (*PP*, p. 455)

This example brings out both the fact that, for change to occur, there must be a new commitment (via the relationship with the therapist), and the fact that mere intellectual assessment of the significance of the past is unlikely to make change possible.

But what makes new commitments more possible for some than for others? One might be tempted to say that a person who cannot change their mode of being is unfree; and then to explain this fact by reference to some causal story involving the person's past.[12] But Merleau-Ponty, as we noted in the first section of this chapter, denies that our behaviour is causally determined. He thus cannot explain why some people are better able to change than others by reference to causal determinants. So his position is to be distinguished from another attempt to resist the alternatives that *either* determinism is true *or* freedom is possible, namely, so-called soft determinism.[13] According to the soft determinist, freedom is possible despite determinism being true. An unfree act involves some *special* sense of necessitation, over and above the mere fact of its being caused. A free act is one which is causally determined, yet is 'free from' such specific forms of necessitation as 'compulsion', 'coercion', and so on. Clearly Merleau-Ponty cannot be a soft determinist, for he denies causal determinism.

Merleau-Ponty's position is more like another response to the metaphysical issue of freedom and determinism. That is, there are philosophers who think that the *metaphysical* questions of free-will and determinism cannot be answered:[14] it is not possible to give a clear 'yes or no' answer to the question whether or not every event has a cause, or to the question whether or not humans have free-will. Instead what these philosophers prefer to do is to pro-vide piece-meal analyses of different cases in which one might say that 'I could have done otherwise', so that one might end up with a continuum of cases: some where it is clear that the person is free, others where it is not so clear, and so on. The issue of determinism, *per se*, is considered irrelevant or dismissed.

In a rather similar way – though switching from conceptual analysis to phenomenological description – Merleau-Ponty would be concerned to describe, for example, the life of a person who seemingly was not able to change; and through this description one would see how this person lives, how difficult it is for them to change, how nevertheless they have some choices, and how even the most deeply rooted habitual patterns express some basic sense of freedom. Thus Merleau-Ponty's main focus is on asking for detailed descriptions of various ways of being in the world rather than asking theoret-ical questions, such as whether there is some sense of 'free' which applies to all human action, or why some people are less free than others (at least if this is understood in causal terms):

Whether it is a question of things or of historical situations, philosophy has no other function than to teach us to see them clearly once more, and it is true to say that it comes into being by destroying itself as separate philosophy. But what is here required is silence, for only the hero lives out his relation to men and the world and it is not fitting that another speak in his name. (*PP*, p. 456)

The suggestion seems to be that philosophical speculation about freedom can be too abstract; freedom should really be of concern only in action. In action one sees freedom's real roots in social and personal history in relation to futures which are never firmly fixed.

Conclusion

In this Conclusion we shall not try to provide a critical assessment either of phenomenology as such, or of the more specific claims to be found in the texts we have been examining. Instead we shall draw together some of the main themes that have emerged, and explore a number of important issues that they raise. In the first section we discuss the relationships between Husserl's transcendental phenomenology and the existential phenomenologies of Merleau-Ponty and Sartre, and some questions raised by this about the nature of philosophical reflection. In section 2 we consider what objections might be made to phenomenology by proponents of scientific realism, and what responses might be made to these objections. In the final section we explore the implications of Merleau-Ponty's criticisms of empiricism and intellectualism for some recent debates in the philosophy of mind.

1 Transcendental and Existential Phenomenology

In section 2 of the Introduction, three closely related questions were briefly noted about the relationship between transcendental phenomenology and existential phenomenology. First, is it possible to consider the two simply as different forms of the same kind of philosophical activity, 'phenomenology'; or are they so much at odds with each other that they cannot both be thus regarded? Second, is the transcendental element essential to Husserl's conception of phenomenology? Third, what significant differences are there between the existential phenomenology found in *Being and Nothingness* and that found in the *Phenomenology of Perception*? The answer to this last question obviously has implications for the answers to the first two.

We shall approach these questions in two stages. First, we will consider Merleau-Ponty's answers to them. His answers are characteristically ambiguous. On one interpretation of 'transcendental', all phenomenology is (or should be) transcendental, and so 'even' existential phenomenology should have a transcendental aspect. Using this interpretation, Merleau-Ponty criticizes Sartre's existential phenomenology for not being properly transcendental, because of its failure to eliminate certain philosophical presuppositions from its descriptions of experience. But on another interpretation of 'transcendental', he thinks that transcendental phenomenology is an inferior form of phenomenology, and hence that the transcendental standpoint is not a necessary feature of phenomenology. The second stage of our approach will involve addressing the question: is Merleau-Ponty correct in his rejection of 'transcendentalism' in the second interpretation he gives to this? In answering this question we will suggest that transcendental and existential phenomenology can be seen as two different versions of the same kind of philosophical activity; and that they each have different emphases which are important in correcting the tendency to describe experience in a way that is not free from presuppositions.

We can begin the first stage of our approach by considering Merleau-Ponty's own, extensive answer to the question 'What is phenomenology?', in the Preface to the *Phenomenology of Perception*. Here he claims both that phenomenology is a transcendental philosophy, and that important aspects of Husserl's transcendental phenomenology are not necessary to phenomenology. Clearly there are two senses of 'transcendental' at work here. In the first sense, Merleau-Ponty is using 'transcendental' to refer to the bracketing of claims that spring from the natural attitude, or from the scientific attitude, or from any other attitude which contains views about the nature and ontological status of the world. In this sense of 'transcendental', all phenomenology is transcendental. It is an essential aspect of the phenomenological project: to describe the experience of the world without any presuppositions about that world. Certainly Merleau-Ponty's existential phenomenology aims to be transcendental in this sense.[1] His positive descriptions of the activity of the body-subject in its engagement with the world are intended to be as free from presuppositions as possible. (How far they can actually be free from presuppositions we will consider later.) His criticisms of empiricism and intellectualism are likewise intended to provide examples of how descriptions of experience are dictated by prior conceptions of the nature of the world, particularly by their shared objectivism. We will also see that Merleau-Ponty thinks that Sartre too did not pursue this transcendental project deeply enough; that his descriptions of being-in-the-world reflect a philosophical prejudice contained in his account of the for-itself and the in-itself.

The second sense of 'transcendental', in Merleau-Ponty's use of the term, is the sense that is attached to Husserl's conception of phenomenology as a form of transcendental idealism.[2] As we saw in Chapter Three, Husserl in the *Cartesian Meditations* sees transcendental idealism as the elucidation of the structures of the transcendental ego. These structures include the ideas that the ego is the identical subject of experience, is the bearer of habitualities, and includes all the intentional life of that subject. Transcendental phenomenology is thus the activity of reducing all experiences to the life of the transcendental ego. Husserl did not abandon this notion of the transcendental in *The Crisis*:

> It is the motif of inquiring back into the ultimate source of all the formations of knowledge, the motif of the knower's reflecting upon himself and his knowing life in which all the scientific structures that are valid for him occur purposefully, are stored up as acquisitions, and have become and continue to become freely available. Working itself out radically, it is the motif of a universal philosophy which is grounded purely in this source and thus ultimately grounded. (*CES*, pp. 97–8)

The 'ultimate source', here, is still the transcendental ego. Thus Husserl, despite the richer descriptions of the lived world which so inspired Merleau-Ponty, never gave up the attempt to display the structures of the experienced world via the description of the structures of the 'I' who reflects, and is reflected upon, in phenomenology (see Chapter Six, section 2). It is this sense of 'transcendental', the uncovering of the transcendental ego, to which Merleau-Ponty, like Sartre, objects. His objection, found repeatedly in his criticisms of intellectualism, is that the phenomenological reduction is presented as

> the return to a transcendental consciousness before which the world is spread out and completely transparent. (*PP*, p. xi)

We have seen, in Chapter Seven, that Merleau-Ponty thinks that the experience of a subject cannot be made totally explicit. If one tries to describe *all* its experiences from the point of view of a timeless, transcendental subject, one is bound to misrepresent those experiences. The attempt to do so takes insufficient cognizance of the facts that the subject whose experience is being investigated operates in time, and exists in the same world as other subjects. The transcendental standpoint fails to acknowledge the opacity of the world, which Merleau-Ponty thinks is revealed by a phenomenology that recognizes the temporal ambiguity of the body-subject's experience. It also fails, despite the gargantuan efforts of Husserl's Fifth Meditation, to capture the sense of 'the other' (see Chapter Eight). It is the rejection of this transcendental standpoint, and the focus instead upon the complex lived experience of the subject in the world, that in Merleau-Ponty's view marks off existential phenomenology from transcendental phenomenology.

But Sartre, as we saw in Chapter Four, section 2, is also critical of Husserl's transcendental idealism, with its twin notions of the transcendental ego, which Sartre cannot discover, and the noematic world, which Sartre thinks is not genuinely transcendent. And Sartre, like Merleau-Ponty, concentrates on providing detailed descriptions of the experience of subjects in the world, where these descriptions make explicit that these subjects are temporal, are bodily, are involved in situations, have histories, and so on. However, Merleau-Ponty thinks that Sartre does not shed all aspects of intellectualism in his descriptions of experience; and that this failure stems from Sartre's employment of the distinction between the for-itself and the in-itself. (Merleau-Ponty rarely talks directly about Sartre in the *Phenomenology of Perception*; and, where he does, it is usually to quote *Being and Nothingness* in support of a position he is defending. But he often talks about and criticizes the distinction between the for-itself and the in-itself; and it is reasonable to suppose that, in doing so, he has Sartre at least partly in mind.)

Sartre, in *Being and Nothingness*, starts with the abstractions of the for-itself and the in-itself; and throughout the book he tries to make these abstractions more concrete by showing how they are related to each other (see Chapter Four, section 3). In response to this programme Merleau-Ponty can be seen as making two basic criticisms. First, Sartre thinks that consciousness, the key feature of the for-itself, is translucent. So the activity of the engaged, pre-reflective consciousness, which is investigated by reflective consciousness, cannot be opaque to that latter consciousness. Sartre accepts that the reflective consciousness often distorts the description of the pre-reflective consciousness; but he thinks that this kind of mistake is wilful. Merleau-Ponty thinks Sartre's account is wrong.

We have seen how, for Merleau-Ponty, the pre-logical bodily engagement in the world (which is the equivalent of Sartre's pre-reflective consciousness) is opaque to reflective consciousness (Chapter Seven, section 3). This is because the subject is situated in time, so that there are always aspects of it not open to a reflecting subject which is also situated in time. This means that phenomenology, for Merleau-Ponty, always has a historical dimension. The world described is subject to change. But the subject trying to understand things and events in this world is also part of this world, and also has a history: the nature of the subject can change, and as a result that subject's understanding of the world can change. The position from which one understands the world is a historical standpoint, encapsulated in a particular body with its particular sedimentation.

Sartre was well aware of the temporality of experience; but it is the implication of Merleau-Ponty's argument that Sartre fails to provide undistorted descriptions of this aspect of experience. This failure is related, in Merleau-Ponty's view, to the target of his second criticism of Sartre's existential phenomenology. Merleau-Ponty thinks that Sartre's starting with the distinction between the for-itself and the in-itself is a basic error. For although Sartre admits that the two poles of this distinction are abstractions from the basic relation of being-in-the-world, Merleau-Ponty considers that they are abstractions which inevitably block the way to capturing the nature of the lived world of the body in action.

This we have seen in Merleau-Ponty's criticisms of intellectualism, which fundamentally operates with a distinction between the for-itself and the in-itself. If one thinks in terms of this distinction then one is bound, according to Merleau-Ponty, to provide distorted descriptions of experience. So, for example, Sartre's descriptions in *Being and Nothingness* of the other, of love, of sexuality and of freedom all have a very different flavour from those found in the *Phenomenology of Perception*. Indeed, Merleau-Ponty might consider that the proper place for Sartre to have begun and ended his phenomenology was the more concrete and complicated world of part 4 of *Being and Nothingness*, where subjects are found to be situated in contexts which are their facticity. Only in this way could Sartre's phenomenology be true to Merleau-Ponty's first sense of 'transcendental', and thus provide descriptions more free of philosophical prejudices.

These criticisms, both of Husserl's transcendental standpoint, and of Sartre's residual intellectualism, raise important issues; for they crucially depend on accepting Merleau-Ponty's own descriptions of experience of the world. So we need to examine more closely the presuppositions of *these* descriptions. But before doing this we will consider a possible response that might be made by the transcendental idealist to Merleau-Ponty's rejection of the transcendental ego.

A basic feature of Merleau-Ponty's attack is that he regards the transcendental idealist as committed to the idea that everything in experience is translucent to consciousness. But in both forms of transcendental idealism we discussed in Chapter Three, namely Kant's and Husserl's, this is not clearly the case. For Kant, it is only the a priori structures of experience, those which make that experience possible, that are transparent to consciousness. The contingent aspects of experience are not transparent: these are dependent on the world. For Husserl, similarly, what the phenomenologist discovers by further reflection on the transcendental ego, in the eidetic reduction, is the *essence* of perception, of experience, of the world, and so on. The phenomenologist's project is seen by Husserl as the discovery of these essences; but this does not mean that *everything* about experience is trans-lucent to consciousness. The life-world is very complex: it depends on many factors – historical, social, physical – and all these factors are contingent.

But Merleau-Ponty has a possible answer in each case. Kant's argument depends upon his distinction between the a priori and the empirical; and this is a distinction which Merleau-Ponty questions. There are two lines of argu-ment in the *Phenomenology of Perception* that are relevant here, one implicit and the other more explicit. The former starts from the link between the con-cept of the a priori in Kant's work, and his concept of the transcendental. Kant's criteria of the a priori are universality and necessity. And the interesting class of non-analytic a priori judgements are seen to be necessary in a very special way: they are necessary for the possibility of experience. This necessity is established via transcendental arguments. (Here the term 'transcendental' concerns what it is that 'makes x possible', where 'x' can range over experience, knowledge, morals, beauty, etc. So this sense of 'transcendental' is different from either of the two senses distinguished earlier.) These transcendental arguments, the most famous example of which is the Transcendental Deduction of the Categories, are attempts to justify the possibility of experience or of types of experience. Merleau-Ponty repeatedly, like Husserl (see Chapter Three, section 4), claims that philosophy should be descriptive, and not concerned with questions of justification. So he would want to eliminate transcendental arguments from philosophy. It follows that he would eliminate Kant's notion of the a priori, in so far as this depends upon the validity of transcendental arguments.[3]

The more explicit form of criticism of Kant's notion of the a priori is in the chapter on Sense-Experience (*PP*, Part Two, chapter 1). Kant argues in The Aesthetic of *The Critique of Pure Reason* that space is a priori. One of Kant's arguments for this is a transcendental one: that space must be a priori, for otherwise the kind of experience we have of space (e.g. its necessary conformity to Euclidean geometry) would not be possible. For Kant, if space is a priori, it follows that the unity of the senses is a priori, i.e. that the different senses yield experience of the same single space.

Merleau-Ponty objects to this on two levels. First, like Husserl in *The Crisis* (see *CES*, pp. 94–5), he thinks that the experience of space is not of the kind that Kant says it is. Kant's starting point, i.e. his acceptance of the necessity of Euclidean geometry, is infected with objectivism. Secondly, and an extension of the first point, the unity of the senses is not a priori:

> The unity of the senses, which was regarded as an *a priori* truth, is no longer anything but the formal expression of a fundamental contingency: the fact that we are in the world – the diversity of the senses, which was regarded as given *a posteriori* ... appears as necessary to this world...; it therefore becomes an *a priori* truth.
>
> The *a priori* is the fact understood, made explicit...; the *a posteriori* is the isolated and implicit fact. (*PP*, p. 221)

What Merleau-Ponty is claiming here is that if one attends without prejudice (e.g. without thinking that one has to justify a certain form of knowledge) to one's experience of space, then the unity of the senses is not obvious. Initially, the senses are experienced as diverse (a contingent fact); but one then discovers that the senses *are* unified, in so far as their operation together enables the subject to have access to one space, or to one world. This claim Merleau-Ponty sees as a priori; but only as the final expression of a fundamental contingency.

Merleau-Ponty's seemingly paradoxical talk of the a priori expressing contingencies, and of what was a posteriori becoming a priori, shows that his notion of the a priori is quite different from Kant's. It is not defined as the opposite of the contingent. (For Kant, a priori judgements cannot be contingent, because a criterion of the a priori is necessity.) So Merleau-Ponty would not accept the transcendental idealist's response to his criticism that transcendental idealism is committed to all experience being transparent to consciousness. For this response depends upon a distinction between the a priori and the a posteriori which Merleau-Ponty considers too sharp.

A further argument against the sharp distinction between the a priori and the a posteriori (or the empirical) can be seen in Merleau-Ponty's response to Husserl's transcendental idealism. His objection to Husserl is not the same as that to Kant. For Husserl's phenomenology is descriptive, and therefore not 'transcendental' in Kant's sense of the term; and Husserl, especially in *The Crisis*, is trying to avoid objectivist presuppositions in his descriptions of experience. But, even there, Husserl does conceive of the ultimate aim of phenomenology as the discovery of essences, through the eidetic reduction (see Chapter Three, section 2). Although this is consistent with there being a whole host of non-essential aspects of experience, which need not be totally transparent to a reflecting consciousness, the discovery of these essences nonetheless depends upon having a complete description of the range of possible experiences. For otherwise one could not be certain one has correctly identified the universal structures. But, as we have seen, Merleau-Ponty denies just this possibility of giving a complete description. Experience is indeterminate. In effect, therefore, Merleau-Ponty is criticizing Husserl for his presupposition that the lived world is subject to determinate descriptions. If it is not, then Husserl's notion of essences collapses; and, with it, his concept of the a priori.

However, Merleau-Ponty does not altogether abandon the conception of phenomenology's aim as discovering essences through the eidetic reduction:

> The eidetic reduction is, on the other hand, the determination to bring the world to light as it is before any falling back on ourselves has occurred, ... I aim at and perceive a world. (*PP*, p. xvi)

Looking for the world's essence is looking for what is a fact for the subject, before that subject has any conception of what the world is like. What is uncovered is the fact that there is a world, and that this is perceived and acted upon by the unified body-subject. This is the fundamental fact of our being-in-the-world. There is a ready-made world to grasp, to gaze at, to wonder at; and this world is harmoniously given to a particular kind of subject, which is able to perceive it. This subject, and the fact that it is fitted to perceive this world, are fundamental facts discovered by phenomenological investigation. The essence of this world is that it is strange, paradoxical and indeterminate: there are no certainties in the experience of such a world. Once again, Merleau-Ponty's argument hinges on his claims about the fundamental nature of the world as experienced. Like his argument against Sartre, his argument against Husserl's conception of 'essences' depends upon the correctness of his descriptions.

It is here that we turn to the second stage of our examination of the relationship between transcendental and existential phenomenology. So far we have noted Merleau-Ponty's acceptance of existential phenomenology as transcendental (in one sense), but his rejection of transcendental phenomenology in Husserl's sense of 'transcendental' (the transcendental ego, and the eidos ego). But is Merleau-Ponty right to reject this second sense of 'transcendental'; or indeed, are both Husserl and Merleau-Ponty right to reject Kant's notion of the transcendental? Might it not be the case that Husserl's (or even Kant's) sense of the transcendental provides the necessary basic framework for understanding Merleau-Ponty's detailed descriptions of temporal bodily experience?[4]

To answer this last question, let us examine the basis for accepting Merleau-Ponty's descriptions of experience of the world. Merleau-Ponty is interested in describing the pre-logical experience of the body-subject. Time and again we have seen Merleau-Ponty point out the difficulties in any such description (e.g. Chapter Seven, section 3). The description is always from the standpoint of the (philosophical) reflector on that experience. So there is always the possibility of a misdescription, not least because the experience described is always in the past. The fact that experience is not translucent is one which Merleau-Ponty thinks crucial. But it is this fact – which a transcendentalist (in Husserl's sense) need not deny – which itself raises important questions that Merleau-Ponty has to answer.

First, there are problems about accepting much of the evidence Merleau-Ponty provides for the nature of pre-logical experience: in particular, his use of reports of scientific studies of abnormal behaviour, as in the case of Schneider (see Chapter Six, sections 3 and 4), and again in the case of hallucinations (see Chapter Seven, section 4). No doubt it is a helpful philosophical technique to highlight what is normal by focusing on the abnormal, since what is normal can be so habitual that one fails to notice its presence (see Chapter Six, section 5). But too often Merleau-Ponty seems to rely on the reports of these experiments without any examination of the experimenter's presuppositions. This seems strange in the midst of sustained attacks on the objectivist presuppositions of scientific descriptions.[5]

Second, and more importantly, there are questions about the presuppositions of Merleau-Ponty's own descriptions of the lived world. Indeed, the two forms of transcendental idealism we have discussed, Kant's and

Husserl's , might themselves provide the basis for challenging the claim of Merleau-Ponty's descriptions to be presuppositionless. Thus one might argue, along Kantian lines, that Merleau-Ponty assumes a specific epistemology in his descriptions of, say, one world, one thing and one subject. Merleau-Ponty seems to assume that there is no problem in accepting that there is only one world that is experienced. But are there not important conditions for identity that need to be established here? One does not have to agree with the detail of Kant's project of trying to show how a particular form of knowledge is possible to agree that there are important questions about the presuppositions of claims to know that the descriptions of an experience are true. For Kant, the central argument concerning these conditions is the 'Transcendental Deduction of the Categories'.[6] Merleau-Ponty (typically) does not discuss this argument directly; and it is arguable that, despite the general validity of his attacks on Kant for presupposing objectivism, there is one place where this criticism does not hold. For in the Transcendental Deduction Kant is concerned to show that objectivism is itself a precondition of being able to ascribe experiences to a single subject. Kant might be unconvincing; but the question about identity needs to be addressed, and Merleau-Ponty does not do this.

Alternatively, one might argue along Husserlian lines that one needs a more thorough examination of the role of the philosophical reflector (in Husserl's view, the transcendental ego) than Merleau-Ponty provides. There are two aspects to the self. There is the pre-logical bodily self; and there is the reflecting self, which describes the bodily self. Merleau-Ponty attends mainly to the former; whereas Husserl might be seen as redressing the balance. There is surely a need to examine the presuppositions of the philosophical reflector, and it is this that Husserl tries to do in his analysis of the transcendental ego. There is a standpoint from which one describes the pre-logical experience; and one does not have to agree with Husserl's descriptions of the essential structures of this standpoint to agree with him that it requires examination.

What Merleau-Ponty does say about the nature of the philosophical standpoint is that it is historical. The philosophical subject, like the body-subject, is historically situated. This suggests that the philosopher is limited in his or her enquiries, and that philosophy is a never-ending process. One way of putting this is to say that the philosopher can never be free of presuppositions.[7] The only hope is to be able to reveal the presuppositions for what they are. The criticism of Merleau-Ponty at this point might be that he has not sufficiently revealed his own presuppositions. And one important area where this may be so concerns the origin of meaning: how meaning arises from our contact with the world. Merleau-Ponty really does no more than assert that meaning emerges out of the interaction between the subject and the world. He wants to resist the idea that meaning can be detached from the world, and then examined for its structure, origin, conditions, and so on. And he takes it as a basic fact that

Phenomenology, as a disclosure of the world, rests on itself, or rather provides
its own foundation. (*PP*, pp. xx–xxi)

Two different critical responses to this might be, first, from the analytical
philosophy tradition, and second, from the hermeneutic tradition. The former
response would be based upon the premiss that language is in some important
way prior to experience. On this basis there are no brute facts: there are
always interpretations of the world. These interpretations must involve the use
of language; and hence it must be wrong to base meaning on experience.
Wittgenstein provides the starting-point for one such line of argument. He
emphasizes language games, rules of grammar, forms of life, shared practices,
as essential conditions for understanding meaning and therefore experience.[8]
Frege is the inspiration for another strand of analytical philosophy, a strand
which sees philosophical method as consisting in the analysis of language.[9]

The second critical response recognizes that language and ontology are
inextricably linked, but insists that more needs to be said about understanding
and interpretation. Gadamer is an important representative of this hermeneutic tradition, who can be seen as extending Merleau-Ponty's insistence on
the historicity of the philosophical subject, and examining this in more detail.
In this way Gadamer offers a more detailed analysis of the presuppositions
behind any description of experience. He provides support for Merleau-
Ponty's views about the unending nature of the philosophical quest, but not
before he has shown how language and ontology are intimately linked.
Gadamer highlights the need to examine the presuppositions of language; for
language is the medium of all understanding. For Gadamer there is no understanding without presuppositions. So presuppositions cannot be eliminated
from philosophical understanding.

This question of the nature of philosophical reflection, and of the possibility
of presuppositionless description, continues to be debated, especially in the
writings of those who are concerned with the relativistic implications of
rooting the ideas of rationality and meaning in historical traditions.[10] Even the
transcendental standpoint (in all its senses) is defended by some. For example,
Habermas, particularly in his debate with Gadamer, argues that one needs a
standpoint outside a tradition (a coherent set of presuppositions), from which
to criticize that tradition.[11] That such a standpoint is possible is one of the
main points of Husserl's transcendental ego.

There are also echoes of Merleau-Ponty's concerns about the nature of
phenomenology, and of philosophy, in current debates about the so-called end
of philosophy.[12] For one implication of Merleau-Ponty's views about the
indeterminacy of the world, the historical nature of the understanding of
experience of the world, and the hazy distinction between the a priori and the
empirical, is that there are likewise hazy borderlines between philosophy and
other disciplines (such as history). Indeed, he says:

True philosophy consists in re-learning to look at the world, and in this sense a historical account can give meaning to the world quite as 'deeply' as a philosophical treatise. (*PP*, p. xx)

If this is true, then perhaps philosophy has no distinctive voice; and phenomenology would be the dialogue between those interested in revealing the fundamental structures of experiences of the world. This is related to one reason why the *Phenomenology of Perception* is so difficult to read for anyone with a specifically philosophical training, namely that such training has presuppositions that are constantly being questioned by the text. The text is not always recognizable as philosophy. Merleau-Ponty is providing a challenge to rethink the nature of philosophy. But he needs challenging himself, to reveal the nature of his own presuppositions. Perhaps, even, he has need of Husserl's transcendental ego (stripped of its eidetic structures). For what this might do is to remind Merleau-Ponty of the possible distortions in *his* descriptions of pre-logical experience. Merleau-Ponty's sensitivity to pre-logical experience reminds the reflecting subject of the danger of imposed thought structures distorting the descriptions given. Kant, Husserl and Sartre are criticized for failing to avoid this danger: their reflective standpoints have failed to avoid the pitfalls of objective thought. One needs the reflective standpoint; its presuppositions do need constant scrutiny; but it need not be objective thought that provides the only pitfalls.

2 Phenomenology and Scientific Realism

Having explored some of the issues raised by the relationship between transcendental and existential phenomenology, we turn now to consider a further set of issues concerning something that they have in common, namely their rejection of scientific realism. According to this philosophical position, not only is there a subject-independent world, which includes within it human subjects and their experiences; but also the empirical sciences have a privileged status in identifying and explaining what happens in this world. Because of this, common-sense or pre-scientific representations of the world may in principle be displaced by scientific ones, where the two are in conflict, and may themselves be regarded as 'objects' for scientific explanation.[13]

What kinds of response might be made by scientific realists to the phenomenologists' arguments against their position? We shall approach this question by returning to a central theme of the *Phenomenology of Perception*, its rejection of 'objective thought', and of its view of the world as consisting of determinate objects in external relations to one another, and hence as an appropriate 'object' for scientific description and explanation. As we noted in Chapter Five, section 1, Merleau-Ponty regards objective thought as shared both by empiricists and by intellectualists; and his critique of objective thought is intended to reveal the deficiencies both of scientific realism and of transcendental idealism. Here we will focus on the implications of this critique for scientific realism.

Merleau-Ponty argues that objective thought misrepresents the character of the lived world. But, even if one accepts that this is so, the scientific realist might well reply that this does not show that the 'real' world, as depicted by the sciences, is not 'objective'. Rather, it may show only that 'the world as experienced by humans' is not the world as it really is, and hence that there may be significant differences between the world as experienced and the 'real' world – the former providing a by no means infallible guide to the character of the latter.

What is suggested by this reply is a typical claim made by the proponents of scientific realism: that there is a fundamental distinction to be drawn between the realms of 'subjective experience' and 'objective reality' – between, for example, what is revealed to perceptual experience and what is discovered by scientific enquiry. Furthermore, it will be maintained, it is a central aim of such enquiry to explain, scientifically, the character of perceptual experience by reference to the nature of the external world, and to the ways in which this interacts with the human perceiver's sensory equipment, neurological mechanisms and/or cognitive structures, and so on. Thus the experience of what Merleau-Ponty terms 'the lived world' itself becomes an 'object' for scientific, causal explanation.[14]

From this standpoint the role of 'phenomenology' would be merely to provide accurate descriptions of perceptual experience, which it is then the legitimate task of the sciences to explain. Such descriptions would, of course, give proper recognition to the intentional, object-directed nature of experience; and, if Merleau-Ponty is right, to the non-determinacy of these intentional objects, and the internality of their relations. Further, the scientific realist could agree with the phenomenologists that many past attempts at such description have indeed misrepresented the experienced world, due to objectivist 'prejudices'. But, it could be argued, there is nothing about the overall project of scientific realism which requires or necessarily generates such misrepresentation; and the insights of the phenomenologists can thus be incorporated within this project, with the philosophical anti-realism that accompanies them being left behind.

The position just sketched out is no mere theoretical possibility, for it was a position of this kind that was in fact adopted by some of the Gestalt psychologists during the period in which Husserl's and Merleau-Ponty's philosophical work was developing – for example by Wolfgang Kohler in his influential book *Gestalt Psychology*, which begins in the following way:

> There seems to be a single starting-point for psychology, exactly as for all the other sciences: the world as I find it, naively and uncritically.... In my case ...

that naive picture consists, at this moment, of a blue lake with dark forests around it, a big grey stone, hard and cool, which I have chosen as a chair, a page on which I write, a faint noise of the wind which hardly moves in the trees, and a strong odour characteristic of boats and fishing. (*Gestalt Psychology*, p. 2)

For Kohler, however, this is *only* 'the starting-point': the task of a scientific psychology is then to explain how such experiences of the world are in fact generated, by a combination of external stimuli and the operations of the central nervous system (or indeed by mental processing of these stimuli – for it makes no difference, in this context, whether such explanations are materialistic or mentalistic). And, in setting out this two-stage programme of 'phenomenological' description followed by scientific explanation, Kohler makes his philosophical commitment to realism quite clear – as, elsewhere, he voiced his suspicions about the phenomenologists' anti-realism.[15]

But Merleau-Ponty would not accept this attempted incorporation of phenomenological description within a realist framework. In the *Phenomenology of Perception* – as he had earlier in *The Structure of Behaviour* – he acknowledges his indebtedness to the work of the Gestalt psychologists in challenging objectivist misrepresentations of perceptual experience (*PP*, pp. 47–51). But he criticizes them for their insufficiently radical rejection of 'naturalism' and 'causal thinking', and for failing to avoid 'the prejudice of determinate being' (*PP*, p. 51, note 1). What exactly does this mean; and does Merleau-Ponty succeed in showing what is wrong with this kind of position?

Given that such forms of 'causal thinking' might accept the non-determinacy of the lived world, and the internality of its relations, and hence do not involve any straightforwardly identifiable misdescription of the phenomena, Merleau-Ponty's basic objection must be that it is simply not possible to provide causal explanations which refer to determinate objects and external relations *for* the (non-determinate, internally related) 'world as it is experienced.' To show that this is not possible, as we have seen, Merleau-Ponty proceeds in an apparently piecemeal fashion, taking one after another a series of attempts that have actually been made by scientists to provide such explanations, and arguing that each of them fails.

But this procedure is itself open to a possible objection: that even if Merleau-Ponty is right about all those attempts which he considers, this may be due to their *specific* failings, and may therefore not reveal anything fundamentally misconceived about the overall project of scientific explanation. Perhaps, that is, the examples he takes are of a rather primitive kind, revealing the inadequacies and immaturity of early twentieth-century psychology and neurophysiology. But these might be improved upon one day – perhaps, indeed, they already have been? So Merleau-Ponty might have done better had he tried to provide an argument to show that the non-determinate and internal cannot *in principle* be explained in terms of the determinate and external. And perhaps such an argument could be provided. But Merleau-Ponty does not do so; and at times he seems to deny that it could be done (e.g. *PP*, p. 8, note 5 – though he might, of course, be wrong about that).[16]

Yet even if no such argument can be provided, and Merleau-Ponty's criticisms of particular explanations are at best inconclusive with respect to the general project of which they are particular instances, there are other kinds of argument which the phenomenologist might use against scientific realism. In particular, there are Husserl's objections, in Part One of *The Crisis*, to what he regarded as the misinterpretation of modern/Galilean science by philosophical realists, including Galileo himself – along with Descartes, Locke and many others. So we will now shift our attention from Merleau-Ponty's concern with the non-determinacy and internality of the lived world to Husserl's concern with the scientific realist's treatment of the secondary qualities.

As was implied in our account of *The Crisis* in Chapter Six, section 1, Husserl does not (unlike Merleau-Ponty, it would seem) straightforwardly deny the possibility of 'explaining' scientifically one's perception of such properties by reference to the (idealized) primary properties of objects. But he *does* deny that such explanations should be taken to imply that the secondary properties – and, more generally, all the properties of things in the life-world – are 'unreal', merely 'subjective', by contrast with the world of objects characterized only by the (idealized) primary properties, as depicted by Galilean science.

Husserl's argument, as we noted, depends upon the claim that Galileo's conception of the 'scientific' world was arrived at by a process of *abstraction* from the lived world. In this process of abstraction, the secondary properties were eliminated because they failed to satisfy the requirements of measurability or quantifiability, and hence could not be represented by the variables of mathematically specifiable scientific laws. Husserl maintains that these abstract conceptual constructs, i.e. of objects with (idealized) primary properties alone, were mistakenly reified by Galileo and his philosophical allies. Instead, he claims, they should be regarded merely *as* 'constructs', which are helpful in contributing to the predictive (and hence explanatory) power of modern science, but have no genuine ontological status – and certainly not one that involves subjectivizing the status of the objects and properties of the life-world.

However, there are a number of possible objections to Husserl's argument here. First, he seems to believe that, because these scientific concepts are formed through a process of abstraction from one domain, they cannot therefore have any genuine referential function in relation to another domain. This may not seem altogether convincing, since it is unclear why any such facts about the *origins* of scientific concepts should imply such restrictions for their referential function. Second, Husserl's argument apparently commits him to an *instrumentalist* view of the cognitive status of scientific theories, which sees them merely as devices for making predictions, and hence regards the nature of scientific explanation as consisting merely in the ability to provide such predictions. This is a far from unchallenged or unchallengeable view of scientific theories.[17] Third, Husserl's account of Galileo seems to ignore some of the reasons which led him and others (such as Descartes and Locke) to regard the secondary properties as 'subjective'. For example, it was claimed that the perception of these properties varies markedly between different external conditions and internal states of the perceiver; and that, although similar variations occur in the perception of primary properties, scientific explanations of the latter variations seem necessarily to make reference to the primary properties of the object, whilst corresponding explanations for the former can be given without reference to any secondary properties of the object.[18]

But there are also a number of broader issues raised by Husserl's rejection of scientific realism in *The Crisis*, which go beyond these somewhat technical problems about his treatment of the primary – secondary property distinction. *The Crisis* was one of a number of philosophical works, published between the two world wars, which protested at the way in which modern science, at least in its dominant cultural interpretations, had denuded the natural world of all 'meaning' – presenting it as a barren, mechanical realm of 'matter in motion', and radically separating it from the 'human' realm of subjectivity and experience.[19] So Husserl's argument in Part One of *The Crisis* can be seen as belonging to a more general form of criticism of 'the separation of humans from nature'. We shall now consider some questions about phenomenology and scientific realism that are raised by this.

The process of separation is said to involve the stripping away from the natural world of all those features which make it a 'meaningful' object of experience for humans in their everyday, pre-scientific existence; and the 'relocation' of these features within the 'inner life' of the human subject. In his opposition to this, Merleau-Ponty's position is very similar to Husserl's. For Merleau-Ponty, the only real world is what he sometimes calls 'the human world' (e.g. *PP*, p. 24), by which he means, not 'the world of other humans', but 'the natural world', invested as it is, in everyday experience, with 'human' qualities and meanings: not just the secondary properties, but aesthetic ones, and many others which have often been deemed by scientific realists to be anthropomorphic (see Chapter Five, section 2).

Before proceeding further, it is important to emphasize the difference between *this* kind of objection to scientific realism, and another which has concerned the supposed illegitimacy of adopting 'scientific' methods in the study of 'the human world', understood in its more usual sense as the realm of human, and hence social, activity. Anti-naturalist philosophers of the social sciences have typically argued that there are various distinctive features of the human world that make it impossible or inappropriate to apply to it the same methods of enquiry and modes of explanation as are employed in the natural sciences. In particular, it has often been argued that what is required in the study of social phenomena is an attempt to 'understand' these by reference to the ways in which human agents experience their activities, and to the 'meanings' which they give to them – or, indeed, the meanings that are given to them by various kinds of social rules, conventions, conceptual frameworks, and so on.[20]

There have been many different versions of this kind of anti-naturalist position. But at least some of them have drawn their philosophical inspiration from phenomenology, with its emphasis upon the unprejudiced, non-scientific description of human experience and meaning.[21] However, despite the possible merits of such approaches in the social sciences, their relationship to phenomenology as a philosophical position is potentially problematic. For in arguing that the human sciences must adopt quite different methods from the natural sciences, because of the distincively 'subjective' character of human existence, they run the risk of at least implicitly accepting precisely that separation between 'subject' and 'object', between the realm of subjective human experience and that of objective nature, which the phenomenologists are concerned to reject.

We can now return to this phenomenological rejection of the separation between experience and nature, and consider some possible difficulties that may face it. Perhaps the most important of these can be introduced in the following way. There is apparently good reason to believe that the 'meanings' in nature experienced by humans are by no means historically or culturally universal: for example, the new ways of 'seeing' nature associated with the Romantic movement, or the different attitudes towards nature and its 'moral status' expressed in different cultural and religious traditions.[22] Such variability might well make it difficult to regard these meanings as residing *in* the world of nature itself, rather than being 'given' or 'attributed' to nature by humans. (Indeed, the socio-historical diversity in human experiences of the world, and the part played in this by differing conceptual structures, presents more general difficulties for phenomenology, since it might seem to undermine both the adequacy of the first-person standpoint in arriving at descriptions of experience, and the supposed primacy of experience *vis-à-vis* the 'meanings' provided by specific conceptual frameworks.)[23]

It may thus seem attractive to maintain, as scientific realism does, that there is indeed a crucial distinction to be made between 'nature' and 'how nature is experienced by humans'; and that one should therefore be on one's guard against the illicit projection of human meanings onto the natural world. A similar conclusion might be supported by considering the existence of other animal species which, like humans, experience the world in certain ways, but in ways that presumably differ from humans. One may, for example, have little if any ability to understand 'what it is like to be a bat' – to take the title of an influential article by Thomas Nagel; but that there *is* some such subjectivity, and that it differs from 'ours', seems a not unreasonable assumption. Furthermore, since non-human species have existed for much longer than the human species, they have presumably, prior to the emergence of humans, inhabited a 'world' which, until quite recently in evolutionary terms, has had no peculiarly 'human' meanings attributed to it, let alone residing in it.

The overall implication of these considerations would be that phenomenology – whether in its transcendental or in its existential forms – is unduly *anthropocentric* in its conception of the world; and correspondingly, that scientific realism is, at least in this respect, less so.[24] Yet there is a curious paradox here, and one that has some significance for current debates within environmental philosophy, concerning what kind(s) of 'attitude towards nature' humans should adopt.[25] For it is often argued that it is scientific realism, at least in its Galilean form, which is itself at fault in supporting a conception of nature that is at the root of contemporary environmental problems: that is, of nature as a mere 'object' of possible human domination and control, rather than as existing 'in its own right' as something whose intrinsic character, and indeed value, humans must learn to respect. According to this line of argument, then, it is scientific realism that is unduly anthropocentric, setting up nature as an object for human, technical control, under the guise of providing 'objective knowledge of reality'.[26]

The issues raised by this apparent paradox are too complex to explore fully here, but two possible responses to it will be briefly considered. The first would be to argue that, even if the scientific realist can show that the phenomenologist's apparent refusal to distinguish between 'the world as experienced' and 'the real world' leads to illicit projections of human meanings onto nature, it does not follow that the world as described by the supposedly objective procedures of the natural sciences is indeed 'the world as it really is', devoid of all human meanings. For science is itself a human, and hence social, activity. The concepts it employs to describe the world, however much they have been constructed so as to eliminate illicit projections of human meanings, *are* nonetheless human, and thus socio-historical, constructions. It would therefore be absurd to regard them as representing 'nature in its own right', and hence as free from the possible influence of such human historical projects as that of the technical control or domination of nature.

The second possible response, one that is more sympathetic to scientific realism, would be this. To the extent that it is true that 'modern science' has conceived of nature as an object of technical control, and has in this respect displayed an objectionable form of anthropocentrism, this has primarily been due to its failure to recognize the distinctive characteristics of the *organic* world – the liv*ing* world, as distinct both from the 'lived world' of the phenomenologists, and from the *in*organic world of 'matter in motion.' But this failure is not inherent in scientific realism which, as such, involves no specific views about the actual character of 'the world discovered by the sciences', and is thus quite consistent with recognizing the distinctive character of the organic world.[27] This organic world includes, *inter alia*, the various non-human animal species; and the members of these species are indeed 'bodily' beings. But this does not mean that their bodies are of a Galilean kind, mere 'matter in motion', whose behaviour is straightforwardly explicable by reference to the laws of physics or mechanics. To regard them in this way would indeed be to misrepresent them.

So in this view, what is objectionable about the kind of duality between 'humans' and 'nature', and relatedly between 'mind' and 'body', which Husserl and Merleau-Ponty were so keen to criticize, is not the scientific realist's insistence on distinguishing between our experience of nature, and 'nature as it is', but the specific characterization of the latter as consisting merely of 'mechanical' bodies, with their exclusively primary properties. Furthermore, it might be argued, amongst these non-mechanical bodies of the organic realm are human bodies; and it may be the case that these display certain characteristics which distinguish them from all other animal bodies. In particular, as we saw in Chapter Six, Merleau-Ponty claims that human bodies possess a certain kind of intentionality, practical knowledge, and so on. According to the view we have been outlining here, there would be no reason why the scientific realist could not, in principle, accept this claim. But what could not be accepted is Merleau-Ponty's further thesis that the human body cannot be understood scientifically: i.e. that these characteristics of the human body cannot be causally explained within the framework of 'objective thought'.

Thus the crucial issue here is whether the intentional properties of the body can be given causal explanations – for example, in neurophysiological, or indeed psychological, terms. Merleau-Ponty clearly believes this is not possible – though there are difficulties for his strategy of argument here, as we noted earlier in this section. Certainly, since the time that Merleau-Ponty wrote the *Phenomenology of Perception*, there have been many attempts to provide such explanations, and of a more sophisticated kind than those he considered there; and, in some of these, 'phenomenological' descriptions of what it is like to live with certain kinds of bodily pathology have been provided by writers who are nonetheless committed to the kind of scientific-explanatory project that Merleau-Ponty regarded as philosophically misconceived.[28]

But this hardly shows that his philosophical claims were mistaken: such writers might simply be wrong in regarding the phenomenological and neurophysiological approaches as compatible with one another. For what is involved here is a strict analogue of the issues traditionally explored within the philosophy of *mind*, about whether it is possible for intentional states to be explained in terms of non-intentional ones. This has usually been regarded as a problem about the relations between 'mind' and 'body', the latter being assumed to be unproblematically characterizable in non-intentional terms. But what Merleau-Ponty's claims about the human body imply, in effect, is that there is a 'body – body problem', not just – or perhaps instead of – a 'mind – body problem': i.e., a problem about the relationship between the intentional properties of the human body, and their supposed neurophysiological bases or correlates.

Yet, at the very least, Merleau-Ponty's own view of this relationship has to be able to account for one apparently undeniable fact: that Schneider's abnormal mode of bodily existence was in some sense due to a bullet damaging his brain (see Chapter Six, section 3). But we shall not try to explore how far Merleau-Ponty can succeed in incorporating this 'fact' in his existential phenomenology.[29] Instead, in the final section of this Conclusion, we shall go on to consider the implications of his criticisms of both empiricist and intellectualist versions of objective thought for some recent debates within the philosophy of mind.

3 Merleau-Ponty and Contemporary Theories of the Mind

In this section of our concluding remarks, we shall indicate in broad outline how some of the criticisms Merleau-Ponty levels at objective thought might be applied to certain current theories of the mind which fall within the analytic tradition of philosophy. We shall focus on what is arguably the heart of Merleau-Ponty's criticism of objective thought, be it empiricist or intellectualist: that it fails to give a satisfactory account of intentionality.[30]

Merleau-Ponty criticizes empiricist theories on the grounds that they adopt an objective, scientific standpoint, in that they make presuppositions, drawn from the natural sciences, about the nature of objects: objects exist independently of each other and stand only in contingent, causal relations to each other. Empiricist theories then construe the problem of intentionality as the problem of explaining how consciousness or the mind can relate to these objects. Characteristically, empiricist theories will emphasize the causal role of objects in the production of mental states and the effects of human activity on objects. But, Merleau-Ponty argues, intentionality cannot be explained in terms of causal relations, since it is essentially an internal relation; items so related cannot be identified except by reference to each other, whereas causation is an external relation, relating only items which can be identified independently of each other.

Intellectualist theories, according to Merleau-Ponty, do acknowledge that intentionality is an internal relation; but they presuppose that all internal relations are relations of meaning and that all meaning has its source in the mind. Hence, intellectualism explains intentionality in terms of relations between mental items: ideas, thoughts or concepts. Merleau-Ponty criticizes such accounts on the grounds that what they characterize is not a relation between subject and object at all, but only a complex state of the subject. No satisfactory account is possible of how these states succeed in relating the conscious subject or the mental states of such a subject to concrete, existent objects.

Modern materialist theories will characteristically give rise to accounts of intentionality similar to those which Merleau-Ponty characterizes as empiricist, and so share, in Merleau-Ponty's eyes, their defects. Materialist theories of the mind are, in origin, developed as a response to the difficulties of explaining interaction between minds and bodies. If, as in mind – brain identity theories, mental states are held to be identical with states of the body, usually the brain, then all interactions between those brain states and physical states of other objects become interactions between kinds of physical states and so can be construed, as all other interactions in the physical world, as causal interactions. Since states of the brain are physical, they do not display intentionality. Intentionality, then, disappears as a distinctive problem. The hypothesis is that all relations between brains and objects in the world are causal, and we must await developments in neurophysiology to find and establish appropriate causal laws. The identity theory, that is to say, offers a causal account of intentionality; hence Merleau-Ponty's criticism of empiricism could be applied equally to it.

Mind-brain identity theories were based on the expectation that 1–1 correlations between mental states and brain states could be found. It ran aground precisely because such correlations were not forthcoming. One reason why 1–1 correlations failed to be found was precisely because of the intentionality of mental states. No distinctive feature of the brain could be identified which corresponded to every occurrence of, for example, perceiving Picasso's *Guernica*, the ambition to be a famous singer, or the belief that one had just paid all one's debts. But finding such brain states is an essential prerequisite for identifying mental states with brain states, and so explaining intentionality in terms of causal relations between events in the brain and events involving other objects in the world.

In the face of such difficulties, Churchland developed 'eliminative materialism'.[31] This is the thesis that, as neurophysiology develops, it will be seen to be a better theory of human activity, and so will replace the current inadequate theory which Churchland calls 'folk psychology'. By 'folk psychology' he understands the loose body of theory, embedded in ordinary talk of the mind, according to which human activity is explained by reference to the existence of minds and mental states. Eliminative materialism can be presented as a diagnosis of why 1–1 correlations between brain states and mental states could not be discovered. We cannot find these correlations because mental states are theoretical entities in a false theory of human beings. As such, there is no reason to suppose that these alleged entities correspond to anything real in the world, and so it is no objection to a different theory that its entities don't correspond to the fictions of folk psychology. Neurophysiology will supersede folk psychology as a better theory; it has no need to be answerable to it, nor share the divisions it makes in its subject matter.

Intentionality, then, on this view would be construed as a feature of folk psychology, a theoretical construct in a false theory. If the mind itself is, as eliminative materialism claims, a fiction, then there is no need to explain how it relates to its objects. Neurophysiology need give no account of intentionality; and so, in particular, is not proposing a causal account of it. Hence, it will not be vulnerable to Merleau-Ponty's claim that no such account can be adequate.

It might, however, seem vulnerable to Merleau-Ponty's charge of adopting the objective standpoint: taking unexamined, from science, presuppositions not only about the nature of objects, as did traditional empiricist theories, but also about the nature of the subject. This charge would not, of course, be made against neurophysiology. That is a science and as such properly adopts the objective standpoint of the natural scientist. It is against the eliminative materialists, as philosophers, that the charge would be levelled. They claim a certain status for neurophysiology: namely, that it does the same work as folk psychology aims to do. But now it might look as if they have an easy defence of their position. They could argue that they are not, as philosophers, adopting the objective standpoint in the way that Merleau-Ponty finds vicious, but only recommending it as a means of dispelling misguided philosophical puzzlement.

However, if we look at the argument in support of eliminative materialism, we find that it is weakened by Merleau-Ponty's criticism. If neurophysiology is to replace folk psychology, then they must, at some level, be theories of the same thing, however generally described – say 'human activity'. If mental states are to be eliminated, they must be the theoretical entities of folk psychology – they must be put forward as somehow 'lying behind' what the theory is aiming to explain, being responsible, and probably causally responsible, for the occurrences to be explained. Now, this is precisely the view of mental states involved in theories which Merleau-Ponty classifies as empiricist theories. They may well qualify to be called 'folk psychologies'; and as such may indeed be candidates for replacement by neurophysiology. Merleau-Ponty could agree with this and even go further in claiming that it is precisely these empiricist theories which have, at least since Descartes, paved the way for eliminative materialism by 'scientizing' philosophy. Their replaceability by neurophysiology is evidence that they never were theories of the mind, never did give an account of the subject or of intentionality. If they had, then they would not be replaceable by neurophysiology; in so far as they are replaceable,

they are shown to have been inadequate. The eliminative materialist standpoint is objective in so far as it fails to acknowledge any standpoint other than
the scientific one.

However, that empiricist theories might be superseded is not sufficient
evidence for the claim that all theories of the mind could be superseded.
Intellectualist theories, Merleau-Ponty might argue, could not be superseded
by neurophysiology because they are not theories of the same thing. They are
exploring, not human activity generally, but specifically the activities of the
mind. To the charge that these are theoretical entities, they could respond by
pointing out that they do not posit mental states as causes of human behaviour, but as logically necessary conditions for the existence of any theory at all.
Any theory, including neurophysiological theory, requires the mind of a theor-
ist, not just to cause it to appear as marks on paper, but to ensure that it is a
meaningful system of explanation. Mental activity is logically prior to all
theory building, including neurophysiological theory building, and hence
must have a more than theoretical existence. Theories of the mind, hence,
have a quite different status from scientific theories.

Further, Merleau-Ponty would claim, that empiricist theories or indeed any
theories of the mind might be superseded by neurophysiology is not evidence
that mental states and their intentionality are theoretical constructs and so
eliminable. Intentionality, he would claim, is not a theoretical entity, but
something which we directly experience. Nor can it be construed, on the
model of secondary qualities, as an appearance which science aims to explain
in terms of the reality which gives rise to it. For, unlike secondary qualities,
intentionality is not an appearance, not something which appears, but rather
the fact that anything appears at all. If science dismisses this as a fiction, then
its entire programme of explaining the reality lying behind appearances is
jeopardized, for it has nothing to explain.

Notice that there is a parallel here between Merleau-Ponty's criticisms and
those which Thomas Nagel explicitly levels against modern materialist
theories of the mind. Nagel, in 'What it is like to be a Bat'[32] and *The View
From Nowhere*,[33] distinguishes objective and subjective standpoint, criticizes
current theories of the mind for adopting the objective standpoint, and argues
that no theory which adopts the objective standpoint can recognize and so
offer an adequate account of the characteristic subjectivity of the mind.[34]

We have seen how modern materialist theories might be vulnerable to
Merleau-Ponty's criticisms of empiricist thought in that they give a causal
account of the relation between the subject and objects in the world, and
hence fail to recognize the true nature of intentionality, that it is an internal
relation. He diagnoses this failure as due to their adopting an objective standpoint, in particular the standpoint of science. We shall now look at some
modern theories of the mind to see how they might be vulnerable to
Merleau-Ponty's criticisms of intellectualist thought.

Intellectualist theories, as we noted in Chapter Five, section 3, construe the mind as a complex system of mental states. A mental state relates to objects in the world by representing them. Merleau-Ponty's criticism of this account of the mind is that it cannot account for intentionality, properly understood, as an unmediated and internal relation between the subject and concrete existing objects. First, the account it gives is of a relation between subject and object mediated by representations, whereas intentionality, as Merleau-Ponty understands it, is an unmediated relation. Second, though it construes the intentional relation between representations and objects as an internal relation, as Merleau-Ponty believes intentionality to be, the relation it in fact describes is one between representations and what Merleau-Ponty calls 'the meanings of objects', and not to the concrete, existing objects in the world. In so far as intellectualism can recognize existent objects at all, it can establish only an external relation between them and representations. This criticism can be put in the form of a dilemma. Intellectualism can explain intentionality either as an internal relation between representation and the meaning of objects or as an external relation between representations and concrete, existing objects. Either way, nowhere does it have an internal relation between a state of the subject and a concrete existing object, and hence misses the essential feature of intentionality as Merleau-Ponty understands it. Merleau-Ponty diagnoses this failure of intellectualism as due to its adoption of an objective standpoint, that of reflective thought. Since intentionality is a pre-reflective phenomenon, any theory built from a reflective standpoint will fail to account for it, because it will fail to recognize it.

Do any modern theories of the mind share these intellectualist features and so prove vulnerable to Merleau-Ponty's criticisms? It might seem prima facie unlikely that any theory in the analytic tradition could be dubbed intellectualist. The legacy of logical positivism and the later work of Wittgenstein has been to direct the philosopher's attention away from theories of the mind as systems of mental items and towards the publicly observable evidence for the existence of such items; for it is these publicly observable 'criteria' which give talk of the mind its sense. In addition, the influence of logic upon analytic philosophy has again been to turn attention away from the mind and towards language. The problem of intentionality has thus been construed as the problem of explaining the logical form of language used for the ascription of intentional, mental states. Indeed, it is this focus on the publicly observable and on language rather than on the mind as the proper way of exploring meaning which chiefly separates the analytic tradition from the intellectualist and phenomenological ones alike. However, this albeit radical difference between analytic and intellectualist thought is not relevant here; for it is not the mental character of the elements in the intellectualist theory that Merleau-Ponty's criticisms are directed towards, but the role those elements, the mental states, are given in the account of intentionality.

Analytic theories, which give rise to accounts of intentionality that Merleau-Ponty would dub intellectualist, take their inspiration from work done in philosophical logic, notably by Frege.[35] A later influence was Chisholm's interpretation of Brentano's thesis that the distinguishing mark of the mental is intentionality.[36] Chisholm reinterprets Brentano's thesis of intentionality as an account of the language necessary to ascribe intentional, mental states. A great deal of work has been done since Chisholm on the logical form of ascriptions of mental states. We noted in Chapter Two, section 4, what the peculiarities of such language were. In brief, ascriptions of mental states give rise to referentially opaque contexts: expressions whose normal function is to refer to objects do not have that function when they occur in referentially opaque contexts.

Frege put forward the view that the function they do have in those contexts is that they refer to what in normal contexts is their meaning or sense. It has become an orthodox view of sentences which ascribe mental states that all terms governed by psychological verbs refer to their customary meaning. In particular, when a psychological verb is followed by a that-clause, since the meaning of a clause is a proposition, the clause refers to a proposition.

Hence, what such sentences state is that a certain relation holds between a subject and a meaning. In particular, when a that-clause follows a psychological verb, since the meaning of the clause is a proposition, the whole sentence states that a relation holds between a subject and a proposition. The relation is one of attitude: belief, disbelief, wanting to be true, etc. Such sentences are said to ascribe propositional attitudes.

Mental states, then, on this view, are attitudes to propositions. Minds relate to the world by having attitudes towards propositions. These propositions describe or represent possible states of affairs in the world. They relate to particular objects in the world by having attitudes to propositions which include descriptions of objects. Propositions, on this view, are abstract objects defined as the meanings of sentences in a language.

The differences between this view of intentionality and that of the intellectualist are that propositions are abstract not mental and that they are defined in terms of language which is public rather than ideas which are private. But the similarities are clear. Propositions play just the role in this theory that mental items, ideas or thoughts, play in intellectualist theories of intentionality. The subject has attitudes to propositions which represent the world. These representations mediate between subject and object in the world. Their relation to existing objects is external or contingent: the existence of the proposition is neutral with respect to the existence of any object it represents. Propositions can be internally or logically related only to items of meaning.

It is clear now how Merleau-Ponty's criticisms would apply to this account of intentionality. First, intentionality is construed as a mediated relation, whereas Merleau-Ponty thinks it is unmediated. Second, the relation between the mediating item, the proposition, and the concrete existing object is an external relation, since the representation can be identified and specified independently of identifying and specifying the concrete, existent object, and vice versa. The representation can be internally related only to other representations, other descriptions of the object, what Merleau-Ponty would call 'the meaning of the object'.

A modern theory which can be seen to share this interpretation of intentionality sufficiently to be categorized as intellectualist and so be a suitable target for Merleau-Ponty's criticisms is functionalism. The claim of functionalism is that mind is whatever produces intelligent behaviour.

Functionalism is inspired by the Artificial Intelligence (AI) programme. The aim of AI is to understand how the human mind works by reference to how computers work. Either of two theses might lie behind the aims of this programme. In 'The Myth of the Computer', his review of Dennett and Hofstadter's *The Mind's I*,[37] Searle calls these theses Strong AI and Weak AI. Strong AI holds that the mind is a program. Weak AI holds that the mind is just like a program and can be understood and studied in terms of our knowledge of computer programs. It doesn't matter for our purposes which we take.[38]

The relevant computers to study will be those which perform tasks commonly believed to require intelligence. The study of computers can throw light on the mind because, not only do they perform 'intelligent' tasks previously thought only to be possible for human beings, they also perform these tasks in the same way – by inferential moves between pieces of information represented by symbols or language. This latter claim is one for which linguistic philosophy and its attempts to understand the mind in linguistic terms, as attitudes to propositions or uses of sentences, paves the way. Merleau-Ponty would not agree that computers do things the same way that humans do, only that they perform as intellectualism holds that humans do.

The relevant part of the computer for AI to study is its program, or software. Hence functionalism claims that mind, in a computer, is the program; in the human it is or can be thought of as the program which the human, in particular the human's brain, instantiates.[39]

One of the chief current exponents of functionalism is Dennett.[40] The functionalist account he offers of intentionality is that intentionality is a feature of a sufficiently complex system. For any such system, there is a variety of different ways in which it can be described. To describe it as an intentional system is to ascribe propositional attitudes to it. The propositions in question would be elements in the program, propositions and programs alike being abstract objects, pieces of information which in the case of a human system would be a representation of the world. Each proposition represents a state of affairs in the world only in virtue of being in a system which contains a model of the world.

We can see now how functionalism would be deemed by Merleau-Ponty to be a form of intellectualism, and so vulnerable to his criticisms. According to functionalism, subjects relate to objects via systems of propositions which represent or model the world. So the relation is a mediated one. Merleau-Ponty in contrast holds intentionality to be an unmediated relation between subject and object. Second, the relation between the model and the world is contingent. Internal relations are possible only between models or elements of models. The existence of the model is independent of the existence of the world which it models, and of any object of which the model includes a representation. Hence Merleau-Ponty would claim that functionalism shares an account of intentionality with other intellectualist theories and fails to acknowledge that it is an unmediated and internal relation between subject and object.

Merleau-Ponty could take support, at least as far as his second criticism goes, from the criticism of strong AI which Searle makes via his Chinese room test.[41] Searle's conclusion is that to run or instantiate a program which models the world does not by itself constitute being intentionally related to the world. His argument is in outline this. A program is a set of rules for transforming input into output. In order to run such a program, applying these rules, one does not need to know what the input or the output mean. They may be in a language which one does not understand; in Searle's example they are in Chinese. But running the program neither requires nor constitutes understanding Chinese. In particular it does not require or constitute understanding what objects in the world any of the symbols in the language represent. So, the relation between a program and objects in the world cannot be explained entirely in terms of the relation between elements of the program. The parallel with Merleau-Ponty's claim is clear. One cannot explain intentionality in terms of the internal relations between representations. No such system of relations will add up to a relation between the representation and what, outside the program, it represents.

Searle's positive view is that, for intentionality, one needs something more. This, he thinks, is that the instantiation of the program should be biological. Merleau-Ponty's point would rather be that one needs to reject the entire project of exploring the mind in terms of computer programs, systems of representations. Instead, the philosopher should look behind any system of representations, or model of the world, to the pre-reflective experience of the world which is the basis of our framing or understanding any model of the world. Our pre-reflective relation to the world is not itself a model of the world, nor does it involve a model of the world. Rather, it is a direct relation with the world unmediated by any model. Reflective thought employs models. Reflective thought is a mediate relation with the world. But it succeeds in relating us to the world only because we are already so related in pre-reflective experience.

He might add that, just as empiricist theories paved the way for eliminative materialism, so intellectualist theories, which construe the mind as a system of representations, paved the way for functionalism and AI. A computer program does not operate as we operate; but only as intellectualist thought claims we operate.

Intellectualism involves taking an objective standpoint, the standpoint of reflective thought. From that standpoint, no adequate account of intentionality is forthcoming. Reflective thought does employ models or representations of the world. These may be construed as ideas, as sentences, as propositions or as elements in computer programs. But these representations get their representational powers, not from their relations with each other, but by being understood as representing the world. It is a prerequisite of so understanding them that one is already related intentionally to the world. This prerequisite is one which intellectualist thought gives no account of, for it fails to recognize that it is a prerequisite.

It is now clear why Merleau-Ponty, in the Preface to the *Phenomenology of Perception*, says that intentionality cannot be properly understood without understanding the reduction.

> We can now consider the notion of intentionality, too often cited as the main discovery of phenomenology, whereas it is understandable only through the reduction. 'All consciousness is consciousness of something'; there is nothing new in that. (*PP*, p. xvii)

Without the reduction, one adopts the standpoint either of science or of reflective thought. From either of these objective standpoints one presupposes that the subject is pre-reflectively aware of the world. Hence, one presupposes instead of explaining what is fundamental to intentionality. Any account of intentionality from an objective standpoint will be, at best, incomplete, and at worst misleading.

Notes

Introduction

1 For an attempt to identify the basic features of phenomenological method, see Part Five of Spiegelberg, *The Phenomenological Movement* – an invaluable guide – which emphasizes the wide range and diversity of this philosophical 'movement'. The remarks we make about phenomenology in this Introduction are deliberately simplistic, and will (hopefully) become less so in the chapters which follow.

2 De Beauvoir, *The Prime of Life*, p. 135.

3 And arguably, perhaps, Heidegger's *Being and Time* represents yet another, though not one that we shall be discussing. Despite its departures from Husserl's transcendental phenomenology, the *Phenomenology of Perception* is much more closely related to Husserl's work than is *Being and Time*, and thus makes for a more fruitful comparison. Further, although Heidegger's work has an important bearing on both Merleau-Ponty's and Sartre's, we think that our relatively brief discussion of *Being and Nothingness*, in Chapter Four, provides a more accessible introduction to the existentialist themes in the *Phenomenology of Perception* than would a correspondingly brief discussion of *Being and Time*.

4 Most of the information in this section is taken from Spiegelberg, *The Phenomenological Movement*. (Note that the most recent, third, edition contains a considerable number of corrections and revisions to what was said in the earlier editions, and should therefore be consulted in preference to them.)

5 On the development of Husserl's work, including his philosophy of mathematics, see Pivcevic, *Husserl and Phenomenology*.

6 Quoted by Carr, in his Translator's Introduction to *The Crisis* (*CES*, p. xxix), upon which our account of the background to this text is mainly based.

7 On Heidegger's relations with Husserl, and with the Nazi Party, see Waterhouse, *A Heidegger Critique*.

8 Cf. Habermas's discussion of Husserl in the course of his own critique of positivism, in the Appendix to *Knowledge and Human Interests*. On the concept of positivism, see Keat, *The Politics of Social Theory*, Chapter 1.

9 As Spiegelberg drily notes: 'Merleau-Ponty's references to Husserl's unpublished MSS usually do not allow identifications in the texts as they have appeared since

in the *Husserliana* edition. Not all these references should be taken at face value'
(*The Phenomenological Movement*, p. 580, note 2).

10   Kojeve, *Introduction to the Reading of Hegel*. See Kline, 'The Existentialist Rediscovery of Hegel and Marx', on the influence of Kojeve's lectures; and Rabil
Merleau-Ponty, Chapter III.

11   On the political disagreements between Merleau-Ponty and Sartre, see Kruks,
The Political Philosophy of Merleau-Ponty. We do not consider the development of
Merleau-Ponty's philosophy after the *Phenomenology of Perception*: on this, see
Kwant, *From Phenomenology to Metaphysics*, and Madison, *The Phenomenology of
Merleau-Ponty*.

12   Sartre, 'Merleau-Ponty (1)'. On de Beauvoir's claims that Merleau-Ponty
misinterpreted Sartre's philosophy, see Rabil, *Merleau-Ponty*, Chapter V, who
argues she was wrong; and Langer, 'Sartre and Merleau-Ponty', who argues she
was right.

13   In particular, we do not consider the important chapter on 'Temporality' (*PP*,
part 3 chapter 2), where the influence of Heidegger is most obvious: cf. notes 3
above. By contrast, Langer's *Merleau-Ponty's Phenomenology of Perception* deals,
most helpfully, with the complete text. (Ricoeur's *Husserl*, Chapters 4 and 5, likewise deals with each of the *Cartesian Meditations* – but not so helpfully.)

Chapter 1:   The Project of Phenomenology

1   We shall not consider the defensibility or otherwise of Husserl's interpretation of
Descartes' philosophy, helpful introductions to which include Cottingham's
Descartes and Kenny's *Descartes*. For an account of Husserl's philosophy broadly
sympathetic to its Cartesian aim, see Kolakowski, *Husserl and the Search for
Certainty*. On the *Cartesian Meditations* see also Hartmann, 'Metaphysics in
Husserlian Phenomenology'; and Ricoeur, *Husserl*, Chapters 4 and 5.

2   See Outhwaite, *Understanding Social Life*, for discussion of various theories about
what distinguishes the human/social 'sciences' (*Geisteswissenschaften*) from the
natural sciences (*Naturwissenschaften*); and Husserl's 'Philosophy as a Rigorous
Science', for his conception of phenomenology as 'science'.

3   See Gadamer, *Truth and Method*, Second Part, Chapter II, section 1, on this idea
of pre-judgement.

4   '*Epoché*' is the transliteration of a Greek word, which initially/literally meant 'a
check or cessation' (as in 'checking an advance'), and later became a technical
term used by the early sceptical philosophers to mean 'a suspension of
judgement'.

5   For an introductory discussion of different forms of realism, see Hospers, *An
Introduction to Philosophical Analysis*, Chapters 18 and 23. On the development of
Husserl's views about mathematics, see Chapters 2 and 3 of Pivčević, *Husserl and
Phenomenology*. For a sophisticated defence of realism about abstract objects,
including numbers, see Hale, *Abstract Objects*.

6   This conception of science is far from unchallengeable: for example, much recent
work in the philosophy of the natural sciences (for a survey, see Chalmers, *What is*

this Thing Called Science?) casts doubt on the idea of indubitable evidential foundations. The existence of competing accounts of 'the idea of science' may itself indicate problems for Husserl's aim of providing an unprejudiced, presuppositionless description of this 'phenomenon'.

7 See Pietersma, 'Husserl's Views on the Evident and the True'.

8 We return briefly to this issue at the end of Section 1 of the Conclusion. See also Chapter Two, section 4.

9 The philosophical rapidity of this move to transcendental idealism may well seem problematic: see, for example, Nakhnikian's comments in his Introduction to Husserl's *Idea of Phenomenology*, pp. xviii–xx

10 The various stages in the development of Husserl's conception of the Ego are discussed by Kockelmans in 'Husserl and Kant on the Pure Ego'.

11 Giving a satisfactory account of the transcendence of the object is a crucial and much debated task in phenomenology. For Husserl's view, see Chapter Two, section 3; for Sartre's criticisms of this, Chapter Four, section 2; and for Merleau-Ponty's account, Chapter Seven, section 4.

12 On the nature and role of these 'principles of natural light', see Chapter 8 of Kenny's *Descartes*. As well as the 'axiomatic' prejudice, Husserl refers to Descartes' 'scholastic' prejudices (*CM*, pp. 23–4): see for example Kenny, Chapter 4, on Descartes' use of the scholastic concept of substance in his account of res cogitans.

13 See Cottingham, *Descartes*, Chapter 4, on the place of 'experiment' in Descartes' philosophy of science.

14 On Husserl's view of imagination, see Casey, 'Imagination and Phenomenological Method'. We return to this in our discussion of the eidetic reduction in Chapter Three, section 2.

15 See especially Kern, 'The Three Ways to the Transcendental Phenomenological Reduction'. But the worry Husserl expresses about the Cartesian way in *The Crisis* (*CES*, p. 155) is somewhat different from the one we focus upon here. See also McKenna, *Husserl's 'Introductions to Phenomenology'*.

Chapter 2:   *Intentionality and Meaning*

1 In what follows, we shall use the expression 'mode of consciousness' to indicate what Husserl calls 'cogito' – the *way* of being conscious or way of meaning as opposed to *object* of consciousness or object meant.

2 'Cogito' means, literally, 'I think'; but Husserl at this stage is not exploring the subject 'I' but only the conscious activity of the subject.

3 In *The Crisis*, Husserl cites Locke as an important exponent of this tradition. See *CES*, Part II, section 22 pp. 84–6.

4 'Die' is the singular of 'dice'. The few examples of phenomenological descriptions which Husserl presents in *CM* are far from fully developed. He has, however, been influential upon others who attempt phenomological descriptions of all manner of phenomena. For examples, see: Barthes, *Camera Lucida* (a phenomenological description of the photograph); Gurwitsch, *Marginal Consciousness*; Attig,

'Re-Learning the World: on the Phenomenology of Grieving"; Relph, *Place and Placelessness*; Casey, *Remembering*; Hamrick (ed.), *Phenomenology in Practice and Theory*.

5 Husserl explores the temporality of consciousness further in his *The Phenomenology of Internal Time Consciousness*.

6 Kahn (trans.), *The Art and Thought of Heraclitus*.

7 In the main, Husserl uses 'existence' and also 'actuality' of particular objects, 'being' when he is concerned more generally with what it is for objects to exist or 'have being'. In either case, being or existence is what, in performing the epoché, the philosopher has bracketed, put out of play.

8 For other comparisons, see Brown and Mays, *Linguistic Analysis and Phenomenology*; Durfee, *Analytic Philosophy and Phenomenology*; Harney, *Intentionality, Sense and the Mind*; Pivčević (ed.), *Phenomenology and Philosophical Understanding*; Ryle, 'Phenomenology' and 'Phenomenology and "The Concept of Mind"' both in *Collected Papers*; and, for related issues, see Baldwin and Bell, 'Phenomenology, Solipsism and Egocentric Thought'; Mohanty, *Husserl and Frege*; Smith and MacIntyre, *Husserl and Intentionality*.

9 Brentano, *Psychology from an Empirical Standpoint*, pp. 88–9. Works on Brentano include: Howarth, 'Franz Brentano and Object-Directedness'; MacAlister (ed.), *The Philosophy of Brentano*.

10 Chisholm, 'Sentences about Believing'.

11 For examples, see Davidson, *Essays on Actions and Events*; Prior, *Objects of Thought*; Ryle, *The Concept of Mind*; Searle, *Intentionality*.

12 If this is not immediately convincing, suppose that Jones's thought consisted in wondering who wove the mat in the garden. If it is not clearly false, it is at least not unproblematically true that he is, thereby, wondering who wove the mat I wove last year. Clearly, something has changed concerning our attempt to characterize Jones's thought. If intuitions differ as to whether the truth value has changed, this, in the present context, might simply be cited as throwing some doubt on the 'exactness' often claimed for linguistic philosophy by those who wish to compare phenomenology unfavourably with it. For some fairly unorthodox intuitions, see Howarth, 'On Thinking of What One Fears'.

13 See Austin, *Sense and Sensibilia*; Wittgenstein, *The Blue and Brown Books, Philosophical Investigations*; Pitcher (ed.), *Truth*.

Chapter 3:   *Phenomenology and Transcendental Idealism*

1 For reading on Husserl's Fourth Meditation, see Ricouer, *Husserl*, chapter 4, section VII; Solomon, *From Rationalism to Existentialism*, chapter 5.

2 Leibniz, *Monadology*.

3 The reader should be warned against the danger of reading examples naturalistically (see Chapter Two, section 1). When considering examples which cite people or things, there is a 'natural' temptation to adopt the view that what one is talking about exists and has 'real' properties. This temptation should be resisted: the examples should be read with the epoché in mind. Likewise

statements about the condition making possible a certain kind of transcendental Ego should not be read as *causal* statements.

4 If one's imagination is limited by the kind of person one has become then any eidetic description will fail fully to transcend these limitations. A cooperative exercise of transcendental Egos would seem to be called for so that each transcendental Ego can see how its imagination, too, is limited by its habitualities. That this is so is argued by Gadamer in *Truth and Method*, Second Part, chapter II, section 1.

5 Hume, *Treatise*, Book I, Part III.

6 This claim from Augustine is also quoted in part by Merleau-Ponty in the preface to the *Phenomenology of Perception* (p. xi). Merleau-Ponty, however, has a quite different attitude towards it (see Chapter Five, section 4 below).

7 Kant's arguments are found in 'The Paralogisms of Pure Reason', *The Critique of Pure Reason*, trans. Kemp Smith, pp. 328–83.

8 For an introduction to Kant's thought, see Kemp, *The Philosophy of Kant*.

9 '*KS*' refers to the Kemp Smith edition of Kant, *The Critique of Pure Reason*.

10 '*CPR*' refers to Kant, *The Critique of Pure Reason*.

11 Popper, in *Conjectures and Refutations*, is an heir to this Kantian thought: see especially the title essay.

Chapter 4:   *Existentialism and Phenomenology*

1 For writings on phenomenology and existentialism, see Grossmann, *Phenomenology and Existentialism*; Kockelmans (ed.), *Phenomenology*; Lee and Mandelbaum (eds.), *Phenomenology and Existentialism*; Pivčević, *Husserl and Phenomenology*.

2 This is tantamount to rejecting the epoché, as Husserl understood it, since, for Husserl, the role of the epoché was precisely to reveal the standpoint of the philosophizing subject outside the world and to bracket the objective world in order to focus on the world as meant. Yet Sartre and Merleau-Ponty do not explicitly reject the epoché; and they both applaud Husserl's method, of which the epoché is a central feature. Broadly speaking, what they commend is the requirement that phenomenological description should be free from philosophical presupposition, and that philosophical reflection should be free from the sort of prejudices which can 'colour' ordinary, introspective reflection.

3 Sartre introduces his notion of 'conduct' on p. 4 of *BN*.

4 Translated by Joseph P. Fell in *The Journal of the British Society for Phenomenology*, vol. 1, no. 2, May 1970.

5 We use the abbreviation '*I*' for Sartre's article 'Intentionality'.

6 In Sartre's dramatic depiction, we can detect the view which Husserl called 'sensualism' (see Chapter Two, section 1).

7 For other discussions of *The Transcendence of the Ego* and Sartre's notion of consciousness, see papers by Glynn, 'The Eye/I of the Paradox', and Morris, 'Sartre on the Transcendence of the Ego', both in Glynn (ed.), *Sartre*.

8 This criticism that Husserl has ignored Being was also made by Heidegger.

9 We use the abbreviation '*TE*' to refer to Sartre's *The Transcendence of the Ego*.

10 In supposing that Husserl's aim is one of 'explanation' and 'need', Sartre's reading of Husserl may be too Kantian (see Chapter Three, section 5).

11 For discussions of Sartre on the unconscious, expecially in its relation to his notion of bad faith, see *BN*, Part 1, chapter 2, section 1; Fingarette, *Self-Deception*; Mirvish 'Gestalt Mechanisms and Believing Beliefs'; Neu, 'Divided Minds'; Pears, 'Freud, Sartre and Self-Deception', in Wollheim (ed.), *Freud*.

12 *Nausea*, pp. 182–93.

13 Sartre might be criticized here for switching from talk of 'the being of the phenomenon' to talking of a 'region of being'. He insists on the difference between his notion of being and Kant's notion of a noumenal realm, but at this point it is not easy to focus on a clear difference. We shall not pursue this issue here.

14 The influence on Sartre of the work of the Gestalt psychologists is evident here.

15 The obvious objection to make to Sartre here is that, since non-being depends on expectations, it fails to satisfy a crucial condition for objectivity, namely inter-subjectivity. Sartre, however, would respond to this by pointing out, first, that it is inter-subjective in the sense that anyone with the expectation may experience the phenomenon; and, second, that all phenomena depend on the state of the subject and so no phenomena are, in the sense of the objection, inter-subjective.

16 Discussions of Sartre's notion of bad faith include: Phillips, 'Bad Faith and Sartre's Waiter'; Manser, 'Unfair to Waiters' and 'A New Look at Bad Faith'; see also note 11 above.

17 Leibniz's definition of identity says that an object a is identical with an object b if, and only if, a and b share all their properties, which seems to entail that an object is the set of its properties.

18 The 'of' is put in brackets to indicate that here it introduces, not an *object* of consciousness, but a state of consciousness which, because it is a conscious state, is conscious that it is that state.

19 Sartre does argue in the context of relations between people (*BN*, Part. 3, chapter 3, section 3) that the character of such 'collective' experiences is ultimately dependent upon individual experience.

20 Sartre also gives descriptions of 'engaged' conduct – usually of himself writing. But these are unstable states which are always implicitly under threat and whose onset is essentially mysterious.

Chapter 5: The Critique of Objective Thought

1 We discuss Merleau-Ponty's view of intentionality in Chapter Six, section 5; and his interpretations of transcendental reduction, and essences, in section 1 of the Conclusion.

2 This account of Merleau-Ponty's overall strategy of argument involves a good deal of extrapolation from the text. One diffculty is an apparent lack of consistency in his use of various key terms: for example, 'objectivism' is sometimes used with specifically empiricist and/or realist implications, at odds with his claim that this is a view shared shared by intellectualists and empiricists. Another is that, although he occasionally talks explicitly of 'realism' (e.g. *PP*, p. 31), he also uses other terms to refer to this position, including 'naturalism' (e.g. *PP*, p. 47). For a helpful overview of Merleau-Ponty's arguments in both *PP* and *SB*, see Spurling, *Phenomenology and the Social World*, Chapter 1.

3   See Gregory's *Eye and Brain*, chapter 9, for a discussion (in Merleau-Ponty's terms, intellectualist) of this and other well-known visual illusions; and his *The Intelligent Eye*, Chapter 3, for a (similarly intellectualist) explanation of perceptual ambiguities and paradoxes.

4   Nagel, in *The Structure of Science*, Chapter 1, argues that the determinacy of scientific concepts is one of several related features which make science different from, and in many respects superior to, common-sense. Cf. Hospers's more sympathetic discussion of 'vagueness' in *An Introduction to Philosophical Analysis*, Chapter 3; and Waismann's argument, in 'Verifiability', that all descriptive concepts are inevitably 'open-textured'.

5   It is unclear whether Merleau-Ponty's claim here implies rejection of the Law of Non-Contradiction; and likewise, for his preceding claim, rejection of the Law of Excluded Middle. For discussion of the meaning and status of these 'Laws', see Hospers, *An Introduction to Philosophical Analysis*, Chapter 11.

6   For an influential statement of the 'internal relations' view of human (and hence social) action, see Winch, *The Idea of a Social Science*, especially Chapters II and V; and for an equally influential statement of the opposing view. Davidson's 'Actions, Reasons and Causes'.

7   For a similar contrast between 'objective' and 'lived' spatiality, see Straus, *Selected Papers: Phenomenological Psychology*, Chapter 1; and for more recent phenomenological explorations of spatiality, see Pickles, *Phenomenology, Science and Geography*, and Relph, *Place and Placelessness*.

8   We return to the issues raised here in section 2 of the Conclusion.

9   See Plomer, 'Merleau-Ponty on Sensations'.

10 Merleau-Ponty's argument here seems to rely on the intellectualist's regarding such judgements as being made *consciously*; and it is unclear why this should be assumed.

11 On empiricist philosophers of the seventeenth and eighteenth centuries, see Woolhouse, *The Empiricists*; and on their influence in the history of psychology, Peters and Mace, 'Psychology'.

12 See Skinner, *Science and Human Behaviour*, for a defence of radical behaviourism in psychology; and Atkinson et al., *Introduction to Psychology*, Chapters 10 and 11, for a discussion of (what Merleau-Ponty would regard as) typically empiricist theories of motivation and the emotions.

13 See Cottingham's *Rationalism*, on the history of rationalist philosophy and its influence on twentieth-century linguistics and psychology. Gregory's *Intelligent Eye* and Miller et al.'s *Plans and the Structure of Behaviour* could be seen as examples of intellectualist approaches to perception and action, as could more recent developments in artificial intelligence and cognitive psychology: see Boden, *Artificial Intelligence and Natural Man*, and section 3 of the Conclusion.

14 Hence Merleau-Ponty gives a good deal of attention to the French neo-Kantians, such as Alain, Brunschvicg and Lachelier, who might be seen by some as providing an improperly 'psychologized' version of Kantian philosophy.

15 See Lakatos, 'Falsification and the Methodology of Scientific Research Programmes': for critical discussion of his position, see Chalmers, *What is this Thing Called Science?*, Chapters 7 and 9, and Feyerabend, *Against Method*, Chapter 16.

16 See Norman, *Hegel's Phenomenology*, Chapter 1, for a discussion of Hegel's conception of dialectical critique and of the 'phenomenological' character of Hegel's philosophy.

17 Cf. the discussion in section 1, Chapter Four, of Sartre's attempt to 'steer a course between realism and idealism'.

18 The centrality of this concept of the body-subject is rightly emphasized by Kwant, in *The Phenomenological Philosophy of Merleau-Ponty*.

Chapter 6: The Body as Subject

1 On Husserl's conception of philosophy as a 'science', see Chapter One, section 1, and note 2.

2 See Carr, 'Husserl's Problematic Concept of the Life-World' and *Phenomenology and the Problem of History*. In discussing Husserl, we shall keep to the term 'life-world', whilst continuing to use 'lived world' when discussing Merleau-Ponty; but we shall ignore possible differences between the two concepts.

3 We return to the question of Husserl's instrumentalism in section 2 of the Conclusion (see conclusion, note 17, for references).

4 An alternative form of such an 'extension' was provided by Berkeley's idealism, which rejected Locke's distinction between primary/objective and secondary/subjective: for discussion, see Alexander, *Ideas, Qualities and Corpuscles*. See also Koyré, *Metaphysics and Measurement*, Chapter 1, on the Platonist elements in Galileo's 'mathematical' conception of nature.

5 This idea of 'analogizing apperception' had played an important part in Husserl's account of the recognition of other Egos in the Fifth of the *Cartesian Meditations*: see Chapter Eight, section 2, for discussion of this.

6 In section 1 of the Conclusion we consider some of the issues raised by this rejection of Husserl's transcendental reduction.

7 Zaner, in *The Problem of Embodiment*, emphasizes the importance of the idea of 'one's own body' in Marcel's philosophy, and its influence on Merleau-Ponty; and he compares both with Sartre's account of 'the body for-itself' in Part Three of *Being and Nothingness*. We consider Merleau-Ponty's criticisms of Sartre's distinction between the in-itself and the for-itself, which imply corresponding criticisms of Sartre's account of the body, in section 3 of Chapter Nine; for a sympathetic analysis of Merleau-Ponty's position *vis-à-vis* Sartre's, see De Waelhens, 'A Philosophy of the Ambiguous'. See also Straus, *Selected Papers: Phenomenological Psychology*, especially Chapters 2, 7 and 10, for a discussion of 'the lived body' that is in many ways similar to Merleau-Ponty's .

8 A classic discussion of this can be found in Schilder, *The Image and Appearance of the Human Body* (first published in 1935: Merleau-Ponty refers only to an earlier work by Schilder, published in 1923).

9 In his analysis of this phenomenon, Merleau-Ponty also explores the possible relevance of the idea of an 'organic repression' (*PP*, pp. 77–8). To understand what he says about this, it is helpful to consult Chapter III of his *Structure of Behaviour*, and his discussion of the psychoanalytic concept of repression in *PP*, Part One, Chapter 5.

10 See Tiemersma, '"Body-Image" and "Body-Schema" in the Existential Phenomenology of Merleau-Ponty'. Goldstein and Gelb worked in an institute set up during the First World War to treat patients suffering from brain injuries. Both were strongly influenced by Gestalt psychology, and Goldstein was an influential proponent of anti-reductionist biology: see *The Organism*, and *A Kurt Goldstein Reader*. For a brief account of his work, see Misiak and Sexton, *Phenomenological, Existential, and Humanistic Psychologies*.

11 On the functions of different areas of the brain, and the effects of damage to them, see Williams, *Brain Damage and the Mind*, and Luria's *The Working Brain*; and also Luria's moving neuropsychological study of a patient with difficulties partly similar to Schneider's, *The Man with the Shattered World*.

12 See Hempel, *Philosophy of Natural Science*, Chapters 2 to 4, for a discussion of scientific theory-testing which takes account of these problems.

13 See also *PP*, pp. 171–3, where Merleau-Ponty talks both of the 'necessity' and of the 'contingency' of the body as a feature of human existence, a view that is related to his rejection of the Kantian distinction between the a priori and the a posteriori: cf. section 1 of our Conclusion. In *What Computers Can't Do*, Dreyfus draws upon Merleau-Ponty to argue, *inter alia*, that they cannot think because they do not have bodies.

14 There are interesting parallels here with Ryle's distinction between 'knowing how' and 'knowing that'; and more generally, between Merleau-Ponty's rejection of 'intellectualism' and Ryle's: see *The Concept of Mind*, especially Chapters II and IX.

15 See Zaner, *The Problem of Embodiment*, Part III, Chapter III, for a Husserlian criticism of Merleau-Ponty on this point. This raises more general issues about the relations between existential and transcendental phenomenology, and about Merleau-Ponty's 'non-representationalist' view of intentionality, which we discuss in sections 1 and 3, respectively, of the Conclusion.

16 From a Foucauldian perspective, Merleau-Ponty might himself be criticized for complicity in the 'normalizing' procedures of modern forms of power (see Foucault, *Discipline and Punish*); and, more generally, for ignoring historical and social specificities in modes of bodily practice. However, it might be replied that Foucault's own account of the disciplining of bodies suffers from its lack of adequate phenomenological description; and that such descriptions can be given in ways that recognize both socio-historical diversity and relations of power. See, for example, Connerton's *How Societies Remember* and Young's 'Throwing Like a Girl'.

Chapter 7: The Perception of Objects

1 However, the 'conventionalist' approach involved in the psychologist's explanation that Merleau-Ponty considers is arguably not the only one that an empiricist might take. For an account of more recent psychological explanations of size, shape and colour constancies, see Atkinson et al., *Introduction to Psychology*, pp. 139–45.

2 The claim that the properties of things are dependent on the type of thing which is the bearer of the properties would rule out any analysis of things (e.g. phenomenalism) which consider the perception of properties (sense-data) as logically prior to the perception of things. For a discussion of phenomenalism and its problems, see Hospers, *An Introduction to Philosophical Analysis*, Chapter 25.

3 Merleau-Ponty's use of 'kinaesthetic', here, is similar to Husserl's in *The Crisis*: see *CES*, pp. 106–7 and 161–2, and the brief account of Husserl's claims about kinaesthesis in Chapter Six, section 2. The term does not have specifically physiological connotations for either of them.

4 Merleau-Ponty's emphasis on the sedimented stock of knowledge may have its roots in his reading of Husserl's account of the life-world in *The Crisis*. Both can also be seen as extensions of Husserl's discussion of habitualities and passive synthesis in the *Cartesian Meditations*: see Chapter Three, section 3.

5 Cf. Husserl's account of the meaning of transcendence, of the sense of objects independent of one, which is given in terms of the infinite number of possible perceptions of the same object from different perspectives, etc.: see Chapter Two, section 3.

6 Notice that the meaning of the term 'transcendence' here, in talking of the 'transcendence of the world', is different from at least one meaning that Sartre gives to the term, according to which 'transcendence of the world' would mean the subject 'going beyond' the world (see Chapter Four, section 5). In Merleau-Ponty's use of the term it means, rather, the world being beyond the subject. This is closer to what Sartre means by the term when he talks of the 'transcendence of the ego', i.e. as the opposite of immanence: see Chapter Four, section 2.

7 Merleau-Ponty is here criticizing Husserl's account of the eidetic reduction: see Chapter Three, section 2. For further comparison of their views on this, see section 1 of the Conclusion.

8 Merleau-Ponty extends his discussion of the importance of temporal considerations for understanding the nature of perception in the later chapter on 'Temporality' (*PP*, Part Three, Chapter 2). There he argues for a non-objectivist understanding of time.

9 A parallel argument about the experience of illusions can be found in Austin's *Sense and Sensibilia*. Arguing in the mode of analytical philosophy, he focuses on the (ordinary) language used to describe the facts of perception. Austin says: 'our ordinary words are much subtler in their uses, and mark many more distinctions, than philosophers have realised' (*Sense and Sensibilia*, p. 3). On the relationship between the analytical philosopher's methods and the phenomenologist's, see Chapter Two, section 4.

Chapter 8: The Recognition of Other Selves

1 For other reading on Husserl's Fifth Meditation, see Haney, 'A Critique of Criticism of Husserl's Use of Analogy'; Schutz; *Collected Papers*, vol. 3; Ricoeur *Husserl*, chapter 5. For a comparison between the three authors discussed in this chapter, see Theunissen, *The Other*.

2   For reading on other minds problem, see Hamlyn, *The Theory of Knowledge*, chapter 8; Dancy, *Introduction to Contemporary Epistemology*, chapter 5.

3   Descartes, *Meditations*, Second Meditation.

4   For an exposition of an empiricist theory of knowledge, see Ayer, *The Foundations of Empirical Knowledge*.

5   See Ayer, 'One's Knowledge of Other Minds', in *Philosophical Essays*.

6   For their analysis of mental concepts, see Ryle, *The Concept of Mind*; Wittgenstein, *Philosophical Investigations*: Strawson, *Individuals*, chapter 3.

7   Husserl in the Fourth Meditation introduced the 'monadic' concrete Ego (see Chapter Three, section 1, above).

8   Leibniz too uses the term 'apperception' to indicate some element of self-perception or self-awareness in the perception.

9   Husserl referred to this in his Second Meditation as 'the ego's marvellous being-for-itself' (see Chapter Two, section 2, above).

10 For a literary example of one's being for others, see Sartre's *Intimacy and other Short Stories*, especially the title story. See also Natanson, 'The Problem of Others in *Being and Nothingness*', pp. 326–344, in Schilpp (ed.); Spiegelberg, 'Phenomenology of the Look'.

11 For a dramatic presentation of this, see Sartre, *Huis clos*, variously translated as *In Camera*, *No Exit*, *Vicious Circle*. See also Spiegelberg, 'Phenomenology of the Look'.

12 For Sartre's criticisms of Hegel, see *BN*, Part Three, Chapter One, section III. Hegel disagrees with Sartre about the *essentially* conflictual character of interpersonal relations; but there is agreement that the primary experience is one of conflict. See Hegel, *The Phenomenology of Mind*, trans. Baillie, pp. 218–40. Norman, *Hegel's Phenomenology*.

13 It is not clear that, for Sartre, the body is in any simple way an object. See *BN*, Part 3, chapters 2 and 3.

14 For discussions of Merleau-Ponty's view of communality, see Rabil, *Merleau-Ponty: Existentialist of the Social World*; Spurling, *Phenomenology and the Social World*.

15 For an account of what Merleau-Ponty means by 'objective thought', see Chapter Five, section 2, above.

16 Sartre would want to make some such criticism; see his discussion in *BN*, Part 3, chapter 3, section III.

Chapter 9:   Freedom and its Limits

1   For an account of Merleau-Ponty's 'dialectical' strategy, see Chapter Five, section 4.

2   Skinner is a clear example of such a determinist. See Skinner, *Beyond Freedom and Dignity*.

3   Merleau-Ponty does not explicitly characterize the thesis of absolute freedom in this way.

4 See Ryle, *The Concept of Mind*, chapters III, V; and Anscombe, *Intention*.

5 See Hume, *Treatise*, Book II, Part III, section III; and Nietszche, *Human All Too Human, Twilight of the Idols*.

6 For an introduction to Kant's thought, see Action, *Kant's Moral Philosophy*.

7 Kant, *The Groundwork of the Metaphysic of Morals*, Prussian Akademy edition, p. 113.

8 Kant, *The Critique of Pure Reason*, A189/B232–A211/B256, Kemp Smith translation, pp. 218–33.

9 There is room for a different interpretation of Part 4 of Sartre's *BN* respecting rather more than perhaps Merleau-Ponty does Sartre's claim that he is revising throughout *BN* his account of being-for-itself (see Chapter Four, section 3 above). See also Langer, 'Sartre and Merleau-Ponty: A Reappraisal', in Schilpp (ed.), pp. 300–25; and de Beauvoir, 'Merleau-Ponty et le pseudo-Sartrisme'.

10 It is important for understanding Sartre's account that one realizes he believes that people often choose failure.

11 Certain of Sartre's fictional characters may seem a clear illustration that Sartre too believes that this intellectual way of living is possible; but also that it is not inevitable, nor indeed a good way to be. It is, however, a fundamental problem, a perpetual risk, according to Sartre, that one might slip into this way of living.

12 This would of course be a specifically objectivist temptation.

13 For reading on soft determinism, see Ayer, 'Freedom and Necessity', in *Philosophical Essays*; Hospers, *An Introduction to Philosophical Analysis*, pp. 321–48.

14 For expositions of this view, see Austin, 'Ifs and Cans', in *Philosophical Papers*, pp. 153–80; Dennett, *Elbow Room*.

Conclusion

1 This argument is to be distinguished from one with a similar conclusion in Ricoeur's *Husserl*, Chapter 8, p. 203. Ricoeur suggests that 'If one calls "transcendental" any attempt at relating the conditions of the appearance of things to the structure of human subjectivity ... then it will be said that all phenomenology is transcendental.' For Ricoeur, existential phenomenology is not 'another division juxtaposed to "transcendental phenomenology"'. Rather, it is phenomenology placed in the service of solving the problems of existence: of the role of the body, of death, of finitude, of freedom, etc. Ricoeur's notion of 'transcendental' has affinities with the more Husserlian sense that Merleau-Ponty criticizes. However, the generality of Ricoeur's sense of 'transcendental' allows it to admit of an interpretation that Merleau-Ponty could accept.

2 As we saw in Chapter Six, section 2, Merleau-Ponty regarded Husserl as having retained his commitment to this transcendental perspective even in the works published in his last period, including, presumably, *The Crisis* (see *PP*, p. 60, note 1).

3 Merleau-Ponty's claims about the indeterminacy of experience are relevant to more recent debates about the possibility of transcendental arguments. Any attempt to show that a certain concept or principle is absolutely necessary for experience is apparently vulnerable to the possibility of new types of experience. Merleau-Ponty accepts this possibility, and so for him no transcendental argument could be successful. See Körner, 'The Impossibility of Transcendental Arguments'.

4 Affirmative answers to this question are given in Zaner, *The Problem of Embodiment* which is an interpretation of Merleau-Ponty's phenomenology from a Husserlian perspective; and in Mohanty, *Transcendental Phenomenology*, especially Chapter 3, which attempts to justify phenomenology as transcendental, as an antidote to relativistically inclined contemporary hermeneutics, such as Gadamer's *Truth and Method*.

5 Langer raises this problem, amongst others, in considering Merleau-Ponty's philosophical method. She criticizes him for not supplying the necessary methodological discussion to convince those wedded to different philosophical approaches of the adequacy of his descriptions. See *Merleau-Ponty's Phenomenology of Perception*, pp. 169–72.

6 More recent discussions include: Strawson, *The Bounds of Sense*, Part Two, Section II; and Allison, *Kant's Transcendental Idealism*, Part Three, Chapter 7.

7 This is Gadamer's position in *Truth and Method*.

8 Hacker, in *Insight and Illusion*, argues that there is a Kantian, transcendental tone to Wittgenstein's enquiries in the *Tractatus* and the *Philosophical Investigations*. Wittgenstein is seen as investigating the features of language as the conditions of the possibility of experience.

9 For instance, in 'Can Analytical Philosophy Be Systematic?', in *Truth and Other Enigmas*, p. 458, Dummett claims that:

> Only with Frege was the proper object of philosophy finally established: namely, first that the goal of philosophy is the analysis of the structure of *thought*; secondly, that the study of *thought* is to be sharply distinguished from the study of the psychological process of *thinking*; and finally that the only proper method for analysing thought consists in the analysis of *language*.... The acceptance of these three tenets is common to the entire analytical school.

10 See, e.g. Bernstein, *Beyond Objectivism and Relativism*; MacIntyre, *Whose Justice?* Chapters XVIII – XX; and Mohanty, *Transcendental Phenomenology*, Chapter 3.

11 See Habermas, 'A Review of Gadamer's *Truth and Method*'; and Thompson and Held, eds., *Habermas: Critical Debates*.

12 See Rorty, *Philosophy and the Mirror of Nature*: and Baynes et al., *After Philosophy*.

13 See Bernstein, *The Restructuring of Social and Political Theory*, pp. 117–35, on the conflict between scientific realism and Husserl's position in Part Two of *The Crisis*.

14 So, for example, in the case of the Müller-Lyer illusion (see Chapter Five, section 2), the scientific realist will insist that the two lines really *are* equal, and then try

to explain why they are not perceived as such: for attempts to do this, see note 3, Chapter Five.

15   On the relations between the phenomenologists and the Gestalt psychologists, see Misiak and Sexton, *Phenomenological, Existential, and Humanistic Psychologies*: Kohler's attitude to Husserl is discussed on pp. 15–16.

16   Cf. the analogy suggested in Chapter Five, section 4, with Lakatos's concept of a degenerating research programme. One can never be sure that a programme that is degenerating at one time will not become progressive later on. This is Feyerabend's objection, in *Against Method*, Chapter 16 – though his own arguments 'against method' may be open to a similar objection.

17   On realism and instrumentalism, see Chalmers, *What is this Thing Called Science?*, Chapters 13 and 14; and O'Hear, *An Introduction to the Philosophy of Science*, Chapter 6.

18   Galileo's arguments are presented in *The Assayer*; and a discussion of Descartes' arguments, in relation to recent philosophical work on these issues, is provided by Cottingham in *Descartes*, Chapter 6.

19   For example, Burtt, *The Metaphysical Foundations of Modern Physical Science*; Whitehead, *Science and the Modern World*; and some elements in the work of the early Frankfurt School (see note 26 below).

20   See Fay, *Social Theory and Political Practice*, Chapters 3 and 4, and Outhwaite, *Understanding Social Life*.

21   See Bernstein, *The Restructuring of Social and Political Theory*, pp. 135–69, for a discussion of the central figure here, Alfred Schutz; Luckman (ed.), *Phenomenology and Sociology*; and Roche , *Phenomenology, Language and the Social Sciences*.

22   See Thomas, *Man and the Natural World*, especially Chapters I and VI, on changing views of nature in England between 1600 and 1800, including artistic representations of landscape; and Attfield, *The Ethics of Environmental Concern*, Part One, on religious traditions and their attitudes toward nature.

23   Hence the rejection of phenomenology as a 'philosophy of the individual subject' by both structuralists and post-structuralist: see Descombes, *Modern French Philosophy*; Solomon, *Continental Philosophy since 1750*; and Soper, *Humanism and Anti-Humanism*. It is arguable that the kinds of wholesale rejection of phenomenology by the theorists discussed in these works fail in relation to some of the specific claims of the phenomenologists we have been considering: for example, Merleau-Ponty's emphasis on the 'historical', pre-conscious, practical character of existence.

24   But cf. Merleau-Ponty's claims about the 'alien' character of things and the natural world, discussed in Chapter Seven, section 4; and, more generally, his acceptance of certain aspects of realism. But his opposition to *scientific* realism is not affected by these qualifications.

25   See Passmore, *Man's Responsibility for Nature*, especially the Appendix to the second edition, 'Attitudes to Nature'; and Attfield, *The Ethics of Environmental Concern*, Part Two, and Brennan, *Thinking About Nature*, Chapters 9 and 10, on whether nature has 'intrinsic value'.

26   The best-known versions of the 'science and technical control' thesis stem from

the work of the Frankfurt School: see Held, *Introduction to Critical Theory*; Leiss, *The Domination of Nature*; and Fay, *Social Theory and Political Practice*, Chapters 2 and 3. See Keat, *The Politics of Social Theory*, Chapter 3, for criticism of Habermas's and Fay's arguments. Marcuse's version draws its inspiration partly from *The Crisis*: for criticism of his interpretation of Husserl, see O'Neill, 'Marcuse, Husserl, and the Crisis of the Sciences'.

27 See Beckner, *The Biological Way of Thought*; and Brennan, *Thinking About Nature*. Cf. also Merleau-Ponty's discussion of what he calls 'The Vital Order', in *The Structure of Behaviour*.

28 See e.g. Luria, *The Man with a Shattered World*; Sacks, *The Man Who Mistook his Wife for a Hat*; and a much older work, Schilder's *The Image and Appearance of the Human Body*. Indeed, unlike these, Merleau-Ponty's descriptions of Schneider give little sense of Schneider's *own* experience of his bodily existence: cf. note 5 above.

29 Merleau-Ponty's solution to this problem is best approached through his discussion of the 'Three Orders' – Physical, Vital and Human – in Part Three of *SB*. Here he argues for what is, in effect, an 'existential' version of teleological holism, in which human meanings function as the highest level goals of the system, and the operations of the lower levels (organic and physical) are explained in terms of their contributions to the higher levels. Thus the biological and physical sciences are 'integrated' in an existential-phenomenological synthesis, and by no means straightforwardly rejected.

30 This comparison owes much to frequent and lengthy discussions over many years with Aurora Plomer. For her analysis of Merleau-Ponty's criticisms of theories of perception, see her 'Merleau-Ponty on Sensations'. For other comparisons between Merleau-Ponty's views and theories of the mind, see Evans, 'Behaviourism as Existentialism'; Russow, 'Merleau-Ponty and the Myth of Bodily Intentionality'.

31 Churchland, *Matter and Consciousness*.

32 Nagel, 'What it is like to be a Bat'.

33 Nagel, *The View from Nowhere*.

34 Nagel distinguishes subjectivity and intentionality, saying that intentionality does not entail consciousness. But this is the account of intentionality of objective thought, i.e. in terms of propositional attitudes, and so not Merleau-Ponty's, and so Nagel and Merleau-Ponty are not actually in opposition on this.

35 Frege, 'On Sense and Reference'.

36 Chisholm, 'Sentences about Believing'.

37 Searle, 'The Myth of the Computer'; 'Minds, Brains and Programs'. For other discussions of intentionality and artificial intelligence, see Dreyfus, *Husserl, Intentionality and Cognitive Science* and *What Computers Can't Do*; for an account of AI, see Pratt, *Thinking Machines*.

38 It does matter for Searle – that is because he thinks that minds are or are very like programs; but mental states occur only when the program is instantiated in a brain. Merleau-Ponty, in contrast, would reject the computer model completely. For Searle's positive views, see Searle, *Intentionality*; *Minds, Brains and Science*.

39 It might look as if functionalism, with its emphasis on the *causal* properties of the

mind, should be classified, for present purposes, as empiricist. However, when functionalism combined with AI theory, the claim must be that it is the *instantiated* program which has causal powers; whereas it is the abstract program which is deemed to be or be like the mind.

40 Dennett, 'Intentional Systems' in *Brainstorms*, pp. 3–22. See also Dennett, *Content and Consciousness*; *The Intentional Stance*.
41 Searle, 'the Myth of the Computer'.

Bibliography

We have included in our bibliography only those works to which we refer in the text. From the vast literature on phenomenology and on the writers we have considered, the following works are, we think, especially helpful as introductions:

on Husserl:
Elliston and McCormick (eds.), *Husserl: Expositions and Appraisals*; Kolakowski, *Husserl and the Search for Certitude*; Pivčević, *Husserl and Phenomenology*.

on Sartre:
Catalano, *A Commentary on J. – P. Sartre's Being and Nothingness*; Danto, *Sartre*.

on Merleau-Ponty:
Kwant, *The Phenomenological Philosophy of Merleau-Ponty*; Langer, *Merleau-Ponty's Phenomenology of Perception*.

Works which consider more than one phenomenologist:
Kockelmans (ed.), *Phenomenology*; Spiegelberg, *The Phenomenological Movement*; Warnock, *Existentialism*; Zaner, *The Problem of Embodiment* – this last work is scarcely introductory, but it raises important questions about Merleau-Ponty's phenomenology of the body.

Suggestions for further reading on particular issues are made in the footnotes.

Acton, H. B., *Kant's Moral Philosophy*, Macmillan, London, 1970.
Alexander, P., *Ideas, Qualities and Corpuscles*, Cambridge University Press, Cambridge, 1985.
Allison, H. E., *Kant's Transcendental Idealism*, Yale University Press, New Haven, CT, 1983.
Anscombe, G. E. M., *Intention*, Basil Blackwell, Oxford, 1957.
Atkinson, R. L., Atkinson, R. C., and Hilgard, E. R., *Introduction to Psychology*, 8th edn, Harcourt Brace Jovanovich, New York, 1983.
Attfield, R., *The Ethics of Environmental Concern*, Basil Blackwell, Oxford, 1983.
Attig, Thomas, 'Re-Learning the World: On the Phenomenology of Grieving', *Journal of the British Society for Phenomenology*, 21, 1, January 1990.

Austin, J. L., *Philosophical Papers*, Clarendon Press, Oxford, 1961.

——, *Sense and Sensibilia*, ed G. J. Warnock, Oxford University Press, Oxford, 1962.

Ayer, A. J., *The Foundations of Empirical Knowledge*, Macmillan, London, 1959.

——, *Philosophical Essays*, Macmillan, London, 1959.

Baldwin, Thomas and Bell, David, 'Phenomenology, Solipsism and Egocentric Thought', *Aristotelian Society Supplementary Volume*, 62, 1988.

Barthes, Roland, *Camera Lucida – Reflections on Photography*, trans. Richard Howard, Hill & Wang, New York, 1981.

Baynes, K., Bohman, J., and McCarthy, T. (eds.), *After Philosophy*, MIT Press, Cambridge, MA, 1987.

Beauvoir, Simone de, *The Prime of Life*, Trans. P. Green, Penguin, Harmondsworth, 1965.

——, 'Merleau-Ponty et le pseudo-Sartrisme', *Les Temps modernes*, 10, 1955, pp. 2072–2123; repr. in *Privilège*, Gallimard, Paris, 1955.

Beckner, M., *The Biological Way of Thought*, University of California Press, Berkeley, 1968.

Berkeley, George, 'Principles of Human Knowledge', in David M. Armstrong (ed.), *Berkeley's Philosophical Writings*, Collier, London, 1965.

Bernstein, Richard, *Beyond Objectivism and Relativism*, Basil Blackwell, Oxford, 1983.

——, *The Restructuring of Social and Political Theory*, Basil Blackwell, Oxford, 1976.

Boden, Margaret, *Artificial Intelligence and Natural Man*, 2nd edn, MIT Press, Cambridge, MA, 1987.

Boden, Margaret (ed.), *The Philosophy of Artificial Intelligence*, Oxford University Press, Oxford, 1990.

Bowie, G. Lee., Michaels, Meredith W., and Solomon, Robert C. (eds.), *Twenty Questions*, Harcourt Brace Jovanovich, New York, 1988.

Brennan, A., *Thinking About Nature*, Routledge, London, 1988.

Brentano, Franz, *Psychology from an Empirical Standpoint*, ed. L. McAlister, trans. A. Rancurello and D. Terrell, Routledge & Kegan Paul, London, 1973.

Brown, S., and Mays, Wolfe (eds.), *Linguistic Analysis and Phenomenology*, Macmillan, London, 1972.

Burtt, E. A., *The Metaphysical Foundations of Modern Physical Science*, 2nd edn, Routledge, London, 1932.

Carr, David, 'Husserl's Problematic Concept of the Life-World', *American Philosophical Quarterly*, 7, 1970; repr. in Elliston and McCormick.

——, *Phenomenology and the Problem of History*, Northwestern University Press, Evanston, IL, 1974.

Casey, E. S., 'Imagination and Phenomenological Method', in Elliston and McCormick.

——, *Remembering: A Phenomenological Study*, Indiana University Press, Bloomington, 1987.

Catalano, J. S., *A Commentary on J.-P. Sartre's Being and Nothingness*, University of Chicago Press, Chicago, 1986.

Chalmers, A. F., *What is this Thing Called Science?*, 2nd edn, Open University Press, Milton Keynes, 1982.

Chisholm, R., 'Sentences about Believing', *Proceedings of the Aristotelian Society*, 61, 1955–6.

Churchland, P. M., *Matter and Consciousness*, MIT Press, Cambridge, MA, 1988.

Connerton, P., *How Societies Remember*, Cambridge University Press, Cambridge, 1989.

Cottingham, J., *Descartes*, Basil Blackwell, Oxford, 1986.

——, *Rationalism*, Paladin Books, London, 1984.

Dallmayr, F., and McCarthy, T. (eds.), *Understanding and Social Inquiry*, Notre Dame University Press, Notre Dame, IN, 1977.

Dancy, Jonathan, *Introduction to Contemporary Epistemology*, Basil Blackwell, Oxford, 1985.

Danto, A. C., *Sartre*, Fontana, London, 1975.

Davidson, Donald, 'Actions, Reasons and Causes', repr. in *Essays on Actions and Events*, Clarendon Press, Oxford, 1980, pp. 3–20.

Dennett, D.C., *Brainstorms*, Harvester, Brighton 1981.

——, *Content and Consciousness*, Routledge & Kegan Paul, London, 1969.

——, *Elbow Room: The Varieties of Free Will Worth Wanting*, Clarendon Press, Oxford, 1984.

——, *The Intentional Stance*, MIT Press, Cambridge, MA, 1987.

Descartes, R., 'Meditations on First Philosophy', in *Descartes: Philosophical Writings*, trans. and ed. E. Anscombe and P. T. Geach, Nelson, London, 1954.

Descombes, V., *Modern French Philosophy*, trans. L. Scott-Fox and J. M. Harding, Cambridge University Press, Cambridge, 1980.

De Waelhens, Alphonse, 'The Phenomenology of the Body', in Lawrence and O'Connor, pp. 149–67.

——, 'A Philosophy of the Ambiguous', in Merleau-Ponty, *The Structure of Behaviour*, pp. xviii–xxviii.

Dreyfus, Hubert L., *What Computers Can't Do: The Limits of Artificial Intelligence*, Harper & Row, New York, 1979.

——, *Husserl, Intentionality and Cognitive Science*, MIT Press, Cambridge, MA, 1982.

Dummett, M., *Truth and Other Enigmas*, Duckworth, London, 1978.

Durfee, Harold A., *Analytic Philosophy and Phenomenology*, Martinus Nijhoff, The Hague, 1976.

Elliston, F. A., and McCormick, P. (eds.), *Husserl: Expositions and Appraisals*, University of Notre Dame Press, Notre Dame, IN, and London, 1977.

Evans, C. Stephan, 'Behaviourism as Existentialism: Ryle and Merleau-Ponty on the Mind', *Journal of the British Society for Phenomenology*, 14, 1, January 1983, pp. 65-78.

Fay, B., *Social Theory and Political Practice*, Allen & Unwin, London, 1975.

Feyerabend, P., *Against Method*, New Left Books, London, 1975.

Fingarette, Herbert, *Self-Deception*, Routledge & Kegan Paul, London, 1969.

Foucault, M., *Discipline and Punish*, trans. A. Sheridan, Penguin, Harmondsworth, 1979.

Frege, Gottlob, 'On Sense and Reference', in Frege, *Philosophical Writings*, trans. P. T. Geach and M. Black, Basil Blackwell, Oxford, 1952.

Gadamer, Hans-Georg, *Truth and Method*, Sheed and Ward, London, 1975.

Galileo, G., *The Assayer*, in S. Drake, *Discoveries and Opinions of Galileo*, Doubleday Anchor, New York, 1957.

Glynn, Simon, 'The Eye/I of the Paradox: Sartre's View of Consciousness', in Glynn (ed.), *Sartre*.

—— (ed.) *Sartre: An Investigation of Some Major Themes*, Avebury, Aldershot, 1987.

Goldstein, K., *A Kurt Goldstein Reader: The Shaping of Neurophysiology*, AMS Press, New York, 1986.

——, *The Organism: A Holistic Approach to Biology* (first pubd 1933; English translation 1939), Beacon Press, Boston, 1963.

Gregory, R. L., *Eye and Brain*, 3rd edn, Weidenfeld & Nicolson, London, 1977.

——, *The Intelligent Eye*, Weidenfeld Nicolson, London, 1977.

Grossman, Reinhardt, *Phenomenology and Existentialism: An Introduction*, Routledge & Kegan Paul, London, 1984.

Gurwitsch, Aron, 'Husserl's Theory of the Intentionality of Consciousness in Historical Perspective', in Lee and Mandelbaum, pp. 25–58.

——, *Marginal Consciousness*, ed. C. Embree, Ohio University Press, Athens, OH, 1985.

——, 'A Non-egological Conception of Consciousness', in *Philosophy and Phenomenological Research*, 1, 1940–1, pp. 325–38; repr. in Glynn (ed.), *Sartre*.

Habermas, J., 'A Review of Gadamer's *Truth and Method*', in Fred R. Dallmayr and Thomas McCarthy, *Understanding and Social Inquiry*, University of Notre Dame Press, Notre Dame, 1977, pp. 335–63.

Hacker P., *Insight and Illusion*, Oxford University Press, Oxford, 1972.

Hale, R. L. V., *Abstract Objects*, Basil Blackwell, Oxford, 1987.

Hamlyn, D. W., *The Theory of Knowledge*, Macmillan, London, 1971.

Hamrick, W. S. (ed.), *Phenomenology in Practice and Theory*, Martinus Nijhoff, The Hague, 1985.

Haney, Kathleen, 'A Critique of Criticism of Husserl's Use of Analogy', *Journal of the British Society for Phenomenology*, 17, 2, May 1986, pp. 143–54.

Harney, Maurita J., *Intentionality, Sense and the Mind*, Martinus Nijhoff, The Hague, 1984.

Hartmann, K., 'Metaphysics in Husserlian Phenomenology', *Journal of the British Society for Phenomenology*, 16, 3, 1985, pp. 279–93.

Hegel, G. W. F., *The Phenomenology of Mind*, 2nd edn, trans. J. B. Baillie, Macmillan, New York, 1931.

Heidegger, Martin, *Being and Time*, trans. John Macquarrie and Edward Robinson, Basil Blackwell, Oxford, 1962.

Held, D., *Introduction to Critical Theory: Horkheimer to Habermas*, Hutchinson, London, 1980.

Hempel, C. G., *Philosophy of Natural Science*, Prentice-Hall, Englewood Cliffs, NJ, 1966.

Heraclitus, *The Art and Thought of Heraclitus*, fragments trans. and with commentary by Charles H. Kahn, Cambridge University Press, Cambridge, 1979.

Hospers, J., *An Introduction to Philosophical Analysis*, 2nd edn, Routledge & Kegan Paul, London, 1967.

Howarth, J. M., 'Franz Brentano and Object-Directedness', *Journal of the British Society for Phenomenology*, 11, 3, October 1980, pp. 239–54.

——, 'On Thinking of What One Fears', *Proceedings of the Aristotelian Society*, 76, 1975–6, pp. 53–74.

Hume, David, *Treatise on Human Nature*, ed. Selby Bigge, Clarendon Press, Oxford, 1888.

Husserl, Edmund, *Cartesian Meditations*, trans. Dorion Cairns, Martinus Nijhoff, The Hague, 1977; French trans. by Gabrielle Peiffer and Emmanuel Levinas, as *Meditations cartésiennes* (first pubd 1931), Vrin, Paris, 1953.

———, *The Crisis of European Sciences and Transcendental Phenomenology*, trans. David Carr, Northwestern University Press, Evanston, IL, 1970.

———, *The Idea of Phenomenology*, trans. William P. Alston and George Nakhnikian, Martinus Nijhoff, The Hague, 1964.

———, *Ideas*, trans. W. R. Boyce Gibson, Collier, New York, 1962.

———, *Logical Investigations*, 2 vols., trans. J. N. Findley, Routledge & Kegan Paul, London, 1970.

———, *The Paris Lectures*, trans. Peter Koestenbaum, Martinus Nijhoff, The Hague, 1967.

———, 'Phenomenology', in *Encyclopaedia Britannica*, 14th edn, 17; repr. in R. Chisholm (ed.), *Realism and the Background of Phenomenology*, Free Press, Glencoe, IL, 1960.

———, *The Phenomenology of Internal Time Consciousness*, trans. James S. Churchill, Martinus Nijhoff, The Hague, 1964.

———, 'Philosophy as Rigorous Science', trans. Q. Lauer, in his *Phenomenology and the Crisis of Philosophy*, Harper & Row, New York, 1965.

Kahn, C. H. (trans.), *The Art and Thought of Heraclitus*, Cambridge University Press, Cambridge, 1979.

Kant, Immanuel, *The Groundwork of the Metaphysic of Morals*, trans. H. J. Paton, with analysis and notes, as *The Moral Law*, Hutchinson, London, 1948 (3rd edn, 1956); also trans. L.W. Beck as *Foundations of the Metaphysics of Morals*, Liberal Arts, New York, 1959.

———, *The Critique of Practical Reason*, trans. L. W. Beck, Bobbs-Merrill, New York, 1965.

———, *The Critique of Pure Reason*, trans. N. Kemp Smith, Macmillan, London, 1964.

Keat, R. N., *The Politics of Social Theory*, Basil Blackwell, Oxford, 1981.

Kemp, J., *The Philosophy of Kant*, Oxford University Press, Oxford, 1926.

Kenny, Anthony, *Descartes: A Study of his Philosophy*, Random House, London, 1968.

Kern, Iso, 'The Three Ways to the Transcendental Phenomenological Reduction in the Philosophy of Edmund Husserl', in Elliston and McCormick.

Kline, P., 'The Existentialist Rediscovery of Hegel and Marx', in Lee and Mandelbaum.

Kockelmans, J.J., 'Husserl and Kant on the Pure Ego' in Elliston and McCormick.

——— (ed.), *Phenomenology*, Anchor Books, New York, 1967.

Kohler, Wolfgang, *Gestalt Psychology*, G. Bell & Sons, London, 1930.

Kojève, A., *Introduction to the Reading of Hegel*, ed. A. Bloom, trans. J. H. Nichols, Basic Books, New York, 1969.

Kolakowski, Leszek, *Husserl and the Search for Certitude*, University of Chicago Press, Chicago, 1987.

Körner, S., 'The Impossibility of Transcendental Arguments', *The Monist*, 51, 1967, pp. 317–31; also in L. W. Beck (ed.), *Kant Studies Today*, Open Court, La Salle, IL, 1969, pp. 230–44.

Koyré, A., *Metaphysics and Measurement*, Chapman & Hall, London, 1968.

Kruks, Sonia, *The Political Philosophy of Merleau-Ponty*, Harvester Press, Brighton, 1981.

Kwant, Remy C., *The Phenomenological Philosophy of Merleau-Ponty*, Duquesne University Press, Pittsburgh, 1963.

——, *From Phenomenology to Metaphysics*, Duquesne University Press, Pittsburgh, 1966.

Lakatos, I., 'Falsification and the Methodology of Scientific Research Programmes', in I. Lakatos and A. Musgrave (eds.), *Criticism and the Growth of Knowledge*, Cambridge University Press, Cambridge, 1974.

Langer, Monika M., *Merleau-Ponty's Phenomenology of Perception : A Guide and Commentary*, Macmillan, London, 1989.

——, 'Sartre and Merleau-Ponty: A Reappraisal', in Schilpp.

Lawrence, Nathaniel, and O'Connor, Daniel (eds.) *Readings in Existential Phenomenology*, Prentice-Hall, Englewood Cliffs, NJ, 1967.

Lee, Edward N. and Mandelbaum, Maurice (eds.), *Phenomenology and Existentialism*, Johns Hopkins University Press, Baltimore, 1967.

Leibniz, G., *Monadology*, trans. D. L. A. Schrecher, Library of Liberal Arts, Bobbs Merrill, New York, 1965.

Leiss, W., *The Domination of Nature*, George Braziller, New York, 1972.

——, 'Husserl's Crisis', *Telos*, 7, 1971.

Luckmann, T. (ed.), *Phenomenology and Sociology*, Penguin, Harmondsworth, 1978.

Luria, A. R., *The Man with a Shattered World*, Harvard University Press, Cambridge, MA, 1987.

——, *The Working Brain*, Basic Books, New York, 1973.

McAlister, Linda (ed.), *The Philosophy of Brentano*, Duckworth, London, 1976.

MacIntyre, A., *Whose Justice? Which Rationality?*, Duckworth, London, 1988.

McKenna, W. R., *Husserl's 'Introductions to Phenomenology': Interpretation and Critique*, Martinus Nijhoff, The Hague, 1982.

Madison, G. B., *The Phenomenology of Merleau-Ponty*, Ohio University Press, Athens, OH, 1981.

Manser, Anthony, 'Unfair to Waiters', in *Philosophy*, 58, 1983.

——, 'A New Look at Bad Faith', in Glynn (ed.), *Sartre*.

Merleau-Ponty, Maurice, *Adventures of the Dialectic*, trans. Joseph Bien, Heinemann, London, 1974.

——, *Phenomenology of Perception*, trans. Colin Smith, Routledge & Kegan Paul, London, 1962; reprinted with revised translation, 1981.

——, *The Structure of Behaviour*, trans. Alden Fisher, Methuen, London, 1965.

Miller, G. A., Gallanter, E., and Pribram, K. H., *Plans and the Structure of Behaviour*, Holt Rhinehart, New York, 1960.

Mirvish, Adrian, 'Gestalt Mechanisms and Believing Beliefs: Sartre's Analysis of the Phenomenon of Bad Faith', *British Journal of the Society for Phenomenology*, 18, 3, October 1987, pp. 245–62.

Misiak, H., and Sexton, V. S., *Phenomenological, Existential, and Humanistic Psychologies*, Grune & Stratton, New York, 1973.

Mohanty, J. N., *Husserl and Frege*, University of Indiana Press, Bloomington, 1982.

——, *The Possibility of Transcendental Philosophy*, Martinus Nijhoff, Dordrecht, Boston and Lancaster, 1985.

——, *Transcendental Phenomenology*, Basil Blackwell, Oxford, 1989.

Morris, Phyllis Sutton, 'Sartre on the Transcendence of the Ego', *Philosophy and Phenomenological Research*, 46, 2, pp. 179–98; repr. in Glynn (ed.), *Sartre*, pp. 1–21.

Nagel, E., *The Structure of Science*, Routledge & Kegan Paul, New York, 1961.

Nagel, Thomas, *The View from Nowhere*, Oxford University Press, New York, 1986.

——, 'What it is like to be a Bat', *Philosophical Review*, 83, October 1974, pp. 435–50; repr. in T. Nagel, *Mortal Questions*, Cambridge University Press, Cambridge, 1979.

Natanson, Maurice, 'The Problem of Others in *Being and Nothingness*', in Schilpp, pp. 326–44.

New, Jerome, 'Divided Minds: Sartre's "Bad Faith" Critique of Freud', *Review of Metaphysics*, 42, 1, September 1988.

Nietzsche, F., *Human All Too Human*, trans. H. Zimmern and Paul V. Cohn, in Oscar Levy (ed.), *The Complete Works of Freidrich Nietzsche*, 6., Macmillan, New York, 1909–11; reissued Russell & Russell, New York, 1964; trans. Marion Faber with Stephen Lehmann, University of Nebraska Press, Lincoln and London, 1984.

——, *Twilight of the Idols and The Anti-Christ*, trans. R. J. Hollingdale, Penguin, Harmondsworth, 1968.

Norman, Richard, *Hegel's Phenomenology: A Philosophical Introduction*, Harvester, Brighton, 1976.

O'Hear, A., *An Introduction to the Philosophy of Science*, Oxford University Press, Oxford, 1989.

O'Neill, J., 'Marcuse, Husserl, and the Crisis of the Sciences', *Philosophy of the Social Sciences*, 18, 1988, pp. 327–43.

Outhwaite, W., *Understanding Social Life*, 2nd edn, Jean Stroud, Lewes, Sussex, 1986.

Passmore, J., *Man's Responsibility for Nature*, 2nd edn, Duckworth, London, 1980.

Pears, David, 'Freud, Sartre and Self-Deception', in Wollheim (ed.), *Freud*.

Peters, R., and Mace, C. A., 'Psychology', in P. Edwards (ed.), *The Encyclopedia of Philosophy*, 7, Macmillan, London, 1967, pp. 1–27.

Phillips, D. Z., 'Bad Faith and Sartre's Waiter', *Philosophy*, January 1981, pp. 23–31.

Pickles, John, *Phenomenology, Science and Geography: Spatiality and the Human Sciences*, Cambridge University Press, Cambridge, 1985.

Pietersma, H., 'Husserl's Views on the Evident and the True', in Elliston and McCormick.

Pitcher, George (ed.), *Truth*, Prentice Hall, New York, 1964.

Pivčević, Edo, *Husserl and Phenomenology*, Hutchinson, London, 1970.

Pivčević, Edo (ed.), *Phenomenology and Philosophical Understanding*, Cambridge University Press, Cambridge, 1975.

Plomer, Aurora, 'Merleau-Ponty on Sensations', *Journal of the British Society for Phenomenology*, 21, 2, May 1990, pp. 153–63.

Popper, Karl, *Conjectures and Refutations*, Routlege & Kegan Paul, London, 1974.

Pratt, Vernon, *Thinking Machines*, Basil Blackwell, Oxford, 1987.

Prior, Arthur N., *Objects of Thought*, ed. P. T. Geach and A. J. P. Kenny, Clarendon Press, Oxford, 1971.

Rabil, Albert, *Merleau-Ponty: Existentialist of the Social World*, Columbia University Press, New York, 1967.

Relph, Edward, *Place and Placelessness*, Pion, London, 1976.

Ricoeur, Paul, *Husserl: An Analysis of his Phenomenology*, Northwestern University Press, Evanston, IL, 1967.

Roche, Maurice, *Phenomenology, Language and the Social Sciences*, Routledge & Kegan Paul, London, 1973.

Rorty, R., *Philosophy and the Mirror of Nature*, Basil Blackwell, London, 1980.

Russow, Lilly-Marlene, 'Merleau-Ponty and the Myth of Bodily Intentionality', *Nous*, 22, 1988, pp. 35–47.

Ryle, Gilbert, *Collected Papers*, 1, Hutchinson, London, 1971.

——, *The Concept of Mind* (orig. pubd Hutchinson, London, 1949), Penguin, Harmondsworth, 1988.

Sacks, Oliver, *The Man Who Mistook his Wife for a Hat*, Duckworth, London, 1985.

Sartre, Jean-Paul, *The Age of Reason*, trans. Eric Sutton, Penguin, Harmondsworth, 1986 [part I of the trilogy *The Roads to Freedom*]; part II, *The Reprieve*, trans. Gerard Hopkins, Penguin, Harmondsworth, 1986; part III, *Iron in the Soul*, trans. Eric Sutton, Penguin, Harmondsworth, 1985 [all with introductions by David Caute].

——, *Being and Nothingness*, trans. Hazel Barnes, Methuen, London, 1958.

——, 'Intentionality: A Fundamental Idea of Husserl's Phenomenology', trans. Joseph P. Fell, *Journal of the British Society for Phenomenology*, 1, 2, May 1970, pp. 4–5.

——, *In Camera*, trans. Stuart Gilbert, in *Three European Plays*, Penguin, Harmondsworth, 1958.

——, *Intimacy and other Short Stories*, trans. Lloyd Alexander, Panther Books, St Albans, 1960.

——, 'Merleau-Ponty [1]', trans. with an Introduction by William S. Hanrick, *Journal of the British Society for Phenomenology*, 15, 2, May 1984, pp. 123–54.

——, 'Merleau-Ponty vivant', *Les Temps modernes*, 17, 1961, pp. 304–76; repr. in *Situations*, trans. B. Eisler, Fawcett World Library, New York, 1966.

——, *Nausea*, trans. Robert Baldwick, Penguin, Harmondsworth, 1963.

——, *The Transcendence of the Ego*, trans. Forrest Williams and Robert Kirkpatrick, Noonday Press, New York, 1957.

Schilder, P., *The Image and Appearance of the Human Body*, International Universities Press, New York, 1950.

Schilpp, P. A. (ed.), *The Philosophy of Jean-Paul Sartre*, Northwestern University Press, Evanston, IL, 1981.

Schmitt, Richard, *Husserl*, in P. Edwards (ed.), *The Encyclopedia of Philosophy*, 4, Collier Macmillan, London, 1967.

——, 'Phenomenology', in P. Edwards (ed.), *The Encyclopedia of Philosophy*, 6, Collier Macmillan, London, 1967.

Shutz, A., 'The Problem of Transcendental Subjectivity', trans. F. Kersten in collaboration with A. Gurwitsch and T. Luckmann, in *Collected Papers, vol. 3: Studies in Phenomenological Philosophy*, Martinus Nijhoff, The Hague, 1966, pp. 51–83.

Searle, John R., *Intentionality: An Essay in the Philosophy of Mind*, Cambridge University Press, Cambridge, 1983.

——, 'Minds, Brains and Programs', in Boden, M. (ed.), *The Philosophy of Artificial Intelligence*.

——, *Minds, Brains and Science*, Harvard University Press, Cambridge, MA, 1984.

——, 'The Myth of the Computer': a review of D. C. Dennett and D. R. Hofstadter, *The Mind's I* [Searle's review appeared in *The New York Review of Books*, 1987; the relevant extract is repr. in Bowie, Michaels, and Solomon (eds.), *Twenty Questions*]

Skinner, B. F., *Beyond Freedom and Dignity*, Cape, London, 1972.

——, *Science and Human Behaviour*, Collier-Macmillan, London, 1965.

Smith, David Woodruff, and MacIntyre, Ronald, *Husserl and Intentionality: A Study of Mind, Meaning and Language*, D. Reidel, Dordrecht, 1982.

Solomon, Robert C., *Continental Philosophy since 1750: The Rise and Fall of the Subject*, Oxford University Press, Oxford, 1988.

——, *From Rationalism to Existentialism*, Harvester, Brighton, 1978.

Soper, K., *Humanism and Anti-Humanism*, Methuen, London, 1986.

Spiegelberg, Herbert, *The Phenomenological Movement*, 3rd rev. and enlarged edn, Martinus Nijhoff, The Hague, 1982.

——, 'Phenomenology of the Look', *Journal of the British Society for Phenomenology*, 20, 2, May 1989, pp. 107–14.

Spurling, Laurie, *Phenomenology and the Social World*, Routledge & Kegan Paul, London, 1977.

Straus, Erwin W., *Selected Papers: Phenomenological Psychology*, trans. in part by Erling Eng, Tavistock, London, 1966.

Strawson, Peter, *The Bounds of Sense*, Methuen, London, 1966.

——, *Individuals*, Methuen, London, 1963.

Theunissen, M., *The Other: Studies in the Social Ontology of Husserl, Heidegger, Sartre and Buber*, MIT Press, Cambridge, MA, 1984.

Thomas, K., *Man and the Natural World*, Penguin, Harmondsworth, 1984.

Thompson, John B., and Held, David (eds.), *Habermas: Critical Debates*, MIT Press, Cambridge, MA, 1982.

Tiemersma, Douwe, ' "Body-Image" and "Body-Schema" in the Existenial Phenomenology of Merleau-Ponty', *Journal of the British Society for Phenomenology*, 13, 3, 1982, pp. 246–55.

Waismann, F., 'Verifiability', in G.H. Parkinson (ed.), *The Theory of Meaning*, Oxford University Press, Oxford, 1968.

Walsh, W. H., *Kant's Criticism of Metaphysics*, Edinburgh University Press, Edinburgh, 1975.

Warnock, Mary, *Existentialism*, Oxford University Press, Oxford, 1970.

Waterhouse, Roger, *A Heidegger Critique*, Harvester, Brighton, 1981.

Whitehead, A. N., *Science and the Modern World* (first pubd 1926), Free Associations Books, London, 1985.

Williams, M., *Brain Damage and the Mind*, Penguin, Harmondsworth, 1979.

Winch, P., *The Idea of a Social Science*, Routledge & Kegan Paul, London, 1958.

Wittgenstein, Ludwig, *The Blue and Brown Books*, Basil Blackwell, Oxford, 1969.

——, *Philosophical Investigations*, trans. G. E. M. Anscombe, Basil Blackwell, Oxford, 1967.

——, *Tractatus Logico-Philosophicus*, Routledge & Kegan Paul, London, 1922.

Wollheim, Richard (ed.), *Freud: A Collection of Critical Essays*, Anchor, New York. 1974.

Woolhouse, R. S., *The Empiricists*, Oxford University Press, Oxford, 1988.

Young, I. M., 'Throwing Like A Girl: A Phenomenology of Feminine Bodily Comportment, Motility, and Spatiality', *Human Studies*, 3, 1980.

Zaner, Richard M., *The Problem of Embodiment*, 2nd edn, Martinus Nijhoff, The Hague, 1971.

Index